Daily Survival Guide
for Divorced Men

Carole,
You have been a
great friend!
Thank you for hanging
in there with me!
— Dale

Daily Survival Guide for Divorced Men

SURVIVING & THRIVING BEYOND YOUR DIVORCE

Dale J. Brown, Ph.D.

Amazon Create Space
2017

Praise for

A Daily Survival Guide for Divorced Men

"I get 2-4 requests a day for a book endorsement and I must refuse most of them, but everywhere I open this book there is wisdom—and hard won wisdom—plus the need is so urgent and so widespread! So I want to go on record in support of Dale Brown's fine book. I know its truth from years of working with men."

- Fr. Richard Rohr, author of *Falling Upward: A Spirituality for the Two Halves of Life*
  Founder of the Center for Action and Contemplation

"In *Daily Survival Guide for Divorced Men* Dale Brown has written a book that challenges, inspires, and comforts men who have experienced divorce—and other losses—and are confronting the pain of it. As a hospice chaplain, Brown is acquainted with loss. Even more, he has experienced the deep pain of divorce himself and he writes out of the wellspring of experience. God is for us. Jesus is the healer. The Holy Spirit is the comforter, helper, and one who comes alongside. This devotional speaks directly to wounded men and walks with them on a daily journey to healing, wholeness, and forgiveness."

- Everett L. Worthington, Jr., author of *Forgiving and Reconciling: Bridges to Wholeness and Hope* Professor of Psychology, Virginia Commonwealth University

Daily Survival Guide For Divorced Men: Surviving and Thriving Beyond Your Divorce

Copyright © 2017 by Dale J Brown
Library of Congress Cataloging-in-Publication Data
Brown, Dale J., 1961—
The Daily Survival Guide for Divorced Men: Surviving and Thriving Beyond Your Divorce / Dale Brown.
p. cm.
ISBN 978-1-56507-098-1 (Hardcover)
ISBN 978-0-7369-0151-2 (Soft cover)
1. Devotional calendars. 2. Devotional literature, English. I. Title.
BV4811. A535 1993
242.'2—dc20 93-18858

Copyright © 2017 Dale J. Brown, Ph.D.
All rights reserved.
ISBN: 9780692952399
ISBN: 069295239X

To

Kelly
Sarah
Ken
Francisco
Mary Martha
Rex
Pat
Richard
Lindsey
Davis
&
Aaron

Without you I would not still be here.

Acknowledgements

WE STAND ON THE SHOULDERS—hopefully not the backs—of those who have gone before us and those who have spoken most deeply into our lives. In the context of this book, I am most grateful for those who helped me stand when I wanted to fall, to rise up when I felt beaten down, to keep going when I wanted to stop.

My three children—Lindsey, Davis and Aaron—are strong, compassionate, smart, resilient people who have overcome much and stood by me. I am privileged to be their earthly dad and grateful for their love.

My parents, both now in heaven, were resilient innovative people who kept going. I get my grit and many other things from them.

When things fell apart at my New England church, I was surprised at who stood by me, who came against me and who didn't seem to care. Richard, Matt, Bill, Donna, Jim Grant, Ken and many others come to mind of those who stood strong with me. The members of Celebrate Recovery met me at the bottom—they know what it's like to lose and they welcomed this 'loser' into their fold. I found Jesus there among them most of all.

Many of the members at Immanuel Baptist Church hung in there with me—Rex, Mary Martha, Pat, Carl and others.

I am most grateful to Kelly. She has listened to my heart cries, steadied me when I stumbled, spoken for me when I stuttered and, most of all, kept believing in me.

A special thank you to Richard Collins who carefully read this manuscript.

The Sycamore

In the place that is my own place, whose earth
I am shaped in and must bear,
there is an old tree growing,
a great sycamore that is a wondrous healer of itself.
Fences have been tied to it, nails driven into it,
hacks and whittles cut in it, the
lightning has burned it.
There is no year it has flourished in
that has not harmed it. There is a hollow in it
that is its death, though its living brims whitely
at the lip of the darkness and flows outward.
Over all its scars has come the seamless white
of the bark. It bears the gnarls of its history
healed over. It has risen to a strange perfection
in the warp and bending of its long growth.
It has gathered all accidents into its purpose.
It has become the intention and
radiance of its dark fate.
It is a fact, sublime, mystical and unassailable.
In all the country there is no other like it.
I recognize in it a principle, an indwelling
the same as itself, and greater,
that I would be ruled by.
I see that it stands in its place and feeds upon it,
and is fed upon, and is native, and maker.[1]

~ WENDELL BERRY ~

Contents

Where to Find Topic Series

———⊶⊷———

Introduction

I STOOD WHERE A HOUSE has been just a few weeks before. Along with thousands of houses on the beach and for miles inland, a 27-foot storm surge had wiped the slab clean. Hurricane Katrina had made landfall just two months before right where I stood. Concrete foundations were all that was left of this community in Mississippi. There wasn't much debris—most of the houses and the stuff in them had been swept into the Gulf of Mexico.

I wasn't from Mississippi. I was a Texas boy transplanted to Massachusetts to be Senior Pastor of a church of about 500. When TV images of Katrina's destruction reached a diligent and godly member of my church named Caroline, God told her that our church would have a big part in helping a church and its surrounding community come back to life. God hooked us up with Pastor Don Elbourne of Lakeshore Baptist Church, and so began a long relationship that would send dozens of Yankees to the Deep South some twenty times in the coming years.

Our first trip was a reconnoiter mission consisting of Caroline, my wife and myself. And so, on that afternoon in early November in Lakeshore, Mississippi, I stood in the midst of what could only be described as utter destruction. Katrina made landfall on August 29, 2005 with winds of 135 mph and a 27-foot storm surge that raced inland six to twelve miles. The superintendent of the county later told me that of the 10,000 buildings in his county, he could count on both hands those that were still standing. Unimaginably powerful winds and enormous waves took the lives of 300 people and destroyed nearly everything.

As I stood in a state of shock in the yard of one of the destroyed homes, I looked down and saw something any man would recognize: the plastic emblem from a Craftsman toolbox. Here is a picture of that very emblem:

I reached down and picked it up. Though scratched, it still proudly bore the name we all know so well: *Craftsman.*

How did this 6" x 1" lightweight chunk of plastic manage to stay in the yard of its owner with 135 mph winds screaming over it and 27 feet of water pounding it? I was bewildered. But I was also proud. I was proud of this little hunk of toughness. It had survived! I put it in my pocket that day. It has found a place on my desk ever since.

Through the years, my desktop plastic 'Craftsman' faithfully bore witness to pure survival as I counseled dozens of people through every crisis known to humanity. Sadly, far too many of the people who sat in my office were living through the storm of divorce. Hurricanes are not preventable. Divorces are. Yet men and women sat before me crushed at what their spouse had done to them through divorce. A few sat in my office burdened by guilt at what they had done to their wife or husband that led to divorce.

As I journeyed with these bruised and bleeding people, two thoughts ran through my mind. First, I was thankful that I was not in their situation, and I was strongly confident that I would *never* be in their situation. I was a pastor after all! I loved my wife and worked hard to keep her happy. My second thought was how glad I was that I did not have to get into the dating scene at my age!

Little did I know how all that would change. My downward spiral began on December 16, 2013. That evening I attended a regular monthly meeting of the Leadership Council (elders) of the church I had pastored for twelve years. I knew these men and women intimately. I had *served them* and served *with them* for over a decade. We traveled on mission trips, worked side-by-side ministering to people and sweat out the tough decisions together. When their businesses failed I was there. When one was falsely accused of child abuse, I was there. When babies were born and parents died, I walked beside them. I had no reason to believe they had questions about my leadership or any other aspect of my job as Senior Pastor. In fact, just a few months earlier they had delivered their annual review to me with the usual, *"You are doing a great job but working too hard."*

But by the time this December meeting was over, the faith I had vested in them vanished. As I sat in the meeting and fielded their questions which seemed odd and out of place, it slowly dawned on me that they had been meeting behind my back, I could not trust them or my staff, and I couldn't go to anyone in the church for help. I felt utterly betrayed by the people I had loved and trusted, served and served with for over a decade. Not only did I *feel* betrayed, I actually had been. The pain I would experience over the next six months was unspeakably deep.

This group kept me in suspense for the next months, never directly accusing me of anything but also never transparently working toward a solution to whatever problem they thought we had. It was as if I had committed some unspeakable sin that even I didn't know about! In the end, they forced my termination. June 29, 2014 was my last Sunday. For the first time in decades, I was unemployed.[2]

The church in America today is not a growth industry. Pharmaceuticals? Now *there* is a growth industry! People will pay anything for their physical health but don't seem to care much about their spiritual health. The few churches looking for pastors or staff want young energetic bucks who, in their minds, can attract young families, the supposed *sine qua non* of successful churches. My youthful energy doesn't usually come through on resumes quickly perused by search teams.

---

[2] Our culture rightly honors those who serve with sacrifice such as firefighters, police, teachers, military personnel, etc. Pastors are left out of this group but they shouldn't be. Most pastors are brilliant people who could have invested themselves in lucrative careers. Instead, they give themselves to the sacrificial and usual brutal service of humanity for low salaries and minimal benefits. Your pastor is an unsung hero. Tell him or her you appreciate them. And if you really want to help, get on the finance team of your church and make sure your pastor has good health insurance and a comparable retirement program. If you don't do it, I can assure you no one else will.

The job market for unjustly terminated 52-year-old pastors is slim. Six months of working my network, combing job websites and sending resumes yielded nothing.

So in December 2014 we moved back to Austin, our hometown. I remember sitting in a Starbucks searching and sending via their Wi-Fi. I thought to myself, *So far there are no bites on ministry jobs. I will apply to Starbucks!* So I did. They never called me.

But God came through as he always does. In April I landed a part time job as a Hospice Chaplain. Meanwhile, a small rural Baptist church of German heritage was interested in us. The church was located in Kyle, just south of Austin. Grateful for the opportunity to serve again as a pastor and convinced this was exactly where God wanted me, I was happy to go from pastoring a church of 500 to being the new pastor of a church of 50. Life finally seemed to be getting back on track. Little did I know that this was to be the shortest pastorate of my life.

My wife of 32 years was the founder and director of a non-profit organization that rescues children in Tanzania and Kenya. We had served together teaching in Tanzania for nearly a year in the mid-1990s and through the intervening years God had called her to rescue children in East Africa as the AIDS epidemic decimated the middle generation of adults, leaving millions of kids without parents. I was fully supportive of her work and did all I could to help her fulfill God's call on her life.

Her work involved her traveling to Africa about three times a year. Just as I began the new pastorate in Kyle, she left for an extended trip to Tanzania. My 14-year-old son and I moved into the parsonage while she was gone. After she returned in mid-September, I left on a two-week teaching trip to Kenya and Tanzania where I would be teaching pastors and their churches about leadership and (ironically) family life. Care of our son usually prevented us from traveling together.

On October 22, 2015, I began the 38-hour trip from Tanzania to home. At 5:15 pm on October 23, 2015, I pulled into the carport at the parsonage in Kyle. My wife and I had many common friends in East Africa and I was excited to share news of them and the rest of my trip with her.

As I entered the carport that evening, my wife stepped from the back door of the parsonage with her mother in tow. I thought this was a bit strange but reasoned that perhaps they were greeting me after the long trip. I was in for the shock of my life. She met me in front of her car and told me that she was leaving me, and had, in fact, moved out of the church parsonage into an apartment while I was gone, taking our son with her.

In utter shock, I mumbled something, then went into the parsonage, immediately noticing how empty it was. On the kitchen counter was a manila envelope. Inside were legal documents, one of which stated that if I did not get a certain document signed and notarized by a certain date, the county constable would come to the parsonage and serve me papers. The thought of a constable coming to the parsonage of the church I pastored to serve me papers as if I were some kind of criminal horrified me.

As I pushed those papers aside I entered a surreal world in which everything I held dear was drifting away. It dawned on me that, try as I might, those things would never come back. I would lose my church, my chance at ever being a pastor again, my children, my hard-earned reputation, and the fulfillment of the dream and goal of growing old with the same person. I would now be a statistic—I would now be classified as 'divorced.'

All these things flooded into my mind and heart as I sat in a sparsely furnished house, alone. I walked into my son's room, now nearly empty. My heart was crushed. But I was exhausted. Two weeks of intense teaching and the long journey home left me empty. I determined to go to bed.

The next morning I crashed. The weight of being unjustly terminated from the church I loved and now being abandoned by my wife of 32 years came crashing down. A hospice chaplain describes better than I can what that moment feels like: *All meaning seems to have evaporated leaving behind in its wake an empty sinking hollowness filled with darkness.*[3]

It was Saturday morning and I would be preaching to my new church in less than 24 hours. What did the future hold for these dear people who had embraced my family and who my wife had pretended to embrace in kind? What would I tell the church and when? Would it be possible to continue being pastor of these people I had just gotten to know but whom I already dearly loved? I wasn't a dentist who could separate my personal from professional life. A pastor's *professional life* is integrally bound up in who he/she is *personally.* Whatever happened with my job would be directly related

---

[3] Mark LaRocca-Pitts, "Four FACTs Spiritual Assessment Tool," *Journal of Health Care Chaplaincy*, 21:2 (2015): 51-59., accessed January 3, 2017, DOI: 10.1080/08854726.2015.1015303.

to my now shattered personal life. The thought of losing another church was unbearable.

It was ALL unbearable. My body wracked with grief as the weight of the disaster came crashing down. I sobbed and yelled and cursed the world. I shouted out my hatred of the leaders of the church who had terminated me and of my wife who had made life so difficult and now seemingly impossible. My mind (and heart and soul) overflowed with thoughts, including suicide. Getting into my car and just driving away was an attractive option.

In that moment on that Saturday morning I reached out to Ken, my good friend and fellow traveler. It helped that he was (and remains) a brilliant psychotherapist.[4] He immediately understood where I was psychologically. He gently talked me off the ledge and made sure I had someone I could be with in this intense agony (Ken was 2,000 miles away in Massachusetts). Ken instantly recognized that my soul was crushed and could break at any moment. His heart opened up to my extreme distress and he absorbed some of my pain. He calmly and quietly listened, and when he spoke it was clear he understood my state of mind and the condition of my soul. He knew exactly what I needed to hear. Saturday morning, October 24, 2015 was a critical moment for me. Things could have gone in several directions. Ken's availability, his compassionate, understanding heart, and his gentle instructions kept me on a track that would lead to healing and recovery.

When I look back on those first days and then the weeks and months that follow, I ask myself:

---

[4] Ken is a Licensed Mental Health Counselor in the state of Massachusetts.

* What would have happened if I had chosen self-destruction rather than reconstruction?
* What was saved in my life then, now, and in my future by the compassionate and courageous help given to me by those closest to me (in addition to Ken, Sarah, my oldest sister, and Francisco, a counselor stepped up to help me)?
* How many men are in this very place at this very moment—dying a million deaths from crushed dreams, destroyed reputations, families lost?
* How many kids are silently suffering through their parents' divorce, and how could their dads be helped to rescue their children from needless guilt and wasted opportunities?

God used these and many other questions through the past three years to lead me to begin a ministry to divorced men. When I was facing the black hole of divorce, three people stepped in to build a bridge across the gaping chasm looming in front of me. God has called me to do for other men what these three people did for me. God called me to be here for you in your pain and agony. That's what the ***Daily Survival Guide for Divorced Men*** is all about. In my fractured state I rediscovered that time with God each morning and the wisdom offered by others through daily readings were the superglue that slowly put my fragmented soul back together.

Right now you are in pain and you are looking for relief. Know this: *Our God who created a world of immense variety has many tools to get back on your feet and back in the game.* And he will do it! ***You will get through this!*** But right now you are face down on the turf wondering if your playing days are over.

They're not. You are God's son, and he doesn't leave his kids on the field alone and bleeding. His specialty, in fact, is taking wounded warriors and rehabilitating them into magnificent men who give back to the very world that beat them to the ground.

Through this process you will be transformed in remarkable ways. You may be thinking: *I've been hammered with everyone telling me to change! I'm sick of it! I don't have the desire or energy to change!*

Maybe there are things in you that really do need to change, patterns of thinking and behaviors that contributed to your divorce. Addiction to pornography (or the real thing), working too much, being a bear at home come to mind. Or maybe you have been picked apart from head to toe for inconsequential things and you are sick of being criticized. *The last thing you want to hear from me is that you need to change!*

I get that. That's why I used the word *transform* instead of *change.* What I *don't* mean by the word *"transform"* is to make you feel guilty or ashamed or afraid. When people change out of guilt, shame or fear, it doesn't last. And that kind of 'transformation' is not what is really need or want. What I mean by *transformed* is the changing of your inward soul through a love relationship with God that is soul-nourishing and soul-building. Transformation is about God's good and powerful grace reshaping your mind, heart, soul and emotions for his glory and for your your good. That's a good thing. It's good for God, good for you, and good for the world.

In fact, if you ride this kayak all the way to the ocean, you will actually be thankful for the pain you are in right now because you will recognize that what you have gained in really knowing and being known by God is far better than anything bad the world can throw at you and anything good the world can entice you with.

Weird huh? That God can take something so terrible as your divorce and bring something spectacular out of it? But that's our God! He can take the crucifixion of his Son on Friday and turn it into a glorious resurrection on Sunday.

Just to be clear as to where we are headed with all this: God doesn't want to squeeze you from the outside until you fit some kind of mold that is acceptable to the people around you who have been squeezing you ever since you can remember. God wants to move in your life in a way you have never experienced, and through his powerful and amazing love, shift your heart and life in a direction that you will find deeply satisfying and fantastically rewarding. As God does this work inside you, all the outside stuff that everyone has been griping at you about will naturally change. Some people will like what they see you becoming. Others will not. Oh well! We want to please God *first.*

Now is your chance to grow into the man God intended you to be. You will discover that *the man he wants you to be* is that man *you really wanted to be all along.* You will experience a confidence and peace that seems to 'fit' you and your particular universe. You will experience a solid grip that holds firm through the storms that try to uproot you and send you out to sea.

For you engineer types, you know that *work = energy.* God's work in our souls is his energy working in the unseen depths of your soul (yes, engineer, you *do* have a soul!). God is not a drill sergeant who wants to erase who you are inside so you conform to some external standard. God's energy in you is motivated by his persistent love which relentlessly pursues you, his beloved son, so he can lavish his love on you and so you can really know him as your dad, perhaps the dad you never had.

Are you ready to experience God's love this way? Maybe all this seems daunting to you, perhaps overwhelming right now. As I look back on those first months following October 23, 2015, I remember that all I wanted was (1) relief from the pain and (2) hope for the future. Surviving through each day was about as much as my soul could grasp. I also remember that taking a few minutes each morning to spend time with God *saved my life from suicide, gave me comfort knowing that I was loved beyond imagination, and kept alive a tiny ember of hope that this terrible time in my life would not last forever.*

You may be down, but brother, you are not out. You may be crushed, but my friend, you are not dead. You may be face down on the turf, but *you will get up, take a deep breath, and get back in the game.* Know this: *No life has failed if God transforms and transmits his grace, love and power in, to and through you.*

Now a word regarding blame. Some of you reading this see yourself as the victim. You feel as if you have been on the receiving end of a raw deal. Others of you are perpetrators. You did something that was really wrong, like cheating on your wife. Understand this: there are two sides (or more) to every story. When a couple divorces, both are at fault. But it is also true that usually one is more responsible for the dissolution of the marriage than the other. The bottom line: whether you see yourself as the victim or the perpetrator, this daily guide is for you. The reality is that all of us are both vics and perps. We have *all* fallen short of the glory of God, of the ideal husband, of the perfect father.

But there is tremendous hope. By his power and through his grace, God can *repair* the damage done *to you*. By his power and through his grace, God can *forgive* the damage you have done *to others*, including your ex-wife and your family. We are damaged and we cause damage. We are messed up and we mess up others. A significant piece of the healing journey is to understand this simple concept—*we all need to be repaired and we all need to be forgiven*.

When we enter this process something amazing happens: As we experience God's gracious healing and gentle conviction he begins to use us to clean up our messes and help repair others. I know this all sounds daunting right now but it is doable by

* Taking one day at a time,
* Seeking God's grace and strength, and
* Holding on to hope in this moment and for the future.

Sitting next to my computer in front of me is that 6" x 1" chunk of toughness, that Craftsman emblem that began its journey attached to a brand new shiny toolbox bought by some guy in Lakeshore, Mississippi. Little did it know that it would end up on the desk of a newly single ex-pastor now living in a one-bedroom apartment in Kyle, Texas. But it did and here we are—survivors! That emblem has made it so far and so have I!

But friend, I want to do more than survive. I want to thrive! Hence this daily guide to help you survive *and* thrive.

If a non-descript hunk of plastic can ride out Hurricane Katrina and give inspiration to you and me, who knows what God has in store for you! My scratched-up Craftsman emblem still bears witness to survival and inspires me to keep going. I want you to keep going too. God has a bright future for you.

Nulla tenaci invia est via...
For the tenacious, no road is impassable.

How to Use This Guide

———∞———

* **Choose a time**... morning, lunch, evening. Mornings are best because you can usually control when you get up. Everything in your mind and body will tell you that getting up 30 minutes earlier than normal is *not normal!* Trust God to make up the energy you lose from a little lost sleep, and he will do it. I promise.

* **Find a quiet place**... free from distractions.

* **Settle your mind**. Ask God to quiet your thoughts. Don't worry if your brain is still cluttered. God is just glad we show up.

* **Ask God to give you peace**. Take a deep breath and rest in his care. For guys this is tough because we want to be in control. Surprise! You are not in control and in the end, that's a good thing. Recognize this reality by giving yourself into God's care. Imagine him giving you a huge bear hug.

* Listen to, play or sing along with some **worship songs** if this is helpful.

* **Read this Daily Guide** beginning with the first day. The readings are designed to carry you along a journey of healing. Note that some days will involve more reading than others. Hang in there and read each day completely. Nothing is more important than your recovery, so giving yourself time to it is a worthy investment.

* **Take time to pray**. Prayer is not complicated. Just tell God what the heck you want to tell him. If you are new to this, this will be a one-way conversation—you

will talk and God will listen. With time and patience, however, you will begin to hear the voice of the Shepherd.

* If writing stuff down (**journaling**) helps, do it. For decades I've heard how wonderful journaling is. Frankly, I've been too busy to journal. But if it helps to put your thoughts down, do it. You may write out what is going on in your life or perhaps write out a prayer to God.

* When you are in a bad spot emotionally—say you are in a rage—**use either the table of contents or the index at the back of this book to find all the daily readings that relate to any topic** (*anger* for example). Just the act of slowing down, finding this book, looking up the topic and reading a helpful word will dispel your rage in amazing ways!

A Few Notes on What to Expect

---

* Some of the language is raw. My writing is not squeaky clean.

* Some of the quotes will not be expressions of what I believe to be true. They are meant to get you to think. Take them as they are and consider whether they express truth or not.

* Many of the readings are designed to be in a short series. In other words, we will explore one topic over a series of several days. Each day will give you something to think about and help you on this road to recovery. But some days may not be wrapped up neatly. Keep reading, keep thinking, keep praying! A table with the series titles and places they show up is found here.

* This is not intended in any way to be legal advice. In my research I found that most resources for divorced men are of the nature of giving legal advice. This is not that.

* I will not cover dating in this devotional. The only advice I will give is that if you are newly divorced, it is generally recommended not to date until you get your feet on the ground and experience significant personal growth. The general rule is to wait two years.

The journey you are on is hard. REMEMBER: You will get through this. *You will get through this.* **You will get through this. You will Survive and Thrive beyond your divorce.**

What you are experiencing now doesn't define you and will not last forever. Healing and hope are ahead of you. Believe it because it is true. I know. I've been there.

Critical Things to Think About Now

- **Invest in time with God.** Spending time with God will give you energy, not take it away. Getting up 30 minutes earlier each day to be with God will *not* make you more tired. Your true strength comes from God. Time with him will put energy *into* you, not take it away. For more on this **GO TO DAYS 116-122.**

- **Lower your expectations of what you can accomplish**. No one expects a patient after open-heart surgery to run a marathon the next day. Or week. Or year. Dial back what you expect to accomplish in this tough season of life. This will most likely *not* be the most productive time in your life. That's OK. As you heal, strength will return. There will be times of amazing productivity in the future. It is winter now, not spring. Be easy on yourself. For more on this **GO TO DAY 174.**

- **Invest in your children.** Divorce takes energy and attention away from kids and puts it squarely on adults. Your kids are hurting and now, more than ever, need your attention. Don't rail about your spouse to them. Love them, listen to them, hug them. For more on this **GO TO DAYS 160 and 176.**

- **You must keep working**, so think about what you must do at work to get by. When you are working, *work*. Concentrate, focus, get the job done. Don't waste time at work worrying about your personal life.

- As painful and distasteful as it is, invest concentrated energy on the **legal and financial** aspects of divorce. Bear down and focus. Push through.
- **Exercise.** I can't emphasize enough how sweating will give you energy. Don't go for the marathon, just get moving at least a little every day. Small steps lead to big strides. You will be surprised how a little physical energy invested when you least feel like it will energize you for the rest of the day. For more on this **GO TO DAY 55.**
- **Sleep.** A common experience for the newly divorced is to want to curl up in bed and escape through sleep. This is normal since your mind is working hard to process all that is happening. Sleep, but don't sleep too much. If you *just* want to sleep that could be a sign of depression. You will need more sleep but not too much. For more on this **GO TO DAY 54.**
- **Don't waste your energy** or money on anxiety, drugs, alcohol, pornography, buying stuff or escaping to the Caribbean. That's stupid and only makes things worse. *Don't make things worse.*

Sources for Immediate Help

———⊶⊷⊶———

IF YOU ARE IN IMMEDIATE crisis thinking you may do harm to yourself or someone else, call one of the numbers below or go to their website now (services with only a website do not have a crisis phone line):

- For direct and immediate help, **<u>Dial 911</u>**.
- **National Suicide Prevention Lifeline: 800-273-8255** *www.suicidepreventionlifeline.org*
- **Homicide Prevention Hotline & website: 800-273-8255** *www.savingcain.org*
- **Alcoholics Anonymous**: *www.aa.org*
- **Celebrate Recovery** (A Christian-based recovery program for all addictions meeting in local churches): www.celebraterecovery.com
- **Divorce Recovery**: 800-489-7778 *www.divorcecare.org*
- Help with Pornography:
- *www.faithfulandtrue.com* (Faithful & True Ministries, Mark Laaser)
- *www.puredesire.org*
- www.2.bebroken.com

You Will Get Through This Because God is For You

— ✦ —

THE WORD

In the day when I cried out, you answered me,
and made me bold with strength in my soul.

— PSALM 138.3

THOUGHT FOR THE DAY:

You start with a darkness to move through, but
sometimes the darkness moves through you.

~ DEAN YOUNG

THE MOST IMPORTANT QUESTION ON my mind growing up was, "Am I good enough?" The answers from my dad and others were conflicted. On one hand, I was told I was special and nothing could stop me. I would be spectacular. On the other hand, if I was anything less than spectacular, it was my fault. Given the deluge of criticism I received, it seemed that though I was special, I never seemed to measure up to my specialness!

Not to kick a dead horse till its teeth fall out, but most of us men grew up with this double message from our parents, our schools, our peers. To be accepted we had to jump through hoops that were just out of reach. The message we received was, *you can do it... but you probably won't.*

Implicit in this message was that people were both *for me* and *against me,* both my friend and my enemy, my companion and my challenger. People were as likely to push me down as they were to help me up.

God is not like that. *Did you get that?* God is not a super-sized human being who acts like the people who raise us and cast us off into adulthood. God is *for* you. He is *with* you. He is *on your side.* He wants you to *win,* to *succeed,* to have *peace.* He is not capricious, he does not change his ways or his thoughts. He is not human. He is God.

So what about this God? Whose side is he on? Romans 8.31 says, *"If God is for us, who can be against us?"* God IS for you!

This is the truth you need to let sink deep in your soul: God **IS** for you, and because he is for you, **you will get through this.**

Paul goes on to say in verse 32, *He who did not spare his own Son, but gave him up for us all—how will he not also, along with him, graciously give us all things?*

Perhaps you cheated on your wife and the bed you now lie in is the bed you made. Maybe you came home from work to find your stuff on the curb with a note attached, *"Get out!"* Perhaps you came home to find your wife and kids gone, the house empty. Maybe you and your wife had a terrible argument and one of you stormed out. It could even be that you hit your wife and now you are facing criminal charges of abuse.

There are perps and vics, and the reality is that we are all some of each. Whatever your situation, whoever you think are, God is *for* you. He wants you to know him and experience his presence and his power to sustain you through this time and transform you into the man he made you to be.

Just start with this simple reality: **God is FOR you.**

If you don't believe that right now, give God some time and space to work. Ask him to show himself to you. He will do it, I guarantee it!

In the day when I cried out, you answered me, and made me bold with strength in my soul. (Psalm 138.3)

THINK ABOUT IT...

* Who do you imagine God to be?
* If you were face-to-face with God, what would he look like? What would he say? What would he do?
* Where do you think your images of God came from?

LIFE COMMITMENT:

I choose to believe God is for me and that he is on my side. I choose to believe that despite what circumstances may say about my life, God has my best interests in mind and I can trust him with my present and with my future.

Pain and What to Do with It

The Word

*What I feared has come upon me; what I
dreaded has happened to me. I have no peace, no
quietness; I have no rest, but only turmoil.*

— Job 3.25–26

Thought for the Day:

*All meaning seems to have evaporated
leaving behind in its wake an empty sinking
hollowness filled with darkness.*[5]

~ Mark LaRocca-Pitts

Wikipedia defines pain as *"A distressing feeling often caused by
intense or damaging stimuli...."*

But you don't know pain until you have experienced
pain; then you *know* pain.

The moment I knew I was being divorced, my soul was
transported to a place it had never been before. The pain

---

[5] Mark LaRocca-Pitts, Four FACTs Spiritual Assessment Tool, *Journal of
Health Care Chaplaincy*, 21:2, 2015, 51-59.

I experienced cannot be explained, only experienced. Millions of men experience this pain, but it goes unspoken and unaddressed because our culture says that men cannot feel that way. But I did.

After about six months of spiraling black thoughts, emotions tumbling all over the place and living through the sheer agony of what I was going through, I wondered what would happen if I just started posting *all* my thoughts on Facebook. What if I posted raw, unfiltered comments on what I thought, what I felt, and what I considered doing?

The few times I actually did reveal my inner reality through posting on Facebook, the pushback was swift and trite—the theme of the message being, *"God will take care of you, suck it up, have faith. Get over it."*[6]

In other words, "We don't really want to hear about your problems, and we certainly don't want to listen to you whine about them."

But the reality is that I was dying inside. My heart was crushed, my soul was disintegrating inside me.

---

[6] For more insight, see Andrew Root, *"There's No Crying on Social Media!"* accessed March 24, 2017, http://www.christianitytoday.com/ct/2017/march/theres-no-crying-on-social-media.html?utm_source=ctweeklyhtml&utm_medium=Newsletter&utm_term=14285049&utm_content=502739904&utm_campaign=email.

Then I found this verse in Job.[7] I think of Job as a fairly manly guy. I mean, he was super successful and seemed to be a genuinely good and humble man, but strong as well. But when his world came crashing down, he told it like it was: *What I feared has come upon me; what I dreaded has happened to me. I have no peace, no quietness; I have no rest, but only turmoil."*

If you think you are not in pain, check again. If you think you cannot feel your pain, step back and observe what you are feeling. If you think it is unmanly to name your pain and try to offload it, then consider Job. Job hurt and he said how much he hurt.

Here's the thing: *God did not cause your pain but he knows about it.* And he knows that he can do something with your pain—like ease it up over time and even transform it. God doesn't waste pain. Think about that: *God does not waste pain.*

One of my favorite thinkers states, *You will be wounded. Your work is to find God and grace inside the wounds.*[8]

You're in pain—deep pain. The world may not want to hear about it or even care, but God does. Tell him about your pain. Then ask him to do something with it. If you keep your heart open, you will *find God and grace inside the wounds.* That's what this journey is about. Hang in here with me.

---

[7] The story of Job (pronounced like it rhymes with 'robe') is found in the Bible, the 18th book in the Hebrew Bible (the Old Testament). Job was a righteous, prosperous man who loved God. But Job lost everything—his family, his wealth, his health—very quickly to various disasters.

[8] Richard Rohr, Joseph Durepos, and Tom McGrath, *On the Threshold of Transformation: Daily Meditations for Men* (Chicago: Loyola Press, 2010), p. 255.

THINK ABOUT IT...

* Think back to a time when someone caused you pain. What did you feel? Anger? Sadness? Resignation? Hopelessness? Helplessness?
* What did you do? Rage? Retreat? Learn something new?
* What do you feel right now?

LIFE REALITY CHECK:

I acknowledge my pain. It hurts and it hurts deep in my soul.

Transformed or Transmitted?[9]

—∞∞∞—

THE WORD

> *A bruised reed he will not break, and a smoldering*
> *wick he will not snuff out. In faithfulness he*
> *will bring forth justice; he will not falter or be*
> *discouraged till he establishes justice on earth.*

— ISAIAH 42.3–4

THOUGHT FOR THE DAY:

> *We can choose to throw stones, to stumble on them,*
> *to climb over them, or to build with them.*

~ WILLIAM ARTHUR WARD

PAIN COMES TO ALL LIVING creatures, but the unique pain of divorce comes to only some of us. Whatever the source, the question before you is, *What will I do with my pain?* This is an extraordinarily hard question to answer and however you answer it now will be challenged in the days, weeks and

---

[9] This phrase comes from Richard Rohr whose wisdom and ability to turn a phrase I greatly admire. I can't think of a better way to say this so with humility I shamelessly borrow from Fr. Rohr. He gave me permission!

months ahead. You will be asking this question of yourself many times and will have to struggle with the answer each time.

When others have answered this question poorly, untold misery has been visited upon our world. That's because of a fundamental law of the universe: *Pain that is not transformed is transmitted.*[10]

Untransformed pain turned *outward* becomes violence against others. Pain turned *inward* turns to violence against oneself. Neither is a healthy option.

Untransformed pain lashes out at others and self. Untransformed pain only multiplies as the victims of our untransformed pain must decide what to do with the pain *we* have inflicted on *them.* And so the cycle that began in the Garden continues into the world today.[11] Untransformed pain is like spilling oil on a pond—it keeps spreading and is impossible to put back into the jar.

We lash out at others because we think that if we unload our pain we will be rid of it. But hurting others only increases our pain, it never diminishes it. If we turn our pain against ourselves, we somehow believe that we can kill our pain with

---

[10] "Richard Rohr Quote." A-Z Quotes, accessed December 28, 2016, http://www.azquotes.com/quote/814475.

[11] The 'Garden' to which I refer is the Garden of Eden. The story of humanity's creation, fall and redemption starts in this remarkable story found in Genesis, the first book of the Bible, the first four chapters (Genesis 1-4). I recommend reading these chapters. It explains a lot of how we got here, what went wrong, and God's purpose in bringing us back. For a different (but I believe to be thorough and true) view of these chapters, see John H. Walton, *The Lost World of Genesis One: Ancient Cosmology and The Origins Debate* (Downers Grove, IL: IVP Academic, 2009) and John H. Walton, *The Lost World of Adam And Eve: Genesis 2-3 and the Human Origins Debate* (Downers Grove, IL: IVP Academic, 2015).

pain. That's like trying to quench your thirst by not drinking. To think we can use pain against others or ourselves to lessen our own pain doesn't make sense. But it is what most of us do.

You hurt. Like Job you *have no rest, only turmoil.* What to do with your hurt? There is a better way. Today, would you commit to continuing the journey to find that better way?

THINK ABOUT IT...

As you begin your journey toward recovery, think about what you are doing with your pain...

* In what ways are you offloading your pain onto *others?*
  __ I lash out at others.

  __ My mind is dominated by thoughts of revenge.

  __ I am seeking ways to hurt those who have hurt me.
* In what ways are you turning your pain inward onto *yourself?*

  __ I have serious thoughts of suicide. (If so, call the Suicide Prevention Hotline: 800-273-8255)

  __ I am depressed.

  __ I am choosing risky behaviors, not caring what happens to me.

  __ I am medicating myself with alcohol and/or drugs.
* Is your strategy working?

  __ Yes, I feel better and believe that lashing out is a productive strategy for dealing with my pain.

  __ No, though it seems that transmitting my pain would get rid of it, I still feel the pain.

  __ I'm not sure... still thinking about it.

LIFE COMMITMENT:

I have a choice as to what to do with my pain. Though at this moment I don't fully understand what this means, I choose to let God transform my pain. I choose not to transmit it.

Giving Your Pain Away

———— ◦◦◦ ————

THE WORD

*Therefore, since we are surrounded by such a great
cloud of witnesses, let us throw off everything that
hinders and the sin that so easily entangles, and let
us run with perseverance the race marked out for us.
Let us fix our eyes on Jesus, the author and
perfecter of our faith, who for the joy set before him
endured the cross, scorning its shame, and sat
down at the right hand of the throne of God.
Consider him who endured such opposition from sinful
men, so that you will not grow weary and lose heart.*

— HEBREWS 12.1–3

THOUGHT FOR THE DAY:

*Even if the whole world refuses to understand or validate
the anguish one is experiencing, yet Jesus Christ never
changes. He always understands and remains willing
to help and bring healing to every throbbing emotion.*[12]

~ KETURAH MARTIN

---

[12] Keturah C. Martin, *Jesus Never Wastes Pain but Can Bring Eternal Gain*
(Bloomington, IN: Xlibris Corp, 2014), 392.

IT WAS THE LAST RUN of the day. The sun was setting, the slopes beginning to clear of skiers. I pushed off the mountain and fairly screamed down the course. All was well until the bottom of the run. My ski caught the top of a stump protruding through the snow. I tumbled end-over-end, the skis whirling around me. Blood gushed down my face when I sat up. Damage assessment revealed a deep gash on my head.

An hour later a doctor used needle and thread to sew my head back together. It hurt.

I got through it by focusing on something else: the amazing story I had to tell back in school!

When we hurt we naturally focus on ourselves and the source of our pain. When we hurt from divorce, there is no glory in the pain, only the pain. This frustrating dynamic of the pain of divorce can tempt us to transmit our pain to the ones who have caused it, including ourselves. And rare is the man (including myself) who has not transmitted his pain in some way—or a lot of ways.

There is another way, a third element that can lift us out of the cycle of feeling pain and transmitting it, only to get slammed again, and transmitting it... you get the picture. It is possible to break this cycle through the transformation of our pain. The catalyst (and source) of our transformation is Jesus himself.

Let us fix our eyes on Jesus...

When I was sitting in the doctor's office my pain was transformed by fixing my eyes on myself and the glory the story would bring to myself.

When you are sitting alone with the horrendous pain of divorce, you may fix your eyes on yourself out of pity or guilt, or you may fix your eyes on your ex out of anger. There's no glory in that.

Instead, look to Christ and consider what he did with his pain. Jesus was perfectly innocent—he had never sinned. Yet he suffered the worst injustice—and the most painful consequences—death on a Roman cross. What did he do with his pain?

Jesus knew God was transforming his pain into glory for God and for our good. Through the amazing story of Jesus' sacrifice for us, God would be the hero of the greatest love story ever told, and the object of his suffering (us), would be saved from an eternity in hell and, instead, spend eternity in heaven.

Jesus didn't focus on the people who nailed him to the cross. Jesus lifted his eyes to God. God's glory came first, not personal revenge. To Jesus our salvation was a higher priority than personal comfort. Jesus could sit with his pain knowing that enduring his pain well would glorify God and save us from hell.

You are in pain. There is no personal glory in this pain, no great story to tell your friends when you get back to school. Your pain is embarrassing, frustrating, maddening. But your pain is not beyond transformation and redemption. Take your eyes off yourself and *Consider him who endured such opposition from sinful men, so that you will not grow weary and lose heart.*

Reality check: I know this may be nearly impossible to read much less think about actually doing. In fact, you may be about to throw this book through the window! Hang in there with me. God will do a work in you. It will take time.

By looking to Jesus you are taking your eyes off yourself and those who have caused the pain in your life. In the days ahead we will explore exactly how to focus on Jesus, but for now, commit to looking to Christ rather than focusing on yourself or your ex.

THINK ABOUT IT...

* Who is Jesus to you? Was he weak or strong? Was he a man or a wimp?
* What do you think Jesus thought when he was being nailed to the cross? If you were Jesus, what would you have been thinking?
* What would have happened if Jesus had chosen revenge while hanging on the cross, sending death angels to take out those who had unjustly nailed him on those wooden beams?

LIFE COMMITMENT:

Though I don't understand all that this means right now, I choose to let God transform my pain by fixing my eyes on Jesus. I deliberately choose to trust that Jesus can transform my pain for God's glory and my good.

What Does a Win Look Like?

———— ✑ ————

THE WORD:

*For we are God's workmanship, created in
Christ Jesus to do good works, which God
prepared in advance for us to do.*

— EPHESIANS 2.10

THOUGHT FOR THE DAY:

Information is not necessarily transformation.

~ RICHARD ROHR

AT ANY POINT ALONG OUR journey we need to ask ourselves, *"What does a win look like right now?"* If we have the wrong answer to this question, all our efforts are for nothing. All this PAIN is for nothing!

Charlie Strong became the head coach of the University of Texas football team in 2014. At the time, UT President Bill Powers said that one of the reasons Strong was attractive was that he focused on the overall development of the student-athletes. Strong said *"I want to see [the players] develop on the field as well as off the field.... The program is always going to be about physical and mental toughness.*"[13]

After three losing seasons, Strong was fired. In his press release after being fired Strong stated: *"I do understand that it comes down to wins and losses, and we have not done our job in that area yet."*[14]

What does a win look like at UT? The President of UT said that it looked like well-developed athletes. Strong agreed. But after three years it became apparent that for powerful alumni, the *real* win was a football program that won games, player development be damned.

What does a win look like in your life right now?

Now is the best time to sit back and ask yourself how you want this moment remembered. As you think about what a win looks like for you, ask yourself, *How do I want my kids to remember me in this moment? What do I want people to say of me at the end of the day?*

In the next few days I want to suggest five 'wins' for you to consider. They are:

* Clarity
* Passion
* Solidarity with Others
* Solid Decisions
* Integrity

---

[13] Ted Madden, *"UT introduces Charlie Strong as new Longhorns coach | kvue. com Austin,"* (January 6, 2014) from Wikipedia, "Charlie Strong," accessed January 15, 2017, https://en.wikipedia.org/wiki/Charlie_Strong.

[14] *"Texas football coach Charlie Strong fired after 3 years"* Last updated November 26, 2016, accessed January 06, 2017, http://kxan.com/2016/11/26/texas-football-coach-charlie-strong-fired-after-3-years/.

THINK ABOUT IT...

* What has winning looked like in your life up to now? How has that worked out for you?
* Do others consider you a winner? Why or why not?
* What does winning look like to God?

LIFE COMMITMENT:

I commit to giving serious consideration to what really matters at the end of the season.

The Win—*Clarity*

—∞∞—

THE WORD

A bruised reed he will not break, and a
smoldering wick he will not snuff out. In
faithfulness he will bring forth justice.

— ISAIAH 42.3

THOUGHT FOR THE DAY:

The pessimist complains about the wind; the optimist
expects it to change; the realist adjusts the sails.

~ WILLIAM ARTHUR WARD

A FRIEND OF MINE WAS a mechanic at Carswell Air Force Base in Fort Worth, Texas. One day he came to church shaken. I asked what happened. He said that the day before, a French pilot was training in a fighter. The pilot came screaming over the runway upside down, then the pilot pulled 'up.' The problem was that 'up' to the pilot was, in reality, straight down onto the tarmac just outside the hanger where my friend was working on a plane. Imagine an F-16 slamming into the pavement at that kind of speed. This disaster happened because the pilot thought he was right-side-up when he was really up-side-down.[15]

Though the pilot was far more qualified and accomplished than probably almost anyone reading this, the *lack of clarity* on his part led to death and destruction. He visualized the path ahead upside down, and that is where he ended up... or rather down.

Clarity begins with how you view God. He is for you, remember? He did not cause your pain but he can transform it. He will strengthen you so that in the end so that *you will get through this*. These are points of clarity you will want to drill into your mind and soul. You need to be clear about these truths about God and about yourself. Take a moment to visualize in your mind how these truths can work themselves out in your future.

Tony Dungy was head coach of the Indianapolis Colts from 2002 to 2008. He was the first African American football coach to win a Super Bowl (2006). He knows something about being clear about football and about life. He writes:

> *Visualization increases chances of success—not just in football but in any area of life. If we can't see ourselves succeeding... we won't have any confidence in those roles and be able to perform them well. But if we can see ourselves fulfilling our responsibilities effectively, achieving our goals, and relating to others healthily, we are much more likely to have the vision and the*

---

[15] *"List of accidents and incidents involving military aircraft (1980–89)."* Wikipedia, accessed January 05, 2017, https://en.wikipedia.org/wiki/List_of_accidents_and_incidents_involving_military_aircraft_%281980%E2%80%9389%29.

confidence to do those things. We tend to be able to accomplish what we can see.[16]

In the wake of divorce you feel anything but successful. Don't let your present circumstances determine your future success. Picture yourself as successfully navigating through this storm and emerging stronger and more resilient than ever.

THINK ABOUT IT...

* Thinking back on your life, can you remember a time being really clear about what to do or what the future could hold for you?
* Are you confused or clear about things now?
* What specific areas are you confused about?

LIFE COMMITMENT:
I commit to asking God to give me clarity about himself, his view of me, and how to think about and respond to my current situation.

---

[16] Tony Dungy and Nathan Whitaker, *The One Year Uncommon Life Daily Challenge* (Carol Stream, IL: Tyndale House Publishers, 2011), Kindle Location 199.

The Win—*Passion*

—⁂—

THE WORD

The heart of a man is like deep water.

— PROVERBS 20.5

THOUGHT FOR THE DAY:

Do more than belong: participate. Do more than
care: help. Do more than believe: practice.
Do more than be fair: be kind. Do more than
forgive: forget. Do more than dream: work.

~ WILLIAM ARTHUR WARD

I RODE MY BIKE OVER 5,000 miles last year. On one ride I was only two miles away from home when I noticed my front tire making an odd noise. Then it got really hard to peddle. My tire went flat to the ground. Most flats are slow leaks. Not this one. My tire was at zero psi and there was no moving forward without a fix. The culprit was a big Texas thorn that made short work of my tire and tube.

Divorce is a thorn that takes the air right out of your life. Whatever passion you had before is gone. But why do we view the flat tire of divorce as a permanent state of deflation? When my bike stopped on the highway I didn't believe for a second that I would spend the rest of my life sitting on the side of the road with a flat tire. I didn't even believe that this flat could hold me up for more than 15 minutes!

But there is a difference between a tire and your soul. When a tire is flat, we know how to fix it. When the soul deflates we may not know how to blow it back up and get back to speed. But lack of knowledge is no excuse to sink into despair. It is possible to regain your passion. Or, more likely, to actually get a real passion for life perhaps for the very first time.

The truth is most men are stumbling through life with no sense of mission or purpose. If you are one of those guys, *now is your chance to discover who you are and what you are made to do.* In other words, this is your opportunity to slow down and look into the deep waters of your soul to find your passion.

John Maxwell asks penetrating questions: *Do you know your life's mission? What stirs your heart? What do you dream about?*[17]

If your highest goal in life is to have the best lawn in the neighborhood, you are off track. Now is the time to find out who you are and what you are made for. We will unpack this in the weeks ahead but for now, *know that your flat tire can be fixed!* Determine to seriously pursue finding and fulfilling your passion.

Here are some suggestions from Maxwell on discovering your passion:

---

[17] John C. Maxwell, *The Maxwell Daily Reader: 365 Days of Insight to Develop the Leader Within You and Influence Those Around You* (Nashville: Thomas Nelson, 2007), 385.

1. *Get next to people who possess great desire [passion].*
2. *Develop discontent with the status quo.*
3. *Search for a goal that excites you.*
4. *Put your most vital possessions into that goal.*
5. *Visualize yourself enjoying the rewards of that goal.*[18]

A win looks like being CLEAR about *where you are now* and clear about your PASSION *for your future.*

THINK ABOUT IT...

* Do you know your life's mission?
* What stirs your heart?
* What do you dream about?

LIFE COMMITMENT:

I commit to asking God to give me clarity about who he wants me to be and what he wants me to do with the rest of my life.

---

[18] John C. Maxwell, *Failing Forward: Turning Mistakes into Stepping-Stones for Success* (Nashville: Thomas Nelson Publishers, 2000), 171.

The Win—*Solidarity with Others*

———◊◊◊———

THE WORD

> *Two are better than one, because they*
> *have a good return for their work:*
> *If one falls down, his friend can help him up.*
> *But pity the man who falls and has no one to help him up!*
> *Though one may be overpowered,*
> *two can defend themselves.*

— ECCLESIASTES 4.9–12

THOUGHT FOR THE DAY:

> *A true friend knows your weaknesses but shows you*
> *your strengths; feels your fears but fortifies your faith;*
> *sees your anxieties but frees your spirit; recognizes*
> *your disabilities but emphasizes your possibilities.*

~ WILLIAM ARTHUR WARD

EVERY THIRD SATURDAY AT 7.30 in the morning a group of about 80 guys would meet in the basement of the church to have breakfast together, sing a few songs and hear words of encouragement and challenge. One morning I watched two men talk together. One was the owner of a large business he had built himself—marvelously successful by any measure of the world's standards.

The wealthy man was deep in a conversation with a man who had just lost his job. The amazing thing about this conversation was that this was just a conversation between two guys who loved God. The rich guy didn't see himself as better than the poor guy. The guy who just lost his job wasn't groveling before the rich guy. Instead, this was just two men, equal in the eyes of God, sharing life together.

This kind of camaraderie doesn't happen in our culture because men are made to go it alone. We are designed to compete. In the old days only one guy killed the deer for his family, so you better be that guy. Only one boy got the girl, so you better beat the other boys to the girl. It's all about competition. We are wired to find our place in the male order of things. I must find out who is above me and who is below me.

The problem with this way of doing life is that, by definition, *no one is beside me.* That's a lonely place.

When divorce slams you in the face, the loneliness only increases. Since men are not supposed to feel pain, we think we can't tell anyone, and if we do actually tell someone what's going on, we must pretend we are handling it with no problem.

But inside we're dying. We may find solace in a bottle or a pill or the internet. We may turtle up, hunkering down to ride out the storm. The problem with this strategy is that it never produces anything good. Left to our own thoughts, we go down destructive pathways. Left alone with no one to prop us up, we are unbalanced and eventually tump over.

Everything in you will tell you to pull back from life. Don't do it. Instead, believe what King Solomon said: *Two are better than one, because they have a good return for their work: If one falls down, his friend can help him up.*[19]

THINK ABOUT IT...

* On a scale of 0 to 10, (0 being not lonely at all to 10, absolutely completely lonely), how lonely are you?

  0—1—2—3—4—5—6—7—8—9—10

* List two guys you know you can call anytime day or night for help.

  _____ Phone # _____
  _____ Phone # _____

* If the two lines above are BLANK, list two guys who you **THINK** might be willing to be your friend:

  _____ Phone # _____
  _____ Phone # _____

* Call the first one on your list. Take him to lunch or something. Be creative. It really can't be that hard to get together. Dogs do it. We can too.

* If none of the above work (or you just want to talk) give me a call or send me an email!

---

[19] King Solomon, King David's son, ruled over Israel during its most prosperous and powerful days (970-931 BCE). He was famous for his wisdom, but in later life he gave up his godly principles to pursue pleasure at all costs. Like most men, Solomon did not finish well. Let's not be like most men!

LIFE COMMITMENT:

I commit to resisting the urge to turtle. I am asking God to bring into my life some other men who can walk beside me.

The Win—*Solid Decisions*

——— ✦ ———

THE WORD

*If any of you lacks wisdom, he should ask God, who
gives generously to all without finding fault, and it
will be given to him. But when he asks, he must believe
and not doubt, because he who doubts is like a wave
of the sea, blown and tossed by the wind. That man
should not think he will receive anything from the Lord;
he is a double-minded man, unstable in all he does.*

— JAMES 1.5–8

THOUGHT FOR THE DAY:

*The optimist lives on the peninsula of infinite
possibilities; the pessimist is stranded on
the island of perpetual indecision.*

~ WILLIAM ARTHUR WARD

AS MY LIFE UNRAVELED, DECISIONS had to be made but I was
not sure my heart, soul and mind were in a healthy place to

move forward with any confidence. But another factor was at work. When life tumbles down you can become so disheartened that you really don't care what you decide.

God is not surprised at what has happened. He knows about your situation and he cares for you and is *for you*, even if the cause of the divorce lies mainly with you. He wants you to *do the next right thing* even if you have made many bad decisions up to now.

The best decision you can make right now is to make good decisions. Poor decisions now will only further tangle up the mess, and you really don't want that.

When divorce was headed my way, I yelled a lot. I cried. I cursed. But I did not put a .380 bullet into my head. I didn't get in the car and start driving. I didn't go onto Facebook and write a hate-filled treatise. Instead I called a good friend. Together we assessed the situation and made some short-term decisions to get me through the immediate crisis.

Now is the time when wins in the areas of CLARITY and SOLIDARITY will really pay off.

Seek clarity by *first* seeking God and asking him to guide you. James says, *If any of you lacks wisdom, he should ask God.* There's no *if* when it comes to whether I lack wisdom or not! I lack! But God is ready and eager to fill my lack.

Notice the promise that follows the invitation: *[Wisdom] will be given to him* because God is a generous giver and he gives to all, *without finding fault.* Whether perp or vic, God wants to guide you every step of this painful way. God speaks first and foremost through his Bible. Get a Bible and start reading. Start with reading the book of Psalms for right now. Seek God.

Second, trust that God will speak through smart people. This is where solidarity with a few good people will really get you through. Who do you need to contact? That depends on your situation, but you will most likely be helped by (1) a trusted friend, (2) a pastor, (3) a professional counselor, and, (4) a lawyer.

The world may seem to be shifting under your feet. You may feel you are in a free fall. You may be raging at yourself, at your wife (or ex-wife), you may be sad beyond belief. You may be *like a wave of the sea, blown and tossed by the wind.* But right now ask God for wisdom and let him lead you to smart people to get you through.

Your goal is to *do the next right thing.* The reality is that your emotions may get in the way of making solid decisions. Ask God for direction and then get in touch with good people to stand with you and guide you.

THINK ABOUT IT...

* Do you believe God is the smartest being in all the Universe (and beyond) and that he wants to guide you for his glory and your good?
* If you are not sure, would you be willing to give him the chance to lead you?

LIFE COMMITMENT:

I commit to praying for God's help and guidance and contacting smart people to help me through this.
I will call... _____

My good friend _____.
My pastor _____.
A counselor _____.
A lawyer _____.

The Win—*Integrity*

—⚬⚬⚬—

THE WORD

> *But seek first his kingdom and his righteousness,*
> *and all these things will be given to you as well.*

— MATTHEW 6:33

THOUGHT FOR THE DAY:

> *We do not think ourselves into new ways of living,*
> *we live ourselves into new ways of thinking.*

~ RICHARD ROHR

A NEW COUPLE AT CHURCH asked to visit with me. We made the appointment and met a few days later. The issue at hand had to do with the husband's previous divorce. In the divorce process the man had not fully disclosed all his financial information. His ex-wife was suspicious (imagine that) and was pushing the issue through legal action. The man in my office wanted to know what to do.

Both the man and his new wife claimed to be good Christians, people of integrity. I sat there wondering why we were sitting there! Was there really a question here? I told the man he had to disclose all his financials. That was easy! Well, it was easy for me to say because it was easy for me to see. But when we are under fire, maintaining our integrity can be challenging.

The word integrity means *sound, whole, complete.* We get the word *integer* from it, which means a whole number. Integrity means being solid through and through. It means that what you see on the inside is reflected on the outside. It means that if you cut a watermelon in half you find watermelon inside. It means being undivided and true.

The only way to gain and maintain integrity is to *seek first [God's] kingdom and his righteousness.* In seeking his kingdom *first* we are trusting that *all these things will be given to [us] as well* because God is for us and is on our side, bending things toward his glory and for our good and the good of the world around us.

The man in my office that day was not seeking God's kingdom first. Though he said he was a follower of God, he really was not trusting God for his financial future. By not trusting God's provision for him he thought he had to lie to keep more of his money for himself and away from his ex-wife. Though he looked like a Christian on the outside, his decisions about his money indicated that he was not really seeking God's kingdom first.

Whether out of anger, fear, hurt, guilt, shame or desperation, when we are in the throes of divorce we may choose to take some shortcuts. Now is the perfect time to seek God, trusting that if you do the next right thing he will take care of all the rest. Don't compromise. Take the high road. You will not regret it and you will see God's incredible provision for you in every way.

THINK ABOUT IT...

* In what areas have you been tempted to compromise?
* What steps can you take to keep you whole, sound, and complete?

LIFE COMMITMENT:
I commit to seeking God first, trusting him for my future and proving my trust in him by making decisions that maintain my integrity.

Larger Than Life

———— ✤ ————

THE WORD

He who began a good work in you will carry it on
to completion until the day of Christ Jesus.

— PHILIPPIANS 1:6

THOUGHT FOR THE DAY:

The rat race speeds up... but it is still a race for rats.

~ OS GUINNESS

I SLIPPED. I RAGED ON Facebook against the unfairness I had
experienced. The conversation began when an old friend
(literally, 81 years old, and a friend for 30+ years) asked how
I was doing. The scab was pulled back and the blood began
to flow. My friend is a saint—back in the 1980s when the
AIDS epidemic was ravaging the homosexual population,
she bucked the evangelical detestation of gays and embraced
men who were dying young.

I knew she could take what I had to dish out, so I un-
loaded my anger and grief right there on Facebook. But a few
days later I realized I had let my smaller self gain the upper

hand. This was *not* how I wanted to be remembered. I wanted to be remembered as *larger than life*...

Richard Rohr describers this well:

> *We describe some people as larger than life. If we could see their history, we would learn that at some point they were led to the edge of their own resources and found the actual Source. They suffered a breakdown, which felt like dying. But instead of breaking down, they broke through!*
>
> *Instead of avoiding, shortchanging, or raging against death, they went through death—a death to their old self, their small life, their imperfections, their illusory dreams, their wounds, their grudges, and their limited sense of their own destiny. When they did this, they came out on the other side knowing that death henceforth could do them no harm.*
>
> *"What did I ever lose by dying?" they say. This process is supposed to be the baptismal initiation rite into Christianity, where we first "join him in the tomb" and then afterwards "join him in his resurrection" (Romans 5:4-5). We are all supposed to be larger-than-death men, appearing to the world as larger than life. This should be the definition of a Christian man.*[20]

God began a good work when he brought you to the planet. That good work, however, is a work in progress and requires your cooperation. When we cooperate with him, we move past the big and little 'deaths' in our lives to his resurrection beyond. If we hang in there with him, he will bring this good work (you!) to completion.

---

[20] Rohr, Durepos and McGrath, *On the Threshold of Transformation*, 283. Used with permission.

What if we don't cooperate? Of all the mass shootings from 1982 to 2016, 79 were male shooters and three female.[21] That tells us something of the crisis among men in our world today. Obviously not all who fail to cooperate with God's transforming energy end up mass shooters. But those who fail to live within God's jet stream do end up causing death and destruction in many big and small ways along life's journey.

The pain of divorce squeezes our soul. What is leaking out of your soul today? What comes out will be how others define you... Larger than life or... crushed by death?

THINK ABOUT IT...

* Size matters. In your own eyes, are you small or large?
* When you are squeezed, what comes out? Patience, endurance, kindness? Or wrath, bitterness, rage?
* How do you want to be remembered?

LIFE COMMITMENT:

I have a choice as to how cooperative I am with God's working in me. I commit to jumping into his jetstream and allowing him to do his work in me.

---

[21] Taryn Hillin, *"Nearly All Mass Shooters Have One Thing in Common,"* Fusion, accessed January 10, 2017, http://fusion.net/story/314137/what-mass-shooters-have-in-common/.

Mission—*Empower*

———— ∞∞ ————

THE WORD

In the day when I cried out, you answered me,
and made me bold with strength in my soul.

— PSALM 138.3

THOUGHT FOR THE DAY:

Men's Divorce Recovery exists to Empower Divorced
Men through Support, Knowledge and Encouragement
to Survive and Thrive beyond their divorce to become
Resilient, Strong and Wise men in their world.

~ MISSION STATEMENT, MEN'S DIVORCE RECOVERY

SEVERAL MONTHS AFTER MY DIVORCE was final, God spoke to me, clearly inviting/commanding me to start a ministry to men like myself who had experienced the shock and pain of divorce.

The call God has placed upon me came in the way he usually speaks to me—words come into my mind I know are not from me. I have experienced his call several times in my lifetime—the call to go into ministry, the call to spend a year teaching in Tanzania, the call to pastor each of the churches I have been privileged to serve. But this call to Men's Divorce Recovery was different. In each of my previous calls, God's voice was mixed with my own unhealthy (but probably unavoidable) dose of personal ambition.

I was a 'career pastor.' I had worked hard on my Ph.D. to have all the external qualifications I could acquire to lead churches to new-found greatness. I was bound up in the throes of the first half of a man's spiritual journey—building up the 'kingdom of me'. Don't get me wrong. I served these churches and cared for them from the very depths of my heart. As a pastor/leader, I duly shared the credit and took the blame. I enthusiastically worked to fulfill God's call upon my life to pastor each church diligently and faithfully. But the pressure to take the church to the 'next level,' to grow ever bigger and brighter, to bring back the 'glory days' was unrelenting.

At the time of this writing I am 55 years old. Despite my best efforts, I have lost a wife and two churches in eighteen months, surely some sort of record. Personal losses have multiplied—hundreds of thousands of dollars in lost wages, my hard-earned reputation, my career as a pastor and teacher. My losses look different than yours, but *they are all losses and loss hurts.*

But I am not despairing because God has called me from the midst of what the world perceives as a failed life to reach other men hammered by divorce and/or personal failure.

The mission statement of Men's Divorce Recovery (above) reflects my own personal desires regarding the goals, the means to reach the goals, and the outcomes of Men's Divorce Recovery. Let's spend a few days unpacking the important truths in MDR's mission statement.

FIRST, Men's Divorce Recovery exists to **Empower** Divorced Men...

The last thing a divorced man feels is empowered. Quite the opposite in fact. We feel *neutered.*

Yet we know that the amazing grace of God finds its home in the midst of devastation and desolation. What emerges from the combination of a yielded heart and God's grace is a man humbly empowered to fulfill his purpose with courage and conviction.

So far you have been living on your own power. Though you may have thought you were powerful, you weren't. Divorce and other life blows reveal how little power we really have.

But God *is* powerful—fantastically more powerful than we can imagine, and we have pretty good imaginations. The journey through the pain and loss of divorce can lead you away from reliance upon your own power to tapping into God's amazing power. Though you have been drained of power in so many ways, *do not despair.* God is ready to take up the slack where you lack.

Time after time I have heard God say to me, *Hold on, I've got you, I am sustaining you, I will see you through this, you will get through this!*

I let God take my pain, heartache and worries. When I let go and relax into him, I am relinquishing dependence on my own power and letting him handle things in his power. My mind clears, my tight chest relaxes, and I am off the ledge once again.

The key is *hearing God's invitation* to take the load and then *consciously allowing him to have it.* Having trouble hearing

God? Don't worry, we will talk a lot about that more later (see Day 116).[22]

THINK ABOUT IT...

* What or who is the source of the power for your life?
* What or who makes you powerless (or less powerful)?
* How do you feel when you are powerless (or less powerful)?
* What do you do when you are powerless (or less powerful)?

LIFE COMMITMENT:

I give up. I give up trying to be strong, powerful, mighty and important based on who I believe myself to be. God is bigger and better. He is stronger and wiser. I defer to him. I give him control over my life. I let him be my power source.

---

[22] Dallas Willard writes, *God wants to be wanted, to be wanted enough that we are ready, predisposed, to find him present with us. And if, by contrast, we are ready and set to find ways of explaining away his gentle overtures, he will rarely respond with fire from heaven. More likely, he will simply leave us alone; and we shall have the satisfaction of thinking ourselves not to be gullible.* Dallas Willard, *Hearing God: Developing A Conversational Relationship with God* (Downers Grove: InterVarsity Press, 1999), 273.

DAY 13

Mission—*Survive*

⸺ ⚬⚬⚬ ⸺

The Word

This poor man called, and the Lord heard
him; he saved him out of all his troubles.
The angel of the Lord encamps around those
who fear him, and he delivers them.[23]

— Psalm 34:6-7

Thought for the Day:

You see, if you quit, you lose. But so long as you
stick it out, you're still in with a chance.

~ Bear Grylls

---

[23] To fear God in the Bible means to have a reverential awe of him. Part of that awe is to literally fear him—he is the most powerful being in the universe and is rightly feared (Matthew 10.28). At the same time, to be in awe of God is to be amazed by him and his handiwork in creation and beyond. William Eisenhower says, *As I walk with the Lord, I discover that God poses an ominous threat to my ego, but not to me. He rescues me from my delusions, so he may reveal the truth that sets me free. He casts me down, only to lift me up again. He sits in judgment of my sin, but forgives me nevertheless. Fear of the Lord is the beginning of wisdom, but love from the Lord is its completion.* William Eisenhower, "Fearing God," *Christianity Today*, March 1986.

THIS POOR MAN CALLED... WHEN I read this verse I hear the cry of a guy who has had to deal with so much he just hangs his head and sings, *"Nobody knows the trouble I've seen, nobody knows but Jesus."* Brother, I've been that poor man!

Men's Divorce Recovery exists to Empower Divorced Men through Support, Knowledge and Encouragement to **Survive**...

Divorce is a body blow that takes you to the mat. Our first priority is to survive this take down and eventually get back on our feet to fight another day.

I have never been in armed combat, but I understand that when a soldier goes down, several things happen. First, the wounded man cries for help. Next, his buddies respond by immediately coming to his aid. Third, they protect their fallen comrade from further harm. Fourth, they stabilize the wounded man and, lastly, they get him out.

Divorce is not the same as an RPG going off in your Humvee, but the impact of divorce on the soul is a slashing wound which cuts through the heart. In the midst of your pain, call on God. When you call on the Lord, he sets into motion the same process that happens on the battlefield.

He *Hears.* God hears all our prayers, but when he hears the cry of a desperate man, he bends his ear in a way that gives special attention to the one crying out. God hears that cry, whether the pain is of the body or of the soul. Like a mother who instantly recognizes the wail of her baby from ten other screeching babies, your cry to God is instantly heard and given special attention.

He *Encamps.* When a soldier goes down, his buddies immediately surround him with weapons facing outward to protect the wounded warrior from further harm. In the same way, God surrounds you. He is a refuge, a place of safety. The attacks may continue but the impact of those attacks on your soul are shared by God who is beside you and all around you. He's got your back (and your front).

He **Saves**. The Hebrew word used here means *victory*. The poor man is surrounded by God's mighty protecting angels and help is immediately given to heal and restore. Just as treatment of the wounded soldier begins on the battlefield, so does God begin to stop the bleeding in your soul *right now*.

He **Delivers**. The Hebrew word basically means *he gets you out of there!* Just as powerful forces are marshaled to get a wounded soldier off the battlefield and into a field hospital, so too God gets us out of the painful place we are in. It will take a while, but to know you will not always be in pain is a ray of hope giving you resolve to hang on.

Survival begins with calling out to God. As proud men who are defined by our ability to go it alone and live a self-sufficient life, this is a hard and humble place to be. But the smart poor man is going to do one simple thing: *Call on the Lord.* God is coming to your aid right now.

One other thing: If you are in survival mode, **set realistic expectations**. No one expects a wounded soldier to function at the same level he was before he was shot. In the same way, when you are in the middle of divorce, your ability to function will be diminished. Learn to be OK with that (see Day 174).

When things were really hard, I had less energy or motivation to do things. I wanted to sleep more and things looked gloomy, even good things. I lost a big chunk of that *oomph* that I relied on to get through the day. To cope, I cut the things in my daily schedule that weren't necessary. But I kept doing the things that I knew gave me life—my morning time with God, eating right and exercising, and fulfilling my commitments to work.

THINK ABOUT IT...

* Where are you in the journey? Have you just been 'hit' and are lying on the battlefield with serious wounds? If so, have you called out to God for help?
* How have you experienced God's rescue before?

LIFE COMMITMENT:

I am calling on the Lord for help right now. Just as there is no shame for the wounded soldier to admit he is hit and needs immediate help, I declare that there is no shame for me to call on God to save, deliver and heal me. God, help me!

Mission—*Thrive*

———❧———

THE WORD

> *He is like a tree planted by streams of water,*
> *which yields its fruit in season and whose leaf*
> *does not wither. Whatever he does prospers.*

— PSALM 1:3

THOUGHT FOR THE DAY:

> *Success is the ability to go from one failure*
> *to another with no loss of enthusiasm.*

~ WINSTON CHURCHILL

FOR THE FIRST MONTHS AFTER I was body-slammed by divorce, survival was my goal. I could not look beyond getting through that day. Whereas before I had been full of energy and fire, now I was a dull ember just trying to keep a little glow going. Whereas before my mind was happily jumbled with all kinds of new ideas and ways of doing things, now my brain was struggling to just wrap itself around this new reality of unwanted events. During those days, I counted surviving the day a huge victory.

But there came a day when I realized that just surviving was not going to do it for me. I was meant for more than just muddling through the day, collapsing into bed at night for sleep's sweet escape once again. I am made to fulfill a larger purpose. I am part of a grander design.

Most people survive major crises. The power of the human being to keep going is truly remarkable. But we are made for more than surviving. We're meant to *thrive*.

That's why thriving is a huge part of our mission statement: *Men's Divorce Recovery exists to Empower Divorced Men through Support, Knowledge and Encouragement* **to Survive and Thrive beyond their divorce**...

MDR exists to 'catch' you in your pain with the initial aim of rescuing you from disastrous decisions often made when one is in extreme misery. Beyond *survival*, however, we embrace the amazing reality that God never wastes pain but turns it on the enemy for Kingdom good. The goal is to help you move beyond surviving to thriving. True thriving is to live out the purpose for which you were made.

Business consultant Paul Stoltz says that for you to first survive and then thrive through setbacks you must *"Identify your mountain, your purpose in life, so that the work you do is meaningful."*[24]

Stoltz goes on to write,

> *I've discovered that people seem to share a core human drive to ascend, to move forward and up along one's mountain or purpose in one's life. But it's tough. If*

---

[24] John Maxwell, *The Maxwell Daily Reader*, 379.

defining—let alone staying true to a worthy aspiration for one's life—were easy, more people would make it happen. The vast majority stop short or bail out.[25]

If you're in survival mode right now, so be it. Set your expectations accordingly. But expect that God has more for you than merely getting through the next day. God has a plan to use this intense pain for his glory and for your good. It may seem inconceivable right now, but it is true. I have seen it over and over again with men who have been hammered by divorce—God has a plan and a future for you—and it is good!

THINK ABOUT IT...

* Think back on a time when you were thriving. What energized you? What fulfilled you?
* Where are you now? Surviving? Ready to Thrive? Just making it through the day? Feeling a little renewed energy?

LIFE COMMITMENT:

Though I find it hard to see right now, I am choosing to trust God not to waste my pain. I commit to being receptive to his greater call on my life and I look forward to hearing his call and fulfilling his greater purpose in my life.

---

[25] Paul Gordon Stoltz, *Grit: The New Science of What It Takes to Persevere, Flourish, Succeed* (Climb Strong Press, 2014), Kindle Location 1106.

Mission—*Resilient*

———⚮———

THE WORD

I am able to do all things through
Him who strengthens me.

— PHILIPPIANS 4:13

THOUGHT FOR THE DAY:

The special characteristic of a great person is to
triumph over the disasters and panics of human life.

~ SENECA

TO PUT IT SIMPLY, RESILIENCE is the ability to bounce back. Technically, the definition goes like this: *Resilience is the capability of a strained body to recover its size and shape after deformation caused especially by compressive stress.* The Latin base of resilient is *salire*, a verb meaning "to leap."[26]

Resilience is the ability of the football player who has been 'shaken up' to shake it off and stand up to play again. It is the ability of the runner to push through the last mile of the race.

---

[26] *Merriam-Webster Dictionary*, *s.v.* "Resilience," accessed January 16, 2017, https://www.merriam-webster.com/dictionary/resilience.

I love the White Mountains of New Hampshire. One of my favorite hikes is up Mt. Lafayette. Combined with Mt. Lincoln and Little Haystack, it's a grueling nine miles with 3,860 feet of elevation.

One particular trip I was leading a group from my church. One of the men, Mike, slipped off a wet rock and twisted his knee. He grimaced in pain as we assessed what to do. Nearly halfway through the hike, Mike determined to keep on going. As happens with the wounded, Mike lagged.

As we began our descent I was with two of Mike's kids further along the trail. The kids and I stopped for a breather. Mike eventually caught up to us. As Mike approached, one of his kids said, *Hey look, Dad's alive!* Mike *was* alive, and still in the game, though moving slower than the rest of us. Mike was resilient![27]

Men's Divorce Recovery exists to Empower Divorced Men through Support, Knowledge and Encouragement to Survive and Thrive beyond their divorce to become **Resilient**, *Strong and Wise men in their world.*

Quitters are remembered for, well, quitting! And then they are quickly forgotten. But those who persevere are remembered not for what put them down but how they managed to get back up.

How will you get through this? Where does your resilience come from?

The only enduring answer is that our ability to bounce back comes from God. When we *reach the end* of our strength, smart men *reach out* to God. If my survival is up to me, my

---

[27] In case you are wondering, we didn't abandon Mike on the trail! My team took turns helping him while walking with the rest of the team members.

strength is limited which means I will give up which means I will not be resilient.

Not so God. His strength is unlimited as is his unswerving commitment to you. For his **glory** he wants you to endure. For your **good** he wants you to bounce back. He is invested in your success, and your success depends on you getting back up. And getting back up depends on God.

When Paul wrote *I am able to do all things through Him who strengthens me,* he was not talking about leaping over tall buildings or building a wildly successful corporation. He was talking about resilience. *Through Christ* I can get back up and keep going. Tell God right now that you need him to pick you back up. Tell him that you need his strength to get through this day. Then take a deep breath. You are in good hands.

Think About It...

* When have you been down and then gotten back up? How did it feel to get back in the game?
* When have you walked away from the challenge to get back up? Do you regret the decision to quit?
* What does getting back up look like right now?
* What does relying on God for your strength look like?

Life Commitment:

The easiest thing to do when down is to stay down and then slink off unnoticed. I will not do the easy thing. With God's strength, I will get back up and get back in the game.

Mission—*Strong*

———∞———

THE WORD

> *God is our refuge and strength, an ever-present*
> *help in trouble. Therefore we will not fear, though*
> *the earth give way and the mountains fall into the*
> *heart of the sea, though its waters roar and foam*
> *and the mountains quake with their surging.*

— PSALM 46:1–3

THOUGHT FOR THE DAY:

> *How do you become an adult in a society that*
> *doesn't ask for sacrifice? How do you become a*
> *man in a world that doesn't require courage?*

~ SEBASTIAN JUNGER

IT WAS THE DARKEST DAY in human history. The very best man who offered the best shot at justice and reform was—just like all the rebels before him— nailed to cross timbers and left to die a slow and agonizing death. The message the government wanted to send was simple: *We are strong, you are not. Obey us or you will be bones on a cross.*

But death was not to hold him. Three days later the Rebel came back to life. But the Rebel had to die before he could legitimately say he had conquered death. To beat the power of Rome and the power of sin and Satan, Jesus had to restrain himself. He had to stay on the cross. And staying on the cross took all the strength he had.

Ironically, to be powerless enough to accomplish our salvation, Jesus had to reach deep within himself for incredible strength to tap another kind of power, the power to overcome without leaving footprints on the backs of those before him. This was a new kind of strength. It's the kind of power and strength God calls men to.

*Men's Divorce Recovery exists to Empower Divorced Men through Support, Knowledge and Encouragement to Survive and Thrive beyond their divorce to become Resilient, **<u>Strong</u>** and Wise men in their world.*

Being strong does **not** mean *wielding power over others*. Being strong means *yielding power to God* and following him and his way. His way is distinguished by a quiet, humble power that nothing can shake.

That's why the writer of Hebrews lifts up Jesus as our hero:

Let us fix our eyes on Jesus, the author and perfecter of our faith, who for the joy set before him endured the cross, scorning its shame, and sat down at the right hand of the throne of God. Consider him who endured such opposition from sinful men, so that you will not grow weary and lose heart. (Hebrews 12.1–3)

In a world weakened by so much dissension, dissolution and anemic leadership, MDR exists to guide men into their true role as men of God. Godly men are strong in a humble yet unyielding way.

THINK ABOUT IT...

* When do you feel most powerful?
* When have you powered over another through sheer strength? What was the outcome?
* When have you restrained yourself? What was the outcome?

LIFE COMMITMENT:

The next time I want to use power to lash out someone I will restrain myself. I will know that this is true strength.

Mission—*Wise*

———— ⊗ ————

THE WORD

Get wisdom, get understanding; do not forget my words
or swerve from them. Do not forsake wisdom, and she
will protect you; love her, and she will watch over you.
Wisdom is supreme; therefore get wisdom. Though it cost
all you have, get understanding. Esteem her, and she
will exalt you; embrace her, and she will honor you.

— PROVERBS 4:5–9

THOUGHT FOR THE DAY:

Talent is God given. Be humble. Fame is man-given.
Be grateful. Conceit is self-given. Be careful.

~ JOHN WOODEN

A DISTINCT MEMORY I HAVE of my first days at the University of Texas was that I was sure all the other incoming freshmen had it figured out and I was the only one who was still trying to. Much to my surprise, I learned that everyone else was still trying to figure it out too!

Thirty-five years later as a hospice chaplain I sit with the old to the extremely old. I have learned that they are still trying to figure it out too. Even the 99-year-old retired pastor has his moments of wondering. Somehow that is both comforting and disturbing.

Wisdom is of two elements: *seeing clearly* and *deciding correctly*. To make wise decisions takes clarity of vision. You will remember that having clarity is one of our 'wins'. The pilot who plowed his fighter jet into the tarmac at Carswell Air Force Base in Fort Worth (see Day 6) was unclear as to where he was. His lack of clarity led to a lethal decision and a devastating outcome.

During this time when your life has been turned upside down by divorce, you need clarity.

But just because you have clarity doesn't mean you will make winning decisions. Wisdom means more than just seeing the world clearly. Wisdom entails making decisions based on the right motivation.

For instance, let's say that the pilot mentioned above really did understand that he was flying upside down but he flew his plane into the tarmac anyway. Why would he make such a decision? The only answer would be that he wanted to take his own life and that of his co-pilot. In that case, he was clear about where he was, but his darkened heart led him to make a terrible decision.

It is critical during this time of upheaval that you make wise choices. You need to think with a clear head and decide with a pure heart.

To do this requires that you look outside yourself for wisdom. You must relocate the source of your wisdom from yourself to God. The source of all wisdom is God, and God showed himself most clearly to us in his Son, Jesus Christ. If you want to know how to live wisely in this world, listen to everything Jesus said and watch what he did.[28]

One of the goals of MDR is that you Survive and Thrive beyond your divorce to become a Resilient, Strong and **Wise** man in your world.

Will you relocate the source of your wisdom from yourself to God? Will you follow Jesus in finding clarity and courage to make wise decisions?

If so, you can take some steps right now to make that happen:

- **Ask God for wisdom**. Expect him to give it.[29]
- **Read the Bible**. A good place to learn about Jesus is to begin reading the book of John. Just read a few verses each day asking yourself *"What did Jesus say and what did he do?"*
- **Find a church** that is following Jesus. Go and listen. Ask questions.

---

[28] Dallas Willard writes, *[Jesus] is not just nice, he is brilliant. He is the smartest man who ever lived. He is now supervising the entire course of world history (Rev. 1:5) while simultaneously preparing the rest of the universe for our future role in it (John 14:2). He always has the best information on everything and certainly also on the things that matter most in human life. Let us now hear his teachings on who has the good life, on who is among the truly blessed.* Dallas Willard, *The Divine Conspiracy: Rediscovering Our Hidden Life in God* (San Francisco: HarperSanFrancisco, 1998), 96.

[29] *If any of you lacks wisdom, he should ask God, who gives generously to all without finding fault, and it will be given to him. But when he asks, he must believe and not doubt, because he who doubts is like a wave of the sea, blown and tossed by the wind. That man should not think he will receive anything from the Lord; he is a double-minded man, unstable in all he does.* (James 1.5–8)

   ❖   **Find some other guys** who are following Jesus. Get together to bounce your ideas off them. Allow God to use other godly men to help you gain clarity of mind purity of heart.

Wisdom is the art of being successful, of forming the correct plan to gain the desired results. Its seat is the heart, the centre of moral and intellectual decision. [30]

THINK ABOUT IT...

   ❖   *First we make our choices, then our choices make us.* Consider the past year. What choices did you make and what were the consequences?

   ❖   If you made poor choices, determine now to make better choices from this moment on (beginning with following the steps above for gaining wisdom!)

LIFE COMMITMENT:

I can choose my source of wisdom. I choose to follow Jesus. He's a lot smarter than me! Choosing Jesus is my first good choice!

---

[30] D. A. Hubbard, "*Wisdom*," ed. D. R. W. Wood et al., *New Bible Dictionary* (Leicester, England; Downers Grove: InterVarsity Press, 1996), 1244.

How Thinking Works (1)

———— ∞∞∞ ————

THE WORD

> *Then God said, "Let us make man in our image, in our*
> *likeness, and let them rule over the fish of the sea and*
> *the birds of the air, over the livestock, over all the earth,*
> *and over all the creatures that move along the ground."*
> *So God created man in his own image, in the image of*
> *God he created him; male and female he created them.*

— GENESIS 1:26–27

THOUGHT FOR THE DAY:

> *The difference between losers and winners*
> *is often determined between the ears.*

~ TONY DUNGY

ONE OF THE MOST AMAZING events to watch is the launch of the
Space Shuttle. I have even interrupted staff meetings so we
could all marvel at this magnificent sight on the TV screen.
Not everyone on my staff had the same appreciation as me.

At launch the Space Shuttle and launch vehicle weigh 4.4
million pounds. The fuel, which weighs 20 times more than

the shuttle itself, propels the shuttle from zero to 17,500 mph in just over eight minutes. That, my friend, is simply stunning! The engines generate 37 million horsepower. Just the fuel pumps alone deliver 71,000 horsepower!

Why do I rattle on about the space shuttle and its amazing launch? Simply because *this magnificent event started in someone's brain.* Someone thought of the idea of the space shuttle. The reality we witness on television began as a thought in someone's head. That's amazing!

In fact, your brain is the second most incredible thing in all the universe. Did you get that? That three-pound mass of cells in your head is the *second most astounding thing in the entire universe!* The first is, of course, God himself.

Only the human brain can remember the past and make meaning from those memories. Only the human brain can project into the future with an imagination powerful enough to shape that future. Only the human brain can conceptualize spiritual reality and tap the resources of the soul to access that reality. Only the human brain can think abstractly and from that abstraction and careful observation, describe reality with mathematical equations and scientific laws.

All this is because we are created in God's image. Dogs are wonderful and they think, but they don't think like us. Dolphins are cool and smart. But dolphins don't build dolphin hospitals or dolphin universities. Our ability to reason is above and beyond any other created thing.

We are more than our thoughts but in our lived experience, we are *mostly* our thoughts. That's because if you are awake, you are, by definition, thinking. This is a blessing and a curse.

We try to maintain our thoughts by controlling our external environment so inputs are comprehendible and manageable. We regulate our thinking by slowing our thoughts enough to process them. We try to control our emotions with our thoughts so emotions don't send our thoughts cascading into a downward spiral of chaos.

But when circumstances run out of control, thoughts come fast and furious and conflicting emotions build one upon another until everything in us—mind, emotions and soul—are overwhelmed. In those moments our thoughts can go in multiple directions which adds to the cascading effect. This out-of-control spiral can lead to drastic and destructive behaviors.

On January 28, 1986, the Space Shuttle *Challenger* lifted off the Florida launchpad only to disintegrate in a massive fireball 73 seconds into its flight, ending the lives of seven extraordinary people. A small separation at an O-ring allowed flaming gas from the solid rocket booster to burn through to the external fuel tank, causing cascading structural failures.

The Space Shuttle transformed much of what we know of space and brought everyday discoveries to useful applications in our everyday lives. But on that January day in 1986 things got out of control and disaster was the consequence.

Over the next few days we want to explore how we think and how we can keep our thoughts on track so we don't let our thoughts take us out in a ball of fire.

Today, however, think about this: Your brain is the second most amazing and incredible thing in all the universe! That's amazing!

THINK ABOUT IT...

*   What do you think is amazing? How much more amazing is your brain than the most amazing thing you can think of?
*   How does knowing you have the second most amazing thing in all the universe change how you think of yourself?

LIFE COMMITMENT:

Even though I may feel like s**t at times, in reality I know that I possess the second most amazing thing in <u>all the universe</u>! That, in itself, is enough to get some positive thoughts going!

How Thinking Works (2)

———— ∞∞∞ ————

THE WORD

We demolish arguments and every pretension that sets itself up against the knowledge of God, and we take captive every thought to make it obedient to Christ.

— 2 CORINTHIANS 10:5

THOUGHT FOR THE DAY:

When U.S. senator Mark Hatfield was asked what was the greatest challenge facing the senate today, he quickly responded: "Not enough time to think."

~ ROBERT J. WICKS

SOMEONE SAID, *THERE IS NOTHING so easy as thinking, and there is nothing so hard as thinking well.*

We all wake up thinking, but how many of us learn to think well?

The **first step** in thinking well is to **become your own observer.** By that I mean that you step back from yourself and analyze your thoughts, emotions and actions. You step outside yourself and evaluate yourself as if you were studying someone else.

Then you think about what you are thinking. Are my thoughts productive? Is my thinking leading me down a path that is helpful or harmful? If I doggedly pursue this line of thinking, what will be the result?

The **second step** in thinking well is to realize that **you make your thoughts**.

Because our thoughts are so close to us, we forget that we are making them. You make your thoughts like you make a toy car in the workshop or a cake in the kitchen. The inner 'you' is making thoughts. The proof of this is that you can think a thought. You can choose this moment to think about what you are reading or where you will watch the football game coming up this weekend.

The **third step** is to recognize the unproductive thoughts you are making and then **throw them out**! Like a birdhouse that looks like a rat trap, **you can throw your thoughts away!**

This is what the writer of Psalm 42 does:

Why are you downcast, O my soul? Why so disturbed within me? Put your hope in God, for I will yet praise him, my Savior and my God. (Psalm 42:5–6)

The writer tells himself to throw out those bad thoughts!

I love woodworking but I'm not great at it. A few times I have started a project that, despite my best efforts, was not coming together. When I decided that my work was beyond hope, everything I had made so far went into the scrapheap.

If a line of thinking is just not doing it for you, throw it out!

The process for this to happen is that you take a step back and evaluate what you were thinking. You think about where this line of thinking is taking you. If you're not satisfied with the direction of your thinking, choose to push those thoughts out and begin a new thought.

Inside your head is the second most amazing thing in all the universe! Why waste it by letting negative thoughts pile up?[31]

THINK ABOUT IT...

* Pause every few hours and just observe yourself as you would someone else. What are you doing? What are you feeling? What are you thinking?

LIFE COMMITMENT:

I choose to think about what I am thinking and throw out thoughts I make that are not helpful.

---

[31] *Resilient people are self-aware enough to notice when their thinking is counterproductive. They don't fall into thinking traps such as jumping to conclusions or making assumptions. Instead, they gather the facts they need to move around obstacles and face the challenge head on.* "Things Resilient People Do" Beliefnet, accessed January 15, 2017, http://www.beliefnet.com/inspiration/galleries/5-things-resilient-people-do.aspx.

How Thinking Works (3)

———∞∞———

THE WORD

> *"For my thoughts are not your thoughts, neither are*
> *your ways my ways," declares the Lord. "As the heavens*
> *are higher than the earth, so are my ways higher than*
> *your ways and my thoughts than your thoughts."*

— ISAIAH 55:8–9

THOUGHT FOR THE DAY:

> *Deep in the human unconscious is a pervasive*
> *need for a logical universe that makes sense. But*
> *the real universe is always one step beyond logic.*

~ FRANK HERBERT, *DUNE*

WHAT IS THE SHORTEST DISTANCE between two points? A straight line, right? That's what I learned in geometry. But in God's geometry, the shortest distance between two points may not be the *best* way to get between two points.

Take the Israelites under the oppression of the Egyptians for example. God rescued them, promising them a homeland in what is today modern Israel. From modern Cairo to Jerusalem is only 264 miles. But in God's plan, the trip took 40 years and covered hundreds of miles.

To us men, this is insane! We want to get the job done as quickly and efficiently as possible. We don't stop for potty breaks on the family vacation because we have a destination to reach! We don't plant flowers in our garden. You can't eat flowers. What's the use of flowers?

Humans (especially men) are built to think, to analyze, to figure things out. We are driven to understand our world and what is happening to us. In the three years of my greatest travail, my mind worked overtime trying to figure out the *hows* and the *whys*. I didn't get it. I simply didn't understand.

Albert Einstein said, *Any fool can know. The point is to understand.* But I didn't understand. I didn't even know all the facts but I worked hard at trying to discover them!

Søren Kierkegaard wrote, *Life can only be understood backwards; but it must be lived forwards.* OK, but I can't wrap my mind around what happened. I don't understand why people would do what they did.

Here's the deal: *you and I won't understand.* No matter how much we dissect and analyze and try to figure it out, we can't. Much of the information we would need to figure it out is inaccessible to us. We can't get into the heads and hearts of those who have caused us pain. Even if we had all the info, our own thinking processes are distorted. We even struggle to understand our own ways of thinking and the true content of our hearts.

If your happiness and ability to move forward depend on you understanding what happened, you will be unhappy and stuck where you are. Instead, *start letting go of your burning need to figure it out* and let God take what is *now* and build a better future for you.

God's thoughts are not our thoughts and his ways are not our ways. The key is to trust that his thoughts are better than our thoughts and his ways better than our ways.

Paul David Tripp writes, *There will be moments when you simply don't understand what is going on. In fact, you will face moments when what the God who has declared himself to be good brings into your life won't seem good. It may even seem bad, very bad.*[32]

It's here that you must push against everything that is driving you to figure it out and rest in him who knows it is best to make a 264-mile journey stretch to many hundreds of miles. Trust in the God who can take a terrible Friday (the Crucifixion) and transform it into a victorious Sunday (the Resurrection). If you're in Friday, Sunday is coming. On Friday you won't get it. But come Sunday morning when Jesus is standing in front of you, you *will* get it!

Tripp writes: *You need to remind yourself again and again of his wise and loving control, not because that will immediately make your life make sense, but because it will give you rest and peace in those moments that all of us face at one time or another—when life doesn't seem to make any sense.*[33]

Isaiah writes: *You will keep in perfect peace him whose mind is steadfast, because he trusts in you. Trust in the Lord forever, for the Lord, the Lord, is the Rock eternal.* (Isaiah 26.3-4)

Confession: Even as I am writing this I am still frustrated that I can't figure it out! I was born and bred on the scientific method. I spent decades reading and learning and thinking

---

[32] Paul David Tripp, *New Morning Mercies: A Daily Gospel Devotional* (Wheaton, IL: Crossway, 2014), Kindle Location 615.

[33] Ibid., Kindle Location 629.

and writing. I'm not stupid. I should be able to figure this thing out. Dang it.

THINK ABOUT IT...

* How much of your time and energy is going to figuring it out?
* What would change even if you could figure it all out?

LIFE COMMITMENT:

I confess that though I am hard-wired to figure it out, this time I won't be able to despite my best effort. I commit to resting in God's better thoughts and ways. He has it figured out. He's got me covered.

Understanding Your Emotions (1)

———⊶⊷———

THE WORD

> *A happy heart makes the face cheerful,*
> *but heartache crushes the spirit.*

— PROVERBS 15:13.

THOUGHT FOR THE DAY:

> *We should allow feelings and emotions to run their*
> *course, teaching us and forming us. No feeling lasts*
> *forever. Feelings are not right or wrong; they have*
> *no moral meaning. They are merely indicators of*
> *what's happening in our lives on other levels.*

~ RICHARD ROHR

I AM AMAZED AT HOW sensitive we are to temperature. A few degrees up, we are hot. A few degrees down, we are shivering.

When I feel warm, I don't get up and start yelling at the thermometer. Instead, I go to the thermostat and turn it down so the air conditioner kicks on.

A thermometer only tells you how fast air molecules are bouncing around—the faster they go, the higher the temp. The slower they go, the lower the temp. A thermometer cannot *change* anything, it only *reveals* something—the speed of moving air molecules.

The same is true for your emotions. Emotions are real. They exist because something in the 'atmosphere' of your life is happening. The part of you that God gave to you to react to that 'something' going on inside you is reacting. You cannot not have emotions just as you cannot not have moving air molecules (I realize this is terrible grammar but it makes the point, hopefully!)

For some reason we men can relish moving air molecules! We study this phenomenon, measuring it, making up equations to describe it, using it to produce something. But when it comes to our emotions, we pretend we don't have them. We push them down and we tell others they should not have them either—think of when we tell our kids they should not be angry or upset. That's like telling air molecules moving at the speed that makes the thermometer read 100° that they shouldn't be moving that fast! We instantly recognize the absurdity of commanding molecules not to move at a particular speed. But we fail to recognize the same absurdity in commanding ourselves not to feel what we are feeling.

The reality of our emotions is independent of whether or not you acknowledge their existence. But because emotions are *only* like a thermometer—telling us something about ourselves—they are not to be feared or denied, just acknowledged and appropriately expressed.

Emotions in and of themselves are morally neutral. It's not wrong to feel angry, irritated, sad or happy. Those emotions are only reflecting what is happening inside us as we engage our world. What we *do* in response to our emotions has huge moral and practical implications. But the actual emotion itself is only telling us something about ourselves.

This may be completely new information to you: Emotions are real. Emotions are like a thermometer, only indicating to us what is happening inside us. Emotions are morally neutral.

In the Bible we read of men who experienced anger, fear, jealousy, lust, terror, hatred, greed, depression, guilt, resentment, bitterness, pride, sorrow, peace, happiness, joy, contentment and the list goes on and on.

If you are still not convinced you have emotions, go to this website to see a list of 147 emotions at *http://bit.ly/2jTlT6a*.

THINK ABOUT IT...

* What emotion or emotions are you experiencing right now?
* What emotions have you experienced through this divorce process?
* If someone were to be asked what one emotion they see in you, what would they say?
* What have you done in response to your emotions?
* What emotions do you want to experience?

LIFE COMMITMENT:

I will acknowledge I have emotions and recognize that my emotions (and the emotions of others) are only like a thermometer, telling me something about myself, not defining who I am or who I am destined to be.

Understanding Your Emotions (2)

———⟨⟨⟨⟩⟩⟩———

THE WORD

Do not be anxious about anything, but in everything,
by prayer and petition, with thanksgiving, present
your requests to God. And the peace of God,
which transcends all understanding, will guard
your hearts and your minds in Christ Jesus.

— PHILIPPIANS 4.6–7

THOUGHT FOR THE DAY:

... for there is nothing either good or
bad but thinking makes it so.

~ William Shakespeare, *Hamlet*, Act 2, Scene 2

THE PROPHET ISAIAH LIVED THROUGH incredibly tumultuous times. After a period of prosperity, Israel was overrun by the Assyrians. Isaiah served through several administrations, most of them dysfunctional and destructive.

Isaiah's message through prosperity and tremendous adversity was always the same: *God is with you and for you. Trust in him.*

Isaiah makes an important point when he writes, *You [God] will keep in perfect **peace** him whose **mind** is steadfast, because he trusts in you.* (Isaiah 26:3)

The critical connection here is between *mind* and *emotions*. If you set your mind (thoughts) on God, you will experience peace (an emotion).

Here's the underlying dynamic at work: *Almost every emotion begins with a thought.* You can't feel something without the initial thought. Thinking comes before feeling. In fact, most of our thoughts will be reflected *back* to us and *out* to those around us as emotions. We think something and that thought generates an emotion. That emotion is experienced by us and, if we outwardly express it, to those around us.

A few days ago we said that the first step in training yourself to think well is to **become your own observer**. Step outside yourself and ask yourself what you are thinking.

Today take this one step further. When you feel an emotion, put a label on your emotion (anger, sadness, exuberance) and then *trace that emotion back to the thought that preceded it.*

Remember that you think first, and whatever you are thinking produces an emotion. You cannot have an emotion without a thought. Your emotions are linked to your thoughts.

THINK ABOUT IT...

* Is it possible to have an emotion without first having a thought?

     *   What emotion do you experience most? What thoughts usually precede that emotion?

LIFE COMMITMENT:

Today I will step back and analyze what I am feeling. I will then trace what I am feeling back to the thought that produced that feeling.

Understanding Your Emotions (3)

—— ∞∞ ——

THE WORD

Like a city whose walls are broken down
is a man who lacks self-control.

— PROVERBS 5.28

THOUGHT FOR THE DAY:

Your reactions determine your reach.

~ LYSA TERKEURST

I HAVE LOTS OF FRIENDS in Africa, fellow pastors mostly. One of my African friends made his first trip to a first world country when he came to America as part of a seminary training program. He—along with dozens of other pastors from around the world—convened at the seminary in the southeastern US for their six weeks of classes. They were housed in student dorms on the seminary campus while the regular students were on summer break.

They had a problem: they nearly froze to death even though it was summertime! The dorm was equipped with air conditioning, and it really worked! In fact, it kept their rooms at 60° F or below. Night after night the students bundled up as best they could to survive the uncomfortably cold temps.

When one of their teachers heard a student complaining about the cold, the teacher went to the dorm and showed the third-world visitors how to use the thermostat. Yep, it was that simple!

Most of us reading this will be amazed that these students didn't know how to use a thermostat. But we who may laugh at these students fail to understand a simple truth about ourselves: *our emotions operate like a thermometer and thermostat.* Our emotions are like a thermometer—they simply tell us what is going on inside us. Like the uncomfortably cold air in the dorm rooms of the students, our emotions can't be ignored for long.

But like that cold air in the dorm, our emotions can be controlled. But you have to know how.

We are like the students who were clueless as to how first world air conditioning works. We experience our emotions and then rage about what we are feeling! Don't rage at the thermometer, instead, let's figure out how to use the thermostat.

The thermometer *describes* reality; the thermostat *sets* reality.

What is the thermostat for your emotions? Hint: go back and look at yesterday's reading! *Every emotion begins with a thought.* Our emotions are a product of our thoughts just like the temperature in a room is the product (in part) of where the thermostat is set.

So go back to yesterday. The challenge yesterday was to step back and analyze your emotions (that is, 'read the thermometer'). Then you were to trace what you were feeling back to the thought that produced that feeling ('see what the thermostat is set on').

The next obvious move is to reset the thermostat. How do you do that?

Go back to Day 19. If you re-read Day 19 you will recall that one of the key points is that **you make your thoughts**. You have the power to set the thermostat of your emotions through the power of your thoughts. *So, to reset the thermostat of your emotions, reset your thoughts.*

If you have negative thoughts that are producing negative and damaging emotions, *reset the thermostat of your emotions by throwing those thoughts out!*

That's what the writer of Psalm 42 does: *Why are you downcast, O my soul? Why so disturbed within me? Put your hope in God, for I will yet praise him, my Savior and my God.* (Psalm 42.5–6)

This guy has found the thermostat: he tells himself to throw out those disturbing thoughts and instead, think about the awesomeness of God (a lot more on that later!).

THINK ABOUT IT...

* Today add to the process you have already begun: Step outside yourself and analyze what you are feeling. Trace that feeling back to its root thought. Now throw that thought out (if it is negative) and replace it with a good thought.
* Be easy on yourself! This is a lifelong exercise.

LIFE COMMITMENT:

Today I will think about what I am feeling and then reset the thermostat of my emotions by thinking different and better thoughts.

Understanding Your Emotions (4)

———— ⌀⌀⌀ ————

THE WORD

*Let us hold unswervingly to the hope we
profess, for he who promised is faithful.*

— HEBREWS 10.23

THOUGHT FOR THE DAY:

*The greatest discovery of my generation is that a human
being can alter his life by altering his attitude.*

~ WILLIAM JAMES

I WAS A YOUNG SEMINARY student moving into the first home we
would own, 900 square feet of vintage 1950 small town Fort
Worth. First on the list of repairs was a new deadbolt lock on
the front door.

Eager to impress my young wife with my handyman
skills, I set out installing the new lock. First thing: drill
that really big hole in the door the dead bolt fits into.
What did I do? Drill the hole TOO BIG! Dang it. It's really

hard to make a smaller hole out of a bigger hole. And remember, the hole that I drilled too big was in our *front door*!

I sat there and ruminated about this situation. My thoughts were not leading to solutions and the lack of solutions let me to think angry thoughts, and my angry thoughts led to angry emotions. I then expressed my anger by throwing my screwdriver hard on the floor.

The screwdriver bounced off the floor, then up and off the couch. From there it sailed even higher and, with a thud, smashed into the door jam right next to where my young wife was standing. She was definitely impressed with me, just not the kind of impression I had been aiming for. Dang.

For the record, *I never did anything as drastic or violent as that again.* The image of something as lethal as a screwdriver screaming uncontrolled through the air stopped me in my tracks.

Emotions are real and they are morally neutral. You cannot not have emotions. But you *can* learn to recognize your emotions and express them appropriately. Right now you may be experiencing emotions with an intensity that is new to you. As I wrote in the introduction, my own life experience in a period of three years led to a ferocity of emotions that was new to me. I felt pushed to my limits.

We *can* control how we express our emotions, no matter the intensity. Whatever you do, *don't cause damage to yourself or others in this time of intense emotions.* I guarantee you will regret it.

Here are some ways to diffuse the intensity of your emotions:

* **Talk** about what is going on to a trusted friend, counselor, and/or pastor. Like heating up a sealed pressure cooker inevitably leads to an explosion, so too does keeping all that stuff inside you lead to an emotional explosion. Talking releases the pressure inside you. *You cannot do this alone.*

* **Get moving.** Exercise is proven to release stress. Intense exercise will not make you forget but it will release pent up energy. Some of my fastest times on my bike have been when I have been raging inside. I have *never* ended a ride angrier than when I began!

* **Keep reading!** The truths you read here and from other sources influence your mind which controls your emotions. But you have to keep at it. Our brains can only hold so much—we leak! To hold truth in our heads we have to keep it coming in.

* **Pray.** Prayer was never intended to be a fourth-down punting situation in which we ask God to bail us out of our hasty decisions. It was intended to be a first-down huddle.[34] Prayer is just talking with God. The best way to pray is to pray, that is, just start talking with God. No instructions needed, just stop and do it.

---

[34] Neil T. Anderson and Joanne, *Daily in Christ: A Devotional* (Eugene: Harvest House Publishers, 1993), 93.

THINK ABOUT IT...

- Think back to a time when you expressed an emotion in a destructive way. How did you feel after you cut loose?
- When you feel rage or depression or some other strong emotion now, what actions have you considered to relieve that feeling? Suicide? Homicide? Alcohol? Exercise? A weekend trip? Reading?

LIFE COMMITMENT:

I choose to work through my emotions instead of letting them work through me. Today, right now, I will stop and pray. Today I will physically move in such a way that my heart rate significantly increases. Today I will call someone to talk about what is going on with me.

Understanding Your Soul (1)

———— ✸ ————

THE WORD

He has set eternity in the hearts of men; yet they cannot fathom what God has done from beginning to end.

— ECCLESIASTES 311

THOUGHT FOR THE DAY:

The spiritual life cannot be made suburban. It is always frontier, and we who live in it must accept and even rejoice that it remains untamed.

~ HOWARD MACEY

WE WERE ON A STAFF retreat in a beautiful home on the shores of Lake Winnipesaukee in New Hampshire. The first question I had for my staff was simple: "What is the soul?" This would be like a professor at a medical school asking first year students, "What is the body?" I got mostly blank stares in response to my question! We don't have a solid, succinct, clear answer to this simple question, *What is the soul?*

The dictionary says that the soul is *A part of humans regarded as immaterial, immortal, separable from the body at death, capable of moral judgment, and susceptible to happiness or misery in a future state.*[35]

Despite a concerted effort to deny the reality of the human soul, we know we have one. And we know that it is invisible and yet at the core of everything we are. John Ortberg has a book titled, *You Have a Soul: It Weighs Nothing but Means Everything.*[36] That says it all.

The Hebrew word translated as *soul* or *heart* means "the center of things." Your soul is your inner self. It is the 'you' that you are talking to when you have conversations with yourself, which you have most of the time.

The Bible says God breathed his spirit into us and in so doing, brought ordinary dirt to spectacular life. Our unique human soul not only animates our lives in a unique way while living on earth, but it is also that which is the 'eternity' that God has set into our hearts. Your soul is the thing that God gave us to access the spiritual world just as your body is given by God to access the material world.

Maybe you haven't thought about your soul much. You should because it is just as real and vital as your body. You need to know that the soul can be wounded, and often is, and that divorce is one of the most serious wounds the soul can receive.

If you crashed your car on the way to work this morning and your leg was broken and bleeding, no one would deny that you should drop everything and get your leg tended

---

[35] *The American Heritage Dictionary*, s.v. "soul," accessed January 27, 2017, https://ahdictionary.com/word/search.html?q=soul&submit.x=24&submit.y=29.

[36] John Ortberg, John. *You Have a Soul: It Weighs Nothing But Means Everything* (Grand Rapids: Zondervan, 2014).

to. But our culture fails to recognize the same urgency and need for the care of the wounded soul.

Your soul needs care and careful tending... *Only take care, and keep your soul diligently.* (Deuteronomy 4.9 ESV)

When you feel deep pain right now, the *part of you* that is feeling that pain is your soul. Just as a needle through the toe will create pain in your toe, so a blow to your soul will make your soul hurt.

But there is hope! The God who made you, body and soul, can heal and restore your soul.

Dallas Willard writes:

> *The human soul is a vast spiritual (nonphysical) landscape, with resources and relationships that exceed human comprehension; and it also exists within an infinite environment of which, at our best, we have little knowledge. We only know that God is over it all and that the soul, if it can only acknowledge its wounded condition, manifests amazing capacities for recovery when it finds its home in God and receives his grace.*[37]

Did you get that last sentence? *If [I] can acknowledge [my soul's] wounded condition, [my soul] manifests amazing capacities for recovery when it finds its home in God and receives his grace.*

THINK ABOUT IT...

---

[37] Dallas Willard, *Renovation of The Heart: Putting on The Character of Christ* (Colorado Springs: NavPress, 2002), Kindle Location 2820.

- How would you have answered the question I posed to my staff, "What is the soul?"
- If someone were to ask you what it is that is hurting inside you because of your divorce, what would you tell them?
- How is your soul?

LIFE COMMITMENT:

I know I have a soul and I know it is hurting. I commit to tending to my soul and caring for it and its recovery.

Understanding Your Soul (2)

—⊗⊗⊗—

THE WORD

Come to me, all you who are weary and burdened,
and I will give you rest. Take my yoke upon you
and learn from me, for I am gentle and humble
in heart, and you will find rest for your souls.
For my yoke is easy and my burden is light.

—JESUS AS RECORDED IN MATTHEW 11.28–30

THOUGHT FOR THE DAY:

A self-made man is a poorly made man.

~ PAUL DAVID TRIPP

NATURA ABHORRET VACUUM. THIS IS a Latin phrase that describes a foundational truth of reality: *Nature abhors a vacuum.* The proof of this is when you break wind the embarrassing smell pervades the room. The molecules of your gas seek to reach equilibrium (equal density) throughout the room.

Now that I have your attention, what is true of gas is true of our souls. Your soul is real but it is empty. It is empty because back in the beginning, Adam and Eve decided to turn against the one Being in the universe for whom their souls were made. When Adam and Eve believed Satan's lie that God was not the true soul-filler, they turned away from God.

The teaching of Christianity is that man chose to be independent of God and confirmed his choice by deliberately disobeying a divine command. This act violated the relationship that normally existed between God and His creature; it rejected God as the ground of existence and threw man back upon himself.[38]

We have a God-shaped hole in our souls because our first parents kicked God out of their lives. As Rick Warren says, *Your heart is designed to contain God.*[39] Anything less than God doesn't fit and won't work.

It's amazing how dense we are about this. Some of you are mechanics. You know that engines are built to amazing tolerances. A particular bolt fits in a particular hole *and anything less than a near perfect match will not work and has potential to do real damage to the engine.*

Some of you are software engineers. You know that code has to be precise or it will send commands to the CPU that will throw everything off.

Some of you are homebuilders. In your case my analogy breaks down because we all know that caulk can cover a multitude of sins!

Your soul has the same tolerance requirements as a Lamborghini. Would you put honey instead of oil in your brand new Huracán? Would you fill your tank with water

---

[38] A. W. Tozer, *The Knowledge of The Holy: The Attributes of God, Their Meaning in The Christian Life* (New York: Harper & Row, 1961), 54.

[39] Rick Warren, *"Your Heart is Designed for God to Fill,"* accessed January 27, 2017, http://pastorrick.com/devotional/english/your-heart-is-designed-for-god-to-fill.

instead of 90 octane (or higher) gasoline? Would you staple a tarp over your seats to protect them?

Some of you are literally shaking with horror while reading this! But when it comes to our souls we give little thought to what goes into our souls and if what we are putting in our souls is fitting or not. I can drive my car and detect the slightest noise or 'feel' and know something is wrong. But our souls can be falling apart and we are clueless.

Blaise Pascal (d. 1662) was a brilliant French Christian philosopher as well as an inventor, mathematician, and scientist. The Pascal programming language is named in his honor for his work as a mathematician and inventor of a mechanical adding machine.[40] Pascal, among other things, proved that nature actually has a vacuum. What he proved of nature as a scientist he applied to the soul as a Christian. The soul, without God, is a vacuum. Only God can fill the vacuum:

> *What else does this craving, and this helplessness, proclaim but that there was once in man a true happiness, of which all that now remains is the empty print and trace? This he tries in vain to fill with everything around him, seeking in*

---

[40] Blaise Pascal was a French mathematical genius. At the age of 19 Pascal invented a machine, which he called the *Pascaline* that could do addition and subtraction to help his father, who was also a mathematician. Pascal's machine consisted of a series of gears with 10 teeth each, representing the numbers 0 to 9. As each gear made one turn it would trip the next gear up to make 1/10 of a revolution. This principle remained the foundation of all mechanical adding machines for centuries after his death. The Pascal programming language was named in his honor. "A Brief History of Computers," accessed January 30, 2017, http://www.cs.uah.edu/~rcoleman/Common/History/History.html.

things that are not there the help he cannot find in those that are, though none can help, since this abyss can be filled only with an infinite and immutable object; in other words by God himself.

God alone is man's true good, and since man abandoned him it is a strange fact that nothing in nature has been found to take his place: stars, sky, earth, elements, plants, cabbages, leeks, animals, insects, calves, serpents, fever, plague, war, famine, vice, adultery, incest. Since losing his true good, man is capable of seeing it in anything, even his own destruction, although it is so contrary at once to God, to reason and to nature.[41]

THINK ABOUT IT...

* What kind of fuel are you putting into your car?
* What kind of fuel are you putting into your soul?
* Which is more important, your car or your soul?
* To learn what it takes to put the good stuff into your soul, go to Days 113 to 138.

LIFE COMMITMENT:
I will pay attention to my soul and what I fill it with.

---

[41] Blaise Pascal, *Pensées* (Harmondsworth: Penguin Books, 1966), 125.

Understanding Your Soul (3)

—— ⊶⊷ ——

THE WORD

My soul finds rest in God alone; my
salvation comes from him.

— PSALM 62.1

THOUGHT FOR THE DAY:

It is dangerous to explain too clearly to man how
like he is to the animals without pointing out his
greatness. It is also dangerous to make too much
of his greatness without his vileness. It is still more
dangerous to leave him in ignorance of both.

~ BLAISE PASCAL

I'VE HAD MY CAR FOR eight years now. It has had more stuff in it, on it and behind it as it has carried me and many friends to adventures far and wide. At the time of this writing I have driven it the equivalent of six times around the earth. I know my car. I know precisely how it 'feels' under my hand and foot. I know every sound it makes. When it doesn't 'feel' right or I hear a new sound, however subtle, I pay attention to it and begin to diagnose possible causes.

Amazing how we know much more about our cars/trucks than we do about our souls. Amazing how we pay so much more attention to our vehicles than we do to the core of our very being! But we do and I think there's a reason for that: we can see, touch, hear and smell our cars. Our souls, on the other hand, are invisible. They are like the wind—we see the effects of the wind but we can't see the air molecules that make the trees move.

How do you determine the condition of your soul? Hey, this is critically important! According to AAA, the average American spends 293 hours per year in his/her car. In comparison, you spend 8,760 hours in your soul per year! That's 3.3% of your life in your car vs. 100% of your life in your soul.

Dallas Willard says that, *In the person with the "well-kept heart," the soul will be itself properly ordered under God and in harmony with reality.*[42]

What happens when your soul is not in harmony with God and reality? Well, just like your car has an idiot light (OBD) so too does your soul!

Willard was a brilliant philosopher and theologian. But when asked how he tested the condition of his soul, Willard asked himself two questions:

Am I growing more or less irritable these days?
Am I more or less easily discouraged these days?

Irritability with others and discouragement within yourself are your soul's idiot lights.

---

[42] Willard, *Renovation of the Heart*, Kindle Location 2790.

THINK ABOUT IT...

* What is the condition of your soul?
* Are you more or less irritable with people?
* Are you more or less discouraged?

LIFE COMMITMENT:

I commit to paying as much attention to the condition of my soul as I do to the condition of my car!

Understanding Relationships (1)

—⟨≈≈≈⟩—

THE WORD

He who walks with the wise grows wise, but
a companion of fools suffers harm.

— PROVERBS 13:20

THOUGHT FOR THE DAY:

"I think, therefore I am."

~ DESCARTES

"I am because we are."

~ AFRICAN PROVERB

WHY DO MEN HAVE SUCH a hard time connecting with other men while women naturally gather into beehives of love and hugs? The answer is, *competition*. Men are born to be competitive, and when it comes to competition, it's all about food and sex.

In the old days (as in the hunter-gatherer days), it was a first-come, first serve world. The guy who got the Zebra got to eat and his family got to eat too. Hunting was usually a zero-sum game. Limited food meant the scramble for survival was on.

It was all about getting the girl as well (has anything changed?). Only one guy would get that girl, so to be the guy you had to shove the other guys to the back of the line.

One January day in New Hampshire I was driving my sixth-grade son to school. He asked that I pray that the girl he liked in his class would be impressed with him. He was distressed because he thought that she liked another boy. That led to a discussion about what we thought girls might be impressed with.

At about that point in the conversation we passed a most spectacular display: six tom turkeys were in full plume, tail feathers spread to the max! These *six* turkeys were chasing *one* hen! Man or turkey, it is about getting the girl, and getting the girl is *not* a team sport!

All this competition means that we men have a hard time seeing ourselves in peer relationships. We view other guys as either above us or below us. We submit to those above us and lord it over those who are below us. We have trouble being shoulder to shoulder.

There *is* a place for competition. When it comes to promotions at work and chasing the girl, game on!

But when your soul is wounded, put aside the competitive spirit and *find a team to get you through*. Now is *not* the time for you to withdraw and go it alone.

The lion chasing a herd of gazelles is not going after the leader of the pack. He is looking for the limping wounded, the slow, lonely straggler.

Your soul is wounded. You are in pain and your life has slowed down. The temptation is to pull back and disconnect from the people in your world. The enemy knows this and will zero in on you.

As head coach of the Super Bowl winning Indianapolis Colts, Tony Dungy knows something about competition and teamwork. He writes:

> *God doesn't ask us to walk alone. God specifically created us to be in relationship, relationship with Him and relationship with others. God is always bringing other people into our lives to walk with us, to help us do what He's called us to do even better.*[43]

Can you trust God to bring other guys into your life to walk this thing through with you?

Dungy goes on to write:

> *Successful, high-performance teams are aware of individual team members and the distractions and temptations they might be facing. Individuals don't have to walk alone on those teams—others come alongside them and keep them focused and encouraged.*[44]

Bottom-line: We need each other... so don't withdraw!

---

[43] Dungy and Whitaker, *The One Year Uncommon Life Daily Challenge*, Kindle Locations 704-713.

[44] Ibid.

THINK ABOUT IT...

* On a scale of 1 to 10, where are in your desire to connect with other people?

  0 = No Desire, 10 = Strong Desire
  0—1—2—3—4—5—6—7—8—9—10

* Who can you call in the middle of the night when you are in a crisis? Think of someone you could connect with and determine to begin building that relationship right now.

LIFE COMMITMENT:

I am determined to not do this alone. I am asking God to send me another man who can walk shoulder-to-shoulder with me.

Understanding Relationships (2)

—⦇∞⦈—

THE WORD

*The evening meal was being served, and the devil
had already prompted Judas Iscariot, son of Simon,
to betray Jesus. Jesus knew that the Father had
put all things under his power, and that he had
come from God and was returning to God;
So he got up from the meal, took off his outer clothing, and
wrapped a towel around his waist. After that, he poured
water into a basin and began to wash his disciples' feet,
drying them with the towel that was wrapped around him.*

—JOHN 13.2–5

THOUGHT FOR THE DAY:

An enemy is one whose story we have not heard.

~ AFRICAN PROVERB

WE ARE MADE FOR RELATIONSHIPS with other human beings.
As painful as that might sound, it is true. As a pastor I would
always say that *the best committee is a committee of three with two
absent.* Everyone would laugh because we know that working
with others is a challenge. But I would admit that planning

and executing as a team is usually more fun than going it alone.

Relationships are great when they go well. They are hell when they don't. Right now you are in the hell of a broken marriage. No relationship is more central to our being than marriage. Divorce rips apart what God put together, and the depth of pain we feel from divorce is proportional to the vitality we experienced at some point in the marriage.

The next several days we will look at a concept that can help you function better in all your relationships. This concept is **Self-Differentiation**.

Self-differentiation is about **separation** and **connection**. Jesus is a perfect example of the *separation* part of self-differentiation. He never let what anyone thought about him take him off mission. Laser focused, nothing anyone said or did got him off track. For example, some people—such as his disciples—thought that going to the cross for humanity was a stupid idea. But what they thought didn't matter to Jesus—he carried through on his mission anyway.

To be perfectly differentiated from others means that what you think, feel and do is not influenced by what others think, feel or do.

At the same time, self-differentiation is all about *connection*. Again, Jesus is our example. Jesus radically connected to *all* people. Jesus connected with the rich (Nicodemus in John 3) and the outcast (the Samaritan woman at the well in John 4). In the passage from John 13 (see above), Jesus washes his disciples' feet, humbly serving them, demonstrating his willingness to connect with them at every level. He died for us—*all* of us—even the people who nailed him to the cross. His love is unsurpassed, and at the care of love is connecting.

In summary:

> **Separation** means that I will not be controlled (emotionally and physically) by the behaviors and attitudes of others. I am comfortable being in my own company.
>
> **Connection** means that I will remain connected to people—despite what they may think of me. I am also comfortable being in the company of others.

Here are a couple of sample questions to help you determine your degree of self-differentiation:

> *How do you feel and behave if you must confront someone?* **If your anxiety is high and you seek to avoid the confrontation, you are not separated from people— they control you to some degree.**
>
> *How do you feel when you are criticized?* **If anxiety goes up when you are criticized, then you are not adequately separated** from people.

Disclaimer: I am still working on this and I always will be. This is more about direction than destination. Only Jesus was perfectly self-differentiated. The rest of us have a long way to go.

THINK ABOUT IT...

* What would be different in your relationships if you were not so influenced by what others thought about you?
* What is one step you can take today to be less influenced by what others think about you?
* What would happen if you radically loved everyone in your sphere of influence?
* What is one thing you can do today to demonstrate more love to one person in your life?

LIFE COMMITMENT:

I will not be controlled (emotionally and physically) by the behaviors and attitudes of others. At the same time, I will remain connected to people—despite what they may think of me.

Understanding Relationships (3)

—◦◦◦◦—

THE WORD

Jesus knew that the Father had put all things under his power, and that he had come from God and was returning to God; So he got up from the meal, took off his outer clothing, and wrapped a towel around his waist. After that, he poured water into a basin and began to wash his disciples' feet, drying them with the towel that was wrapped around him.

— JOHN 13.3–5

THOUGHT FOR THE DAY:

Today I will give myself the chance to have new kinds of relationships.... Disagreeing and learning to accept differences are a part of intimacy.... Genuine trust and understanding make room for moving apart and coming together again.

~ TIAN DAYTON

HOW WAS JESUS SO SELF-DIFFERENTIATED? The answer is that his identity did not come from people but from God. Notice what John says in 13.3: *Jesus **knew that the Father had put all***

things under his power, *and that* **he had come from God** *and was* **returning to God.**

Jesus knew who he was—he was God's Son and nothing anyone thought about him could change that fact. Because his identity was firmly anchored in God, no person could deter him from his mission. In addition, he was totally confident around all people because what they thought about him was secondary to what God thought about him.

Jesus could love everyone without condition because his identity was completely rooted in God. Notice in the passage below how Jesus' identity led to his ability to radically love his disciples:

> *Jesus* **knew** *that the Father had put all things under his power, and that* **he had come from God and was returning to God;** **So** *he got up from the meal, took off his outer clothing, and wrapped a towel around his waist. After that, he poured water into a basin and* **began to wash his disciples' feet.**

How could Jesus be willing to stoop so low to do the work of a servant? Because *[He] knew... that he had come from God and was returning to God.*

Most of us are unwilling to stoop so low because we are in competing with others for status and standing. Jesus didn't play that game because he didn't have to—his identity was securely anchored in God. Jesus could demonstrate such radical love in complete freedom because he was free from what people thought about him. He was free from being at the mercy of others. This freedom allowed him to love others completely— no strings attached.

Here are some real-time benefits of self-differentiation:

* Freedom from anxiety of what others think about us.
* Freedom to live out our God-given mission rather than being limited and controlled by others.
* The capacity to connect to others despite how we think or feel about them.
* The ability and willingness to obey Christ's command to love one another no matter what.
* Our own personal growth and the joy of seeing God use us to help others grow.

THINK ABOUT IT...

* What do you fear?
* What is the root of that fear?
* How could living a self-differentiated life relieve that fear?

LIFE COMMITMENT:

I commit to living with less fear and more courage because I know my identity is anchored in Christ.

Understanding Relationships (4)

THE WORD

Yet to all who received him, to those who believed in his name, he gave the right to become children of God— children born not of natural descent, nor of human decision or a husband's will, but born of God.

— JOHN 1:12–13

THOUGHT FOR THE DAY:

God loved his Son and was pleased with him not based on how he was performing but simply because Jesus is his Son.

~ LYSA TERKEURST

A FEW DAYS AGO WE said that in this time of distress, the last thing you need is to withdraw, trying to go it alone. But how do we do relationships well? How do we connect in a way that gives energy and life to us and others? How can we run with the pack with strength and wisdom? The answer is to live a self-differentiated life.

Self-differentiation is about separation and connection. To be self-differentiated is to live free from being controlled by the thoughts, emotions and actions of others. To be self-differentiated is to live a life so rooted in God that you are free to radically love (connect) with the people God puts into your sphere of influence. Self-differentiated people are radically disconnected from people and radically connected to people at the same time.

Self-differentiated people live lives of freedom—freedom from the anxiety of what others think about them and freedom to live out their God-given mission rather than being limited and controlled by others.

Follow these steps toward living a self-differentiated life:

* **<u>Anchor your identity in God</u>**, not people, places or things. Jesus *knew that the Father had put all things under his power, and that he had come from God and was returning to God.* (John 13.3) You are *not* defined by others! You are not defined by your worldly success or failures. You are not defined by your status and position in society. You are not defined by the size of your boat or how your NFL team is doing. You are a son of God. Your identity comes from him, not from anything in this world. For more on rooting your identity in God, go back to Day 30.

* **<u>Discover God's purpose for your life</u>** and live unbendingly for his purpose. As God's son you have a specific mission he wants you to fulfill. To live out his purpose for your life will be the most rewarding and most challenging thing you ever do. But in the end, living out

his purpose for your life is all that matters. For more about finding and living God's purpose of your life, go to Days 7, 14, 48-49, 67, 80, 163, 178, and 180.

* **<u>Learn to observe how you act/react in anxiety-producing situations</u>**. Practice what we have already talked about—stepping outside yourself and analyzing what the heck is going on inside you. Why am I anxious? What is causing this fear in me? What is ramping up my anger right now? For more about becoming your own best observer, go back to Days 18 through 20 (*How Thinking Works*).

* **<u>Own what is your part, and let others own their part</u>**. In my work as a hospice chaplain I deal with many adult men taking care of their dying parents. Some of these men have done an amazing job of caring for mom and/or dad, and yet they are often filled with regrets. Though they have given 110% they still beat themselves up. Other men don't seem to give a damn about their parents.

    In both cases there is a failure of men to own what is theirs and let go of what isn't theirs. For the men taking good care of their parents, they need to celebrate what they have done and let go of what is beyond their control. For the men who don't seem to care about their parents, they need to own up to their responsibility and do their part. Taking responsibility for what is yours and letting others own their part is a huge step toward self-differentiation.

* **<u>Seek to understand the other rather than change him/her</u>**. How many of us have failed marriages because we wanted to win the argument rather than

simply understand our partner? Self-differentiated men have less need to win and more desire to understand. Here is a simple step toward self-differentiation: Shut up! Listen first. Listen hard. Listen slow. You really *don't* have to talk all the time! You really *don't* have to win the damned argument! Brothers, there is freedom in this!

* **Practice!** Guess what? Life is an experiment. If something is not working, try something else. Experiment, test, evaluate. Step back and let the games begin!

Years ago I found this quote from John Gardner to be most helpful. I just wish I had perfectly practiced what he suggested:

> *The things you learn in maturity aren't simple things such as acquiring information and skills. You learn not to engage in self-destructive behavior.*
>
> *You learn not to burn up energy in anxiety. You discover how to manage your tensions.*
>
> *You learn that self-pity and resentment are the most toxic of drugs.*
>
> *You find that the world loves talent but pays off on character.*
>
> *You come to understand that most people are neither for you nor against you; they are thinking of themselves.*

You learn that no matter how hard you try to please, some people in this world are not going to love you—a lesson that is at first troubling and then really quite relaxing.[45]

THINK ABOUT IT...

   *   What anchors your identity? Another way to ask this question is, *What would I think about me if I lost* _____*? What would I feel if* _____ *were taken away from me?* Fill the blanks in with *job, house, wife, kids, career, 401k, summer house, boat, hobby, health, reputation,* etc., etc., etc.

   *   How would you answer the question: God's mission for my life is _____.

LIFE COMMITMENT:
I will anchor my identity in God alone.

---

[45] *John Gardner's Writings,* accessed August 06, 2017, http://www.pbs.org/johngardner/sections/writings_speech_1.html.

Understanding Relationships (5)

─────❧❧❧─────

The Word

*My dear brothers, take note of this: Everyone
should be quick to listen, slow to speak and slow
to become angry, for man's anger does not bring
about the righteous life that God desires.*

—James 1.19–20

Thought for the Day:

*After collecting a few disasters [in life] we learn
that actions are forever, opportunities seldom
return and that consequences are relentless.*

~ Dallas Willard

I was never so thrilled as when I attended my second
meeting of the local Volunteer Fire Department which I had
just joined. I was the new pastor in town and eager to jump
on a truck and spray water on a fire.

The occasion for my joy was that the Assistant Fire Chief
was not there. When I arrived the buzz was that a spat had

arisen between the Chief and his assistant. The assistant had resigned in a huff.

Why did this make me so happy? I wasn't happy because the Assistant Fire Chief had resigned—I barely knew the guy! I was happy because I realized *that the church was not the only place adults acted like two-year-olds!* It was a revelation! Since then I have had many occasions to marvel at the utter immaturity of people and to regret my own.

Today and tomorrow we will look at a second dynamic that will help you understand and function better in your relationships. This will also explain a lot of (immature) human behavior.

In a perfect world everyone would talk *only* to one another, encouraging one another and gently and lovingly confronting each other to work out problems. In this ideal world we would perfectly live out Ephesians 4.15 which says, *Speaking the truth in love, we will in all things grow up into him who is the Head, that is, Christ.*

This is not an ideal world (shocker). When tensions increase between two people the natural tendency is for one or both parties in the relationship to 'triangle' in a third person or issue. Working out problems face-to-face takes emotional investment and risks the relationship. It just seems easier to talk about your problems to someone else. This is called *triangling.*

We form relational triangles because they appear to help us. Triangling serves to:

* Absorb anxiety.
* Cover over basic differences and conflicts in a relationship.

* Give us a sense of self-importance.
* Lure us into thinking we are working on the problem.

THINK ABOUT IT...

* Think about your relationships at work, home, school, etc. Where are the triangles?
* What would change in your world if you truly [spoke] the truth in love, that is, handled the tensions in your relationships by gently stating your opinion and waiting patiently for a response, really trying to understand the other person?

LIFE COMMITMENT:
I will step back and analyze my relationships looking for the triangles that have formed right under my nose!

Understanding Relationships (6)

———⟨oᴇᴇᴏ⟩———

THE WORD

*Speaking the truth in love, we will in all things
grow up into him who is the Head, that is, Christ.
From him the whole body, joined and held together
by every supporting ligament, grows and builds
itself up in love, as each part does its work.*

— EPHESIANS 4.15–16

THOUGHT FOR THE DAY:

*I count myself in nothing else so happy / As
in a soul rememb'ring my good friends.*

~ WILLIAM SHAKESPEARE, *KING
RICHARD II*, ACT 2, SCENE 3

WE LIVE IN A WORLD of triangles where seemingly successful people deal with one another in stunningly immature ways. We form triangles because one-to-one conversation and confrontation is emotionally risky and can be painful. It's just easier to gripe about someone behind their back than to talk face-to-face. Triangles work to ease our anxiety and decrease personal tension, but they don't work in the long run.

Triangles...

* Perpetuate problems instead of solving them.
* Limit growth because they push down anxiety.
* Have potential to lead to adulterous affairs.
* Maintain distance in relationships.
* Give the appearance of working on the problem when nothing really changes.

For us to grow in our relationships, we need to de-triangle as much as possible and encourage others to not triangle us into their relationships. This sounds like a ton of work, and it is, but in the end you will be glad that you are aware of this dynamic and your relationships will be more authentic and life-giving.

How to handle triangles:

* Observe yourself and those around you—where are the triangles? What is your role in these triangles?
* Reposition yourself by helping the person who has drawn you into a triangle to see his/her own responsibility in the situation. Try to move yourself and others from victimhood to responsibility.
* When anxiety occurs in your relationships, resist the urge to triangle and instead, speak the truth in love.
* Test yourself: In your normal daily conversation with others, how much time do you spend talking about people who are not present, rather than talking about yourself, the person with you, or your relationship with each other?

THINK ABOUT IT...

❋   Think of one relationship in your life that would benefit from taking the steps above. Pick a step and do it today.

LIFE COMMITMENT:

I commit to being more mature in my relationships by avoiding triangles and seeking to speak the truth in love.

Accepted by God (1)

———⧉———

THE WORD

Accept one another, then, just as Christ accepted
you, in order to bring praise to God.

— ROMANS 15:7

THOUGHT FOR THE DAY:

People are suffering from an identity crisis. It
seems everywhere we turn we see people striving
to become someone or something that they
perceive will bring them some sort of contentment
when in reality the opposite is true.[46]

~ PERRY NOBLE

FROM THE BEGINNING OF MY Christian experience I
was told the amazing truth that I was accepted by God.
Everyone seemed so excited to tell me this wonderful
news. But try as I might, I could not wrap my head around
what being accepted by God really meant. The reason is

---

[46] Perry Noble quoted in Mark Driscoll, *Who Do You Think You Are? Finding
Your True Identity in* Christ (Nashville: Thomas Nelson, 2013), 7.

that my understanding of acceptance was based on my experiences of human 'acceptance.'

We are told that to accept others is a noble thing, part of our unique American experience of one another. Despite the mantra that we need to accept one another, my actual experience is that we don't accept each other for who we are. Instead, the relationships I have lived in have been unpleasantly based on a cost-benefit analysis. If I can do something for you, you like me. If I am no use to you, you push me aside and move on to the next person to use. And I usually treat others the same way.

For this reason, all this talk of acceptance was muddied in my brain until I ran across a new (and biblical) way of looking at things from the smart folks at an organization called Victorious Christian Living.[47]

Here's how this works: when someone says to me that God accepts me I automatically filter that statement through what I know of acceptance, which is to say, I define the word 'acceptance' by my experience of acceptance. The only experience I know of acceptance is from my life in the world.

How do I gain the world's acceptance? To get the world's ultimate approval/acceptance I follow a specific path:

First, someone in the world (an **AUTHORITY** in my life) gives me their expectations. This authority can be parents, a teacher, an employer or anyone or anything in the world that has a measure of control over my life.

Next, I have to work to meet those expectations. I strive to *do* the things that I have been told I should do. I jump through all the right hoops to reach the goal, *which is acceptance by that authority in my life.*

---

[47] The teachings for the next several days come primary from *"Seven Areas of Life Training."* Victorious Christian Living International, accessed February 03, 2017. http://www.vcli.org/salt/.

I wrote on the first day of this guide:

The only question on my mind growing up was, "Am I good enough?" The answers from my dad and others were conflicted. On one hand, I was told I was special and nothing could stop me. I would be spectacular. On the other hand, if I was anything less than spectacular, it was my fault. Given the deluge of criticism I received, it seemed that though I was special, I pretty much never measured up to my specialness!

Not to kick a dead horse till its teeth fall out, but most of us men grew up with this double message from our parents, our schools, our peers. To be accepted we had to jump through hoops that were just out of reach. The message we received was, you can do it but... you probably won't.

Implicit in this message was that people were both for me and against me, both my friend and my enemy, my companion and my challenger. People were as likely to push me down as they were to help me up.

Is this your experience of 'acceptance'? If this is the way God 'accepts' me, I think I will pass!

To be continued...

Think About It...

* When you hear the word 'acceptance' what first comes to your mind?
* What have you been told you must do to be accepted by the authorities in your life? Parents? Teachers? Employers?

* When have you measured up? What were the consequences?
* When have you failed to measure up? What were the consequences?

LIFE COMMITMENT:

It could be true that what I think about God's love and acceptance for me has been informed more by my experience of how the world defines love and acceptance than by what God says about me.

Accepted by God (2)

———∞∞∞———

THE WORD

We have the free gift of being accepted by God,
even though we are guilty of many sins.

— ROMANS 5.16 (NLT)

THOUGHT FOR THE DAY:

I renounce the lie that I am too worthless to ever be
accepted by God or people. I acknowledge that my
value before God is so great He sent Jesus to die for me,
and it is the value in His eyes which truly counts.

~ KETURAH MARTIN

I WAS OFTEN TOLD I was loved and accepted without condition, but it seemed to me that love and acceptance came with a lot of conditions. When I came home with A's on my report card, I got showered with praise and affection. When I came home with a C in algebra, all hell broke loose. All those A's didn't seem to cover over a single C. The question I was always asking (and still ask in my weaker moments) is, *"Am I good enough?"* And often the answer was, *"Almost."*

When I worked hard to be good enough for the **AUTHORITIES** in my life, I got **AFFIRMATION**.

Affirmation is the second step in being accepted by the world. First, authorities lay out their **expectations**. If you meet these expectations, you get **affirmed**.

This is the way the world works whether you working on a Ph.D. or trying to get into a gang. The group says, "Do this, and we will accept you." You jump through the hoops, and if you succeed, they affirm you. If you keep it up, affirmation turns into **ACCEPTANCE**. You're in!

The downside of this is that if you fail to keep jumping through the hoops, you can be pushed back out. You can go from being *acceptable* to *unacceptable*.

This is the way of the world. Authorities give us expectations. We work hard to meet those expectations. If we do, we are affirmed, and if consistently affirmed, we are accepted.

Here's the thing: The motivation behind this dynamic at work in our world is *control*. Parents, teachers, employers—they all have to control us. The way they control us is to give or take away their acceptance of us. The emotion that accompanies and drives this process is *fear*. We *fear* not being accepted, and that fear motivates us to follow the rules.

Now think about it: Do you think God accepts or rejects you based on your obedience to his authority?

If you do, please explain these words from the Bible:

[We] know and rely on the love God has for us. God is love.... There is no fear in love. But perfect love drives out

fear, because fear has to do with punishment.... (1 John 4.16–18)

Hopefully you are beginning to realize that being accepted by God means something significantly different than how the world accepts us.

THINK ABOUT IT...

* What is the most ridiculous thing you ever did in order to be accepted by a group?
* What are some ridiculous things people do to earn God's acceptance?
* Was there a time you felt like God accepted you?
* Was there a time when you believed God rejected you?

LIFE COMMITMENT:

I believe God's way of accepting me must be different than the world's way of acceptance.

Accepted by God (3)

———— ∝∝∝ ————

THE WORD

Do you want to get well?

—JESUS, ASKED OF A LAME MAN AS RECORDED IN JOHN 5.6

THOUGHT FOR THE DAY:

If you obey for a thousand years, you're no more
accepted than when you first believed; your acceptance
is based on Christ's righteousness and not yours.

~ PAUL DAVID TRIPP

FOR THE PAST TWO DAYS I have explained the way the authorities in our world accepts us. The **authorities** in our lives give us expectations. We try to meet them. If we do, we are **affirmed**. If we are affirmed enough, we are **accepted**. If we screw up, we can be unaccepted.

The purpose of this dynamic is *control*, and the emotion used to control us is *fear*.

Now, two simple questions: *Is this the way God works? Is God's main goal to control you?*

That leads to a next question: *Do you think God can control you?*

The small town of Bertram is located northwest of Austin. This little town has the irritating habit of positioning one of their police cruisers somewhere along the highway that goes through their town. The cruiser is empty. But it is menacing. Every time I go through Bertram *I know the empty cruiser will be there. And every time I see that cruiser my heart skips a beat and I slow down out of fear of getting a speeding ticket!*

Guys, if an empty police cruiser can control my behavior and strike fear in my heart, what can an all-powerful God do?

The prophet Jeremiah said,

God made the earth by his power; he founded the world by his wisdom and stretched out the heavens by his understanding. When he thunders, the waters in the heavens roar; he makes clouds rise from the ends of the earth. He sends lightning with the rain and brings out the wind from his storehouses. (Jeremiah 10.12–13)

That's a powerful God! God could make you bend over double with excruciating pain right now. He could pop your head off or send you careening through space. *God can do to you whatever he wants!* So the question is, *What does God want?*

Here's what God wants: God wants you to experience his love so that you can respond to him in love.

God does not want to control you out of fear but to woo you with his love!

That's why God's acceptance of us begins with his love, not his expectations.

First John 4.16 plainly states, *God is love. Whoever lives in love lives in God, and God in him.*

In the world's way of acceptance, you must earn the approval of the authorities. In God's Kingdom, **God already approves you on the basis of what Jesus, his Son did for you on the cross.**

God's way starts with acceptance. He accepts you right now before you do anything. He doesn't accept you based on your ability to obey His commands. You are accepted because Christ's death on the cross made you acceptable.[48]

When God looks at you he doesn't see your shortcomings, he sees his Son's righteousness. When God looks at you he doesn't see where you have fallen short he sees where his Son has lifted you up.

That means that you have nothing to prove to God. Jesus has already bought God's approval of you. You cannot earn God's approval; his approval of you has already been purchased by his Son.

Neil and Joann Anderson say it like this:

> *We are not on a performance basis with God. He doesn't say, "Here are My standards, now you measure up." He knows you can't solve the problem of an old sinful self by simply improving your behavior. He must change your nature, give you an entirely new self—the life of Christ in you.*[49]

The world says, **Perform**! God says, **Receive**!

---

[48] *Seven Areas of Life Training*, Book 1, Lesson 4. VCLi, Version 2.0, 51.

[49] Anderson and Anderson, *Daily in Christ: A Devotional*, 105.

There is nothing you can do to add to or take away his love from you. When you do something good, God does not love you more. When you mess up, God does not love you less. His love is based on who he is *not on what you do or don't do.*

God's acceptance of us begins with his love for us, not his expectations of us.

THINK ABOUT IT...

* In what ways have you tried to earn God's approval?
* If you tried to earn God's approval, how did you know you got it (or not)?
* God's acceptance of us begins with his love for us, not his expectations of us. What could change in your life if you really believed this?

LIFE COMMITMENT:

I give up! I give up trying to earn God's approval and love. Instead, I choose to simply receive his steadfast, never-changing love for me.

Accepted by God (4)

———<small>∞</small>———

THE WORD

*For you did not receive a spirit that makes you a slave
again to fear, but you received the Spirit of sonship.
And by him we cry, "Abba, Father." The Spirit himself
testifies with our spirit that we are God's children.*

— ROMANS 8.16-17

THOUGHT FOR THE DAY:

*Every day you preach to yourself some kind of
gospel—a false "I can't do this" gospel or the
true "I have all I need in Christ" gospel.*

~ PAUL DAVID TRIPP

WHEN MY WIFE MET ME upon my return from Africa and told
me she was leaving me, the weight of her rejection drove
me into the ground. I had worked hard all my life to earn
the approval, affirmation and acceptance of the people
in my life. No person's approval meant more to me than
her's.

Just a few weeks before this happened, she had been on a business trip. On the way home she posted on Facebook that she could not wait to get home and go to church to hear her favorite preacher. She meant me! I beamed inside! A month later she told me she was leaving me. Coming to grips with these double messages is a challenge yet before me.

Every single rejection stings because rejection goes against all that we have tried so hard to attain—the love, approval and acceptance of others. As now famously disgraced Lance Armstrong once said, "A boo is a lot louder than a cheer."

The only thing that kept me going through that time was knowing that God did not reject me. Even though I am a divorced pastor, God has not divorced me. Though to many people in the world I am a failure because my wife rejected me, I know that in God's eyes, I am accepted and loved *no matter what.*

God begins by accepting us out of his love for us and based on Christ's death on our behalf. When we understand this amazing truth we understand and experience God's **AFFIRMATION**. God's affirmation of us is experienced as an emotion. We *feel* God's love for us. Just like we feel the fear of the rejection of the world, we can feel God's amazing love and acceptance of us!

The Apostle Paul wrote, *The Spirit himself testifies with our spirit that we are God's children.* (Romans 8.16). This is really good news! When we experience God's Spirit testifying with our spirit that we are his kids, accepted *because we are his kids,* we experience joy, peace, gladness... and the list of positive emotions goes on!

To the depth that I felt crushed by all that I was going through, God met me equally and even beyond with his Spirit gently holding my soul and reassuring me that I would be OK. I kept hearing him say, *I love you, you are OK. Just hold on and we will get through this. I will never leave you or forsake you.*

I could receive no greater affirmation than that.

God first **ACCEPTS** us based on his love for us, not our performance for him. He then **AFFIRMS** us by reassuring us that we his kids and he will never leave us or forsake us.

Think About It...

* Have you experienced God's **peace** equal to or greater than your **anxiety**?
* Have you experienced God's **joy** equal to or greater than your **anguish**?
* Have you experienced God's **love** equal to or greater than your **anger**?
* If not, ask his Spirit to testify with your spirit that you are his son, and that you are accepted, affirmed and loved *no matter what* anyone else may say or do. Ask him to allow you to experience this truth deep in your soul as a good and strong emotion.

Life Commitment:
I choose to believe that God has accepted me first, and that he actually wants me to experience the reality of his acceptance of me resulting in emotions of peace, joy and love.

Accepted by God (5)

———◦∞◦———

THE WORD

Before I formed you in the womb I knew you,
before you were born I set you apart.

—JEREMIAH 1.5

THOUGHT FOR THE DAY:

Because the Spirit of the Lord is in you, you are free to
choose to live a responsible and moral life. You are no
longer compelled to walk according to the flesh as you were
before conversion. And now you are not even compelled to
walk according to the Spirit. You are free to choose to walk
according to the Spirit or to walk according to the flesh.

~ NEIL ANDERSON

EVERYONE DEMANDS IT FOR OTHERS but few want it for themselves. We decry others when they avoid it, but we crumple into a heap when others require it of us. We rail at others when it catches them in the act, but curl up into a ball of excuses when it exposes our shortcomings. What am I talking about? Accountability.

Everywhere we turn we hear the incessant call for more accountability. And yet when we are held accountable, we squeal and squirm. We scream at the referee who fails to call pass interference on the opposing team, but run like a hen when the finger is pointed at us.

From the world's perspective, accountability is all about fear. The boss lays down expectations. Then he holds us accountable. The thought of failing creates fear in us, and fear motivates us to meet expectations. If we meet expectations we get affirmed, and if affirmed enough, we feel accepted. Accountability is a big piece of the way the systems in the world work.

How does accountability work in God's Kingdom? If God starts with accepting us, and then he affirms us, where does accountability fit in?

Look at the first few lines of the 23rd Psalm:

The Lord is my shepherd, I shall not be in want.
He makes me lie down in green pastures, he leads me beside quiet waters, he restores my soul.
He guides me in paths of righteousness for his name's sake. (Psalm 23.1–3)

This Psalm affirms what we have said about the way God accepts us. It starts off with the assurance that God is our good shepherd, and we know that shepherds accept their sheep the way they are.

The next few lines are all about affirmation: God leads me to green, abundant pastures and quenches my thirst at no cost. Green pastures and still waters are given to all sheep regardless of how 'good' or 'bad' they have been. He restores my soul *at no cost*. In other words, God accepts us and provides for us because he loves us, not because we have done anything to earn it.

But then comes accountability. Notice how David describes accountability in God's Kingdom: *He [God] guides me in paths of righteousness for his name's sake.*

God *does* hold us accountable. He doesn't let us live without limits. But the limits he sets are *for our good* and *for his glory*. God sets boundaries for us, but the purpose of those boundaries is that we may flourish into what we were meant to be. When we grow into his Kingdom people, the world takes notice and God gets the glory!

He *guides* us—he doesn't *drive* us—into the paths of righteousness so that we may flourish and in our flourishing, he may get the glory. God wants the best for us.

I confess that a few times I disciplined my children more to release my own anger than to guide them in life. Not God. His discipline is never to vent his own anger but *always* to nudge us back onto the path toward green pastures, smooth waters and soul restoration.

What if we stray *way* off the path? The Shepherd will pursue us (not hunt us down) to bring us back to the abundant pasture and thirst-quenching stream (see Luke 15.4-7).

God holds us accountable for our good and for his glory. He is motivated by his love for us, trusting that by loving us we will respond in love back to him. There is no fear in this equation. The world operates on the basis of fear. God operates on the basis of love. The difference between the two is utterly profound.

Think About It...

* If you go to church, why do you go?
* If you give money to your church or another charity, why do you give?
* If you pray, why do you pray?

Life Commitment:

I choose to believe that God is for me and has my best interests in mind, and that he holds me accountable not out of a motivation of control but out of pure love for me.

Accepted by God (6)

———◦◦◦◦———

THE WORD

> *Brothers and sisters, I do not consider myself yet to*
> *have taken hold of it. But one thing I do: Forgetting*
> *what is behind and straining toward what is ahead,*
> *I press on toward the goal to win the prize for which*
> *God has called me heavenward in Christ Jesus.*

— PHILIPPIANS 3:13-14

THOUGHT FOR THE DAY:

> *Jesus paid it all! There are no bills due for your*
> *sin! You are now free to simply trust and obey.*

~ PAUL DAVID TRIPP

ONE DAY I WAS DRIVING along and I had a profoundly terrible thought. It was terrible because it was so incredibly untrue. The thought I had was this: *I bet I will get into heaven. I mean, I am a pastor! Don't all pastors go to heaven because we are so good?*

The moment I thought it I realized how idiotic this was. The first bad thing about this thought was that whatever *good*

I did could *never* add to God's love for me. I could *never* increase God's love for me by any good thing I did. He loves me now as much as he did when he decided in eternity past to create me. He loves me now as much as he did when his Son hung on a cross taking the hell I rightfully deserved for every sin I would commit in my lifetime. There is nothing good I could ever do to increase God's love for me. He loves me, period.

The second bad thing about this thought was that I am *not nearly as good as I had led myself to believe!* I am a self-centered sinful creature like everyone else. Which led me to this awesome reality: *There is nothing bad that I could ever do that would take away God's love for me.* He loves me, period. His love for me never changes.

God is not like the Greek gods who were just super-sized humans who pretty much screwed up the world with their super-sized but misdirected powers. God does not act like we do—he doesn't keep score of our good deeds and misdeeds—and love us depending on the score.

The world begins with rules to follow which may or may not lead to its acceptance of us. God is just the opposite—he begins by accepting us! No hoops to jump through, no demands to meet, no fear of falling short. God *begins* with accepting you because he profoundly, deeply and incessantly loves you.

If he wanted to control you out of fear, he could. Oh... he could! Instead of controlling you through fear he wants to woo you with his love. The basis of God's acceptance of you is love, not fear.

THINK ABOUT IT...

* Do you fear God or love him?
* What could you do to make God love you more?
* What does God think when you screw up?

LIFE COMMITMENT:
I will live my life based on God's unchangeable love for me, not based on the fear of not meeting his or people's expectations of me.

Walden Pond or the North Atlantic?

—⊶⊶—

THE WORD

There is a time for everything, and a season
for every activity under heaven.

— ECCLESIASTES 3.1

THOUGHT FOR THE DAY:

I believe in process. I believe in four seasons. I believe
that winter's tough, but spring's coming. I believe
that there's a growing season. And I think that you
realize that in life, you grow. You get better.

~ STEVE SOUTHERLAND

I CAN'T REMEMBER WHERE I read it, but someone said that while we yearn for a peaceful life on Walden Pond, real life is more like the North Atlantic in winter! For the most part, we try to live on Walden Pond, and for most of our lives we may be able to manage life closer to Walden than the North Atlantic.

But inevitably something happens that flings you into the North Atlantic where the waves are huge and the water frigid.

Divorce did that for me. All the things I had worked for, the *stability and security* I sought, slipped right out of my hands. Maybe you had this same experience. You worked hard to provide for your family. You tried to be there for your kids, you sacrificed to secure a safe and stable home. Then the bottom dropped out.

The reality is this: Walden is an illusion. But so is the North Atlantic. Life is never as peaceful as Walden and it is never as completely terrifying as the North Atlantic.

I've had a 'Walden Pond' moment or two. It was great, but fleeting and still not deeply satisfying.

For three years I was flailing around in the North Atlantic with wind, water and waves crashing all around me. But just as Walden was not that great as promised, the North Atlantic was not as terrifying as imagined. The reason Walden disappoints and the North Atlantic not so terrifying is that our security and stability are not found in earthly circumstances.

Look at Psalm 46:

> *God is our refuge and strength, an ever-present help in trouble. Therefore we will not fear, **though the earth give way** and **the mountains fall into the heart of the sea**, though its waters roar and foam and the mountains quake with their surging.* (Psalm 46:1–3, emphasis mine).

Did you get that second sentence: *Therefore we will not fear, though the earth give way and the mountains fall into the heart of the sea.*

Earth and mountains are supposed to be *stable*. They don't just collapse. Their collapse represents the Psalmist's worst calamity. But, he says, *because God is our refuge,* we will not fear *even if the most stable things we can imagine actually do collapse.*

If your life is more like flailing in the North Atlantic than sitting peacefully by Walden Pond, know that God is your refuge and strength and that, ultimately, nothing can shake you.

THINK ABOUT IT...

* Where are you right now: Walden Pond, the North Atlantic, or somewhere in between?
* Have you experienced moments of true peace due to positive circumstances? Did the peace last?
* When circumstances have felt like drowning in the North Atlantic, how did you feel? What did you do?
* What does it mean that God is our *refuge and strength*?

LIFE COMMITMENT:

I am coming to realize that life is never as peaceful as Walden nor as completely terrifying as the North Atlantic. Security and safety are only found in turning to God to be my refuge and strength.

Go With the Flow

—⬥—

THE WORD

*See, I am doing a new thing! Now it springs
up; do you not perceive it? I am making a way
in the desert and streams in the wasteland.*

— ISAIAH 43.19

THOUGHT FOR THE DAY:

*Often in the growth process we do not know what
to do, or we do not want to do what we know we
should do. This is where the "control" of the Spirit
comes into play, and we must yield. We must submit
to what the Spirit is telling us to do and allow him
to have the reins of control moment by moment.*

~ HENRY CLOUD

I MAPPED OUT MY LIFE carefully. I would get educated, get
married, get a steady job, have some kids, retire comfortably
and die peacefully. I would spend my last days in a house by a
lake, reading good books by the water in summer and by the

fire in winter. My life would be predictable. My life would be peaceful. Most of all, my life would be stable.

In some ways that happened. I got educated. I pastored stable churches (or so I thought). We had the big house and the kids. I loved walking with my kids in the New England woods behind our home, working in the yard in the summer and working with wood in the basement in the winter. I really craved this stability and worked hard to get it and protect it. I wanted what scientists and engineers call *homeostasis*.

The problem with stability is that life is intrinsically unstable. Life is not a quiet pool of water. It's a flowing river. Life is in motion and motion means change.

God knows this. The Bible is about a God who is in motion and it tells the stories of this God-in-motion sending his people in motion.

God calls Abram to get moving from the city of Ur to the yet-undisclosed Promised Land. He sends Jacob north to get a wife and Joseph south to Egypt by the most unlikely of means. God pulls his chosen people out of Egyptian slavery and then has them live a life of constant motion in the desert until they finally get a few hard-fought lessons under their belts.

God sends a very pregnant Mary in motion from Nazareth to Bethlehem, then he sends the young family fleeing to Egypt as refugees. Jesus sends his disciples on all kinds of missions. He is always on the move, teaching and healing wherever he is.

God scatters the early church when they became too comfortable in their Jerusalem digs. He knocks Saul off a donkey and then Saul becomes Paul, the most in-motion man who ever lived, traveling well over 11,000 miles in his four recorded journeys.

A persecution in Rome sends Priscilla and Aquila fleeing to Corinth and then to Ephesus. Along the way they faithfully teach about the Jesus who had saved them... and who seemed to want them to keep moving!

If your life has been turned upside down by divorce and/ or other circumstances, welcome to life. Life is about movement and change. Since nothing surprises God and God himself seems to relish movement, determine to quit fighting for stability in your circumstances and simply *go with the flow.*

God has you covered. He is *with* you and he is even *in front of you,* preparing your future for you. Stability is an illusion. Real life is in the river!

THINK ABOUT IT...

* How important is stability to you?
* When your life has been turned upside-down in the past, how did you handle that? Did you go with the flow or fight it every step of the way?
* What possibilities do you see for God to work in your future?

LIFE COMMITMENT:
God is a God in motion. I will move with him.

Flow With the Go

———— ∞ ————

THE WORD

> *But as surely as God is faithful, our message to you*
> *is not "Yes" and "No." For the Son of God, Jesus*
> *Christ, who was preached among you by me and Silas*
> *and Timothy, was not "Yes" and "No," but in him*
> *it has always been "Yes." For no matter how many*
> *promises God has made, they are "Yes" in Christ.*

— 2 CORINTHIANS 1.18–21

THOUGHT FOR THE DAY:

> *Security is mostly a superstition. It does not*
> *exist in nature, nor do the children of men as a*
> *whole experience it. Avoiding danger is no safer*
> *in the long run than outright exposure. Life*
> *is a daring adventure or nothing at all.*

~ HELEN KELLER

WHEN HAMMERED BY LIFE, RECOVERY begins with a surrender to the flow... *Go with the flow.* The only way you can
go with the flow with any sense of peace is to know that

God controls the flow. God is *with you*, and he is *in front of you*. He has your future—he is *in* your future preparing a way for you.

But when life is caving all around us our natural reaction is to withdraw, hunker down and ride out the storm. We tend to pull back rather than risk reaching out.

For men, this can be deadly. We can easily get lost in booze, pornography, video games, television... anything we think can fill the hole left by the rejection of our spouse or by the guilt of our own poor choices. We just want to be left alone and try to forget our pain.

Another factor is fatigue. When struggling through divorce our energy level drops. Getting through each day is like trudging through a snow-covered field with the wind howling around us rather than strolling through a green meadow with sunshine beaming down on us.

This is definitely *not* the time to make major decisions. But it is also a mistake to turtle up and get lost in booze and porn.

God knows this and so he will send you opportunities to crawl out of the hole. Say yes to these opportunities.

Bear Grylls is a man who has said *yes* to the opportunities that have come his way.

Once he spent 18 months recovering from a skydiving accident. But when the opportunity came to say *yes* to jumping out of a plane again, he took it! His advice? *Say yes and try something, rather than saying no because you fear where a yes will take you.*[50]

---

[50] Bear Grylls, *A Survival Guide for Life: How to Achieve Your Goals, Thrive in Adversity, and Grow in Character* (New York: William Morrow, 2014), 36. Reprinted by permission of Peters Fraser & Dunlop (www.petersfraserdunlop.com) on behalf of Bear Grylls.

He goes on to write, *More often than not, saying no means that nothing will change in your life. A yes, however, has the power to create change. And change is where we create room for success.*[51]

SAY YES! Say yes to God and the invitations he sends your way to get out of the hole. Say yes to people when they reach out to you. Say yes to opportunities to get out. Say yes to your own ideas... go take a hike, go on a trip, go to a movie. Go to church, a men's conference, a small group. Take a chance! What do you have to lose?

Think About It...

- What invitations have come your way that you have said no to? Was it helpful to stay hunkered down?
- What happened when you said yes?
- What can you say yes to today?

Life Commitment:
I choose to believe that saying yes to the opportunities God puts in my path is better in the long run than playing it safe.

---

[51] Ibid.

Our Life with God (1)

———∞∞∞———

THE WORD

Therefore we do not lose heart. Though outwardly
we are wasting away, yet inwardly we are being
renewed day by day. For our light and momentary
troubles are achieving for us an eternal glory that
far outweighs them all. So we fix our eyes not on
what is seen, but on what is unseen. For what is
seen is temporary, but what is unseen is eternal.

— 2 CORINTHIANS 4.16–18

THOUGHT FOR THE DAY:

God sent me 1,000 hints that he didn't want
me to keep doing what I was doing. But I
didn't listen, so he set off a nuclear bomb.

~ JACK ABRAMOFF [52]

---

[52] In January 2006, Jack Abramoff was sentenced to six years in federal prison for mail fraud, conspiracy to bribe public officials, and tax evasion. "Jack Abramoff," Wikipedia, accessed February 10, 2017. https://en.wikipedia.org/wiki/Jack_Abramoff.

IT ALL BEGAN WELL ENOUGH. God made two humans for fellowship. He walked with them every day in the Paradise he fashioned just for them. But love isn't love unless it can be rejected, otherwise God would have two robots in his Paradise, not two humans. So he put a temptation in Paradise in the form of a tree. The warning was that if his two humans ate the fruit from that tree, God would see it as a rejection of all that he had provided for them, and he would view that as a rejection of himself.

Sure enough, the two humans were persuaded that God was less than he said he was and that he was holding out on them. So they turned against God's amazing love and provision. They demonstrated their decision by eating from the one tree God had warned them about. Humanity would now live 'East of Eden,' out from under the provision and protection of God.

Our original sin is that we believed we could go it alone. Our fatal flaw is believing the lie that we don't need God. So the first step in understanding how God works is coming to the realization that we do, indeed, need him.

My oldest daughter is smart and beautiful... and stubborn. When she was about eight she decided to run away. So... she packed her pink Little Mermaid suitcase and headed out the front door *at night!*

How absolutely ridiculous of her! How did she think she would survive alone at night at the tender age of eight? How could she have been so dense?

Well, go look in the mirror! You and I are like my daughter. We are like eight-year-olds running away from a good and kind Father.

The further into the night my daughter went the less sure she was about leaving and the more she questioned her decision. It wasn't far (maybe 100 yards) until she turned around. And when she turned around she found me just behind her, eager to receive her back.

How does God work? He provides for us, but we turn away from him. We fly off into the dark. We stumble along, tripping on that situation here, bumping into that problem there. It's usually not until we are flat on our face that we get it. It's when we're face down on the sidewalk with a bloody nose that we comprehend our profound need for God.

Think About It...

* Did you ever run away from home? If so, what did that feel like? Did it work?
* Do you know you need God? How do you know?
* What do you think God thinks when you realize how much you need him?

Life Commitment:

I realize that I have been running away from God. I am ready to take steps to go back to him.

Our Life with God (2)

—∞∞∞—

THE WORD

Therefore do not worry about tomorrow, for tomorrow will worry about itself. Each day has enough trouble of its own.

—JESUS AS RECORDED IN MATTHEW 6.34

THOUGHT FOR THE DAY:

God can't fix what you pretend isn't broken.

~ RYAN LEEK

I WAS NOT IN MY daughter's head when she stomped off into the dark one spring evening, determined to run away from her 'mean' parents. But I know what it is like to come to the stark realization that without God I am in deep trouble.

How do you know you are in that moment?

Ask yourself these three questions:

* Am I paralyzed by my PAST? Am I lost in regrets, saying to myself *I should have* rather than *I will*?

* Am I slipping into a Pity Pit in the PRESENT, sliding down a slimy sinkhole where I find only me, myself and I at the bottom?[53]
* Am I tangled up in the Worry Webs of the FUTURE, my mind racing with all the terrible things that could be but aren't yet?

Being paralyzed by the past, sinking into self-pity in the present and/or worrying about your future are sure signs that you aren't connected to God. That's OK for now. Like a thermometer, how you are thinking now is only an indication of where you are *now*. Diagnosis is the first step toward an effective treatment.

Know this: God does NOT want you paralyzed by your past, stuck at the bottom of the pity pit or caught in the worry webs of your future. By experiencing his presence and living in trust and gratitude, God will free you from your past, pull you out of the pity pit and untangle you from worry webs.

Think About It...

* Am I OK with my *past*? Or am I lost in regrets?
* Am I taking responsibility for where I am *now* or lost in self-pity?
* Am I looking forward to my *future* or dreading what might come?

---

[53] I am indebted to Sarah Young and her book *Jesus Calling* for the concepts of the *Pity Pit* and the *Worry Web*. Sarah Young, *Jesus Calling: Enjoying Peace in His Presence: Devotions for Every Day of the Year* (Nashville: Integrity Publishers, 2016), Kindle Locations 335 and 458.

LIFE COMMITMENT:
I believe God has a better way for me. I commit to finding and following his way for my life.

Our Life with God (3)

———— ∞∞ ————

THE WORD

Be strong and courageous. Do not be terrified;
do not be discouraged, for the Lord your
God will be with you wherever you go.

— JOSHUA 1.9

THOUGHT FOR THE DAY:

Breakdowns often lead to breakthroughs.

~ J.R. BRIGGS

I'VE READ THE BIBLE THROUGH from cover to cover multiple times. The two over-arching themes I see throughout Scripture are **(1) GOD IS WITH US** and **(2) GOD PROVIDES FOR US**.

God made us to be with him. The startling thing is that he doesn't need us. He can and does exist completely outside and independently of us. At first this is a troubling thought because our earthly experience regarding the security of our relationships is based on the need of the other for us. For example, we may sometimes say to ourselves, *I won't get fired because my boss needs me.*

God doesn't need us. Yikes! But don't get upset! God's amazing desire for us is not based on *need*, it is based on *desire. God wants us!* He wants to be with us! He wants to be with us so much that his own Son died the most horrible death imaginable to break down the wall we had built between us and God:

> *For God so loved the world that he gave his one and only Son, that whoever believes in him shall not perish but have eternal life.* (John 3.16)

If God went to this much trouble to be with us, don't you think he wants you to actually experience his presence in your life?

When my daughter tromped off down the street and then came to her senses, turning around to find me there, do you think that I coldly told her that I was glad she had finally seen things my way and that we should get back into the house?

Heck no! Scared of the darkness in front of her and dreading what our reaction might be behind her, when she turned around, I picked her up and gave her a huge hug! I was thrilled she wanted to be with me, so I made it clear I wanted to be with her!

As a divorced man you are probably experiencing a deep loneliness. If you aren't you most likely will. Know this: God wants to be with you in a way that *you know he is with you.* He doesn't just want you to know in your head that he is with you. He wants you to know in your heart and soul that he is really with you.

Dallas Willard writes, *The personal presence of Jesus with individuals and groups that trust him was soon understood by Jesus' first students to be the practical reality of the kingdom of God now on earth.*[54]

Living in God's presence is to be the norm for us, not the occasional high we may get at a men's conference or retreat. I admit it's tough. It's tough to experience God's presence all the time because we live in a fog while on earth. It's a challenge to experience the presence of an invisible God. But it is possible and can actually become the norm.

The Bible is clear: God wants us and he wants us to experience his real and powerful presence.

If you are not experiencing God's presence in your life, ask him to show up. I guarantee you there is no greater invitation from you that God wants than this! Keep your eyes and ears open. Things are about to get interesting for you!

A few days ago the Life Commitment was: *I realize that I have been running away from God. I am ready to take steps to go back to him.* Asking God to make himself known to you is one of these steps you can take toward him.

Be strong and courageous.
Do not be terrified;
do not be discouraged,
for the Lord your God will be with you
wherever you go.

---

[54] Willard, *The Divine Conspiracy*, 279.

THINK ABOUT IT...

* What price did God pay to be with you?
* Have you ever experienced what you believe to be the presence of God? What happened?
* What do you think experiencing the presence of God will be like?

LIFE COMMITMENT:

I am asking God to show up in my life. I commit to having an open and receptive soul to his presence in my life.

Our Life with God (4)

> "Am I only a God nearby," declares the Lord, "and
> not a God far away? Can anyone hide in secret places
> so that I cannot see him?" declares the Lord. "Do
> not I fill heaven and earth?" declares the Lord.

— JEREMIAH 23.23–24

THOUGHT FOR THE DAY:

> We live in a broken world full of broken people. But
> isn't it comforting to know God is never broken? He isn't
> ever caught off guard, taken by surprise, or shocked
> by what happens next. He can take our worst and
> add His best. We just have to make the choice to stay
> with Him and keep following Him through it all.

~ LYSA TERKEURST

KIDS ARE AMAZING. THEY NEVER wake up saying to themselves, *Oh no! I wonder if mom and dad got food for me today! I wonder if I will have a house to come home to after school today!*

I have *never* heard a kid say that! Kids have absolute trust in their parents. And where a kid does not have food and shelter, love and affection, shame on the adults for failing those children. And shame on us if we don't do something radical about it.

Most children trust their parents to provide for them. A wise kid will not only trust his/her parents to provide, but express gratitude for that provision.

At the time of this writing I have a 16-year-old son. His life was turned upside-down beginning three years ago. This kid went from a strong, stable situation to a world wrecked by the terrible decisions of some adults that impacted the life of our family in horrendous ways.

A few minutes ago we returned from going out to eat. Despite all that he has been through he said, *Thanks, Dad, for taking me out to eat!* He's that way about everything! He has an amazingly grateful heart.

Our life with God goes something like this: God provides for us. But we foolishly decide we can do this thing on our own. We hit a wall of pain. We cry out to God. God rescues us. Then we get really happy about his rescue!

As we trust him and express our gratitude to him, our souls open wide and we really do know God is with us and for us.

Trusting God and being grateful to him are the two best strategies for staying out of the pity pit and away from the worry webs.

American writer Melody Beattie writes, *Gratitude makes sense of our past, brings peace for today, and creates a vision for tomorrow.*[55] Exactly!

---

[55] *"Melody Beattie Quotes,"* BrainyQuote, accessed February 13, 2017, https://www.brainyquote.com/quotes/quotes/m/melodybeat134462.html.

By experiencing his presence with you and living in trust and gratitude, God will free you from your past, pull you out of the pity pit and untangle you from worry webs.

THINK ABOUT IT...

* What would it look like for you to have the same trust in God that your kids have in you?
* You knew this was coming! Make a list of five things you are grateful for:

_____

_____

_____

_____

_____

LIFE COMMITMENT:

Instead of bitching today, I am going to be thankful. Even if it is just for one thing and even if it really hurts to do so.

Our Life with God (5)

—⟨≋≋⟩—

THE WORD

You did not choose me, but I chose you and appointed
you to go and bear fruit—fruit that will last. Then the
Father will give you whatever you ask in my name.

—JOHN 15.16

THOUGHT FOR THE DAY:

Remembering that I'll be dead soon is the most important
tool I've ever encountered to help me make the big
choices in life. Because almost everything—all external
expectations, all pride, all fear of embarrassment
or failure—these things just fall away in the face
of death, leaving only what is truly important.

~ STEVE JOBS

AS A HOSPICE CHAPLAIN I'VE seen many people die. One
man stands out. He was amazingly accomplished. If I told
you what he did, you would be stunned, but I can't tell you
because of privacy laws.

From the beginning of my only encounter with him, he let me know that he did not have a faith but he was not worried about his death.

He was also in agony. He was gasping for air, frantic and wide-eyed with fright. His was not going to be an easy death. And yet, during the entire visit his family kept telling me of his amazing accomplishments, not only in his work life but around the house we were in. *He built this room, he painted that wall, he fixed this light.*

I left the house that day sad. The self-worth of this family was built exclusively on the achievements of their husband/father. And yet in the end, the man was in physical agony and spiritually bankrupt.

As John Ortberg says, *In the end, it all goes back in the box.*[56] Having been with many people at their deaths, I can assure you that there are no do-overs.

God has more for you than a few earthly accomplishments. Once he has rescued you from yourself and planted a heart of gratitude and trust in you, he calls you to your destiny.

It's hard to see this when you are at the bottom after a divorce. When you're flat on your back with the wind knocked out of you, you can't imagine being back in the game. Winning the game seems totally out of reach.

But God has a plan for you. *In his power* he will lift you up. *In his power* he will heal you. *In his power* he will give you a mission specific to you. And *through his strength* you will accomplish the mission he gives you.

---

[56] John Ortberg, *When the Game Is Over, It All Goes Back in the Box* (Grand Rapids: Zondervan, 2007), 16.

And at the end of the day, when someone like me is sitting beside you, we will celebrate together what God has done in your life for his Kingdom, and we will rejoice together in your final destination.

Think About It...

* If you were on your deathbed right now, what would you tell me about your life?
* What hope would you have for your future?
* What legacy would you be leaving?

Life Commitment:

I want to finish well. Where I am today does not define my future. I trust that God will lift me up and set me on the pathway of his choosing.

Our Life with God (6)

———⊷∞⊶———

THE WORD

> *For my own name's sake I delay my wrath; for the sake*
> *of my praise I hold it back from you, so as not to cut*
> *you off. See, I have refined you, though not as silver; I*
> *have tested you in the furnace of affliction. For my own*
> *sake, for my own sake, I do this. How can I let myself*
> *be defamed?* ***I will not yield my glory to another.***

— ISAIAH 48.9–11 (EMPHASIS MINE)

THOUGHT FOR THE DAY:

Your desire determines your destiny.

~ JOHN MAXWELL

IN HIS BOOK *SACRED MARRIAGE*, Gary Thomas asks a hard question: *What If God Designed Marriage to Make Us Holy More Than to Make Us Happy?*[57]

---

[57] Gary Thomas, *Sacred Marriage: What If God Designed Marriage to Make Us Holy More Than to Make Us Happy?* (Grand Rapids: Zondervan, 2015), 1.

The question Thomas asks of marriage is really a question God asks each of us no matter where we are in life: *Is God's first job to make me happy?*

Rick Warren begins his best-selling book *The Purpose Driven Life* with this simple statement: *It's not about you.*[58] Ouch. We are taught from the moment we come squealing into the world that it IS about us! Nearly every decision we make is filtered through the question, *How will this help or hurt me?*

And yet the fact that Rick Warren's book sold well over 40 million copies, landing 90 weeks on the New York Times Bestseller List, should tell us that deep inside we know we were made for more than just personal happiness.

In Isaiah, God makes clear that our happiness is secondary to his holiness and glory: *I will not yield my glory to another.* If our happiness were God's first job, then he would have to make his glory secondary to our happiness. No, everything is first about God's glory.

Nearly 400 years ago a group of English and Scottish Theologians came to the same conclusion. The Westminster Catechism's first question is: *What is the chief end of man?*

The answer? *Man's chief end is to glorify God, and to enjoy him forever.*[59]

The Hebrew word translated *glory* means '*weight.*' Each of us has only so much 'weight' to throw around. We have only so much 'weight' to give to people and things. Where do you

---

[58] Richard Warren, *The Purpose Driven Life* (Cleveland: Findaway World, 2005), 17.

[59] Philip Schaff, *Creeds of Christendom,* Vol. 1, (New York: Harper & Brothers, 1919), 1659.

throw your weight, toward God's glory or toward your own happiness?

Divorce strips us of so much. I lost my hard-earned reputation, my status in society, a huge chunk of my career, lots of money—the list goes on and on. I went from a beautiful home tucked in the New Hampshire forest to a one-bedroom apartment with a cat. I went from Superhero to Superzero.

If I measured my life in terms of circumstances, I would be very unhappy. But I know that my happiness is secondary to God's glory. God's amazing glory is far bigger than my puny little speck of happiness. What this means is that if I can stay tuned in to God's glory, I am attached to something bigger and better than my little life, and nothing can touch that!

Through these terrible ordeals I have tried to stay focused on glorifying God despite my afflictions. And here's the deal: staying tuned into God's glory has kept me sane. But that's what tomorrow is all about.

THINK ABOUT IT...

* Where do you throw your 'weight'?
* Are you plugged into God's glory or your own happiness?

LIFE COMMITMENT:
Life is first about God's glory, not my happiness.

Our Life With God (7)

THE WORD

All this is for your benefit, so that the grace that
is reaching more and more people may cause
thanksgiving to overflow to the glory of God.

— 2 CORINTHIANS 4:14–15

THOUGHT FOR THE DAY:

To please God... to be a real ingredient in the
divine happiness... to be loved by God, not
merely pitied, but delighted in as an artist
delights in his work or a father in a son—it seems
impossible, a weight or burden of glory which
our thoughts can hardly sustain. But so it is.

~ C.S. LEWIS

THE MAN BEFORE ME WAS shaking like a leaf. He shouldn't have been. He had just retired young with tons of money. To the world he was a raging success. He appeared to have it all. But like so many men, he had reached the top of the mountain only to find that he had climbed the wrong mountain.

As he stood before me trembling with anxiety I told him what I had told many other men in his position: *The second half of his life would be far better than the first half.*

The first half of a man's life is all about me. I work hard to build my life around what the culture tells me will make me happy and significant.

But if we work hard enough and achieve whatever it is that our culture tells us will make us happy and significant, at some point it all comes tumbling down. The tower that we so carefully constructed crashes around us. Divorce is one of those RPG's in life that destroys your tower.

Apart from God, success and adversity are two sides of the same coin. For my newly retired but unhappy friend, success was a hollow shell of what he expected it to be. For other men, adversity tears at us until we are empty inside.

As we saw yesterday, however, it's not first about our happiness, it's about God's glory. God is passionate for his glory. Whatever God does is first for his glory, as he says in Isaiah, *I will not yield my glory to another.* (Isaiah 48.11)

But here's the awesome thing about God's Kingdom: When we make God's glory first in our lives, *we find true and lasting happiness and satisfaction.*

The catechism asks: *What is the chief end of man?* The glorious answer is *Man's chief end is to glorify God, and to enjoy him forever.*

Those old guys got it right! In putting God's glory first we get to enjoy him forever! And when we enjoy him, we enjoy all the things that bring him delight such as his astounding creation, loving others, even working through hard times.

This is the promise Paul makes: *All this is **for your benefit**, so that the grace that is reaching more and more people may cause thanksgiving to **overflow to the glory of God**.* (2 Corinthians 4:14–15, emphasis mine)

God calls us to glorify him with our lives. In putting his glory first, we find our true purpose. When we live out his purpose for us, we find amazing fulfillment, satisfaction and happiness.

Divorce may be the Hellfire missile that you think has destroyed your life. Far from it. God is using all you have lost to highlight what is of first importance: Him and his glory.

When you get this—when you really understand and submit to this truth—you will find relief, joy and an eagerness to discover God's next step for you.

THINK ABOUT IT...

* Fill in the blank: If _____ would happen, I would be happy.
* Is the answer about you or about God and his glory?
* What would living for God's glory look like in your life right now?

LIFE COMMITMENT:

I have lived my life for me, myself and I. It is time to live for God the Father, Jesus the Son, and the Holy Spirit.

Rage

———◦◦◦———

The Word

*My dear brothers, take note of this: Everyone
should be quick to listen, slow to speak and slow
to become angry, for man's anger does not bring
about the righteous life that God desires.*

—James 1.19–20

Thought for the Day:

Anger is the fluid that love bleeds when you cut it.

~ C.S. Lewis

C.S. Lewis was an intellectual titan of the mid-20th century. He still reigns as one of the most brilliant cultural commentators of the modern era. I had the privilege of visiting his home in Oxford, England. As part of the tour we visited his grave at Holy Trinity Church in Headington Quarry.

While standing beside the grave of this amazing and brilliant man who had (possibly) done more for the cause of Christianity than anyone since the Apostle Paul, we were told that the church almost didn't let Lewis be buried there.

The reason? Late in life Lewis married a woman named Joy Davidman. Joy was divorced. Because Lewis had married a divorced woman, the church at first refused to allow his burial in the church yard.

Lewis was wounded in World War I. He helped shepherd England through the unbelievable suffering of World War II. Lewis had seen and known the worst of humanities atrocities. He had cause to be angry and one would wonder how he would feel at this last slight of his church nearly refusing his burial in their cemetery.

I think he would have been angry. But I think that his anger would have moderated into a quiet, well-considered acceptance of the world as it is and things as they are.

Lewis wrote, *Anger [is] the anaesthetic of the mind.*[60] Indeed, it is. In the pain of divorce, anger feels good. It soothes the wounds and allows a way for us to process intellectually and emotionally what has just happened relationally.

Kristin Armstrong writes,

> *[Anger] is a valid reading on the spectrum of human emotion. It is our barometer of injustice. It is sometimes the impetus for great change. It can be the fuel of self-preservation. But we are instructed in Scripture to manage our anger, and this means our anger cannot manage us.*[61]

---

[60] C. S. Lewis and Walter Hooper, *Poems* (San Diego: Harcourt Brace & Co., 1992), 125.

[61] Kristin Armstrong, Happily Ever After: Walking with Peace and Courage Through a Year of Divorce (New York: Faith Words, 2008), Kindle Location 2938.

I have raged. I have yelled and screamed. I have thrown a few things. I have imagined a lot of things. I went to a self-defense class and beat the hell out of 'Century Bob', the martial arts dummy that looks like a guy. I have said the 'F' word in the last three years more than most people say it in three lifetimes. I've gone to the gun range and imagined faces on the targets. Yep, even a pastor can be driven to thoughts like this through pain-induced anger!

I have also learned that in our culture for a man to express anger is strictly forbidden. If you say what's burning in your soul most people immediately cut you off, usually because they simply don't know what to say or do. They won't respond to you on Facebook or text or email. Things go dead once you let it fly.

But the fact is that when you are angry, you *are* angry. Anger is a natural emotional response to pain. As Lewis rightly said, *Anger is the fluid that love bleeds when you cut it.*

The next few days we will look at ways to manage this real and powerful emotion. There is a difference between being a man who is angry and being someone who is defined by anger, that is, an angry man.

Let me leave you with this thought from C.S. Lewis: *To rail is the sad privilege of the loser.*[62]

Maybe that's the heart of our anger. Divorce feels like a huge loss. And that pisses us off. But we don't have to end up angry men.

---

[62] C. S. Lewis and Walter Hooper, *Selected Literary Essays* (New York: Cambridge University Press, 2013), "Addison" (1945), para. 4, p. 156.

THINK ABOUT IT...

* Are you angry?
* Why?
* Think back on a time when you are furious. What did you do? What were the results?
* How can you be angry and yet not become an angry man?

LIFE COMMITMENT:

I am a man who is angry but I don't want to end up being an angry man. God, help me manage this fire in me.

Don't Make Stupid Choices

———∞∞∞———

THE WORD

> *In your anger do not sin; Do not let the sun go down while*
> *you are still angry, and do not give the devil a foothold.*

— EPHESIANS 4.25–27

THOUGHT FOR THE DAY:

> *First we make our choices, then our choices make us.*

~ ANNE FRANK

I'M NOT ABOUT TO TELL you not to be angry. Nothing chaps my hide more than when people tell me not to be angry. I **AM** angry! I lost my family, my career, my reputation, my income. Loss hurts and when I am hurt I get mad.

But being angry and expressing it in non-destructive ways is a good choice that can save you and many others much pain and suffering.

In your anger do not sin. Anger is not a sin but it can lead to sin when it dominates your thoughts and plots.

Psychologist Robin L Goldstein explains the dynamics of anger in a divorced man:

Sadness feels weak and men often experience humiliation when they feel weak. This makes it easy to become angry. Anger feels powerful. It can cause men to say or do things that hurt the person who rejected them. This tough guy stance may come out with friends and family who try to support the bereaved man, pushing them away. The message can be "I don't have a problem, I can handle this fine on my own." A high price is paid for that momentary sense of power; further isolation and often further despair. A greater toll is taken when the anger leads to a more complicated divorce or when children are exposed to the toxicity of a parent's hostility.[63]

What can you do with your anger that will not lead to more despair or drive others away?

Poor choices include drinking yourself under the table, having sex with anyone and anything, isolating yourself from the world, binge watching Netflix, killing yourself or someone else. Those are just a few stupid things men do when they are angry. Don't do anything on this list.

Instead, **TALK**. Talking is God's way of us working it out in our mind and soul. I can't explain why talking works, I just know it's true. You *must* find a trusted and wise friend, counselor, pastor, therapist... someone!

EXERCISE. Burn off anger. In six months I rode my mountain and road bikes over 3,000 miles. The anger in my head and heart was channeled through my legs down into the pavement. Why not use anger to get in better shape?

---

[63] Robin Goldstein, *"Divorce Recovery: Stages of Divorce Recovery for Men Article Series,"* accessed February 16, 2017, http://robingoldstein.net/divorce/stages-of-divorce-recovery-for-men-article-series/.

SOLVE THE PROBLEMS YOU CAN SOLVE. Abraham H. Maslow said, *I suppose it is tempting, if the only tool you have is a hammer, to treat everything as if it were a nail.*[64] Time to expand your toolbox. You will get energy from solving problems instead of raging against them.

These are just a few ways to deal with anger... the next several days we will look at these and other suggestions in more detail.

The main point is to not give in to what your anger is tempting you to do. Believe me, I *thought* about doing all kinds of things, many of them illegal! But thinking about doing something and actually doing it are two very different things. Though anger tempts us with the rationalization of justification, in the end, to choose the hard way of venting anger constructively makes you stronger, not weaker.

I like what Ben Horowitz says about the impact of our decisions: *Every time you make the hard, correct decision you become a bit more courageous, and every time you make the easy, wrong decision you become a bit more cowardly.*[65]

Determine that a temporary state [will not become] a permanent trait.[66]

---

[64] Abraham H. Maslow, *"Toward a Psychology of Being Quotes by Abraham H. Maslow,"* accessed February 17, 2017, http://www.goodreads.com/work/quotes/2216557-toward-a-psychology-of-being.

[65] *"Ben Horowitz Quotes,"* BrainyQuote, accessed February 17, 2017, https://www.brainyquote.com/quotes/quotes/b/benhorowit529646.html?src=t_wrong_decision.

[66] Armstrong, *Happily Ever After*, Kindle Location 2554.

Think About It...

* Why do I always feel right when I am angry?
* Is my anger a temporary state or is it becoming a permanent trait?

Life Commitment:

I am angry but I don't want to be known for my anger. I commit to actively seeking out ways to express my anger appropriately.

Play Your Position

—⊷⊶⊷—

THE WORD

In his heart a man plans his course, but
the Lord determines his steps.

— PROVERBS 16.9

THOUGHT FOR THE DAY:

No one ever healed from a blow to the head
by hitting themselves there again.

~ LESLIE BECKER-PHELPS

MY FAVORITE POSITION IN FOOTBALL is linebacker. The line-backer plays the rush and covers the passes. He's on the move, mentally covering the entire field, but singularly focused on where the football might be and then actually is. Linebackers have to be smart, fast and tough.

Imagine being a quarterback looking across the line into those amazing eyes of Mike Singletary (Chicago Bears, 1981-92). Who would want to be a receiver about to receive the earth-shattering impact of Lawrence Taylor (New York Giants, 1981-93)?

Even though linebackers cover more of the football field than any other defensive player, *linebackers still have to play their position.* In fact, everyone does. Success in football requires that each player *knows* his position, *stays* in his position and *plays* his position to the best of his ability.

The quarterback calls a pass play in the huddle. Each guy immediately knows his position. Most important to the success of the play will be the determination of the receiver to know his route and then run it with precision. When the ball is snapped the quarterback drops back and—if the receiver is open—throws the ball to the pre-planned and much-practiced spot on the 57,600 square-foot football field where the receiver will eventually be. Everyone on the team knows the route and believes in it. Each runs here and pushes there, trusting that if everyone plays his position, the plan will work.

But as Helmuth von Moltke said, *No battle plan survives contact with the enemy.*[67] That's why the coaches watch hours of the tapes of the other team's defense. The idea is to anticipate how the enemy will react, and adjust accordingly.

But what if the coaching staff had a video of the game they were *going to play*? Every move could be planned with precision! I know this is a bit *Back to the Future-ish*, but in a way, that's what God does for us. He has a position for us to play. But he knows how everything plays out. Though it seems we have been knocked *out of position*, God helps us recover and get back *in position*.

Divorce is like a quarterback blindsided by a wild-eyed Mike Singletary or hammered by Lawrence Taylor. Divorce

---

[67] Helmuth von Moltke, "No Battle Plan Survives Contact with the Enemy," accessed September 24, 2017, http://www.lexician.com/lexblog/2010/11/no-battle-plan-survives-contact-with-the-enemy/.

knocks you out of position. But God is bigger than this giant blow in your life.

God gave us free will. He doesn't cause these body-blows—we cause them from our poor choices and/or they happen to us because of the terrible choices of others. The amazing thing is that God's grace is stronger than evil and his plan supersedes the chaos of life on earth.

Can you trust the plan? Can you play your position?

Surrendering to God's plan is one of the best ways to handle your anger.

Despite all the chaos around you, know that God is not surprised by what has happened in your life. Trust him to take this pain and transform it into something better than you imagined. When you release control of your present and future to him, you will sense a relief that is far better than any of the other things you might have tried.

God is in the game and so are you. It's not over till it's over. Trust him to get you to victory.

Think About It...

* What position did you play before the divorce? Husband, dad, provider? How have those positions changed?

* Trust God to take you from where you are to where he wants you to be. Trust him that his plan is good and right. Commit your ways to his care, then follow his direction.

LIFE COMMITMENT:

Though I am flat on the turf, I trust that God will get me back up and give me a new route.

Shadows

——— ✦ ———

THE WORD

What causes fights and quarrels among you? Don't
they come from your desires that battle within you? You
want something but don't get it. You kill and covet,
but you cannot have what you want. You quarrel and
fight. You do not have, because you do not ask God.

—JAMES 4:1–2

THOUGHT FOR THE DAY:

Grief that is ignored turns into depression or
hopelessness. Hurt turns into cynicism, lack of trust,
or worse. Anger turns into bitterness and hatred.

~ HENRY CLOUD

I SAT WITH A WOMAN who had been repeatedly abused in
unspeakable ways by multiple male members of her family
of origin. We were at once on a battleground and on holy
ground as she reached deep into her crushed soul and
drew the pain from the depths up to her consciousness.
Then, with incredible courage, she formed the words in

her mind and then actually spoke out loud the trauma that had been done to her. That she had not taken her life years ago was a testimony to her strength and God's power and love.

Over the course of some weeks we learned something together. We learned that while this huge ugly *thing* remained in her, it kept growing and dominated her 'life space.' It defined her, even years later. But once we put the ugly thing out on the table, the light of the truth and God's healing power shrank the thing back to its proper size in her life.

It's not that talking about this thing eliminated it from her life or memory. The *thing* just finally shrank to its right size. Where before it dominated everything about her, now it was remembered as a terrible and ugly thing in her past, but it was *in her past.*

Here's the deal. We all have black and ugly things in our lives. We are all wounded and we carry the wounds of our parents and others with us.

Much of our energy goes to keeping these shadows pushed down. As long as life is good, the shadow stays hidden. As Robert Bly says, *The naïve man who flies directly toward the sun will not be able to see his own shadow. It is far behind him.*[68]

But as John O'Donohue says, *We cannot seal off the eternal. Unexpectedly and disturbingly, it gazes in at us through the sudden apertures in our patterned lives.*[69]

---

[68] Robert Bly, *Iron John: A Book About Men* (Boston: Da Capo Press, 2015), 126.

[69] John O'Donohue, *Anam Ċara: A Book of Celtic Wisdom* (New York: Harper Perennial, 2004), 42.

Divorce knocks us off our course toward our sun and suddenly our shadow becomes glaringly visible. The holding tank we have constructed to keep the ugly in cracks and starts to leak. This can be a terrifying moment for us as the shadow grows and the ugliness leaks out.

Don't be terrified by this. All of us have this stuff inside. Now is the time to recognize it for what it is but not to be terrorized by it, because scared people become angry, destructive people.

Henry Cloud makes the point that *just as you do not want a tumor growing in your brain, you do not want one growing in your heart either. There are no benign tumors of the heart.*[70]

By recognizing that the good, bad and the ugly are in all of us and that God knows this and will get us through it, the shadow becomes less frightening and we are able to deal with it. God is not surprised by what's in us. After all, he took all the terrible things in us and killed them on the cross. He knows more about your shadow than you do, and because he has dealt with it, he has the power to give us healing.

THINK ABOUT IT...

- What lurks in your heart?
- What do you think would happen if you just keep pushing it down?
- What are the potential risks and rewards of bringing it out into the open and dealing with it?

---

[70] Henry Cloud, *9 Things You Simply Must Do to Succeed in Love and Life: A Psychologist Probes The Mystery Of Why Some Lives Really Work And Others Don't* (Detroit: Gale, Cengage Learning, 2008), Kindle Location 333.

LIFE COMMITMENT:

I am strong and weak, good and bad, bright and dark. I can celebrate the good and deal realistically with the bad.

Sleep is the Great Reset Button

———⌾———

THE WORD

> *On my bed I remember you; I think of you through*
> *the watches of the night. Because you are my help,*
> *I sing in the shadow of your wings. My soul*
> *clings to you; your right hand upholds me.*

— PSALM 63.6–8

THOUGHT FOR THE DAY:

> *I love sleep. My life has the tendency to fall*
> *apart when I'm awake, you know?*

~ ERNEST HEMINGWAY

WHO NEEDS SLEEP? NOT BUSY, important people. Not people who want to succeed or climb the ladder. The only people who really need sleep is... *everyone*. Especially when you've been hammered by life.

Elijah was a mighty prophet. He risked everything for God in the face of an overwhelming enemy. You may recall the story—he went head-to-head with evil King Ahab and the priests of Baal. He challenged them to a cosmic dual between Baal and Yahweh. The scene was the top of Mt. Carmel. The priests of Baal built an altar for their god. Elijah built one to Yahweh. The god who burned up the offering would be the winner. The losers would be slaughtered.

The priests called upon Baal to rain down fire. Nothing happened. They cried out more, Elijah taunted, still nothing. Then Elijah called on Yahweh. Fire fell down consuming every part and parcel of the sacrifice. God and Elijah won!

But there was this woman named Jezebel. She was the queen and when she heard the news from Mt. Carmel she was furious. She sent word to Elijah: *I'm coming after you.* And what did this mighty man of God do in response? He ran like hell! The Bible says it like this:

> *Jezebel sent a messenger to Elijah to say, "May the gods deal with me, be it ever so severely, if by this time tomorrow I do not make your life like that of one of them." Elijah was afraid and ran for his life.* (1 Kings 19:1–3)

Amazing how men can go toe-to-toe with each other but one woman can send us running!

Elijah ran for his life. And then, exhausted, he did what all of us should do when life turns upside down—he collapsed under a tree and slept. The next verses describe the tenderness of God: *All at once an angel touched him and said, "Get up and eat." [Elijah] looked around, and there by his head was a cake of bread baked over hot coals, and a jar of water. He ate and drank and then lay down again.* (1 Kings 19:5–6)

Amanda Jameson hiked the 2,650-mile-long Pacific Crest Trail. When asked what she learned on that arduous journey, she said, *Sleep is the great reset button.*[71] I like that.

Men who are Hungry, Angry, Lonely and Tired (HALT) make poor decisions. The fuse is short when we are tired. Give yourself a break... let your body, mind and soul mend through sleep.

Despite all the medical research as we have done, we still don't know much about sleep. It's thought that during sleep your brain runs a sort of garbage pickup routine. Your brain produces by-products as it works through the day. During sleep these byproducts are literally picked up and carried off, performing a cleanup and reset function.[72]

When life tumbles in, your brain is working overtime, hence more toxic byproducts. You need more sleep to clean out your brain. John Steinbeck said that *it is a common experience that a problem difficult at night is resolved in the morning after the committee of sleep has worked on it.*[73]

Elijah didn't know all that was going on in his brain when he collapsed into sleep under the tree in the desert, but God did. The result was that through sleep and good food, Elijah was prepared to hear God and take the next step in his life.

Having trouble with anger? Sleep on it.

---

[71] Amanda "Zuul" Jameson, *"Active Interest Media,"* Backpacker.com, February 14, 2017, accessed February 20, 2017, http://www.backpacker.com/trips/advice-from-a-hiker-who-finished-the-pacific-crest-trail.

[72] *"10 Fascinating Things That Happen While You're Sleeping,"* Prevention, March 21, 2016, accessed February 20, 2017, http://www.prevention.com/health/what-happens-during-sleep/slide/9.

[73] "John Steinbeck Quotes," BrainyQuote, accessed September 24, 2017, https://www.brainyquote.com/quotes/quotes/j/johnsteinb103825.html.

THINK ABOUT IT...

* How much sleep do you get?
* If you are having trouble sleeping ask God for help. Check with your doctor and/or therapist to see what they may be able to do to help you sleep.
* Check out this website from the National Sleep Foundation for tips and tricks in getting and staying asleep: https://goo.gl/gikwV6

LIFE COMMITMENT:

Sleeping doesn't mean I am lazy. Sleep is designed by God to reset and refresh me. If ever I need good sleep, it is now.

DAY 55

Get Moving

∞

THE WORD

Do you not know that your body is a temple of the
Holy Spirit, who is in you, whom you have received
from God? You are not your own; you were bought
at a price. Therefore honor God with your body.

— 1 CORINTHIANS 6.19–20

THOUGHT FOR THE DAY:

Making excuses burns zero calories per hour.

~ ANONYMOUS

TODAY'S ENCOURAGEMENT IS SHORT AND simple. *Start doing something, anything, that gets your heart beating fast and makes you sweat.* You don't have to do it a long time. You don't have to pay anything to do this. You don't have to have any special clothes or shoes. The weather doesn't have to be perfect. You don't have to go anywhere special. All you have to do is *do it.* Do **something** that gets your heart beating and your body sweating.

Study after study after study can give you all the info you could ever want on why exercise is good for you. But the real problem is not *information*, it's *motivation*.

So here's the deal. If you can't do 50 pushups, do 10 today. Do 10 pushups a day for a week. Then next week do 15. Ten pushups today is better than zero.

If you can't walk 100 yards without your heart coming out of your chest, start with 50. Just do it. *Start today, right now.*

It won't be fun. Putting your heart and lungs into chaos can be exhilarating, but it is not *fun* in the traditional sense of the word. It actually feels more like *work*. All those people who tell you this will be easy and exciting set you up for unrealistic expectations.

I'm not going to tell you it is fun but I can tell you it really feels good. It feels good to drop weight. It feels good to know you can eventually handle that five-mile hike or run with your kids or get on a bike and travel on your own power 20 miles.

It feels good to not have sleep apnea, high blood pressure, acid reflux, chest pains and high blood sugar *simply because you consistently put your heart and lungs into chaos for 30 minutes a day*. Is all this fitness stuff really so complicated?

If you eat more calories than you burn, you will get fat. The opposite is true. If you burn more than you eat, you will lose weight. Mean old Mr. Science! But that's the way it works. No matter what anyone tells you, there are no shortcuts or magic pills. Eat less, exercise more, that's it.

Now is the time to get off the couch and do *something*. *Something* is better than *nothing* and a bunch of *somethings* add up to *a lot of good things* for you.

If you need a few inspirational quotes, here they are:

- *Better sore than sorry.*
- *Nothing tastes as good as skinny feels.* (My personal favorite)
- *Sweat is just fat crying.*
- *Get comfortable with being uncomfortable.*
- *Pain is weakness leaving the body.*
- *Three months from now you will thank yourself.*
- *No pain. No Gain. Shut up and train.*
- *Work hard. Stay humble.*
- *Sore? Tired? Out of breath? Sweaty? Good... It's working.*
- *Good things come to those who sweat.*
- *Sore muscles are the new hangover.*
- *Motivation is what gets you started. Habit keeps you going.*
- *Your fitness is 100% mental. Your body won't go where your mind doesn't push it.*

I guarantee you this: No matter how you feel when you start a workout, you will *not* feel worse after your workout. No matter how you feel when you begin a workout, you will not regret having worked out.

Try me on this one. Get moving. And... you will want to check with your doctor before you do anything too strenuous.

THINK ABOUT IT...

- No... don't think about it. Just get up and do SOMETHING to get your heart beating and your body sweating!

LIFE COMMITMENT:
I am getting up to do something that will get my heart beating and my body sweating.

It's a Mess

—⚬⚬⚬—

THE WORD

This is the verdict: Light has come into the
world, but men loved darkness instead of
light because their deeds were evil.

— JOHN 3.19

THOUGHT FOR THE DAY:

Man's greatness and wretchedness are so evident
that the true religion must necessarily teach us that
there is in man some great principle of greatness
and some great principle of wretchedness.

~ BLAISE PASCAL

THAT WE KNOW WE WILL die indicates we are different from
and higher than all other creatures. That we fear this death
indicates that we know something is wrong.

And something *is* wrong. We find ourselves in a story that
has gone awry. And it seems as though we have arrived in
the middle of this story. We are not sure who wrote the story,

what has gone wrong in the story and if the story is currently being edited.

Most people sense that we have been created by something or Someone bigger than us. Even tribal cultures that have many 'gods' usually have one Supreme Creator God. But if this God created us, what happened?

What happened is that the God who created us wanted us to love him, so he gave humans something he didn't give anything else: *the capacity to choose.* We could choose to love God or we could choose to reject him. God's desire is that we love him, but true love is only true love when the object of love can be rejected.

So in one tiny part of the vast universe, for only a brief time, God's will can be deflected and denied. That small temporary place that can push back on God is the human heart.

Our first parents chose in their hearts to deny God. When they chose against God they took themselves (and all of us) out from under his protection and provision. Out from under God's protection and provision, life became a matter of survival. The story of humanity is the story of human survival, each of us out for him/herself, clawing up the backs of others to get to the top—or just to get something to eat.[74]

God graciously allowed the race to continue and like a parent following behind his runaway child, God gives a measure of protection and provision to us. But in the end, our choice against God has created the messy world in which we live.

---

[74] If you want to see this fight for survival being played out today in horrifying detail, watch the 2004 movie *Darwin's Nightmare.*

Neil and Joanne Anderson explain our condition like this:

Eternal life, identity, purpose, significance, security, and a sense of belonging are all attributes of mankind created in the image of God. Adam and Eve experienced these attributes in full measure, and we were destined to enjoy them too. But when Adam sinned, he died spiritually and forfeited everything God had provided. Being separated from God, Adam's glowing attributes became glaring needs.

As children of Adam born separated from God, we come into the world with these same glaring needs. We wander through life striving to make a name for ourselves, looking for security in temporal things, and searching for significance apart from God.[75]

Why is it important for you to know this and how will this help you with your anger?

It is all about knowing reality and having the right expectations. If you buy a 1965 Volkswagen Beetle but you expect it to perform like a 2017 BMW Z4, you will be one very frustrated driver. As much as you believe your VW is a BMW, it just ain't so!

We live in a messed-up world full of heartache and heartbreak. To accept the world as it is will help you deal with the brokenness that you are now experiencing because of divorce.

It took me a long time to understand that good people can be persuaded to do bad things. My heart was broken and remains so from trust torn to shreds by people I loved,

---

[75] Anderson and Anderson, *Daily in Christ*, 66.

trusted and had poured my life into. But one reason my heart was so crushed was that I was expecting people to be a BMW when in fact, everyone, including myself, are just rattily old VW Bugs.

THINK ABOUT IT...

* What expectations do I have of people?
* Where have people failed to live up to my expectations?
* Where have I failed to live up to the expectations of others?

LIFE COMMITMENT:

This world is a mess and I am a part of this mess. Accepting this reality helps me have realistic expectations of myself and others.

Things Can Go to S***t (Fast)

———— ∽∾∽ ————

THE WORD

> *As fish are caught in a cruel net, or birds are*
> *taken in a snare, so men are trapped by evil*
> *times that fall unexpectedly upon them.*

— ECCLESIASTES 9.12

THOUGHT FOR THE DAY:

I love mankind... it's people I can't stand!

~ CHARLES M. SCHULZ, "PEANUTS," 1959 (LINUS)

ON SEPTEMBER 3, 1967, A truly remarkable thing happened. On that day in Sweden all traffic switched from driving on the left side of the road (as the British do) to driving on the right side of the road. This was a profound change involving thousands of people, years of preparation and a lot of money. The Swedish word for this event is *Högertrafikomläggningen,* which means *the right-hand traffic diversion.*

On September 3, traffic was banned from the roads from 1:00 am to 6:00 am. If any vehicle was on the road, it had to come to a complete stop at 4:50 a.m., then switch over to the right-hand side of the road where it had to stop again. At 5:00 a.m. the vehicle could move again.

Before this amazing moment, thousands of traffic lights and signs had been installed and wrapped in plastic. During the wee hours of September 3, the plastic was removed. Buses and bus stops had to be switched to the other side and intersections were re-marked and modified to allow for the change. Remarkably, the number of accidents actually *decreased* after the change, probably due to the perception of heightened risk and thus more cautious driving.

Why do I bring this up? Because life (on the surface) is *not* like a well-orchestrated *Högertrafikomläggningen*. It's more like a traffic change with no preparation. It is more like *skit-prat* (another Swedish word, look it up).

We live in a world that has chosen against God, and God has allowed us to suffer the consequences of our choices. The Bible doesn't sugar-coat this fact.

But the Bible doesn't just describe reality as it is, it also lets us peak behind the scenes. What we find is that ultimately this is not a WYSIWYG world. This is not a *What-You-See-Is-What-You-Get* world. God is at work behind the scenes, weaving the tangled threads of our lives into something that is beautiful and makes sense.

The gap between what you are experiencing in your life right now and the ultimate reality of what God is doing in your life takes faith to grasp and hold onto. Hold on. Hold on for as long as it takes for God to show you how he is turning your disasters into deliverance.

Author and theologian Chris Tiegreen's son was in a terrible car accident only a month after receiving his driver's license. Out of his pain Tiegreen was able to see God work in amazing ways.

Tiegreen writes, *Revelations of light seem to come most often in places of mystifying darkness. And life seems to flourish most plentifully out of deathly wounds. Out of the depths, God speaks.*[76]

The tragic events of our lives create a strong wind that can push our hearts even further away from God. Instead of giving in to this wind, adjust your sails. By faith, lean your heart into God and see where he takes you. The sure and powerful testimony of millions of Christians is that you will not be disappointed.

By the way, the entire heavens and earth will eventually experience a perfectly-executed cosmic *Högertrafikomläggningen.* This is when God remakes heaven and earth, and it will be glorious indeed!

Think About It...

* What disasters led you to this place in your life?
* In your opinion, who caused the pain you are experiencing?
* Do you believe God is at work beneath the surface of your life?

---

[76] Chris Tiegreen, *One Year Hearing His Voice Devotional: 365 Days of Intimate Communication with God* (Tyndale Momentum, 2015), 641.

LIFE COMMITMENT:

Though life feels more like 'skitprat' than 'Högertrafikomläggningen,' I will trust that God is at work behind the scenes for his glory and my good.

It's a War

THE WORD

Finally, be strong in the Lord and in his mighty power.
Put on the full armor of God so that you can take your
stand against the devil's schemes. For our struggle is not
against flesh and blood, but against the rulers, against
the authorities, against the powers of this dark world and
against the spiritual forces of evil in the heavenly realms.

— EPHESIANS 6.10–12

THOUGHT FOR THE DAY:

If you know the enemy and know yourself, you need
not fear the result of a hundred battles. If you know
yourself but not the enemy, for every victory gained
you will also suffer a defeat. If you know neither the
enemy nor yourself, you will succumb in every battle.

~ SUN TZU, THE ART OF WAR

THE WORST THING YOU CAN do when going to war is to underestimate your enemy. The British underestimated the Americans and the Americans underestimated the Viet Cong.

Worse than underestimating your enemy is not realizing you have one. We experienced the terrible results of this fatal error on September 11, 2001. I experienced it in my church in New England. I never knew that guy was my enemy or that he was at war with me.

The reality is that we are at war. This war transcends my enemy who did me in at my last church. This war is even bigger than any battle fought between humans on earth. This war is cosmic. It's huge and it's ancient, going back to the beginning of time.

Before we were created God had a worship leader who wanted to be God. There's only one God and he is (rightfully) jealous of his glory. The worship leader lost his bid to take God's place in the universe. The mutineer and his compatriots were kicked out of heaven. We know this mutinous worship leader as Satan and his fellow mutineers as demons.

Ever since that terrible cosmic tragedy, Satan has done all he can to destroy and defame anything of God. The war was won but skirmishes continue. Since Satan can't get to God, he goes for what God loves—his children. The battleground of this war is our mind and heart.

On June 6, 1944, the largest assault in military history took place when the Allies invaded northern France. We know this as D-Day. The success of this initial battle to retake Europe spelled the end of Hitler and his murderous regime. Everyone knew it except Hitler.

Between Normandy and Berlin were 844 miles of German-infested hedgerows, forests, meadows and mountains. To complete the victory meant retaking all that ground stolen by Hitler.

Victory was *assured* on June 6, 1944, D-Day. But victory was not *fully realized* until May 8, 1945, V-E Day, when the Germans surrendered in Berlin. Between D-Day and V-E Day were 336 days and 844 miles of struggle. But each allied soldier fighting those 336 days and 844 miles knew Hitler was doomed.

We are living between a spiritual D-Day and V-E Day. Jesus stormed the beaches of Satan's stronghold on Good Friday. Jesus emerged victorious on Resurrection Sunday. The victory was won and secured 2,000 years ago. But the full benefits of that victory will not be realized until Jesus comes again and the Great Renovation of heaven and earth is completed.

Meanwhile, we fight on, knowing the victory is ours and the enemy is defeated.

How does this help with anger? It helps to know that the battle is bigger than you, your ex-wife, your boss, your flat tire, your _____ (fill in the blank). The real enemy is not a human or situation or circumstance on earth. Your real enemy is Satan, and his target is your head and heart.

It helps to know that a good choice in the midst of your anger scores a victory that rings throughout heaven.

It helps to know the battles are temporary. Eventually you will have rest from this struggle. It helps to have hope.

It helps to be angry at the real enemy and to know he is ultimately defeated forever.

THINK ABOUT IT...

* Have I been fighting the right enemy?
* If all this is true, what does a real victory look like?

LIFE COMMITMENT:

I will know the enemy and I will know myself and my God, so I need not fear the result of a hundred battles.

God Wins

*Since everything will be destroyed in this way, what kind
of people ought you to be? You ought to live holy and godly
lives as you look forward to the day of God and speed its
coming. That day will bring about the destruction of the
heavens by fire, and the elements will melt in the heat.
But in keeping with his promise we are looking
forward to a new heaven and a new earth, the home
of righteousness. So then, dear friends, since you
are looking forward to this, make every effort to be
found spotless, blameless and at peace with him.*

— 2 PETER 3.11–14

THOUGHT FOR THE DAY:

*This is the good news of the gospel. Peace came. Peace
lived. Peace died. Peace rose again. Peace reigns on
your behalf. Peace indwells you by the Spirit. Peace
graces you with everything you need. Peace convicts,
forgives, and delivers you. Peace will finish his work
in you. Peace will welcome you into glory, where
Peace will live with you in peace and righteousness*

forever. Peace isn't a faded dream. No, Peace is
real. Peace is a person, and his name is Jesus.

~ PAUL DAVID TRIPP

JOHN O'DONOHUE WRITES, *IT IS strange to be here. The mystery never leaves you alone. Behind your image, below your words, above your thoughts, the silence of another world waits.*[77]

This mystery is not only in you but far beyond you. There is far more *in* you than you can possibly imagine, and there is far more *beyond* you than you can possibly fathom.

We live out our earthly lives on an extremely thin line (about 10 feet?) where rock and air meet. We exist on a tiny speck of rock in a universe of perhaps a trillion galaxies. Go outside tonight and look up. You will be humbled. It is indeed, strange to be here.

But we *are* here and we are here because God made us to be here. We are his glorious creation, the ones he has made to love and from whom love is desired. As weird as it is for us as men to hear it, we are in the middle of a love story.

It makes sense, doesn't it? In the end, don't all good things come down to love, and all the *skitprat* to misplaced love (see Day 57)?

All love stories are about love in the midst of conflict and war. The epic stories we tell and the movies Disney makes are not creations of our imagination. They are echoes of a deep reality, a reality we seek to grasp while stumbling around in our foggy world.

---

[77] O'Donohue, *Anam Ċara*, Kindle Location 283.

We are in a love story, but a love story gone awry. The battle rages and casualties mount. But here's the thing: as in our epic tales and delightful movies, **in the end, love wins**.

This is crucial for you to understand. In the end, love wins. In the end, God wins. You are on the winning team.

How does this help you manage your anger? If you know you are on the winning team, you can endure anything until the victory is complete. If you know you on the winning team, everything *now* becomes training for the ultimate victory *later*. You and I can endure hardship because we know the victory is coming.

The Apostle Paul says it like this:

> *For our light and momentary troubles are achieving for us an eternal glory that far outweighs them all. So we fix our eyes not on what is seen, but on what is unseen. For what is seen is temporary, but what is unseen is eternal.* (2 Corinthians 4.17–18)

Knowing you are on the winning team lets you look beyond your current troubles to the victory that is on the way.

THINK ABOUT IT...

* What am I here for?
* If this is a war, whose side am I on?
* What would change in my attitude if I really grasped that in the end, all that matters is that God wins?

LIFE COMMITMENT:

It is Friday, but Sunday's coming! I can make it until Sunday.

Thinking About Forgiveness

—⧥—

THE WORD

He does not deal with us according to our sins, nor repay us according to our iniquities. For as high as the heavens are above the earth, so great is his steadfast love toward those who fear him; as far as the east is from the west, so far does he remove our transgressions from us. As a father shows compassion to his children, so the Lord shows compassion to those who fear him. For he knows our frame; he remembers that we are dust.

— PSALM 103.10-14

THOUGHT FOR THE DAY:

Resentment is like drinking poison and then hoping it will kill your enemies.

~ NELSON MANDELA

FORGIVENESS IS TOUGH. IT'S A journey. It's a process. Today I simply ask you to consider what forgiveness might look like in your life... forgiveness of your ex, forgiveness of yourself, forgiveness of anyone else involved in the pain you find your-self in right now.

THINK ABOUT IT...

* How have I experienced forgiveness from others in my life?
* What barriers to forgiving others are in my life right now?
* What will I gain by forgiving the people in my life who have hurt me?
* What would I gain by not forgiving them?

LIFE COMMITMENT:
I commit to giving consideration to forgiveness.

YOU MAY ALSO LIKE...
Forgiveness; Anger

You Need Jesus (1)

———∽∞∽———

THE WORD

It is appointed for man to die once,
and after that comes judgment.

— HEBREWS 9.27 (ESV)

THOUGHT FOR THE DAY:

Go to Heaven for the climate, Hell for the company.

~ MARK TWAIN

SEVERAL YEARS AGO I WAS called to the bedside of a dying woman named Pat. Pat was a friend of a woman in our church—let's call her Fran. Fran told me about Pat and said she wanted to talk to a pastor. I jumped at the chance.

Fran and I arrived at Pat's apartment. Inside we found Pat in her bed—thin, bald and weak. Death lingered close.

Fran began the conversation: *Pat, you are sure to go to heaven! You have been such a good person. You are always so kind and generous, and you have helped so many people. I know you are going to heaven! You are so good!*

Then I chimed in: *Actually, Pat, you are <u>not</u> good enough to go to heaven. But this is not bad news, it is, in fact, good news.*

THINK ABOUT IT...

- How *does* a person get to heaven? If goodness doesn't get you there, what does?
- If you were Pat and you heard what Fran said to you and what I said to you, who would you believe?
- How could not being good enough to go to heaven be good news?
- Unless you die quickly in an accident or of heart failure, someday you will be where Pat was. What do you think happens when the body quits working?

LIFE COMMITMENT:

I want to settle this matter of my own death once and for all. I commit to an open mind and soft heart to allow God to speak truth to me about this most important of all issues.

You Need Jesus (2)

——— ⊶∞⊷ ———

THE WORD

> *The wrath of God is being revealed from heaven against*
> *all the godlessness and wickedness of men who suppress*
> *the truth by their wickedness, since what may be known*
> *about God is plain to them, because God has made it*
> *plain to them. For since the creation of the world God's*
> *invisible qualities—his eternal power and divine*
> *nature—have been clearly seen, being understood from*
> *what has been made, so that men are without excuse.*
> *For although they knew God, they neither glorified him as*
> *God nor gave thanks to him, but their thinking became*
> *futile and their foolish hearts were darkened. Although*
> *they claimed to be wise, they became fools and exchanged*
> *the glory of the immortal God for images made to look*
> *like mortal man and birds and animals and reptiles.*

> — ROMANS 1.18–23

Thought for the Day:

*I am good, but not an angel. I do sin, but I
am not the devil. I am just a small girl in a
big world trying to find someone to love.*

~ Marilyn Monroe

When I was a kid my friends and I would get into rock fights, that is, we would throw rocks at each other. We also had a tendency to try to shoot each other with BB guns. That's what boys do. Boys like to shoot things, burn things, and blow things up. And I define 'boys' here loosely!

One day my friend and I got into rock fight at my house. My friend threw a rock at me and missed. That was the good news. The bad news was that he hit my dad's car and put a significant dent in it just below the passenger side back window.

Oh, this was very very bad. My dad was definitely *not* the kind of dad where you just walked up and said, *Father, I have failed you. My friend just threw a rock at me and instead of hitting me it hit your car. Please forgive us.* To say such a thing to my dad was to sign your death warrant.

But here's the thing. Even though my dad had no clue what we had done, *my guilt and fear of him compelled me to avoid him.* My fear of what he would do to me if he found out made me not want to be in his presence.

That's the way we are with God. God made us and then gave us rules to live by. Those rules are for our own good but they are also a test of if we love God. If we love God we obey his rules, just like a husband who loves his wife doesn't cheat on her but instead, remains faithful to her, not out of begrudging obligation but from a heart of joyful love.

Ever since Adam and Eve turned against God, however, we've been rebels.

Human beings are not like pebbles on a beach; we're like leaves on a tree. If the root of a tree is diseased, then the disease will spread to every part of the tree.[78] We are all infected with the 'rebellion virus.' All of us have broken the rules.

We may not consciously be aware of it, but deep inside we know we have done what God has told us not to do, and we have failed to do what God requires of us. The Biblical word for rebellion and rule-breaking is *sin. For all have sinned and fall short of the glory of God.* (Romans 3.23)

So, just like I tried to avoid my dad out of fear of what he would do to me, we avoid God out of fear of what he will do to us. Unlike my dad, however, God is all-knowing *and* he is all-powerful. As much as I feared my dad, my dad didn't know everything (though he acted at times as if he did!) and he wasn't all-powerful (though he sure felt powerful in my life).

Sin separates us from God. Our rebellion against God has put a very real gap between God and us. We avoid God because we fear his punishment. If something is not done about this gap between us and God, things will go very poorly for us.

---

[78] Colin S. Smith and Tim Augustyn, *The One Year Unlocking the Bible Devotional* (Carol Stream, IL: Tyndale House, 2012), 698.

THINK ABOUT IT...

* What is sin?
* Are you a sinner?
* In what ways do you think you have rebelled against God?
* In what ways have you avoided God?

LIFE COMMITMENT:

I recognize that I have sinned and fallen (far) short of the glory of God.

You Need Jesus (3)

———∞∞∞———

THE WORD

*For God so loved the world that he gave his one
and only Son, that whoever believes in him shall
not perish but have eternal life. For God did
not send his Son into the world to condemn the
world, but to save the world through him.*

—JOHN 3.16–17

THOUGHT FOR THE DAY:

*Jesus lived the life we should have lived and
died the death we should have died.*

~ TIM KELLER

MANY PEOPLE HAVE SEEN MEL Gibson's *The Passion of the
Christ,* his 2004 movie about the final 12 hours of Jesus' life.
Gibson portrays the flogging and crucifixion of Jesus in
gruesome detail. The movie was rated R because of this violence. Some critics ironically excoriated the film, claiming
the violence was exaggerated and distracting!

The reality is this: Whatever violence you see perpetrated on Jesus in this movie doesn't come close to the reality of what really happened to Christ on the cross. What *actually did* happen to Jesus on the cross? The Bible says that God loved us so much he *gave* his one and only Son. What did God give when he gave us his Son?

Here's the deal: When we sin we sin against a perfect and holy God. Our sin separates us from God. Our sin is the evidence of our running away from God in a hopeless bid for autonomy rather than living in dependence upon him and submission to him. Because of our sin we are far from him. And our sin puts us in debt to God. Our sin causes unspeakable damage to ourselves, to the people around us and to our world. The cost of sin is immeasurable.

When my friend threw the rock that put the dent in my dad's car, damage was done and repairing the car would be costly. Someone would have to pay to have the car fixed.

Because we have turned away from God, we are far from him and the cost to repair the damage is far beyond us.

The great news is this: God loves us too much to leave us in our lost, separated and miserable state. Since we couldn't go to him he came to us. He sent his son Jesus, fully God and fully human, to be the bridge between him and us.

When Jesus hung on the cross he was taking upon himself all the hell you and I rightfully deserve for the damage we have caused by our rebelling against God. When Jesus hung on the cross he not only suffered terribly physically (as portrayed in *The Passion*) but he suffered far, far more spiritually as he paid the price to repair the damage we have caused.

That's why out of the billions of people who have died, only Jesus' death can affect your life on earth and your life after you die.

A really rough and tough man wrote this about Jesus: *[Jesus] himself bore our sins in his body on the tree, so that we might die to sins and live for righteousness.* (1 Peter 2.24)

And Jesus said this about himself: *For even the Son of Man did not come to be served, but to serve, and to give his life as a ransom for many.* (Mark 10.44–45)

Jesus paid this unspeakably high price so our debt to God would be paid and we would be forgiven of every sin we have committed and all the sins we will commit.

When Jesus hung on the cross he took upon himself your sin, and when he died, your sin was killed on that cross. In exchange for our sin, Jesus gives us his righteousness. He exchanged our black for his white, our infection for his healing, our damage for his restoration.

THINK ABOUT IT...

* Most people have heard about Jesus and that he died on the cross. Do you now understand what actually took place when Jesus died on the cross?
* What is new to you it in what you just? What questions you have?

LIFE COMMITMENT:

I commit to understanding as much as I can about what Jesus did for me on the cross so that I can decide to follow him fully... or reject him. Ignoring him and putting this off is no longer an option for me.

You Need Jesus (4)

———— ∽∞∿ ————

THE WORD

[God] made [Jesus] who knew no sin to be sin for us,
that we might become the righteousness of God in Him.

— 2 CORINTHIANS 5.21

THOUGHT FOR THE DAY:

God may thunder His commands from Mount Sinai
and men may fear, yet remain at heart exactly as they
were before. But let a man once see his God down in
the arena as a Man—suffering, tempted, sweating,
and agonized, finally dying a criminal's death—
and he is a hard man indeed who is untouched.

~ J.B. PHILLIPS

I'VE HAD MANY CHURCH FOLK through the years who simply didn't understand a simple concept: *When Jesus died on the cross he took upon himself our sins.* Every single one of them. While on the cross Jesus killed all the sins you have committed up to this very moment. And, he also killed all the sins *you will* commit. It's a done deal.

I was living in the Boston area when the Red Sox beat the St. Louis Cardinals to win their first World Series in 86 years. To get to that exciting victory the Red Sox had come from a 0-3 deficit to beat their arch rivals, the New York Yankees in the American League Championship Series. It was an exciting and unforgettable fall!

Now, suppose it's 2017. You and I are having a conversation and I casually mention that I really hope the Red Sox win the 2004 World Series. Remember, its 2017. You give me a puzzled look. I say again, *I really hope the Red Sox win the 2004 World Series.* You may say something like, *Dale, it's a done deal! The Red Sox DID win the 2004 World Series!*

When Jesus died on the cross *all your sins were put upon him and he paid for every one of your sins on that terrible and amazing day.* It's a done deal. It's not something that *might* happen. *It happened.* It's not something that could be, *it is.* You don't have to hope Jesus paid for your sins. He did. You don't have to plead with him to forgive you. He has.

It's a done deal. God won. Your sins are paid for, your debt erased. You are forgiven.

THINK ABOUT IT...

* If God has already paid for and forgiven all your sins, including the sins you *will* commit in your future, does that give you freedom to sin?
* Has someone graciously pay off a debt that was dragging you down? How did you feel toward that person?

LIFE COMMITMENT:

I am a sinner whose sins have been paid for by Jesus when he died for me on the cross. My debt is erased, my bill paid, my obligation covered by Jesus' amazing sacrifice.

You Need Jesus (5)

———❧———

THE WORD

*For the grace of God that brings salvation
has appeared to all men.*

— TITUS 2.11

THOUGHT FOR THE DAY:

*Mercy is not getting what we deserve. Grace
is getting what we don't deserve.*

~ ANONYMOUS

KING DAVID WAS AT THE top of his game. Things were going swimmingly—he was winning wars, the kingdom was growing, his family was tight. But David let his guard down. In just a few words the Bible tells the story that took down a king:

In the spring, at the time when kings go off to war, David sent Joab out with the king's men and the whole Israelite army. They destroyed the Ammonites and besieged Rabbah. But David remained in Jerusalem. One evening David got up from his bed and walked around on the roof of the palace.

> *From the roof he saw a woman bathing. The woman was very beautiful, and David sent someone to find out about her. The man said, "Isn't this Bathsheba, the daughter of Eliam and the wife of Uriah the Hittite?"*
>
> *Then David sent messengers to get her. She came to him, and he slept with her. Then she went back home. The woman conceived and sent word to David, saying, "I am pregnant."* (2 Samuel 11.1–5)

Have you cheated on your wife? David did. But David did even more. When Bathsheba turned up pregnant, David schemed to get his tail out of the crack. Uriah, Bathsheba's husband, was off fighting David's war. Instead of being grateful, David sent for Uriah, hoping Uriah would sleep with his wife so it would look like the child was Uriah's, not David's. What a swell guy is this King David.

But Uriah was a better man than David. Uriah refused to sleep with his own wife, saying that he couldn't indulge in sex while his fellow soldiers were living in tents and fighting a war.

Desperate, David got Uriah drunk, but Uriah still refused to sleep with Bathsheba.

When that didn't work, David's heart darkened: In the morning David wrote a letter to Joab and sent it with Uriah. In it he wrote, *"Put Uriah in the front line where the fighting is fiercest. Then withdraw from him so he will be struck down and die.* (2 Samuel 11.14–15) Joab did and Uriah died.

Have you committed adultery? If you did, did you have your lover's husband murdered? If you have committed adultery and murder like King David, do you think God could forgive you?

David committed adultery with a man's wife while this man was off fighting David's war. David schemed, lied and manipulated the situation as much as he could, only to end up having the man murdered. It doesn't get any worse than this. And yet, God forgave him.

Why is such a story in the Bible? God put this story in the Bible to teach you and me a most important lesson: *You can't out-sin the reach of God's grace.* There is nothing you have ever done that cannot be forgiven by God. God's grace is bigger than your sin.

In fact, as we saw yesterday, whatever terrible sin you have committed *has already been paid for by Jesus on the cross* 2,000 years ago. Not only *can* you be forgiven, you *have been* forgiven.

The Bible portrays humanity as we really are and God as he really is. Most of us have not sinned as David did, but if we did, we know God can and has forgiven us. Even if we have sins that are, in our minds, worse than David's, we can know that sin is forgiven by God because all sins were paid for by Jesus on the cross.

There is no difference, for all have sinned and fall short of the glory of God, and are justified freely by his grace through the redemption that came by Christ Jesus. (Roman 3.22b–23)

As a divorced man you may be filled with guilt. Maybe you are divorced because you cheated on your wife. Maybe she walked away because you are an alcoholic or hooked on drugs. Even if you feel you are the victim here, you have sinned and your sin has been a factor in your divorce.

Whatever your circumstance, remember that you can't out-sin the reach of God's grace. There is nothing you have ever done that cannot be forgiven by God. God's grace is bigger than your sin.

THINK ABOUT IT...

* Do you understand and believe that God's forgiveness is bigger than your sin?

LIFE COMMITMENT:
Though I have sinned greatly and often, God's grace is bigger than my sin. I believe this and I am grateful to God for his amazing grace.

You Need Jesus (6)

———— ❧ ————

THE WORD

Repent and be baptized, every one of you, in the
name of Jesus Christ for the forgiveness of your sins.
And you will receive the gift of the Holy Spirit.

— ACTS 2:38

THOUGHT FOR THE DAY:

My deepest awareness of myself is that I
am deeply loved by Jesus Christ and I have
done nothing to earn it or deserve it.

~ BRENNAN MANNING

THROUGH MORE THAN THREE DECADES of pastoral ministry many men have sat in my office crushed because their wives have left them. Sometimes it was clearly the man's fault—he cheated on his wife and he got caught. Sometimes it was more the wife's fault.

The men in my office always desperately wanted their wives back. But to me, the bigger issue in each of these men's lives was his relationship with God. No matter *why* that man is sitting in my office, each of those men needed the same thing: to get right with God.

You are hurting because of divorce. The bigger issue, however, is your relationship to God. Are you ready to start over with God? If so, read on. If not, read on anyway!

Ray Pritchard says there are three elements to getting right with God: True saving faith involves the **intellect**, the **emotions**, and the **will**.... Faith starts with **knowledge**, moves to **conviction**, and ends with **commitment**.[79]

To receive forgiveness now and heaven forever, you need to **know some facts**, be **convinced they are true**, and then **make a decision**.

What you need to **KNOW**:

Here are the basics:

* We don't get to heaven based on our goodness. Instead, we get there only by God's grace because **no one is good enough. Our rebellion against God, expressed as sin, separates us from God**.
* Since we can't go to God, he came to us. God sent his son, Jesus, to take the punishment we deserve for our sin. **On the cross Jesus took upon himself your sin**, and when he died, your sin was killed on that cross. In exchange for our sin, Jesus gives us his righteousness.
* After Jesus died on the cross **he rose again**, proving he is who he said he is, and proving his power over our greatest enemy which is death.

---

[79] Ray Pritchard, *An Anchor for the Soul: Help for the Present, Hope for the Future* (Chicago: Moody Publishers, 2011), 123. Emphasis mine.

To solve any problem you have to understand it and then map out the solution. You and I have a problem: we are separated from God because of our sin. God provided the solution by sending his own Son to die in our place. These are the basics of what you need to know about your problem and its solution.

THINK ABOUT IT...

* Do you understand your problem?
* Do you understand how God has solved your problem through Jesus?
* What questions still linger about the facts of what you need to know to be right with God?

LIFE COMMITMENT:

I commit to understanding my problem and how God has taken steps to solve my problem. I will pursue questions I have until I know all I need to know to move to the next step.

You Need Jesus (7)

———∞———

THE WORD

> *For I am the least of the apostles and do not even deserve
> to be called an apostle, because I persecuted the church
> of God. But by the grace of God I am what I am, and
> his grace to me was not without effect. No, I worked
> harder than all of them—yet not I, but the grace of God
> that was with me. Whether, then, it was I or they, this
> is what we preach, and this is what you believed.*

> — 1 CORINTHIANS 15.9–11

THOUGHT FOR THE DAY:

> *The greatest enemy to human souls is the self-righteous
> spirit which makes men look to themselves for salvation.*

> ~ CHARLES SPURGEON

FOR SEVERAL MONTHS I HAD the privilege of homeschooling
our youngest child. Aaron was 13 at the time. We weren't sure
how this experiment would work but our time together turned
into something I will cherish the rest of my life. One advantage

of homeschooling is you get to teach your kids things that will really matter in life.

One morning our assignment was persuasive writing. Aaron had to write a paper persuading me about something. Ahhh... this was *not* a topic to skim over! I told Aaron that we would spend some time here because, in the end, *nearly everything we say and do is all about trying to persuade someone about something.*

Think about the things you think and say. Consider the things you do. Almost everything is about persuasion.

To persuade someone of something you must deliver a set of facts, and then convince him/her that those facts are true.

The same is true as you get right with God. You must **KNOW** the facts about your standing before God and what God has actually done about it.

The last few days we have talked about what the Bible says about the human condition (separated from God because of sin) and God's solution (Jesus died for our sins).

This knowledge is important. Ray Pritchard states:

> *Christian faith is not blind faith. We are called to believe in something—not just anything. True saving faith rests first and foremost in Jesus Christ. This is most important. We must know who He is, why He came, why He died, why He rose from the dead.*[80]

If you have questions about these stated facts, pursue answers. Loads of smart people over the past 2,000 years have

---

[80] Pritchard, *An Anchor for The Soul*, 124-25.

met every intellectual challenge raised against these facts. You can find answers to your questions!

To get right with God at some point you must be convinced that these facts are true. It's like buying a car. You go to the dealership and, of course, they try to convince you to buy their car. They try to convince you by presenting 'facts' about how awesome their car is. You may be persuaded or not, but *eventually you will buy a car,* and the reason you will buy it is because you have been persuaded that this car is the right car for you.

Friend, if you are sucking wind because of your divorce, know that even if you had not gone through this divorce and were married, even happily married, nothing is more important than getting right with God.

The Bible makes claims about our human problem and God's solution. What do you think? True or not?

THINK ABOUT IT...

* What is holding you back from being convinced that what the Bible says about our human problem and God's solution is true?
* Read this statement below from Paul David Tripp. As you read, think about what you have been persuaded to think and do, and why.

We are value-oriented, goal-oriented, purpose-oriented, and importance-oriented human beings. We are constantly rating everything in our lives. We all have things that are important to us and things that are not, things that mean a lot to us and things that mean very little. We willingly make sacrifices for one thing and refuse to sacrifice for another.

We grieve the loss of one thing and celebrate the loss of another. We love what another person hates and we see as a treasure something that another person thinks is trash. We look at something and see beauty while the person next to us sees no beauty in it at all.

Some things are so important to us that they shape the decisions that we make and the actions that we take. Some things command the allegiance of our hearts, while other things barely get our attention. In the center of this value system is our definition of success.[81]

What do you value? How do you define success? What are your goals? What is your purpose?

Life Commitment:

I am convinced that what the Bible says about my problem and God's solution is true.

---

[81] Tripp, *New Morning Mercies*, Kindle Location 1480.

You Need Jesus (8)

———— ∞∞ ————

THE WORD

*I tell you the truth, whoever hears my word and
believes him who sent me has eternal life and will not
be condemned; he has crossed over from death to life.*

—JOHN 5.24

THOUGHT FOR THE DAY:

*While salvation is a free gift, [salvation] can only be
through unreserved consecration and unquestioning
obedience. Nor is this a hardship, but the highest privilege.*

~ HUDSON TAYLOR

FLYING ON AN AIRPLANE IS absolutely amazing. Consider how
few people in the history of the world have seen the earth
from 30,000 feet!

On a recent trip home from teaching in Africa we were
somewhere over the North Atlantic. Getting up to stretch, I
wandered to the back of the plane. I stopped at the window
in the emergency door of the plane and looked down. Five
miles below me the iceberg dotted waters loomed.

I really began to think about this. I was in mid-air in a small aluminum cylinder going 600 miles per hour. My life was completely in the hands of the engines pushing us through the air and the pilots guiding us to a tiny patch of concrete in Houston, Texas. At any moment a bolt could tear loose, a window buckle, a gas line rupture, an electronic component fry. Any number of small failures could lead to an unscheduled trip to the frigid waters below.

I decided it was time to get back to my seat!

In reflecting on my experience it occurred to me how much faith it took me to get on this airplane. At some point in my life I had learned about airplanes and modern day flying. What knowledge I had gained I had deemed as true and trustworthy. I had come to believe that airplanes are remarkably safe and that if I chose to fly, there was a very high probability I would safely arrive at my destination.

But no matter how much I knew about flying or how much I believed in the safety of modern air travel, *I would never get to my destination unless actually I got on the airplane.*

The same is true of getting to heaven. Faith starts with **knowledge**, moves to **conviction**, and ends with **commitment**.[82]

To receive forgiveness now and heaven forever, you need to **know some things**, be **convinced they are true**, and then **make a decision**.

The past several days we have talked about some facts as revealed in the Bible about our problem (sin) and God's solution (Jesus). Do you believe those facts? Do you trust they are true?

---

[82] Pritchard, *An Anchor for The Soul*, 123. Emphasis mine.

If so, now is the time to make a decision. To be right with God you must get on the plane. To get to heaven, you have to walk down the jet way, step into the airplane and take your seat. Your trip is bought and paid for by Jesus Christ. But to get to your final destination, you have to trust the ride.

What does this look like? My experience is that at some point a person's heart that has been leaning away from God *leans toward God*. When your heart leans toward God (and you will know when it does), you are saved.

Another way to think of this is that I ask people to project their lives forward to their deathbed. I ask them to consider who or what they will trust in that moment to get to them to the other side. The only right answer is Jesus.

Pritchard writes, *How much faith does it take to go to heaven? It depends. The answer is not much but all you've got. If you are willing to trust Jesus Christ with as much faith as you happen to have, you can be saved.*[83]

I like that!

Remember my friend Fran and her dying friend, Pat? Remember what I told Pat on her deathbed? *Pat, you are not good enough to go to heaven. But this is not bad news, it is, in fact, good news.*

The good news is that though we are not good enough to get us to heaven, Jesus is. Through his death on the cross he has taken our sins upon himself and given us his righteousness instead.

Pat listened as I shared this good news. She was ready to say *yes* to Jesus—she was ready to get on the airplane. Pat died physically just a few days later. But she was born spiritually and now lives in heaven.

---

[83] Ibid., 129.

THINK ABOUT IT...

* Is your heart leaning *away from* God or *toward* God?
* Imagine that you are on your deathbed. Who or what will you trust to get you to the other side? Science (there *is* no other side)? Your good works? Or Jesus?

LIFE COMMITMENT:

Today I choose to lean my heart toward God, believing that he has forgiven me through the shed blood of Jesus Christ and that through Jesus, I will go to heaven when I die.

You Need Jesus (9)

———⸎———

THE WORD

For I know the plans I have for you," declares the Lord,
"plans to prosper you and not to harm you, plans to
give you hope and a future. Then you will call upon
me and come and pray to me, and I will listen to you.
You will seek me and find me when you seek me with
all your heart. I will be found by you," declares the
Lord, "and will bring you back from captivity."

— JEREMIAH 29.11–14

THOUGHT FOR THE DAY:

Adversity is not simply a tool. It is God's most effective
tool for the advancement of our spiritual lives. The
circumstances and events that we see as setbacks
are oftentimes the very things that launch us into
periods of intense spiritual growth. Once we begin
to understand this, and accept it as a spiritual
fact of life, adversity becomes easier to bear.

~ CHARLES STANLEY

YOU HAVE BEEN THROUGH HELL and you might feel you're still there. But there is hope. Jesus is our ultimate hope for surviving *now* and for thriving in our very near *future*. As difficult as it may be for you to believe, *you will get through this.* Not only will you get through this, but *God will take you from where you are and grow you into the man you were meant to be.*

You may be living in the ruins of shattered dreams, demolished expectations, and the realities of financial loss, a destroyed reputation and diminished social standing. You may feel angry, lonely, exhausted, shamed, embarrassed and sad.

Despite where you are today, God promises that when we come to him, *he will grow you into the man he always wanted you to be.* What looks to us like an ending, can become a new beginning. What looks like a funeral can be a celebration of new birth.

God specializes in taking the horror of Good Friday and turning it into the astonishing victory of Resurrection Sunday. The worse the mess, the more he relishes cleaning it up and bringing forth new life.

The past few days we have talked about salvation—that is, coming to Jesus and trusting him for forgiveness and new life. If you have not made that decision to follow Jesus, I hope you will soon.

If you have already decided to follow Jesus, either in the past few days or years ago, know that he wants you to grow in your faith.

Growing in your faith means that you will become more and more like Jesus. You will come to *love the things God loves and despise the things he despises.* You will react to the situations in your life as Jesus did—with *wisdom and peace, confidence and gentleness.*

You will come to see people as God sees them. You will live with an open hand and warm spirit. You will know what and when to fight, what weapons to use, and what constitutes a victory.

You will change on the inside because you will want to experience God's presence in your life through prayer, reading and consuming his Word (the Bible), being with other Christians, and serving God through your church. God will transform you from the inside out. Following God will not be a burden but a natural outgrowth of your life as you experience more of God's love.

The best is yet to be for you. The second half of your life can be better than the first half. You have a hope and future.

THINK ABOUT IT...

- Am I emotionally, relationally and spiritually where I was five years ago?
- What would it look like for me to grow in these areas?

LIFE COMMITMENT:

Five years from now I don't want to be who I am today. I commit to following God, being transformed by his presence inside so that I will be different on the outside.

You Need Jesus (10)

—∞∞∞—

THE WORD

*On this mountain the Lord Almighty will prepare a
feast of rich food for all peoples, a banquet of aged
wine—the best of meats and the finest of wines. On
this mountain he will destroy the shroud that enfolds
all peoples, the sheet that covers all nations; he will
swallow up death forever. The Sovereign Lord will
wipe away the tears from all faces; he will remove
the disgrace of his people from all the earth.*

— ISAIAH 25.6–8

THOUGHT FOR THE DAY:

Joy is the serious business of heaven.

~ C. S. LEWIS

A FEW DAYS AGO (Day 58) we talked about living between
D-Day and V-E Day. After D-Day nearly everyone knew the
enemy would lose. But it was not until V-E Day that the victory was fully realized. Hitler was dead, Berlin captured, the
war in Europe over.

The point is this: *There will be a day, not too far off, where you and I live in the victory of V-E Day.* For us V-E Day is heaven. If you really understand heaven you will always live with hope because you will know that whatever you are suffering right now is temporary. Your permanent home is heaven.

Heaven is so amazing we simply don't have the language to capture it. As Paul says, *...our light and momentary troubles are achieving for us an eternal glory that **far outweighs them all**.* (2 Corinthians 4.17)

If you think heaven is one long worship service—and that makes you shudder—take heart. If you think heaven will be boring, think again. If you think heaven is one long nap, you are wrong.

Heaven is all about God, and however you feel about that now will be transformed into a burning passion to fulfill those desires as God will empower you. Heaven is about pleasure. The best things that bring you pleasure on earth will be there in heaven in their purest form.

Sarah Young encourages us: *Do not long for the absence of problems in your life. That is an unrealistic goal since in this world you will have trouble. You have an eternity of problem-free living reserved for you in heaven. Rejoice in that inheritance, which no one can take away from you.*[84]

THINK ABOUT IT...

* What images of heaven have been downloaded into your 'hope' drive?

---

[84] Young, *Jesus Calling*, Kindle Location 693.

* Does your picture of heaven encourage you or does heaven seem a distant and rather distasteful destination?
* How would your attitude change if you believed in a heaven that is like a dream vacation destination?

LIFE COMMITMENT:

God's own Son died so that I can have heaven as my final destination. Heaven is a place I want to be and I look forward to going there!

God Can Repair the Damage Done to You (1)

THE WORD

Therefore, as God's chosen people, holy and dearly loved,
clothe yourselves with compassion, kindness, humility,
gentleness and patience. Bear with each other and forgive
whatever grievances you may have against one another.
Forgive as the Lord forgave you. And over all these virtues
put on love, which binds them all together in perfect unity.

— COLOSSIANS 3.12–14

THOUGHT FOR THE DAY:

Thou hast been …
A man that Fortune's buffets and rewards
Has taken with equal thanks …
Give me that man
That is not passion's slave, and I will wear him
In my heart's core, aye, in my heart of hearts
As I do thee.…

~ HAMLET TO HIS FRIEND HORATIO
SHAKESPEARE, *HAMLET*, ACT 3, SCENE 2

WHY IN THE HECK DO we do the things we do? Why did I throw a screwdriver when I was angry during The Great Door Disaster? (See Day 24) Any rational person, including myself, could easily make a determination that throwing a screwdriver inside a house with other people in the room is dangerous and reckless!

When teaching Master-level students an intro class on pastoral ministry I clear stated: *You will never ever benefit from losing your temper. NEVER have I lost my temper as a pastor and later thought it was a good idea.*

Six weeks later on a Sunday night after church I was nose-to-nose with one of my church members! Seriously? I lost my temper *that quickly* after telling 50 students not to?! How can emotions so easily override reason?

The answer is that all of us have been wounded. There is absolutely no way a man will get through childhood without being beat up physically and emotionally.

Painful memories deeply embed themselves into our mind. This is for our survival—we are designed to quickly and efficiently process potentially painful stimuli to avoid dangerous situations. When our senses detect circumstances similar to those from which we were initially wounded, the part of our brain that deals with emotions (the amygdala) takes over from the part of our brain that processes stimuli using reason and sound judgement (the prefrontal cortex). If we touch a hot stove our brain is good at remembering not to do that again. We quickly (without deliberate thought) react emotionally and behaviorally toward self-preservation.

The problem is that all these memories of wounds become tapes we play every time we're in a similar situation.

The summer between second and third grade I went to our school gym to goof around. A bunch of kids were shooting baskets and tossing around those maroon utility balls. One of those utility balls came my way so I kicked it as hard as I could. The ball sailed under the basketball goal, bounced off the wall, and smacked this big fifth grader in the face as he was coming in for a layup! Ouch.

This kid marched over to me and, looking down at me, said something to the effect that he would kill me if I ever did that again. Almost 50 years later this memory is alive and well.

But painful experiences are more than just remembered for a long time. Painful memories inform and instinctively direct our behavior. After I was told I would die at the hands of this fifth grader, *I became afraid of kids older than me and avoided them for years afterward.* That's the power of a single event that took place in less than five minutes.

The events surrounding your divorce have seared new painful memories into your consciousness. What is more, many of the behaviors that led to your divorce were probably instinctive reactions driven by the tapes in your head. In other words, the painful things done to you decades ago can make you do things you would not think possible, like throw a screwdriver across a room.

The great news is that God can *repair* the damage done *to you.* In fact, this is the perfect time to allow God to bring those memories to the surface and heal them.

Determine to get those old tapes out of your head! If you don't, you will continue to *react instinctively* to life rather than *respond thoughtfully* to it.

The second half of your life can be far better than the first half. For that to happen, however, old tapes need to be ejected and tossed in the garbage. More on that the next few days...

Think About It...

* Think back on a time when you reacted in a way that was more instinctive than rational. What were you thinking? What were you feeling?
* What are the most painful memories in your life? How do you think those memories may be influencing your emotions and behaviors today?
* Dredging up old memories can be a daunting task. If you were severely wounded, seek to do this journey with a competent counselor or therapist.

Life Commitment:
I have tapes in my head that short-circuit my thinking. Time to get rid of those old 8-tracks!

God Can Repair the Damage Done to You (2)

—⊷∞⊷—

THE WORD

*Brothers, I do not consider myself yet to have taken
hold of it. But one thing I do: Forgetting what is
behind and straining toward what is ahead, I press
on toward the goal to win the prize for which God
has called me heavenward in Christ Jesus.*

— PHILIPPIANS 3.13-14

THOUGHT FOR THE DAY:

*Nature has placed mankind under the governance
of two sovereign masters, pain and pleasure. It
is for them alone to point out what we ought to
do, as well as to determine what we shall do.*

~ JEREMY BENTHAM

NOBEL PRIZE WINNING PSYCHOLOGIST DANIEL Kahneman[85]
helps us understand how bad memories get out-sized in our

---

[85] Daniel Kahneman, *Thinking, Fast and Slow* (New York: Farrar, Straus
and Giroux, 2015), 912-14.

minds. God can use our understanding of this dynamic to help put our past in perspective.

Kahneman believes we have two selves, the *Experiencing Self* and the *Remembering Self.* The Experiencing Self are the experiences you have in everyday living. For the most part our experiences are not horrifically bad. In fact, for most of us most of the time, we are reasonably physically comfortable and in a state of relative emotional equilibrium.

But even as we experience a mostly comfortable and tolerably happy life, a single bad experience can become the author of our memories. In other words, memories overwrite experiences as we narrate our life history. The *Remembering Self* has power over the *Experiencing Self.*

When I really think back on my childhood I was mostly happy. Seldom was I physically or emotionally uncomfortable. But it's not the normal experiences of day-to-day living that inform most of my memories. I remember the time my dad swung me by ears and threw me into the dining room table. I remember being yelled at and criticized. But I wasn't *always* criticized. And I was tossed around *only one time.* In reality, my dad often affirmed and encouraged me and took good care of me.

What's more, Kahneman has shown that a *good experience that ends badly* will be remembered *only as a bad and painful experience.* Let's say you go on vacation with your spouse. For 99.99% of this vacation things are wonderful. But on the way home from the airport you get into an argument. Years later you will tend to remember the argument, not the great vacation, and you will think of the entire vacation as an unpleasant experience.

What does this mean for you right now? As God repairs your past, consider these points:

- **Allow God to 'right-size' your memories.** Realize that your painful memories describe only a tiny fraction of your overall life experience. What should be a brief memory has overwhelmed how you think about your past. Ask God to shrink these overly huge negative memories to their proper size. Don't let the negative override the positive in your life.
- **Determine to go forward with God.** The Apostle Paul says, *One thing I do: Forgetting what is behind and straining toward what is ahead.* (Philippians 3.13) Paul had a lot to forget. Before he came to Christ Paul focused his considerable energy into destroying Christ's church. But in God's power, Paul put that behind him and reached for the goal in front of him.

God has a future for you. You won't reach God's future for you if the tapes of outsized memories from your past constantly replace thoughts of his presence and power in your life. Paul goes on to say, *I press on toward the goal to win the prize for which God has called me heavenward in Christ Jesus.* How positive is that?!

- Be patient. Paul says, *Brothers, I do not consider myself yet to have taken hold of it.* Amen to honesty! Paul acknowledges that the battle in our minds is constant but it *is* winnable!

THINK ABOUT IT...

* What do you think about most of the time?
* When you recall the past, what thoughts usually come to mind? Are they negative, unhappy remembrances or mostly positive?
* What negative tapes hold you back from the pursuit of God's future for you?

LIFE COMMITMENT:

I do not consider myself yet to have taken hold of it. But one thing I do: Forgetting what is behind and straining toward what is ahead, I press on toward the goal to win the prize for which God has called me heavenward in Christ Jesus.

God Can Repair the Damage Done to You (3)

———— ∞∞∞ ————

THE WORD

Do not conform any longer to the pattern of this world,
but be transformed by the renewing of your mind.

— ROMANS 12.2

THOUGHT FOR THE DAY:

The human capacity for burden is like bamboo—far
more flexible than you'd ever believe at first glance.

~ JODI PICOULT

GOD CAN *REPAIR* THE DAMAGE done *to you.*

In September 2009, my (then) wife and I traveled to Gulu in the northern part of Uganda. Just weeks before, Joseph Kony, the evil leader of the misnamed *Lord's Resistance Army,* had just been pushed out of Uganda into the Central African Republic (CAR). We visited a church and an orphanage in this war-ravaged part of the world.

Kony's brutality is infamous. To build his army, Kony's soldiers raided schools and homes in the night stealing children. As the terror spread, thousands of children in northern Uganda would walk from the countryside into the towns, including Gulu, spending the night wherever they could, usually on the streets.

At least 30,000 children were abducted and became child soldiers. Kids as young as six were taught to shoot and kill. Often they were forced to slaughter family members or friends. The brutality is beyond the capacity of language to describe and the human soul to fully absorb. My wife and I left Gulu on the charter flight back to Kampala amazed that anyone could survive such cruelty.

That night at a conference at Kampala Pentecostal Church we heard several former child soldiers tell their stories. These young men and women had been trapped in Kony's icy grip just a year before. While I had been sleeping in a nice bed and enjoying good food and friends, these young women and men were sleeping on the ground, terrified at what the morning would bring and living with the horror of what they had been forced to do to others.

Remember what we talked about yesterday—how a single bad experience will be remembered over all the good experiences in life. These children's experiences were *not* good. Their experiences were overwhelmingly horrific most of the time. Surely the memories of those horrible experiences would dominate their every waking moment. *But these kids proved that God is bigger than our experiences and he can right-size our memories*—even the most horrific memories.

God's power to repair their past was clear as these young men and women told their stories. Their tales all started the same way—they were happy children sleeping in their home or dorm when LRA soldiers raided their village or school and snatched them. They were ripped from family and friends. They were made to do atrocious things. Then they planned and executed a daring escape.

Here's what stuck out in my mind as I listened. The amount of time each speaker dedicated to the horror of his/her experience was only about 10%. The rest of their story (90%) was about God's victory in their lives.

These kids had experienced more trauma in their short lives than most people in a lifetime. But these young men and women did not let that trauma define them. Instead, they did exactly what Paul encouraged: *Forget what is behind and strain toward what is ahead... press on toward the goal to win the prize for which God has called us heavenward in Christ Jesus.* (Philippians 3.13-14)

With huge smiles and contagious joy, these former child soldiers told of how God rescued them from their plight. They overflowed with gratitude as they shared how God was healing them of the trauma they experienced. They were overwhelmingly hopeful about their future. Filled with optimism of their future with God, each young man and woman knew that telling their story was a rich opportunity to give glory to God and to make him famous. They were *pressing on toward the goal to win the prize for which God has called [them] heavenward in Christ Jesus.*

Repairing your past is not a simple, one-time event accomplished by any single thing you can do. It's a process that takes time. But these young women and men proved that God *can* take our pain, right-size it, and move us into an amazingly bright and hopeful future.

Divorce is an experience where we are *snatched up* into a new and painful reality. It hurts. If you have just been recently snatched into this reality, hold on. Don't give up. God can rescue you and repair your heart and soul from this experience.

Maybe you are further down the road of the divorce journey. The immediate crisis has passed and you are settling into a new but uncomfortable reality. And yet you keep playing over and over the painful tapes in your head of what has happened. You are counting your losses and you alternate between intense anger and sadness. If this is you, don't despair. God can repair the damage done to you. If you cooperate with God, one day you will be able to tell others of God's rescue, repair and restoration of your life.

To repair your past God needs your cooperation. Gary Thomas says, *God is the agent of change, but we have a responsibility to surrender ourselves to God's change.*[86]

If the negative, painful tapes of what has happened to you—either recently or in your distant past—are ruling your mind, surrender to God. Ask him to change the tape. Tell him you are ready to cooperate with his transformative work in your mind.

THINK ABOUT IT...

* When you read the story of the child soldiers of Uganda, what came to mind?
* What childhood memories dominate your thinking? Can you trust God to re-size those memories and repair them?

---

[86] Gary Thomas, *Simply Sacred: Daily Readings* (Grand Rapids: Zondervan, 2011), Kindle Location 1239.

PRAYER:

God, only you can repair me. I surrender myself to you and your power to resize my memories and give me hope for my future.

God Can Repair the Damage Done to You (4)

—⚬⚬⚬—

THE WORD

Finally, brothers, whatever is true, whatever is noble, whatever is right, whatever is pure, whatever is lovely, whatever is admirable—if anything is excellent or praiseworthy—think about such things.

— PHILIPPIANS 4.8–9

THOUGHT FOR THE DAY:

Never let the inmates run the asylum.

~ CHRISSY SCIVICQUE

ALL OF US TALK TO ourselves. The moment we wake up in the morning this conversation from one 'self' to the other 'self' begins. Part of you is talking to your deeper self.

This internal conversation is the stuff of life and determines the course of your life. What are you saying to yourself?

Humans have the unique capacity to step away from ourselves and become our own observers. The more we do this more human we are. The less we do this the more animal-like we are.

So... stop and listen to the conversation you are having with yourself. The content of this conversation will tell you what you believe. Some of the things you believe empower you, moving you forward in life. Some of your beliefs hold you back.

To determine the beliefs that are holding you back, **pay attention to your thoughts that make you feel fear**. Beliefs that cause you to feel fear are mostly likely the beliefs holding you back.

I like adventures—hiking, cycling, kayaking. My favorite is cycling. I have two bikes I ride, one for outside and a second mounted on an indoor trainer. Winters are made for the indoor trainer. Summers are for glorious outside rides. Every year as winter turns to summer *it takes me a while to get on my outside bike!* Why?

Honestly, I am slow to ride outside because my indoor trainer is familiar and safe. In contrast, outside rides pose very real dangers. Last summer I almost got tangled up with a pickup truck and the huge boat he was hauling behind him. A slight miscalculation would have sent me under the wheels of the boat trailer and that couldn't have possibly turned out good.

On another occasion, I ingloriously slid through an intersection on a rainy day. Embarrassing and painful! Another time my wheels caught the edge of the road and I fell over the curb. I wasn't going fast but I jacked my hand when I hit the grass. It took a year for it to not hurt when I shook hands with someone.

So even when the spring brings a much-welcomed warm day, I have a twinge of fear as I think about making the ride outside. *This fear is irrational.* Riding outside is far better than watching Netflix while pounding away on my indoor trainer! And though I have taken a few spills on my bike outside, the reality is that I have ridden tens of thousands of miles accident free!

My irrational and out-sized fear is driven by a belief that is limiting me.

All of us have these limiting beliefs. Divorce will inevitably bring these beliefs to the surface and may even become so dominant as to paralyze you.

Ask God to show you these limiting beliefs that dominate your self-talk. The roots of these limiting beliefs are most likely the result of something traumatic done to you in past, even decades ago.

What are you telling yourself?

Think about this: The truth of the matter is that if we spoke to others the way we speak to ourselves, they'd probably accuse us of emotional abuse.[87]

Wow, that is probably true for most of us! Would you say to others what you are saying to yourself? If you did, how do you think they would feel after you hammered them as you are hammering yourself? How do you think they would eventually begin to behave if you kept pounding away at them?

---

[87] *"How to Delete That Negative Voice in Your Brain,"* accessed March 06, 2017, https://www.dumblittleman.com/how-to-delete-that-negative-voice-in/. I also recommend Chris Thurman, *The Lies We Believe* (Nashville: T. Nelson, 2003).

Now that you have insight into what you are saying, why you are saying what you are saying, and how your internal conversation is probably impacting your attitude, emotions, happiness and behaviors, ***throw those thoughts away!*** Get rid of them.

In their place, put something POSITIVE and TRUE.

For my bike and me, fears of crashing are replaced with the thought of sinking my hot sweaty body into the cool Blanco River at mile 15 on my bike ride! Doubts about if I can make it are met with the truth that I *have* made this 30-mile ride often, and when I finish *I never regret having made the ride!*

What would you tell someone who is going through a hard time? Now, tell those things to yourself!

Think About It...

* Step back and analyze the conversations you have with yourself.
* Write down the fear-based lies you say to yourself:

_____

_____

_____

_____

_____

* Would you say to others any of these things you are saying to yourself?
* Now write down three truths about yourself that you can use to replace the negative self-talk that has been running through your head. If you are having

trouble coming up with something, refer to this website: https://goo.gl/DiOXup.

A brief word: I know you may think this is stupid and trite and a touchy-feely thing that you would never share in your small group (if you have a small group) and you sure as hell would never venture to explore with other guys at the hunting camp. Forget that all that. Just try it and see what happens.

_____

_____

_____

_____

_____

LIFE COMMITMENT:
I am more than the lies I keep telling myself. I refute those lies and replace them with the truth about who I am and what I am capable of.

God Can Forgive the Damage You Have Done to Others (1)

———⊗⊗⊗———

THE WORD

Let the wicked forsake his way and the evil man his thoughts. Let him turn to the Lord, and he will have mercy on him, and to our God, for he will freely pardon.

— ISAIAH 55.7

THOUGHT FOR THE DAY:

Here's some excellent counsel: Become a good repenter. The only way to move forward in God is through repentance. If your pride hinders you from repenting, get over it. You're a wretch. You need mercy so badly it's scary. Wise up and master the art of repentance. Call your sin in its worst possible terms. Grovel. Eat dust.

~ BOB SORGE

THE LIGHT WE SEE WITH our most powerful telescopes has been traveling about 13.8 billion years. Since that light left its source, the universe has continued to expand. It is believed, then, that the actual distance from us to the edge of the observable universe is about 46 billion light years.[88]

I would contend, however, that the greatest distance in the universe is not from one end of the universe to the other but rather *the distance from a man's knee to the ground.*

Men, we are prideful beings. We are taught *not* to bend the knee.

We are taught from the earliest moments of life to suck it up, stand tall, take it like a man. We celebrate men like Clint Eastwood, Charles Bronson, Arnold Schwarzenegger and Sly Stallone. For some weird reason we voraciously consume violent movies where men fight hand-to-hand and blow away anything in sight with a vast array of (cool) weapons. Tough. Strong. Unbending.

But are these guys real? When was the last time you were actually in a fist-fight? When have you pointed a gun at and much less actually shot someone? Where does all this stuff come from? What does it mean?

Our culture celebrates winning at all costs. We revere those who have made it to the top even if we know they got there by climbing on the backs of everyone else. We celebrate images of strength, endurance, toughness and an unyielding, stubborn spirit—especially this unyielding, stubborn spirit.

But it's that unyielding, stubborn, prideful spirit that gets us in trouble. Maybe you are divorced because of your stubborn spirit. Maybe you *did* hit someone such as your (now)

---

[88] *"How big is the universe?"* accessed March 08, 2017, https://phys.org/news/2015-10-big-universe.html.

ex-wife, and that's the reason you are divorced and/or in prison.

Whatever your situation, I can assure you that you and I have caused damage to others because of our prideful, un-yielding, stubborn spirit.

If you honestly believe that your sin has not caused dam-age to others, ask God to show you who he really is and who you really are. That's a daring request. I dare you.

When God reveals to you who you really are, you will be stunned. You will get a glimpse of God as he is—*holy, perfect, all-knowing, all-seeing, all-powerful.*

And you will see yourself as you really are—*tiny, insignifi-cant, dirty, selfish, puny.*

In that moment, *don't despair.*

Even though what God reveals to you is true, the larger truth is that the very same holy, perfect, powerful God who could crush you in a split-second is the same God who will-ingly went to the cross and died the most humiliating death so you could be raised to new life.

Jesus shows us the way: the way up is down. The way for you to really stand tall on sure and steady legs is to bend low on your knees.

The Apostle James was tougher than any man you know. He rallied the church in Jerusalem when Christians were being hunted down and killed. This wasn't a movie—his people really were being killed. James boldly led the church through a huge church squabble (Acts 15) that would have enormous implications for at least the next 2,000 years. Clint Eastwood nor any other man we think strong couldn't hold a candle to James.

James' advice? *Humble yourselves before the Lord, and he will lift you up.* (James 4.10)

To humble ourselves means to go down on the knee before God and admit that he is God and we are not. It's to confess our sins to him. It is to acknowledge the damage our sins have done to others. It's to bend low before God so he can lift us up.

God can *repair* the damage done *to you.* And God can *forgive* the damage you have done *to others,* including your ex-wife. What others have done to you is *repairable.* What you have done to others is *repentable.*

THINK ABOUT IT...

- Have you humbled yourself before God? (If you have, you will know it.)
- If you haven't, I dare you: Ask God to show you things *as they really are.* If you thought prayer was for the weak, you have not prayed this prayer.
- Ask God to show you who he is.
- Next, ask God to show you who you are.
- Lastly, God to reveal to you how to bridge the gap between who you are *now* and who you were meant to be.

PRAYER:

God, show me who you are. Show me who I am. Show me how to be the man you want me to be.

God Can Forgive the Damage You Have Done to Others (2)

———— ✣ ————

THE WORD

From that time on Jesus began to preach,
"Repent, for the kingdom of heaven is near."

— MATTHEW 4.17

THOUGHT FOR THE DAY:

It remains a startling story to those who never
understand that the men and women who are truly
filled with light are those who have gazed deeply
into the darkness of their imperfect existence.

~ BRENNAN MANNING

A WIFE CATCHES HER HUSBAND looking at internet porn. She is devastated. She comes to me (as pastor) for counseling. I call the husband. He agrees to come in. We sit together in my office. He sheepishly confesses to looking at porn. She cries. We begin to probe. He slowly confesses to more. He has seen another woman but they didn't touch. Then he confessed that they did, but only one time. And only one woman. But there's more. More women, more sex, more devastation.

His wife is distraught beyond words. She is furious, sad, terrified. She weeps uncontrollably. He shrinks in his chair. He realizes he is losing her. So he repents. He says he is sorry, he will never do it again, what was he thinking. She cries more. He repents more.

A week later she is back in my office. She has one question: *Has he really repented?*

How does she know if his repentance is real? How does she know he has changed? How does she know he won't do it again, crushing her already fragile and fractured heart? This is a critical question for each of us. How do we know if we are really repenting?

The first thing to know is that *the ability of the male human to rationalize bad behavior is stunning.* Denial is not just a river in Egypt as the saying goes. We must be suspicious about ourselves and how we are thinking.

Every time we excuse, minimize, rationalize, or point the finger of blame, we are participating in that system of denial.[89] Are you making excuses for your behavior? Are you blaming someone else? Are you minimizing the impact of your behavior on others?

The second thing to note is that, *The best ally of God is* <u>*what is*</u>—*not what should be, what could be, or what needs to be.*

---

[89] Tripp, *New Morning*, Kindle Location 3600.

God and grace can always work with the real; it's the unreal, the fabricated, the illusory that God cannot build on. There's nothing there![90]

It takes a big man to face himself squarely. And if you don't face yourself now you will surely be doomed to repeat the same mistakes that got you here in the first place. To become the man God wants you to be takes facing head on who we are right now.

I realize that there are two sides to every story. I also know that in divorce one party is usually more to blame than the other. I realize that you may be less to blame in this divorce than your ex-wife. On the other hand, you may be the principle reason for the divorce. Maybe you are that man who has sat in my office so often: a cheater who is now reaping what you sowed.

Either way, God wants to change us. He wants to transform us so that he is glorified and your life is better. He wants to make you a trophy of his grace.

Yesterday I asked you to take a huge dare: *Ask God to show you who you really are.* Did you pray that prayer? For you and me to get well, we must admit we are sick. Maybe you need a heart transplant. Maybe you just need some tweaking in the gym. Either way, we all have things we need to repent of. Repentance is realizing we are sick and that we desperately need God to transform us.

---

[90] Rohr, Durepos and McGrath, *On the Threshold of Transformation*, 153. Emphasis mine.

Think About It...

* *Excusing, minimizing, rationalizing, blaming...* ouch. Do a personal inventory of where you are guilty of each of these things. Here is a hint: Think about when you have been angry. What makes you angry? Now think about what you are thinking when you are angry. For instance, *I am furious that she left me because I just watched a little bit of porn.* Now, ask yourself about how you may be minimizing watching porn and thus excusing your behavior.

_____

_____

_____

_____

_____

Life Commitment:

I commit to a deep look into myself. For God's glory and my good and the good of those around me, I will look deep inside and face up to who I am, the good, the bad, and the ugly.

God Can Forgive the Damage You Have Done to Others (3) [91]

———— ∞∞∞ ————

THE WORD

Or do you show contempt for the riches of his
kindness, tolerance and patience, not realizing that
God's kindness leads you toward repentance?

— ROMANS 2.4

THOUGHT FOR THE DAY:

People change when they hurt enough that
they have to, learn enough that they want to,
and receive enough that they are able to.

~JOHN MAXWELL

WE BEGAN THIS JOURNEY TO healing from divorce with a discussion of pain. We said, quoting Richard Rohr, that *Pain that is not transformed is transmitted.*[92] The transformation of your pain

---

[91] Much of the teaching in the next several chapters comes from: *S.A.L.T.: Seven Areas of Life Training* (Phoenix, AZ: Victorious Christian Living International, 2006), 149-57.

[92] See Days 2-4.

begins with true repentance. Like the wife in my office who is asking me if her cheating husband's repentance is real or not, you and I need to ask ourselves if our repentance is true or false.

A simple test of if your repentance is true or false is the *direction of your heart*. If your heart, revealed by your thoughts, is focused inward toward the self, you are not truly repenting. If, however, your heart is focused on God and others, you are on the road to true repentance.

The most famous case of false repentance in the Bible is when King Saul, for purely selfish reasons, failed to fully obey God. Saul was commanded to eliminate a group of people (the Amalekites) and their possessions in battle. *Why* God commanded this is a discussion for another day.

Saul failed in his mission because he wanted to keep the spoils of war for himself. He wanted personal glory and riches, so he kept the best of the Amalekite livestock and erected a monument to himself!

But the Prophet Samuel came calling. When Samuel confronted Saul, Saul went on a false repentance binge.

What are the signs of false repentance?

* **<u>Making excuses for self-indulgence</u>**. Saul was to keep nothing of the battle for himself, yet he clearly did. His actions betrayed what he was supposed to do. This is like a man excusing his porn-viewing by saying he has an ugly wife. Porn is porn and it's not to be viewed *no matter the circumstances.*

* **<u>Saul lied about the facts of the case.</u>** The Bible says that *When Samuel reached [Saul], Saul said, "The Lord*

bless you! I have carried out the Lord's instructions. (1 Samuel 15.13)

Uh... no he hadn't. Saul lied about the facts of the case in order to preserve his image and excuse his behavior, plain and simple.

* **He used religion as a cover**: *But Samuel said, "What then is this bleating of sheep in my ears? What is this lowing of cattle that I hear?" Saul answered, "The soldiers brought them from the Amalekites; they spared the best of the sheep and cattle to sacrifice to the Lord your God, but we totally destroyed the rest.* (1 Samuel 15:14–15)

Pardon the pun, but *bull*! Saul wanted those cows and sheep for himself!

* **Saul blamed the people for his pain**: *The soldiers took sheep and cattle from the plunder...* (1 Samuel 15.21)

Shifting blame and playing the victim are sure signs of false repentance. These are classic tactics for image management and avoiding consequences for one's actions.

* **Saul tried to wiggle out of the consequences of his disobedience**: Saul replied, *"I have sinned. But please honor me before the elders of my people and before Israel...* (1 Samuel 15.30) Again, classic image management.

* **Saul becomes demanding**: *Then Saul said to Samuel, "I have sinned. I violated the Lord's command and your instructions. I was afraid of the people and so I gave in to them. Now I beg you, **forgive my sin and come back with me**, so that I may worship the Lord."*

> *But Samuel said to him, "I will not go back with you.*
> *You have rejected the word of the Lord, and the Lord has*
> *rejected you as king over Israel!"*
>
> *As Samuel turned to leave,* **Saul caught hold of the**
> **hem of his robe,** *and it tore. Samuel said to him, "The Lord*
> *has torn the kingdom of Israel from you today and has giv-*
> *en it to one of your neighbors—to one better than you."* (1
> Samuel 15.24–29)

Lying, making excuses, shifting blame, minimizing, playing
the victim, demanding—all drizzled with a slathering of reli-
giosity! False repentance at its best!

False repentance is focused on self-preservation. The
man who is falsely repenting is trying to sell just enough repentance to get himself out of trouble. False repentance says
what you think the other wants to hear in order to make
yourself feel better *rather than genuine concern for how you have
hurt the other.* False repenters have a wounded heart, not a
broken heart.

THINK ABOUT IT...

* *Lying, making excuses, shifting blame, minimizing, playing the victim, demanding...* Which of these is in your
ammo box? When have you loaded them into the
chamber and pulled trigger? What happened?
* Honestly, is your repentance really just false
repentance?

LIFE COMMITMENT:
I am sick of playing these stupid games. God, lead me to and into true repentance.

God Can Forgive the Damage You Have Done to Others (4)

———— ∞ ————

THE WORD

Godly sorrow brings repentance that leads to salvation
and leaves no regret, but worldly sorrow brings death.
See what this godly sorrow has produced in you:
what earnestness, what eagerness to clear yourselves,
what indignation, what alarm, what longing,
what concern, what readiness to see justice done.

— 2 CORINTHIANS 7.10–11

THOUGHT FOR THE DAY:

Real repentance shuts its mouth. Real repentance
has nothing more to say in addition to "I have
sinned." Real repentance makes no demands.
Real repentance accepts the consequences.

~ JEFF CRIPPEN

IF FALSE REPENTANCE IS INWARDLY focused on managing your image and minimizing painful consequences, it stands to reason that true repentance lets go of image management, accepts responsibility for the consequences, and focuses outward toward God and others.

King David (the same King David who received the kingdom after Saul screwed it up) also failed miserably. But his reaction to being confronted in his sin is completely different than Saul. David truly repented.

Briefly, here's what happened, and it's a doozy (refer to Day __**Error! Reference source not found.** for a refresher on this one). Late in his reign, King David decided to take it easy. Instead of leading his men into battle he decided to hang back at the castle and let his second in command lead. While loitering around the castle he noticed a beautiful woman, Bathsheba, taking a bath. *Sans* Viagra, David demanded Bathsheba sleep with him (a serious abuse of power).

Problem: Bathsheba became pregnant.

To fix this problem, David had Bathsheba's husband, Uriah, recalled from the battle field (where Uriah has been risking his life for his king's kingdom while the king slept with his wife!). David was hoping Uriah would use the break from battle to sleep with his wife, thus avoiding the painful consequences of being a cheating and indulgent king while his men died for him in his battles.

Uriah was a better man than David. He simply would not indulge himself while his brothers were struggling on the battlefield. Not one to give up, David tried again. He invited Uriah for dinner, got him drunk and sent him home. Again, Uriah took the high road.

David didn't and it cost Uriah his life. The next day David sent Uriah back to the battlefield with a carefully constructed scheme to have him left alone on the front line—a sure way to get rid of this pesky husband.

So guys, David is an adulterer *and* a murderer! Wow! But in all his male glory, he had convinced himself that he was OK and would get out of this one unscathed.

God had other plans. God revealed to Nathan, David's advisor, what David had done. At great personal risk, Nathan confronted King David (see 2 Samuel 12). In that critical moment David had a decision to make: suck it up and own what he had done or try lying, making excuses, shifting blame, minimizing or playing the victim.

David chose the high road by bending low before the Lord. Psalm 51 is David's response to Nathan's confrontation:

I know my transgressions, and my sin is always before me. Against you, you only, have I sinned and done what so that you are proved right when you speak and justified when you judge. (Psalm 51:3–4)

That is... God, you are right and I am wrong. No excuses. I did it. I committed adultery and murder. I have sinned against Bathsheba, destroying her family. I murdered a good man. And I tried to cover it up and run away from it all. I own it. It's mine—all of it. I am to blame.

While false repentance is inwardly focused on self-preservation, true repentance is a pivot away from yourself toward God and toward others. True repentance confesses all of what one did as wrong *and then shuts up.*

True repentance is really an act of faith. It takes faith to believe that God is good and he will forgive you and that he will preserve you through the storm better than you can preserve yourself.

True repentance speaks the truth, takes the blame and lets go of demands.

THINK ABOUT IT...

* Where are you on this repentance thing? Focused on self or truly broken before God?
* We all want to be men. True men own what is theirs. Can you own up to yourself before God and others? Will you trust that God can preserve your future better than you can? I hope so.

PRAYER:

God, you are right and I am wrong. No excuses. I did it. I have sinned against you and _____. I have tried to cover up my sin and run away from it all. No more. I own it. It's mine—all of it. I am to blame. I ask your forgiveness and humbly place myself in your care. I trust you to forgive me and give me a better future than I could give myself by holding on to false repentance.

Between Surviving & Thriving

———— ∞ ————

THE WORD

It is good and proper for a man to eat and drink, and
to find satisfaction in his toilsome labor under the
sun during the few days of life God has given him.

— ECCLESIASTES 5.18

THOUGHT FOR THE DAY:

If you're going through hell, keep going.

~ WINSTON CHURCHILL

I DESCRIBED EARLIER WHAT I experienced when I walked in from a 38-hour journey from Tanzania that October day only to have my wife inform that she was leaving me. I was crushed beyond words. My thoughts spiraled out of control as my soul struggled to figure out what *had happened*, what *was happening* and *what could possibly happen* to my future.

I distinctly remember saying to myself that my goal was to ride this wave, to grab on to the Rock and hold on through the storm. I knew that whatever my long-term future looked like I would never make it there if I didn't survive the short-term shit storm.

When people are devastated by crushing news the first order of business is survival. But God made us for more than mere survival. He designed us to thrive as we live out the purpose for which he made us.

I fervently believe you will survive and I believe you will thrive. That's why the mission statement for Men's Divorce Recovery says:

*Men's Divorce Recovery exists to Empower Divorced Men through Support, Knowledge and Encouragement to **Survive and Thrive beyond their divorce** to become Resilient, Strong and Wise men in their world.*

You may be in survival mode. You are riding out the storm. You are clinging to the Rock. Survival for you may look doubtful. If surviving seems iffy, thriving will definitely seem a distant, diminishing hope.

But here is some hope for you right now: There is a place between merely surviving and totally thriving. It is in this place that God will give you some moments of enjoyment.

As you move through the survival stage you can expect God to give you moments of enjoyment and happiness. They will probably be brief but these moments are real.

These glimpses of joy and hope may come from the things that gave you joy before like hiking or woodworking or reading or fishing. As you regain strength, try to do some of the things that brought joy to you before.

On the other hand, God may bring some new things into your life. Who knew bird watching could be so energizing! The symphony? Seriously? Country music? Rap? OK, maybe we are pushing the limits! Or maybe not.

You just never know what God will do in your future! Just know this: He loves you and has a plan for you that will include your deepest desires coupled with the world's greatest needs. It is in that happy place that you will know you are thriving. Until then, look for some spots along the trail where the views are stunning, the breeze refreshing, the water crystal clear.

Think About It...

* Where are you on this journey? Are you in survival mode? Are you fully thriving? Or are you somewhere along the path between these two places?
* As you think of your life right now, where are some places of enjoyment and happiness?
* Has God brought into your life some new desires? Has he put you into unexpected places of hope and healing?

Life Commitment:

Even if life looks totally black right now, I can expect God to bring into my life some new places of happiness and enjoyment, even if brief.

What You Hear is Important

THE WORD

Whether you turn to the right or to the left,
your ears will hear a voice behind you,
saying, "This is the way; walk in it.

— ISAIAH 30.21

THOUGHT FOR THE DAY:

Those who trust His voice must learn to hear it above
all other voices out there. And the only way to do that
is to hear the other voices and still choose His.

~ CHRISTIEGREEN

REMEMBER ELIJAH, THE PROPHET? (see Day 54). He was a mighty man when facing off with the prophets of Baal. But when Queen Jezebel threatened his life he ran! The Bible says that *"Elijah was afraid and ran for his life"*! (1 Kings 19.3) Man, that is low!

Elijah hit the mother of all lows: *He came to a broom tree, sat down under it and prayed that he might die. "I have had enough, Lord,"* he said. *"Take my life; I am no better than my ancestors." Then he lay down under the tree and fell asleep.* (vs. 4–5)

Life can turn on a dime. We can go from the mountain-top of success to the pit of despair with just a few shifts in circumstances. We can go from amazing strength and confidence to debilitating weakness. In those moments it may seem God has left us. *Exactly the opposite is true.* God is ready to fill us up when we are emptied out.

In Elijah's 'broom tree' moment God gave him food and sleep. Then God called him to the mountain:

And the word of the Lord came to [Elijah]: "What are you doing here, Elijah?"

He replied, "I have been very zealous for the Lord God Almighty. The Israelites have rejected your covenant, broken down your altars, and put your prophets to death with the sword. I am the only one left, and now they are trying to kill me too."

The Lord said, "Go out and stand on the mountain in the presence of the Lord, for the Lord is about to pass by."

Then a great and powerful wind tore the mountains apart and shattered the rocks before the Lord, but the Lord was not in the wind.

After the wind there was an earthquake, but the Lord was not in the earthquake.

After the earthquake came a fire, but the Lord was not in the fire.

And after the fire came a gentle whisper. *When Elijah heard it, he pulled his cloak over his face and went out and stood at the mouth of the cave.* (1 Kings 19.9–13, emphasis mine)

Earth, wind and fire... we live in a cacophony of sound. Just look at a cable news channel. On one screen there are seven inputs of information—a talking head, pictures, tickers, sidebars. Unbelievable!

God is not in this noise. His voice is above and beneath and beyond the noise.

God wants to guide you. He longs to show you the way. The key is to be still and listen for his gentle whisper. The key is to be still and listen for his *above and beneath and beyond voice.* If you are under the broom tree wishing you had never been born, *you can expect God to speak to you.*

When he does, you can be amazed but don't be surprised. His conversation with us is to be the norm, not the exception.[93]

God knows your troubles. He hears your cry. He is ready to provide for you (food and sleep) and to talk with you (*after the fire came a gentle whisper*). At the right time he will give you a new mission, a new purpose for the rest of your life. And he will let you know that you are not alone.

As you read the end of Elijah's story (below), look for these actions of God:

> *When Elijah heard [God's voice], he pulled his cloak over his face and went out and stood at the mouth of the cave.*
>
> *Then a voice said to him, "What are you doing here, Elijah?"*

---

[93] Willard reminds us that *God wants to be wanted, to be wanted enough that we are ready, predisposed, to find him present with us. And if, by contrast, we are ready and set to find ways of explaining away his gentle overtures, he will rarely respond with fire from heaven. More likely, he will simply leave us alone; and we shall have the satisfaction of thinking ourselves not to be gullible.* Willard and Johnson, *Hearing God*, 273.

He replied, "I have been very zealous for the Lord God Almighty. The Israelites have rejected your covenant, broken down your altars, and put your prophets to death with the sword. I am the only one left, and now they are trying to kill me too."

The Lord said to him, "Go back the way you came, and go to the Desert of Damascus. When you get there, anoint Hazael king over Aram. Also, anoint Jehu son of Nimshi king over Israel, and anoint Elisha son of Shaphat from Abel Meholah to succeed you as prophet.

Jehu will put to death any who escape the sword of Hazael, and Elisha will put to death any who escape the sword of Jehu. **Yet I reserve seven thousand in Israel**—*all whose knees have not bowed down to Baal and all whose mouths have not kissed him." (1 Kings 19.13–18, emphasis mine)*

THINK ABOUT IT...

* How has God spoken to you in the past?
* What did Jesus mean when he said in John 10.27 *"My sheep listen to my voice; I know them, and they follow me"*?
* If you have not heard God speak to you, ask him to. Then take some time to read the Bible (his main voice to us), be still in his presence, and open your heart and mind to the possibility that he really does want to speak to you, guiding you through this storm and giving you a new purpose for your life.

LIFE COMMITMENT:
I believe God wants to speak with me, guiding me through this storm into a future with a mission and purpose.

What You Say is Important

—⚬⚬⚬—

THE WORD

> *From the fruit of his lips a man enjoys good things,*
> *but the unfaithful have a craving for violence.*

— PROVERBS 13.2

THOUGHT FOR THE DAY:

> *What starts out as a sound, ends in a deed.*

~ ABRAHAM JOSHUA HERSCHEL

IT IS ENTIRELY POSSIBLE THAT you are divorced because of things you said or didn't say. In fact, it is *inevitable* that this is the case. As I look back on my marriage I know I should *not* have said some things. And I know that some things were never said that *I most certainly should have said.*

Our words are the currency of relationships. They are the ships that transport our lives, the cars that move us through the days. It is said that only 7% of communication is in our actual words, the rest is through body language. I really doubt that. The content of our words is critical, far beyond a mere 7%.

Gary Thomas says that

The mouth reveals what the heart conceals. If we allow our tongues to become God's servants, there is no end to the good God can do through us. There is no limit to the encouragement he can unleash, the number of people he can turn from their sins, and the communities he can build.[94]

First we make our choices, then our choices make us. We can and must make good choices with our words. The power to hurt or to heal with our words is incredible.

Remember James, the Christian leader who shepherded the early church through incredible persecution? He has some things to say about the tongue:

The tongue is a small part of the body, but it makes great boasts. Consider what a great forest is set on fire by a small spark. The tongue also is a fire, a world of evil among the parts of the body. It corrupts the whole person, sets the whole course of his life on fire, and is itself set on fire by hell.

All kinds of animals, birds, reptiles and creatures of the sea are being tamed and have been tamed by man, but no man can tame the tongue. It is a restless evil, full of deadly poison.

With the tongue we praise our Lord and Father, and with it we curse men, who have been made in God's likeness. Out of the same mouth come praise and cursing. My brothers, this should not be. (James 3.5–10)

---

[94] Gary Thomas, *Holy Available: What If Holiness Is About More Than What We Don't Do?* (Grand Rapids: Zondervan, 2009), 75-76.

The trouble with our words are that we always feel justified in saying them *when we say them.* Always. The fact that we often regret what we have said is proof that we are sometimes not justified in what we say.

Given this reality, choose to use words well in this crisis of divorce. How you and I respond is important and will shape the lives of those around us, especially our children.

A couple of thoughts to leave you with:

Raise your words, not your voice. It is rain that grows flowers, not thunder.

~ RUMI

The secret of being boring is to say everything.

~ VOLTAIRE

THINK ABOUT IT...

* I have most regretted what I have said. My second greatest regret is what I did not say. What do you need to say?
* The Apostle James wrote, *The tongue is a small part of the body, but it makes great boasts. Consider what a great forest is set on fire by a small spark. The tongue also is a fire.* Fires cause damage but they can be put out. What fires have you started with your tongue need to be quenched? What do you need to say to put those fires out?

LIFE COMMITMENT:
Though I feel justified when I say what I say, I know that, in retro-spect, I am often not. I will to think before I speak.

You Aren't as Brilliant as You Think

THE WORD

*He has showed you, O man, what is good. And what
does the Lord require of you? To act justly and to
love mercy and to walk humbly with your God.*

— MICAH 6.8

THOUGHT FOR THE DAY:

*What it all boils down to is this: one day a man must
wake up and realize, "I'm a complete dumb ass, and
I'm sick and tired of being sick and tired." Mature
spirituality might well begin only at that point.*

~ RICHARD ROHR

WHEN MY SON WAS 13-YEARS-OLD he traveled with us to
Tanzania. It so happened that the local Masai clan was gathering from miles around for their annual initiation ceremony. A good friend invited us to the celebrations.

We arrived at the local boma (village) where we joined
the men around campfires feasting on the roasted meat
of freshly slaughtered cattle. Our friend explained to us

that the next morning at dawn all the boys who turned 13 the year before would line up and be circumcised. The manlier the boy, the less noise he made when the knife was applied!

The next morning, back at our hotel, I greeted my 13-year-old son with a well-received salutation: *It's a good day to be an American!*

Every boy wakes up with a simple question: *Am I good enough?* The answer to that question depends entirely on where the boy lives. If he is Masai and lives in Tanzania, the question is answered by silently enduring excruciating pain. If he lives in Vanuatu, a small island nation in the middle of the South Pacific, the answer is found in diving off a 100-foot tower with vines tied around his ankles. The closer he gets to the ground without smashing into it, the more of a man he is considered to be.

The *real* answer to this question is that *apart from walking humbly with God, we are not good enough.* But we sure think we are! The proof of this is our completely culturally conditioned standards of 'manliness.'

John Calvin wrote,

> *Until God reveals himself to us, we do not think we are [persons]... we think we are gods; but when we have seen God, then we begin to feel and know what we are. Hence springs true humility, which consists in this, that a [person] make no claim for himself [herself], and depend wholly on God.*[95]

---

[95] John Calvin, quoted in Robert J. Wicks, *Spiritual Resilience: 30 Days to Refresh Your Soul* (Cincinnati: Franciscan Media, 2015), Kindle Location 910.

Mac Davis was right when he sang, *Oh Lord it's hard to be humble | When you're perfect in every way.*

We really are not as strong, good or as smart as we think. The sooner we realize this, the faster we can start to grow.

Thomas Keating wrote:

> *The spiritual journey is not a career or a success story. It is a series of humiliations of the false self that become more and more profound. These make room inside us for the Holy Spirit to come in and heal. What prevents us from being available to God is gradually evacuated. We keep getting closer and closer to our center. Every now and then God lifts a corner of the veil and enters into our awareness through various channels, as if to say, "Here I am. Where are you? Come and join me.*[96]

We really are not as brilliant as we think, and that's a good thing. When we come to the end of ourselves we find God waiting to get us moving into the real journey to manly success: *To act justly and to love mercy and to walk humbly with your God.*

THINK ABOUT IT...

* What is the most humiliating experience you have ever had? What did it feel like? What did you learn?
* In what ways did your culture define 'manhood'?
* In what ways does God define manhood?

---

[96] Thomas Keating, *The Human Condition: Contemplation and Transformation* (New York: Paulist Press, 1999), 38.

LIFE COMMITMENT:

I am not as smart as I think. And in the end, that's a good thing. God is smarter and stronger than me. I bow before him and submit to his greatness.

Between Fear and Hope

———— ⚬⚬⚬ ————

The Word

So do not fear, for I am with you; do not be dismayed,
for I am your God. I will strengthen you and help you;
I will uphold you with my righteous right hand.

— Isaiah 41.10

Thought for the Day:

Everything can be taken from a man but one thing: the
last of the human freedoms—to choose one's attitude in
any given set of circumstances, to choose one's own way.

~ Viktor E. Frankl

Think about this (I realize this is a big bite, but it's worth it!):

Hope is a disposition of the soul to persuade itself that what
it desires will come to pass, which is caused by a particular
movement of the spirits, namely, by that of mingled joy and
desire. And fear is another disposition of the soul, which
persuades it that the thing will not come to pass.

And it is to be noted that, although these two passions are contrary, one may nonetheless have them both together, that is, when one considers different reasons at the same time, some of which cause one to judge that the fulfilment of one's desires is a straightforward matter, while others make it seem difficult.[97]

Every person lives between hope and fear. When things are going well, hope dominates your 'brain space.' When things get tough, fears can (and do) set in. Your brain is saturated by worrying thoughts provoked by fear.

Your soul is always in a tug-of-war between hope and fear. Usually these two emotions are in balance. But when something really bad or really good happens, hope and fear get out of balance. This creates a sense of disequilibrium that is unsettling to our soul.

There are two things to say about this:

First: Know deep in your soul that **God is the God of hope**, and *he will not be moved*:

Many are saying of me, "God will not deliver him." But you are a shield around me, O Lord; you bestow glory on me and lift up my head. To the Lord I cry aloud, and he answers me from his holy hill. I lie down and sleep; I wake again, because the Lord sustains me. I will not fear the tens of thousands drawn up against me on every side. (Psalm 3.2–6)

---

[97] René Descartes et al., *The Passions of The Soul: And Other Late Philosophical Writings* (Oxford: Oxford University Press, 2015), 264.

God is your anchor, your rock, your foundation. He will not be moved. Though you waver between hope and fear, God will not waver. He is solid when we are not.

Second, know that **your goal is to keep moving**.

There are two ways hope and fear can paralyze your life. First, if hope runs rampant, complacency and laziness can slow or halt our growth. As Descartes says, *When hope is so strong that it altogether drives out fear, its nature changes and it becomes complacency or confidence.*[98]

On the other hand, if fear completely takes over, paralysis can lead to self-destruction. Descartes writes: *When fear is so extreme that it leaves no room at all for hope, it is transformed into despair; and this despair, representing the thing as impossible, extinguishes desire altogether,* ***for desire bears only on possible things****.*[99]

God is the critical ingredient Descartes leaves out: God is the bearer and bringer of impossible things, therefore ***all things are possible for you that fit within God's will****.* Since God is unequivocally for you and on your side, you can be sure that his will is good and right and true.[100]

When fear come crashing in, take a deep breath, pray to God for comfort, peace and wisdom, and allow him to reassure you that you will make it and you will be OK. God will do this. He *longs* to do this for you.

---

[98] Ibid.

[99] Ibid. Emphasis mine.

[100] *Therefore, I urge you, brothers and sisters, in view of God's mercy, to offer your bodies as a living sacrifice, holy and pleasing to God—this is your true and proper worship. Do not conform to the pattern of this world, but be transformed by the renewing of your mind. Then you will be able to test and approve what God's will is—his good, pleasing and perfect will.* (Romans 12.1-2)

THINK ABOUT IT...

* Are you more hopeful or more fearful right now?
* What fears are roiling around your head right now?
* What hope is God giving you?

LIFE COMMITMENT:

I will always live between hope and fear. I choose to give my fears to God and allow him to replace them with hope in his good will toward me and his desire to fulfill his purpose for me.

Ultimate Hope

—∞∞∞—

THE WORD

*Since, then, you have been raised with Christ, set your
hearts on things above, where Christ is seated at the right
hand of God. Set your minds on things above, not on
earthly things. For you died, and your life is now hidden
with Christ in God. When Christ, who is your life,
appears, then you also will appear with him in glory.*

— COLOSSIANS 3.1–4

THOUGHT FOR THE DAY:

*If you don't keep the eyes of your heart focused on
the paradise that is to come, you will try to turn this
poor fallen world into the paradise it will never be.*

~ PAUL DAVID TRIPP

A GOOD FRIEND OF MINE who had been through a hard time
once told me, *If you don't have Jesus, this world is as good as it
gets. If you do have Jesus, this world is as bad as it gets.*

If this world is all there is, *all your happiness depends on how things are going for you <u>now</u>* because now is all you have. Whatever future you have is limited by death, so you are driven to wring out of life all that you can while you can. The clock is ticking.

Charles Darwin wrote, *A man who dares to waste one hour of time has not discovered the value of life.*"[101] He is right. But if death ends it all, time becomes a ruthless taskmaster demanding that you get everything you can out of every minute of this life.

But if you *do* have Jesus, *this life is as bad as it gets* because through Jesus, *this life is not all there is.* In fact, because of Jesus, we have an eternity of problem-free living waiting for us!

Divorce puts an end to many dreams. At the very least, divorce slows life to a crawl. As you emerge from this dark place, you may resent the time you lost as you experience the pain of shattered dreams. If you believe this life is all there is, your resentment and anger will grow into bitterness because of lost time.

But if you believe in heaven, if you believe the best is yet to be, you will be able to bear the losses with patience and grace. I am not saying this is easy, but it is true that heaven gives you an amazing hope. Heaven frees us from the tyranny of having to get it all now. Heaven gives us space to live on earth.

Heaven is our ultimate hope. Heaven is forever and it is good. Heaven is home.

---

[101] Charles Darwin, *Life and Letters of Charles Darwin* (Rare Books Club, 2016), Kindle Location 3485.

THINK ABOUT IT...

* What do you believe about heaven?
* What would change in your thinking, emotions and actions today if you really believed that this life is not all there is, that there is an amazing heaven waiting for you?

PRAYER:

God, deliver me from the tyranny of time. Let heaven settle deep in my soul. Let heaven give me room to breathe, space to live as fully as I can now on earth, knowing that true life awaits me later in heaven.

Thin Skin, Hard Heart Or...

———— ∞ ————

THE WORD

When [Jesus] saw the crowds, he had compassion
on them, because they were harassed and
helpless, like sheep without a shepherd.

— MATTHEW 9.36

THOUGHT FOR THE DAY:

[God] will use the brokenness of the world that is
your present address to complete the loving work
of personal transformation that he has begun.

~ PAUL DAVID TRIPP

IT'S CRAZY HOW OUR CULTURE glorifies people who have a *thin skin* and *hard heart*. Movies and TV celebrate 'tough guys' who take quick and violent action against anyone who slightly provokes them. Their 'toughness' is measured in how violently they respond to the slightest offense rather than their ability to take offenses into themselves without being rattled.

Thin-skinned people are easily provoked. A simple phrase or look can offend them. Everything is about them so anything or anyone who makes them uncomfortable in any way *gets under their skin.* They wear their feelings on their sleeve, which means that everyone knows what they are feeling, which is usually anger at some offense.

Thin-skinned people have a hard heart. Since they believe they are the center of the universe they lack the ability to put themselves in the other's shoes. They can't imagine what it is like to be the other person because all they can imagine is their own limited lives.

Thin-skinned, hard-hearted people are usually angry, resentful, and bitter. And they let the world know it because they don't care how their words fall on others. Though they are easily offended, they believe others should not be. Thin-skinned, hard-hearted people believe they should be allowed to criticize everyone else. But when criticized, thin-skinned, hard-hearted people react with disbelief, anger and hostility.

Thin-skinned, hard-hearted people believe they are powerful and that their angry outbursts show them to be so. In reality, however, thin-skinned, hard-hearted people have given their power away to others.

Thin-skinned, hard-hearted people are the opposite of self-differentiated. Their thoughts, emotions and actions are completely controlled by what other people think, feel, say and do (See Days 29-31). They believe that they are controlling others when, in fact, they are controlled by others.

Jesus was not like this. Jesus had a thick skin, that is, he was able to hear what others said and respond (or not respond) according to what God the Father wanted, not according to his own wants or desires.

For example, during this trial before Pilate, Jesus fearlessly spoke truth to power. At the same time, he allowed

Pilate to send him to the cross for crimes he didn't commit because Jesus knew that his death would bring life to us.

Jesus' thick skin allowed him to take what others were dishing out against him. His soft heart drove him to act with complete compassion toward those who were hurting.

We are to be like Jesus, not Charlie Sheen. We are to be like Jesus, not the Godfather.

Divorce is a radical assault on our soul. It slams through our skin and slashes our heart. If left unchecked, the wounds of divorce can make our skin thinner and our hearts harder.

This is your moment to allow God to transform your thin skin and hard heart. God can thicken up your skin and soften your heart. Everything in you right now is reinforcing the old thin-skinned, hard hearted person you were. Push back on that. Surrender to God's work of transformation. Let him toughen up your skin and soften your heart.

THINK ABOUT IT...

* How thin is your skin? How hard is your heart? You can measure both by simply thinking about what you *think*, how you *feel* and what you *do* when you are criticized.
* What would change in your life if you were more like Jesus—thick-skinned and soft-hearted?

PRAYER:

God, show me where my skin is thin and my heart is hard. I want you to thicken my skin and soften my heart.

Weak Enough, Strong Enough

—⊶∞⊷—

The Word

*This is how we know what love is: Jesus Christ
laid down his life for us. And we ought to
lay down our lives for our brothers.*

— 1 John 3.16

Thought for the Day:

*Love must be learned, and learned again and
again; there is no end to it. Hate needs no
instruction, but waits only to be provoked.*

~ Katherine Anne Porter

A few days ago I mentioned the various ways cultures define manhood. In Boston it is about brains. In Kyle, Texas, it is about having the biggest, baddest truck in the parking lot. Modern western cultures define manhood in terms of power—the more the better.

That hit Sheldon Brown (Philadelphia Eagles) put on Reggie Bush (New Orleans Saints)? Or the Varitek-Alex Rodriguez Brawl of 2004? Or Scott Stevens, NHL's one-man wrecking crew? Somehow when we see these guys we think they are powerful.

Male images of power almost always involve a man *powering over* somebody or something.

That's not the Jesus way. Don't get me wrong. Jesus was powerful. He was the most powerful human walking the earth when his sandaled feet cruised through Israel. He could stop wind and waves and blabbing idiots with his words. He could walk for untold miles and lay his head down for a good sleep anywhere. He could take the flesh-ripping lashing of the Romans and still keep on going.

But the deeper power of Jesus was not in his powering over others but in his willingness to be weak enough to be strong enough to truly love.

Jesus was a warrior. But he was the perfect warrior. He fought the right *enemy* at the right *time against* the right *people for* the right *people* with the right *weapon* with the right *strength* and the *perfect motive.*

Sometimes the power of Jesus was to physically power over the enemy. The cleansing of the Temple comes to mind. He handily overturned the tables of the money changers and cleared the courtyard. But usually Jesus demonstrated his power through what the world would perceive as weakness.

Are you weak enough and strong enough to love?

Perhaps a better way to look at this is to substitute the world 'weak' with 'tender.' Are you tender enough and yet strong enough to love?

Are you tender enough to have an open heart, to have the confidence to express sympathy and compassion toward another?

Are you strong enough to have an identity that can push against the tough guy persona our world loves so much?

THINK ABOUT IT...

* If you could have any super power, what would it be?
* How do you respond when someone powers over you?
* When have you used raw power to get your way? How did that feel?
* When have you expressed your strength through tenderness? What was the result?
* Who in your life needs your strength expressed through tenderness?

PRAYER:

God, show me where I have used power to my advantage. Help me be strong enough to be weak (tender) enough to really love those in my life.

Fail Forward... But Not Flat on Your Face!

THE WORD

My flesh and my heart may fail, but God is the strength of my heart and my portion forever.

— PSALM 73.26

THOUGHT FOR THE DAY:

When we act, uncertainty chases us out into the open where opportunity awaits.

~ MARC AND ANGEL CHERNOFF

MY MOM, WHO WAS 89, lived with us for seven months in New Hampshire. One winter day she determined to go on a walk. By this time we realized that resistance was futile so I told her to have a grand time. I watched all 85 pounds of her slowly make her way down the road. Then I forgot about her. I know. Not good.

About 20 minutes later I heard this 'ooohing' sound coming from the front yard. I jumped up to see her crumpled by the mailbox face down in the gravel between the yard and street. I dashed out the front door sure that one (or more) of our neighbors would call Adult Protective Services on me!

She had literally fallen flat on her face. Gravel was embedded in her forehead, her glasses were broken, and blood oozed from various wounds on her cheek and chin.

After an initial assessment I asked her if she thought she could get up with my help and walk to the house where we could clean her up. She responded with a hearty 'SURE!' She popped up and we went inside to do some first aid!

Whether you are the one who initiated divorce or not, whether the divorce is mostly your fault or not, whether you believe your divorce is justified or not, *divorce feels like a failure.* Divorce is the ripping apart of a sacred bond you made with your partner. At some point, divorce feels like you fell flat on your face.

The question then becomes, what will I do about it?

How you think about, feel toward, and behave in response to failure in general and your divorce in particular has huge consequences for the future. We will explore this topic of failure and how to respond to it in the next several days.

One thing is certain: *Failure will **define** us, **refine** us or **redefine** us, but it will never leave us the same.*[102]

A terrible thing happened. Don't let it define you. Let it **refine** you as you let God **redefine** you. You will not be the same. The question is, will you be better or worse? The answer depends on you.

In the introduction to this book I wrote words that ring true for you today:

---

[102] J. R. Briggs, *Fail: Finding Hope and Grace in The Midst of Ministry Failure* (Downers Grove, 2015), Kindle Location 1319.

You may be down, but brother, you are not out. You may be crushed, but my friend, you are not dead. You may be face down on the turf, but you will get up, take a deep breath, and get back in the game. Know this: No life has failed if God moves in, transforms, and transmits his grace, love and power in, to and through you.

Think About It...

* When you failed as a child, how did people react to you?
* When you hear the word 'fail' what or who do you think about? What emotions come to the surface?

Life Commitment:

Failure sucks. But failing to use my failure as a launchpad into a better future sucks more. I commit to understanding failure and how God can use my failure to move me forward.

Fail Forward (2)

THE WORD

*We also rejoice in our sufferings, because we know
that suffering produces perseverance; perseverance,
character; and character, hope. And hope does not
disappoint us, because God has poured out his love into
our hearts by the Holy Spirit, whom he has given us.*

— ROMANS 5.3–5

THOUGHT FOR THE DAY:

*When we fail we are merely joining the
great parade of humanity that has walked
ahead of us and will follow after us.*

~ RICHARD ROHR

EVER HEARD OF TRAF-O-DATA? IT was Bill Gates' first company.

* Michael Jordan was cut from his high school basketball team.
* Vincent Van Gogh sold only one painting in his lifetime.
* Steven Spielberg was rejected from USC—twice.

* Henry Ford was broke five times because his first businesses failed.
* Twenty-Seven publishers rejected Theodor Geisel's first book. Theodor Geisel is better known as Dr. Seuss.
* J. K. Rowling was divorced, broke and depressed while writing her first novel.
* Colonel Sanders of Kentucky Fried Chicken had his chicken recipe rejected 1,009 times before a restaurant accepted it.
* Walt Disney was fired by a newspaper editor. The reason? He "lacked imagination and had no good ideas."
* Lucille Ball was told by her drama instructors that she would never make it in theater and she should try another profession.
* Elvis Presley was fired by the manager of the Grand Ole Opry after just one performance. The manager told him, "You ain't goin' nowhere, son. You ought to go back to drivin' a truck."
* Jerry Seinfeld's career began when he walked out on stage, froze, and was eventually jeered and booed out of the club.
* For decades Babe Ruth held the record for strikeouts.
* Sidney Poitier was told by the casting director after his first audition, "Why don't you stop wasting people's time and go out and become a dishwasher or something?"
* Thomas Edison was told by teachers that he was "too stupid to learn anything." He was fired from his first two jobs. He attempted over 1,000 times to invent the lightbulb.
* Stephen King's first novel (*Carrie*) was rejected 30 times. King threw it in the trash. His wife retrieved it.

Here is Tom Landry's coaching record of the Dallas Cowboys from 1960 to 1964:

Win	Loss	Tie
0	11	1
4	9	1
5	8	1
4	10	0
5	8	-

Every successful person has failed, some multiple times and some spectacularly (Remember *New Coke?*)

J. M. Barrie wrote, *We are all failures—at least, all the best of us are.*[103]

When we fail we feel like we are the only ones who have failed and that our failure is wildly public and depressingly permanent. *Nothing is further from the truth.* The harder the fall, the more amazing the summit when God pulls you up and out of that pit!

John Maxwell asks a good question: *If you've failed, are you a failure?*[104]

God's answer for you is, *You are not a failure.* Failure is something that happens for a variety of reasons. Failure is a thing, not a person.

---

[103] J.M. Barrie, *"J.M. Barrie Quotes."* BrainyQuote, accessed September 27, 2017 https://www.goodreads.com/quotes/288278-we-are-all-failures--at-least-the-best-of-us.

[104] John C. Maxwell, *Failing Forward: Turning Mistakes into Stepping Stones for Success* (Nashville, TN: Thomas Nelson, 2007), 23.

THINK ABOUT IT...

* When you read the list of names above and hear what others have said to them, what comes to mind?
* What do you think these people thought/have/did that pushed them past their failures?

LIFE COMMITMENT:

If God uses only perfect people, he will have a short list! I'm not perfect but I know God can use me.

Fail Forward (3)

———— ∞∞∞ ————

The Word

*Therefore, if anyone is in Christ, he is a new
creation; the old has gone, the new has come!*

— 2 Corinthians 5.17

Thought for the Day:

Failure is an event. It is not a person.

~ Zig Ziglar

To many people, the Apostle Paul was an incredible failure
by the standards of his day. He didn't start out that way.

As a relatively young man—the man we know as the
Apostle Paul (then named Saul)—was a rising star in the
Jewish academia. Raised in a cosmopolitan city and attending the best schools, Paul's future was bright, his future
secured. Paul's enthusiasm matched his great intellect. He
fervently believed his zeal should be applied to stamping out
the new sect of rebels led by the heretic named Jesus.

Paul was a success according to the world—his zealotry was appreciated by his superiors and made him famous with the general population. The problem, however, was that Paul was using his energy *against* God instead of *for* him. While traveling from Jerusalem to Damascus Jesus confronted Paul in a vision. The experience literally knocked Paul off his feet.

When the Lord revealed himself to Paul (see Acts 9) Paul wisely chose to reject the dead tradition he had been taught for the living God he was encountering. God changed Paul's mind, heart and will that day. Paul went on to become the most effective missionary the world has ever seen. You and I live in a world shaped by God's work through Paul begun nearly 2,000 years ago.

Paul truly experienced that day what he wrote years later: *If anyone is in Christ, he is a new creation; the old has gone, the new has come!* Paul, filled with zealous but misdirected hatred, became the bearer of the loving Good News of the very Christ he was determined to destroy!

If God can do that in Paul's life, he can do it for you. Your moment of failure is only a moment. Failure is an event. It is a thing that happens to you and sometimes because of you. *But it is not you.* Don't allow this failure to define you. Rather, let God *redefine* you!

Paul would later write to the church at Rome: *Do not conform any longer to the pattern of this world, but be transformed by the renewing of your mind.* (Romans 12.1)

What is the pattern of this world? The world sees failure as final. The world rejoices when you are down because, compared to you, they are up. The world loves victims because victims are helpless and easily manipulated. Paul tells us to reject this loser/victim mentality.

Instead, he says, *be transformed by the renewing of your mind.* The Greek word we translate as *transform* is *metamorfoo,* from which we get the word *metamorphosis.*

What happens when a caterpillar rejects the world and cocoons? It emerges transformed. It is metamorphosed into something so spectacular the ground can't hold it down!

The world defines success in a lot of bizarre, ridiculous ways. God defines success by allowing him to transform you into the man he purposed you to be.

Failure events are part of the process of this transformation. Whether you are the vic or the perp (or most likely a combination of the two), God can and will (and is!) using this event to transform you.

J. R. Briggs gives us God's perspective on your current crisis: *God is much more concerned about the transformation going on inside us than the circumstances going on around us.*[105]

Failure is not final. It is simply a launching point for a better you which means a better future *for* you.

THINK ABOUT IT...

* Do you believe that your failure will define you for the rest of your life?
* If you answered *yes* to the question above, open your mind to the possibility that God can use your failure to *refine* and *redefine* you.

---

[105] Briggs, Fail: *Finding Hope And Grace In The Midst Of Ministry Failure,* Kindle Location 1428.

* If you allowed God to use failure to refine and redefine you, what could your life look like?
* What is the cost of not allowing God to use failure to refine and redefine you?

LIFE COMMITMENT:

God, I believe you can do for me what you did for the Apostle Paul. My failure can be the turning point in my life that I have been needing. Here's my life... take me and refine and redefine me.

Fail Forward (4)

———— ∾∾∾ ————

THE WORD

*For my thoughts are not your thoughts, neither are
your ways my ways, declares the Lord. As the heavens
are higher than the earth, so are my ways higher than
your ways and my thoughts than your thoughts.*

— ISAIAH 55:8–9

THOUGHT FOR THE DAY:

*The cross is evidence that in the hands of the
Redeemer, moments of apparent defeat become
wonderful moments of grace and victory.*

~ PAUL DAVID TRIPP

A LONG TIME AGO (20 years) the hottest thing in computing
was WYSIWYG—*What You See Is What You Get.*

In computerese, this meant that what you saw as you
typed a document or presentation is what you would get
when you printed it out. Today everything is WYSIWYG, but
before WYSIWYG, your words appeared on a plain screen

without formatting. The advent of WYSIWYG made writing and making presentations much easier.

Through over 30 years in ministry, one unequivocal truth I have learned is that **this is <u>not</u> a WYSIWYG world**. What appears to be a raging success often isn't. What appears to be utter failure is often a blessing.

The Bible is all over this. Joseph, sold into slavery, becomes second in command in all of Egypt. The weak, depleted and powerless Hebrew slaves are freed from the grips of the world's greatest super-power, eventually to become their own super-power. The Bible is full of these *Great Reversals*.

One of the greatest of Great Reversals is when a teenage Jewish girl is chosen to bear God's own Son into the world. When Mary heard the news she sang a song that is all about Great Reversals. Her song defies any notion that this is a WYSIWIG world:

> *My soul glorifies the Lord*
> *and my spirit rejoices in God my Savior,*
> *for he has been mindful*
> *of the humble state of his servant.*
> *From now on all generations will call me blessed,*
> *for the Mighty One has done great things for me—*
> *holy is his name.*
> *His mercy extends to those who fear him,*
> *from generation to generation.*
> *He has performed mighty deeds with his arm;*
> *he has scattered those who are proud in their inmost thoughts.*
> *He has brought down rulers from their thrones*
> *but has lifted up the humble.*

He has filled the hungry with good things
but has sent the rich away empty.
He has helped his servant Israel,
remembering to be merciful
to Abraham and his descendants forever,
even as he said to our fathers. (Luke 1.46–55)

Men, this song puts to rest the idea that the world or God's Kingdom is only about us! It also denies any thought that things are always as they appear to be. In God's Kingdom, rulers are brought down, the humble are lifted up. Those who *have* become those who *have not*. The hungry are filled. The lowly are esteemed and called blessed.

God is all about Great Reversals. This is not a WYSIWYG world. God is doing things behind the scenes of your life that are far more complex and incredible than you can imagine.

* What you see as a dead-end God sees as a launchpad into a life you never could have imagined.
* What you see as downer in life God sees as an opportunity to lift you up.
* What you see as depletion God sees as an opportunity to fill you up.
* What you see as an *end* God sees as a new *beginning.*

Don't believe me—believe a 15-year-old Jewish girl who lived 2,000 years ago!

Paul David Tripp's advice is timely:

Be careful how you make sense of your life. What looks like a disaster may in fact be grace. What looks like the end may be the beginning. What looks hopeless may be God's instrument to give you real and lasting hope. Your Father is committed to taking what seems so bad and turning it into something that is very, very good.[106]

THINK ABOUT IT...

* Look back on your life. When have you experienced a *Great Reversal?*

LIFE COMMITMENT:

Though things look down now, I believe God can lift me up. Though things feel empty now, I believe God can fill me up. Though things look dark now, I believe God can light me up!

---

[106] Tripp, *New Morning Mercies*, Kindle Location 2285.

Fail Forward (5)

———∽∾∝———

THE WORD

This is what the Lord says:

> *Cursed is the one who trusts in man, who depends on*
> *flesh for his strength and whose heart turns away from the*
> *Lord. He will be like a bush in the wastelands; he will not*
> *see prosperity when it comes. He will dwell in the parched*
> *places of the desert, in a salt land where no one lives.*
> *But blessed is the man who trusts in the Lord, whose*
> *confidence is in him. He will be like a tree planted by the*
> *water that sends out its roots by the stream. It does not fear*
> *when heat comes; its leaves are always green. It has no*
> *worries in a year of drought and never fails to bear fruit.*

—JEREMIAH 17.5–8

THOUGHT FOR THE DAY:

> *During crisis God seems to give us his presence at a depth*
> *we have not experienced in times of peace and calm.*

~ J. R. BRIGGS

WE HAVE A HUGE PROBLEM and it is this: We have thought it best to live without God.

A great teacher and pastor of early last century says it best in his amazing book, *The Knowledge of the Holy*:

> *The teaching of Christianity is that man chose to be indepen-dent of God and confirmed his choice by deliberately disobey-ing a divine command. This act violated the relationship that normally existed between God and His creature; it re-jected God as the ground of existence and threw man back upon himself. Thereafter he became not a planet revolving around the central Sun, but a sun in his own right, around which everything else must revolve.*[107]

I have seen many people take their last breath. Those who don't know God go silently. Those who do know God go with an incredible hope filled with a firm and certain conviction of where they are headed. In the end, *these people know that they are completely dependent on God—nothing they have done, nothing they have acquired, nothing they have achieved will get them through.* The only thing going with them as their bodies fail is God's amazing and all-powerful presence.

The greatest gift this failure can give you is to make you realize you really really really need God. In fact, he is all you need and all you will have. He is all you really have now, you just didn't realize it.

It is true that

> *In the face of your failure, you can wallow in guilt and shame, beating yourself up because you did not do better and*

---

[107] Tozer, *The Knowledge of the Holy*, 61.

working hard to hide your failure from God and others. Or, in the brokenness and grief of conviction, you can run not away from God but to him. You can run into the light of his holy presence utterly unafraid, filled with the confidence that although he is righteous and you are not, he will not turn you away.[108]

In the end, *God can fly faster than we can ever fall, and He swoops in under us to break the fall when He sees that we need His help.*[109]

THINK ABOUT IT...

- Who or what have you relied on in the past to get you through tough times?
- What does relying on God look like to you right now? What does it look like to give your brain a break from trying to figure it out and just trust that he knows what is happening and can turn things around?

LIFE COMMITMENT:

I think I am stubbornly independent but the reality is that I am radically dependent on God and others. Self-made men are poorly made men. I want to be re-made through complete dependence on God. I am unashamed to say that I need God—desperately.

---

[108] Tripp, *New Morning Mercies*, Kindle Location 1711.
[109] Keturah C. Martin, *Jesus Never Wastes Pain*, 333.

Fail Forward (6)

———◦◦◦———

THE WORD

Christ Jesus came into the world to save sinners—of whom I am the worst. But for that very reason I was shown mercy so that in me, the worst of sinners, Christ Jesus might display his unlimited patience as an example for those who would believe on him and receive eternal life. Now to the King eternal, immortal, invisible, the only God, be honor and glory for ever and ever. Amen.

— THE APOSTLE PAUL, 1 TIMOTHY 1.15–17

THOUGHT FOR THE DAY:

The pessimist sees difficulty in every opportunity. The optimist sees the opportunity in every difficulty.

~ WINSTON CHURCHILL

WHETHER WE SURVIVE A FAILURE and then thrive afterward depends entirely on putting failure in perspective. This is a battle in your mind. It is a war for your soul and for your future. It is critical that you right-size your divorce and anything else in your life you or others perceive as failure.

First, know that failure is inevitable. I deluded myself that I could avoid failure if I just worked hard enough and kept everyone happy. While much of my hard work was driven by good motives, underlying it all was the fear of failure. Then I failed, spectacularly, at least in the world's eyes. I thought I could avoid failure. I couldn't. Nobody can. Life is incredibly fragile.

Second, know that failure is not the enemy. No one cruises through life making all the right decisions. No one takes the right path at every fork in the road. John Maxwell calls these 'errors.' What we do with errors makes the difference between people.

Maxwell says, *Errors become mistakes when we perceive them and respond to them incorrectly. Mistakes become failures when we continually respond to them incorrectly.*[110] Mistakes, errors, bad decisions... these are unavoidable. But each of us can choose to respond to them by learning from them.

Third, determine to live life on the edge enough to fail some. *If you are not failing some, you are not living at all.*

At the beginning of every summer, schools put a phrase on their sign that drives me crazy: *Be Safe!*

What kind of message is that to send to our kids? Of course we don't want our kids to live unsafe lives, but we also don't want them to avoid risk! Every kid should have what I call 'summer legs.' Summer legs have scrapes on the knees from climbing over rocks, scratches on their calves from running through the forest, and sore muscles from living life!

---

[110] John C. Maxwell, *Failing Forward: Turning Mistakes into Stepping Stones for Success* (Nashville: Thomas Nelson, 2007), 18.

Sumner Redstone said, *We all have to decide how we are going to fail, by not going far enough or by going too far.* That you are divorced now means that you risked loving and being loved in the most intimate and most demanding of all relationships. Marriage is hard. Some are going to fail. But that you tried says that you were willing to take the risk.

Go back and read Day 88. Look again through that list of people. They either failed miserably or were told they were failures or both. How did they overcome? They viewed failure as a stepping stone instead of a brick wall. When they were told they *couldn't* or *shouldn't*, they dug down deep and determined they *would* just to show the world they *could!*

Read again what the Apostle Paul wrote: *Christ Jesus came into the world to save sinners—of whom I am the worst.* Ouch! Paul says that though he started off strong he eventually was a huge failure.

But Paul could see that what looked like a failure to him was really an opportunity for God to shine through him: *But for that very reason I was shown mercy so that in me, the worst of sinners, Christ Jesus might display his unlimited patience as an example for those who would believe on him and receive eternal life.*

In the long view, Paul could see how God worked in his life so that God could show off his mercy and glory.

God doesn't waste pain. He doesn't waste our mistakes. He doesn't cut us down when we fall short. In God's Kingdom, those who are down are lifted up, those who fall into the deepest pit are elevated to the highest summit. When people see what God does with our failures, they are amazed and know that only God could do such a cool thing!

No wonder Paul concluded his brief biographical foray with this exclamation: *Now to the King eternal, immortal, invisible, the only God, be honor and glory for ever and ever. Amen!*

Let God put that *Amen!* in your life by right-sizing your failures.

Think About It...

* Who is winning that war in your mind right now? The *pessimist* who sees difficulty in every opportunity or the *optimist* who sees the opportunity in every difficulty?

Life Commitment:

Everyone fails. Some right-size their failures and move past them into God's future for them. I choose to move

Fail Forward (7)

———⚬⚬⚬———

THE WORD

*But he said to me, "My grace is sufficient for you, for
my power is made perfect in weakness." Therefore I
will boast all the more gladly about my weaknesses,
so that Christ's power may rest on me. That is
why, for Christ's sake, I delight in weaknesses, in
insults, in hardships, in persecutions, in difficulties.
For when I am weak, then I am strong.*

— 2 CORINTHIANS 12.9–10

THOUGHT FOR THE DAY:

*You have brains in your head. You have feet in your
shoes. You can steer yourself any direction you choose."*

~ DR. SEUSS, *OH, THE PLACES YOU'LL GO!*

WHETHER FAILURE IS A PERIOD or a comma is entirely up to
you. Just know this: *Failure doesn't have to be a period.*

Too many people put a period in their life where a comma belonged. I think of men whose dreams are finished so
they think they are too. They keep living but they are not

alive. They keep going but without direction. They keep waking up but they are still just really sleeping.

Then I think of the tens of thousands of people in our country who put the ultimate period in their lives—they kill themselves.

My oldest sister chose this at the age of 50. She was a vibrant, brilliant, fun, glorious human being. She embraced life to the max. She was the first woman to graduate from Georgia Tech with a masters degree in Mechanical Engineering. She had three amazing children (who are still amazing). She was the ultimate big sister. She took me and others backpacking into the high country of Colorado... for over a week! We traipsed through the Arkansas Ozarks during Christmas vacation. It was 5°.

Suicide is a huge mistake. Suicide is a permanent (and terrible) solution to a temporary problem. Failure is a temporary problem. Don't put a period where a comma belongs.

By the end of World War I, Winston Churchill was washed up as a politician. As Britain's Lord of Admiralty, he had planned and pushed for the attack on Turkey at Gallipoli. A million men fought on both sides. Over the course of eight months, over 135,000 died with nearly 400,000 wounded. Britain lost in total humiliation. Churchill was fired and thereafter excluded from any decisions regarding war.

But nearly 20 years later, it was Prime Minister Churchill who would lead the British when Britain faced the Nazi juggernaut entirely alone. Imagine being Churchill in that moment. Here he was being tested at the very point where he previously had failed miserably.

Later Churchill would write, *Success is not final, failure is not fatal: it is the courage to continue that counts.* Churchill proved that with his life. So can you.

Bear Grylls says it like this: *Ever heard the phrase When you're in a hole, stop digging'? It's the same with mistakes. Don't give the mistake more power than it warrants by squandering precious time worrying about it. Yesterday is not ours to recover, but tomorrow is ours to win or lose.*[111]

Failures are commas, not periods. Don't put a period where a comma belongs!

Think About It...

* If you are contemplating suicide, call this hotline right now: 800-273-8255 (https://suicideprevention-lifeline.org)
* Six days ago we started this short series about failure. What has changed in how you view failure?

LIFE COMMITMENT:

Success is not final, failure is not fatal: it is the courage to continue that counts. Though it is painful and though I don't know what the future holds, I commit to continuing this journey.

---

[111] Bear Grylls, *A Survival Guide for Life*, 235. Reprinted by permission of Peters Fraser & Dunlop (www.petersfraserdunlop.com) on behalf of Bear Grylls.

Finishing Well

———— ∞∞∞ ————

THE WORD

For I am already being poured out like a drink offering,
and the time has come for my departure. I have fought
the good fight, I have finished the race, I have kept
the faith. Now there is in store for me the crown of
righteousness, which the Lord, the righteous Judge,
will award to me on that day—and not only to me,
but also to all who have longed for his appearing.

— 2 Timothy 4.6–8

THOUGHT FOR THE DAY:

According to legend, the Great Plains warriors
would say to their sons first thing in the morning,
"It is a good day to do great things."

~ Richard Rohr

HERE'S WHAT I HAVE OBSERVED from watching men die:

* Few men have thought about life, how they will end theirs, and if they have much to celebrate or regret. Most men, it would seem, really have lived lives of quiet desperation.[112]
* Not a single man has ever said to me, *I had a really kick-ass lawn* or *I wish I had spent more time at the office* or *How 'bout them Cowboys?*
* Most highly successful men (high achievers such as physicians, lawyers, successful businessmen) go out kicking and screaming. They are *pissed* that they have to die.
* Godly men are few and far between. These few men are gentle, humble, and full of joy when they die. They are grateful for the lives they were given and they are full of hope for the new life they know is coming.

These observations bring up important questions:

* Why do so few men think deeply about their lives?
* Why do so many men spend their lives in such trivial pursuits such as football fanaticism or having the perfect lawn?
* Why do highly successful men end life so angry?
* Why are there so few men finishing well?

---

[112] Henry David Thoreau wrote: *The mass of men lead lives of quiet desperation. What is called resignation is confirmed desperation. From the desperate city you go into the desperate country.... A stereotyped but unconscious despair is concealed even under what are called the games and amusements of mankind.* Henry David Thoreau, *Works of Henry David Thoreau* (Boston: MobileReference. com, 2008), Kindle Location 5599.

We've always heard that life is a journey. When we were young we believed the journey would last forever. There comes a time, however, when we know it won't. For many men that time comes in the middle of life and it comes like a train barreling down the tracks.

Perhaps you are in this moment as you face your divorce. *This is a moment all men face* whether brought on by divorce, a job loss, financial ruin, a health crisis or any number of catastrophic events.

It's at this point that you and I decide how we will finish the journey. Imagine your life 30 years from now. When you are an old man, how do you want people to think of you? What do you want to be remembered for? What kind of man do you want to be?

Most men don't think this through and consequently, most men don't finish well. Your personal disaster has given you the opportunity not to be one of those 'most men.'

Life is a journey and to a large degree, that journey has predictable paths, signposts and forks in the road. It really helps to know how the journey goes. It helps to know where you are on the journey. It helps to know where you have come from and to know that most men around the world are traveling the same general path. And it really helps to know what lies ahead. It helps to have a map!

The next several days I will map out the typical spiritual journey of men. As we go through these next days together, determine to be able to say with the Apostle Paul at the end of the journey: *I have fought the good fight, I have finished the race, I have kept the faith.*

To reach this goal will take knowledge and commitment.

THINK ABOUT IT...

* Have you ever wondered if other guys experienced life as you have?

LIFE COMMITMENT:
If life is a journey I want to know the destination and how to get there.

The Big Story

---∞∞∞---

The Word

> *Then God said, "Let us make man in our image, in our*
> *likeness, and let them rule over the fish of the sea and*
> *the birds of the air, over the livestock, over all the earth,*
> *and over all the creatures that move along the ground."*
> *So God created man in his own image, in the image of*
> *God he created him; male and female he created them.*

— Genesis 1.26–27

Thought for the Day:

> *For most of us, life feels like a movie we've*
> *arrived at forty-five minutes late.*

~John Eldredge

I grew up in a family of scientists and engineers. My dad had a master's degree in biochemistry. My oldest sister earned a master's in Mechanical Engineering, my brother a master's in Geology. It goes on from there!

Deeply steeped in an empirical universe, I was recording daily weather data in third grade, and this was not a school project! Shakespeare and Van Gogh were not high on my parents' education agenda. Calculus was.

But the longer I live the more I realize that *story* is as much a fabric of our lives as are quirks and quarks. We are material beings living in a material universe, but that we sense we are in a story and our lives are amazing stories in themselves, point to something beyond a universe experienced, measured and manipulated through our five senses alone.

The ancients understood how important it was to know that we are, indeed, in a story. Each culture, tribe, or clan had its origin story and diligently passed the story down to the next generation. Their grand narrative gave a context in which boys could grow to be men. The elders would teach the boys their place in the bigger story and how they should live out their storyline.

The Enlightenment changed all that for Western culture. A radical turn to individualism left each of us to ourselves. Freedom from the shackles of aristocracy led to a meritocracy where individuals had the space to flourish, and flourish we have. But the price of this freedom is dissociation from The Story. We wonder where we came from and why we're here.

As John Eldredge says, we feel like we woke up 45 minutes into a movie. We are left wondering *What kind of movie are we in? Who wrote the script? How does it end? What is my place in it?*

Western Culture has failed to give us an overarching narrative, a communal story, an arc of life that places our lives in a larger context. If we do have one, it is about being an individual, living life our own way, and, above all, being materially rich.

Radical individualism leaves us to write our own little story. The upside to this way of thinking is that *we get to be the star of our own story!* The downside is that *no one cares about our story* because they are busy writing their own story.

There is, however, a Grand Narrative, a Big Story, an arc to history.

G. K. Chesterton wrote, *I had always felt life first as a story: and if there is a story there is a story-teller.*[113]

C. S. Lewis noted, *To construct plausible and moving 'other worlds' you must draw on the only real 'other world' we know: that of the spirit.*[114]

Your life is bigger than you. You can choose to join this larger, grander story that has meaning and purpose.

Most men in most cultures follow a spiritual pathway through life that can be known and examined. Like a map, this pathway doesn't set one's destiny. Like a map, knowing where things are and the possible routes ahead help orient us and give us insights into where we are headed.

Paying attention to the map of the male spiritual journey can help orient you in this terribly disorienting period in your life.

As we lay out the map of the male spiritual journey in the next few days, look back on your life to examine key events. As you learn more about this journey of male spirituality, try to figure out where you are now. When you know where you are, boldly look ahead to the possibilities of the future so that you will not be surprised at the options ahead for you. Determine to make good choices so that you finish well.

---

[113] G. K. Chesterton, *Orthodoxy* (Centrehouse Press, 2017), 117.

[114] C. S. Lewis and Walter Hooper, *Of Other Worlds: Essays and Stories* (San Francisco: HarperOne, 2017), 12.

THINK ABOUT IT...

* Is reality limited to the material universe, or is there something more?
* If you are the star of your own story, how's it going? How do you think it will end?
* Think of your favorite movie. What do you like about it? What parts of the story resonate with you?

PRAYER:

God, I have been the star of my own little story for too long. Show me the big picture.

Why You Might Feel Lost: The Lost Art of Initiation

———— ∞∞∞ ————

THE WORD

*Then God said to Abraham, "As for you, you must
keep my covenant, you and your descendants after
you for the generations to come. This is my covenant
with you and your descendants after you, the covenant
you are to keep: Every male among you shall be
circumcised. You are to undergo circumcision, and
it will be the sign of the covenant between me and
you. For the generations to come every male among
you who is eight days old must be circumcised...."*

— GENESIS 17.9–12

THOUGHT FOR THE DAY:

*From our earliest beginnings until quite recently,
men were not born; they were consciously made.*

~ RICHARD ROHR

THE MAP OF OUR SPIRITUAL journey begins with something
that, for most of us, is missing. That something is what traditional cultures call *initiation*. Most societies in the history

of the world have intentionally made their boys into men. A huge step in that process is male initiation.

Bret Stephenson has counseled hundreds of high-risk adolescents, mostly boys, for more than two decades. He noticed that all high-risk teens and young adults were missing something.

He writes:

> *All older cultures learned that if you leave adolescents to fend for themselves, they often take the wrong path. They need to be led through adolescence and put in a position that begins with a boy but requires a man for completion, thus encouraging the youth to grow up quickly yet solidly. Native cultures kept adolescence as short as possible, for it drove everyone crazy. Modern American adolescence is now the longest in history, with no end point and a steadily earlier starting point.*[115]

Traditional cultures intentionally *make* their boys into men. A milestone on this journey is *initiation*.

During initiation rituals, boys are pulled away from their mothers and sent alone into nature where they will confront real limits. While alone in the wild the boy bumps up against the dangerous and yet nurturing reality of his existence in nature. Nature sustains us but can also kill us. Boys who think they are more powerful than anything realize that nature is more powerful than them.

After this time apart, the boys are brought back into the gathering of the men of the tribe and other boys.

---

[115] Bret Stephenson, *From Boys to Men: Spiritual Rites of Passage in an Indulgent Age* (Rochester, VT: Park Street Press, 2006), 18. Used with permission.

There they face an initiation ritual, typically circumcision. This ceremony is intended to teach boys that their power is limited. What better way to get this message across than cutting the very thing that men believe gives them so much power!

When this is completed, *the boys are named as men by the elders of the tribe.* By declaring them men, they are given something *to grow into* instead of something *they desperately try to prove* the rest of their lives.

The designation of men by the elders also places them into a position of accountability to the men who did the naming. When the boys—now declared men—violate the rules of manhood in their culture, they are reprimanded and disciplined by the elders.

This entire ritual is designed so that most, if not all boys pass. The tribe wants all their boys to grow into manhood.

Western culture has virtually eliminated the pathway of initiation for males. The only organizations doing anything close to initiation may be the Boy Scouts, sports teams and the military. Organized sports are the most widespread means through which boys encounter themselves and their limits. The problem with organized sports is that only one team wins the championship, or, in the case of solitary sports like tennis, only one boy is crowned the winner. What message is our culture sending if the vast majority of our boys are declared losers?

The results of not showing boys a clear pathway to manhood are numerous and devastating. The most obvious consequence is seen in the 30-year-old young man who can't hold a job or treat a woman well, and whose highlight of his life is playing video games.

The most devastating result is that young men are left without heroic dreams. They have no clear sense of their place in the grander story. They are devoid of a mission that calls them to give themselves away to a cause higher than themselves. Worst of all, their hearts are dulled and the fire of their lives is slowly snuffed out.[116]

The first stop on the map to manhood is initiation. Did you miss this stop? If so, you are, unfortunately, in good company.

THINK ABOUT IT...

- Who told you what it takes to be a man?
- What organizations or events did you participate in that resembled anything close to a traditional initiation?
- Did someone name you as a man or have you always had to prove to others your manhood?

PRAYER:

God, I know that you can make up for what I lack. I give you my life and ask you to show me what kind of man you want me to be and what purpose you have for my life.

---

[116] *Every man wants to play the hero. Every man needs to know that he is powerful.* John Eldredge, *Wild at Heart: Discovering the Secret of a Man's Soul* (HarperCollins Christian Pub, 2011), Kindle Location 284. See also Chuck Stecker, *Men of Honor Women of Virtue: The Power of Rites of Passage into Godly Adulthood*, (Denver: Seismic Publishing Group: 2010).

Who Am I? Really?

———— ∞∞∞ ————

THE WORD

*Wisdom is supreme; therefore get wisdom. Though
it cost all you have, get understanding.*

— PROVERBS 4.7

THOUGHT FOR THE DAY:

*When you get your "Who am I?" question
right, all the "What should I do?" questions
tend to take care of themselves.*

~ RICHARD ROHR

FROM OUR FIRST MOMENTS OF self-awareness, we ask ourselves, *Self, who are you? What are you doing here? Why are you here? Who put you here and why?*

Without a map it's hard to know where you are and what lies ahead. Without a distinct pathway given to us by our culture, we begin this journey toward manhood lost and without a clear identity. Fumbling along, boys try to answer these questions by taking cues from the people around us. We push against others and see how they will respond. We test our limits. We advance, retreat, advance again. Lurking behind and underneath everything we think, say or do is this question: *Who am I?*

When divorce or any other tragedy crashes into our lives, the props that defined our identity fall away, knocked out from under us. Once again we struggle to give coherent answers to these simple questions, *Who am I? What am I doing here? Why am I here? Who put me here and why?*

Mark Driscoll was the influential and controversial pastor of a dynamic, growing church in Seattle. Experiencing phenomenal growth in the church and beyond, things suddenly fell apart. Little did he know that just a year after he wrote the words below, they would come painfully true in his own life. But what he wrote *then* is true *today*:

> *Most of us live unaware of the source of our identity until change occurs, often in the form of hardships and pain. When an individual faces adversity, it leads to a crisis as his marriage, children, appearance, wealth, success, career, religious performance, political party, favorite cause, loving relationship, treasured possession, or something else crumbles under the weight of being a god. Suddenly he realizes that the source of his identity was the idolatry of that treasured thing.[117]*

In our culture many competing voices have told you who you should be. Now is the time to really ask this question of yourself: *Who am I?* Take it one step further: *Who do I want to be?*

---

[117] Mark Driscoll, *Who Do You Think You Are?*, 32.

THINK ABOUT IT...

- What does a successful man look like to you?
- What do you need to add to your life to be 'successful' in your own eyes? What needs to be subtracted?
- In this time of loss, what loss (your role as husband, role as father, your reputation, standard of living, money to settle your divorce and pay your lawyer, living arrangement, etc.) has hurt (or is hurting) the most? Why does that particular loss hurt so much?

LIFE COMMITMENT:

Now is my opportunity to really examine who I am deep inside. It is not too late to change my entire identity or modify elements of it.

Building the Tower Culture Wants

———— ∞∞∞ ————

THE WORD

> *So Jonathan said to his armor-bearer, "Climb up*
> *after me; the Lord has given them into the hand*
> *of Israel." Jonathan climbed up, using his hands*
> *and feet, with his armor-bearer right behind him.*
> *The Philistines fell before Jonathan, and his armor-*
> *bearer followed and killed behind him. In that first*
> *attack Jonathan and his armor-bearer killed some*
> *twenty men in an area of about half an acre.*

— 1 SAMUEL 14.12–14

THOUGHT FOR THE DAY:

> *If there's one thing the recent teen shootings have*
> *taught us it is that no one likes to be on the outside.*

~ BRET STEPHENSON

A MAN'S LIFE IS DIVIDED into two halves.

The first half of life is all about answering the question, *Am I good enough to belong?* The answer to that question is supplied by one's culture. If you grow up in West Texas, the answer lies in how good you are at football and what kind of truck you have. If you grow up in Ethiopia, the answer is in how many cows you can jump over. If you are Jewish, Bar Mitzvah at age 13 signifies the transition from boyhood to manhood when one is now responsible for one's sins. The thing every boy is pushed to shoot for is ascension—keep getting better, stronger, smarter. The only successful way forward is the way *up*.

The transition from boy to man is dependent on society leading to some bizarre ways boys are determined to be men.[118] A few days ago we talked about male initiation. Not all cultures get it right!

In our individualistic, ritual-less culture, we end up planting our adolescents' feet firmly in mid-air. We give them a map with nothing on it and tell them they can go wherever they want. In the name of freedom, we declare that our boys can be anything they want to be. The trouble is that with no guidance, our boys don't know what or who they should be. With no clear path to manhood, our boys are stuck in an

---

[118] Bret Stephenson writes: *The concept of masculinity in our culture has shifted dramatically over time. As we become less and less clear with each generation on what healthy masculinity is, it becomes hard to agree on what is expected of boys as they mature. Differences in just a couple of generations serve as testament to this. For example, in the world of movies there have always been heroes for us to identify with. Typical movie heroes of the 1940s were Bogart, John Wayne, Cary Grant, and Clark Gable. They were strong and tough, but not necessarily the biggest and baddest guys around. They often portrayed fairly ordinary men; their personification of ideal masculinity arose from their confidence, their values, and their resolve. Contrast that with the profile of modern heroes like Arnold Schwarzenegger in the eighties and nineties and Vin Diesel and The Rock today. The current model of a hero is truly larger than life, often assisted by technological invention such as bionics, genetic manipulation, and/or some serious weaponry. This new breed of hero, unlike those of yesteryear, is an image unattainable by the common boy who doesn't have personal trainers and mega-million-dollar computer effects to enhance him.* Stephenson, *From Boys to Men*, 25.

extended adolescence playing video games where they are virtual heroes, *but only virtual.*[119]

Remember the story of Walter Mitty by James Thurber? Whether commanding a Navy hydroplane through a hurricane or performing surgery on *McMillan, the millionaire banker and close personal friend of Roosevelt* who was unfortunate enough to have *obstreosis of the ductal tract*, Mitty was the hero of his own imagination.[120] Walter Mitty's imagination echoes a deeper reality: *Every boy wants to be the hero. Every boy wants to belong.*

The first half of life is about building a tower that everyone will notice. It is about jumping through the right cultural hoops to be declared successful, and most important, to be included.

---

[119] McKay and McKay write: *At the heart of the modern crisis of manhood is the extension of adolescence, a boyhood which is stretching on for a longer and longer period of time. Once thought to end in a man's 20s at the latest, men are extending their adolescence into their 30's and in some especially sad cases, their 40's. But in some ways it's not their fault. It's the fault of a culture in which rites of passage have all but disappeared, leaving men adrift and lost, never sure when and if they've become men. Today's men lack a community of males to initiate them into manhood and to recognize their new status. Across time and place, cultures have inherently understood that without clear markers on the journey to manhood, males have a difficult time making the transition and can drift along indefinitely. Thus, rites of passage were clearly delineated in nearly every culture as one of the community's most important rituals.*
While almost every culture had a rite of passage ritual, there existed a great diversity in what these ceremonies consisted of. The common thread was an experience that involved emotional and physical pain and required a boy to pass the test of manhood: to show courage, endurance, and the ability to control one's emotions. Brett McKay and Kate McKay, "Male Rites of Passages from Around the World," *The Art of Manliness*, last updated December 04, 2015, accessed April 19, 2017, http://www.artofmanliness.com/2010/02/21/male-rites-of-passage-from-around-the-world/.
[120] James Thurber, *Secret Life of Walter Mitty* (Penguin Books, 2016), Kindle Location 27.

American culture clearly holds up money, sex and power as the highest possible achievements for a man. Those goals are most visibly achieved through professional sports and/ or entertainment and business and/or technological genius. Given these realities, no wonder most of us feel we have fallen far short of the American dream.

Richard Rohr writes,

> *Almost all of culture, and even most of religious history, has been invested in the creation and maintenance of first-half-of-life issues: the big three concerns of identity, security, and sexuality and gender. They don't just preoccupy us; they totally take over.*[121]

Western culture places a high emphasis on first half of life issues. We are much more about the external marks of achievement than the internal processes of growth and wisdom. We are much more about building the biggest and tallest tower rather than helping to build a community.

THINK ABOUT IT...

* Looking back on our life, what dreams did you have as a young man? What goal, vision or fantasy captured your imagination? What set your heart on fire?

---

[121] Richard Rohr, *Falling Upward: A Spirituality for the Two Halves of Life: A Companion Journal* (London: Society for Promoting Christian Knowledge, 2013), 3.

* How did you answer the question, If I only _____ I will be happy and successful?

* Did you achieve your goal / dream / fantasy? If so, how did it make you feel? If not, how did (or does) failure make you feel?

LIFE COMMITMENT:

Though culture worships external achievement, I want my life to be about internal growth and maturity. I commit to a journey of inward growth.

The Price of Upside Down

———∞∞∞———

THE WORD

> *For although they knew God, they neither glorified him as*
> *God nor gave thanks to him, but their thinking became*
> *futile and their foolish hearts were darkened. Although*
> *they claimed to be wise, they became fools and exchanged*
> *the glory of the immortal God for images made to look*
> *like mortal man and birds and animals and reptiles.*

— ROMANS 1.21–23

THOUGHT FOR THE DAY:

> *A spiritually deadened person mourns over*
> *things that should bring celebration, yet often*
> *celebrates things that should be mourned.*

~ GARY THOMAS

TRAGEDY HAS BEEN EERILY PROMINENT in the Kennedy
family. On July 16, 1999, John F. Kennedy Jr. was flying in
his Piper Saratoga from New Jersey to Martha's Vineyard.
Kennedy was only qualified to fly under Visual Flight
Rules. Though the weather officially allowed for VFR

flight, a persistent haze made it impossible to distinguish air from water. That evening the horizon and visual landmarks were obscured. Disoriented, Kennedy flew his plane into the Atlantic, eventually descending into the water 50 times faster than normal.

What was physically true of Kennedy and his world that evening is spiritually true for all of us. We live in an upside-down, disorienting world.

I am confident that the prophet Isaiah would describe our world as he described his nearly 3,000 years ago: *Woe to those who call evil good and good evil, who put darkness for light and light for darkness, who put bitter for sweet and sweet for bitter. Woe to those who are wise in their own eyes and clever in their own sight.* (Isaiah 5.20-21)

God designed us to live in dependence upon him in love and trust. Adam and Eve chose to turn against God. Cast out of Eden, Adam and Eve lived out from under God's provision and his protection. In grace God allowed the race to continue and he ever-lovingly guided and provided for Adam and Eve. But the going was hard because Adam and Eve lived in a world turned against them, a world of their own making. They (and we) live in this upside-down world.

As young men we pick up cultural clues, landmarks if you will, to guide us. But these landmarks are false and/ or misplaced because they are landmarks set to guide us through our upside-down world. Eventually we lose our way. The horizon gets blurred, landmarks fade out of sight and we rapidly descend into the cold waters of the vast ocean, joining countless others who have made the same mistake.

Paul David Tripp says it well:

Everybody searches for life somewhere. God has placed this quest in each of our hearts. It is there to drive us to him. It is there because we were made for him. But sadly, in their lifelong quest for life, most people ignore God. In their God amnesia, they look for life where it cannot be found, and because they do, they always come up empty.[122]

As the external pieces of your life crumble around you, take comfort in knowing that many if not most of those elements of your life falling away are part of the upside-down world. Many of the components of your life that propped up your identity were delusions and illusions anyway.[123]

Think About It...

* Do you believe we live in an upside-down world? If so, in what ways does our world get it wrong?
* What is the price of living in an upside-down world?

Prayer:

God, I have built my life on upside-down things. I want to live life in the right-side-up world. Show me the way.

---

[122] Tripp, *New Morning Mercies*, Kindle Location 2629.

[123] Thomas Merton writes, *The logic of worldly success rests on a fallacy: the strange error that our perfection depends on the thoughts and opinions and applause of other men! A weird life it is, indeed, to be living always in somebody else's imagination, as if that were the only place in which one could at last become real!* Thomas Merton, *The Seven Storey Mountain* (London: SPCK, 2009), 362.

The Tower Comes Tumbling Down

THE WORD

What good will it be for a man if he gains the
whole world, yet forfeits his soul? Or what can
a man give in exchange for his soul?

— MATTHEW 16.26

THOUGHT FOR THE DAY:

So we must stumble and fall, I am sorry to say. And
that does not mean reading about falling, as you are
doing here. We must actually be out of the driver's
seat for a while, or we will never learn how to give up
control to the Real Guide. It is the necessary pattern.

~ RICHARD ROHR

THE SPIRITUAL JOURNEY OF MALES follows a predictable pathway. As boys we ask ourselves, *Am I good enough to belong?* We spend the first half of our lives trying to answer that question by building a tower to ourselves that meets cultural expectations. We try to build a tower acceptable to our social group (see Day 98). Most of us build enough of a tower to convince ourselves that we belong. For me, that tower was built out of education (a Ph.D.), status (pastor, teacher, adventurer), and family (husband, father).

But at some point, ***all men in all cultures hit the wall***—their towers come crumbling down. For all men, at some point in midlife, a missile comes careening into the tower we so carefully constructed. This is unavoidable and no one is immune. Think of Steve Jobs who died at age 56. With all his brilliance, drive and wealth, he could not avoid pancreatic cancer.

For you, the most obvious missile is divorce. But the rocket that took down your tower could be unemployment, a wayward or disappointing child, death of a parent, spouse or child, or failure of a project or sales goal or idea. Your tower can even be brought down by success (disappointment when you reach the top that you reached the top of the wrong ladder). Your tower may be crumbling because of more than one of these that hit all at the same time.

This moment in a man's life comes with various names: *The Great Defeat*, *The Humbling*, and so on. Whatever the cause and whatever you want to call it, the pain of this moment reaches into your deepest soul. You spent years and blood, sweat and tears building your tower. You were proud of your tower. You protected your tower. You loved your tower. Now it is tumbling down around you.

Here's the thing: This is a normal part of the journey. For every man in every culture, the tower comes tumbling down.

Robert Bly says it like this:

> *The way down and out doesn't require poverty, homeless-*
> *ness, physical deprivation, dishwasher work, necessarily,*
> *but it does seem to require a fall from status, from a human*
> *being to a spider, from a middle-class person to a derelict.*
> *The emphasis is on the consciousness of the fall.*[124]

The Buddha says that *Life is 10,000 joys. And life is 10,000 suf-*
ferings. You can't avoid the 10,000 sufferings.

When the missile strikes, the certainty you had when
you were 25 is replaced by a deep sense of insecurity. The
hopes and dreams you had when you began the journey are
replaced with hard questions. Pain takes the place of joy; depression seeps in where energy once thrived.

We should not be surprised by this but we are. We are surprised because we believe we are the exception to the rule.
We are surprised because we worked our asses off specifically to avoid the nightmare we are in! We are surprised
because we are Americans (if you are American), and
Americans are immune to this stuff (so we believe)! We are
surprised because we have convinced ourselves that our
wealth and education should be able to reduce our 10,000
sufferings to three, or four at the most.

The collapse of your tower is one of the most, if not the
most, critical moments in your life.

For today, know this: Every man's tower comes down at
some point in their lives (usually mid-life). Don't be surprised—it happens to all of us.

---

[124] Robert Bly, *Iron John*, 121.

THINK ABOUT IT...

* What is your tower made of? Money? Prestige? Power? Status? Physical fitness? A talent or hobby? Being a family man?
* What missiles have slammed into your tower?
* What were/are you *thinking* as you watched your tower come down?
* What were/are you *feeling* as you watched your tower crumble?
* What *actions were/are you contemplating* as you stand in the rubble that was once your life?

PRAYER:

God, I'm pissed. I worked my tail off just so this would not happen. I am at the end of my resources. Show me the way forward. Though I am thinking a lot of unhelpful thoughts and feeling a lot of emotions that could probably put me in jail if I acted on them, I want to do the right thing. I want to take the next steps of this journey with you as my guide.

Choices—*Keep Building Your Tower*

———⊶⊷———

THE WORD

He who trusts in himself is a fool, but he
who walks in wisdom is kept safe.

— PROVERBS 28.26

THOUGHT FOR THE DAY:

Most unhappiness in life is due to the fact that you are
listening to yourself rather than talking to yourself.

~ MARTYN LLOYD-JONES

HERE WE STAND IN THE midst of the ruins of what was once our carefully constructed lives. We invested our blood, sweat, tears, finances, and reputation into our tower. Now it's tumbling down. What do we do?

It's at this point in our journey that we have choices. The next two days I will share the first two of three choices. These pathways are the wrong ones to take, but they are the roads most men venture down.

The first is cling to the old, that is, to keep trying to ascend. We fall down. Then we read a motivational book that tells us that when men fall, real men pick themselves up and keep moving forward *doing the same thing we did before*, which is to say, keep building the tower that culture wants.

Men who choose this path remain stuck in the first half of life. They continue giving their energy to external markers of success. They choose to keep things on the outside, rather than do the hard work of looking inward.

The problem is that most men don't have the resources of time, energy and/or money to rebuild a fallen tower. Most of us can't buy a new Corvette to ease our pain and regain our status.

In American life you often see wealthy older men who are still stuck in the first half of life. They are still boys trying to be men. Those of us in the second half of life see these older men as boys frantically trying to rebuild their original tower.

Examples of men who choose to try to keep ascending are wealthy men who seem to never have enough and men who are old and fat but think they are still attractive to young women. Believe me, if you're one of those guys who think the girls still adore you, you are an *old fool.* Everyone knows it except you! Every time I see an old rich guy in a hot, fast car, I see a little boy who is still trying to be a man. This is a man stuck in the first half of life. This is a 20-year-old stuck in a 60-year-old body.

If you are standing in the middle of the ruins of your tower and you are thinking to yourself, *I can get this back, I can rebuild my life, I can overcome this myself...* you are choosing to keep trying to ascend. You are choosing to 'be the man' according to what culture wants. You are choosing to answer second-half-of-life questions with first-half-of-life answers.

The problem with this is that even if you are successful—even if you manage to build your old tower back—it's vulnerable to come tumbling back down. If you choose this path you are choosing a path of hard and frustrating work that will never lead to deep security and inner peace.

THINK ABOUT IT...

* Name some older men who have chosen to keep trying to ascend, that is, though they are old and ugly, they keep trying to *be the man.*
* What would it take in terms of personal time, energy, motivation and money to get back what you have lost? Is it worth it?

LIFE COMMITMENT:

I tried to answer first-half-life-questions with first-half-of-life answers. That didn't turn out so well. Give me another option.

Choices—*Bitterness*

—⚬⚬⚬—

The Word

See to it that no one misses the grace of God and that no
bitter root grows up to cause trouble and defile many.

— Hebrews12.15

Thought for the Day:

It is a simple but sometimes forgotten truth that
the greatest enemy to present joy and high hopes
is the cultivation of retrospective bitterness.

~ Robert Menzies

A SECOND CHOICE WHEN OUR tower comes tumbling down is to make camp in the middle of the rubble. It is to choose bitterness. I think most men choose this dark and lonely path.

To choose bitterness is to deeply feel the losses and *choose to keep feeling those losses*. It is to do a mental income/expense report of your life and dwell on the huge *minus* sign on the bottom line. It's to let anger—perhaps justified—find its vent in ruminating over and over about *what has been done to you* and *what has been taken from you.*

To choose bitterness is to deny God's work in your life. It is to say that the universe is set against you, and if there is a God, he has either forgotten you or wants you damaged.

To choose bitterness is to allow your dreams to die. It is to give up on what you hoped life would be or could be.

To choose bitterness is to choose to remain stuck. It's to decide to be alone the rest of your life.

I remember a wonderful patient in a nursing home. She was 92-years-old. She was *always happy* when I visited her! She was thrilled to be in the nursing home and proudly proclaimed that they treated her like a queen! I have a feeling that because she said she was treated like a queen the staff made sure she was...with delight! Most of us shudder at the thought of spending our last days in a nursing home. Not this amazing woman.

One day I asked her the secret to her happiness. She said, *My mama used to say: "Smile, and the world will smile with you. Frown, and you frown alone!"* I needed to hear that message that day. I have done my share of bitching. So far no one has wanted to hear it, except me, myself and I, and we are a boring lot.

Kristin Armstrong experienced disappointment and heartache in her marriage to and then divorce from Lance Armstrong. Her advice: *Don't go sour. Don't settle for less than a healed heart. Don't stop believing.*[125]

---

[125] Armstrong, *Happily Ever After*, Kindle Location 2842.

To sink into bitterness is to choose to settle for less than you are now and to steal the world of what you were meant to be and what you will contribute in the future.

I realize the struggle. I'm still in the fight. Part of me wants to sit in the rubble and stop thinking, trying, praying and believing. But if I choose to sit and brood, my life will be over. I will have said to the world that my God really isn't big enough to rescue and rebuild me. It will be to say that my future days are not worth living. It would be to deny God's plans for me. It would be to deny the amazing promises of the Bible to heal and restore me.

Henry Cloud writes, *Grief that is ignored turns into depression or hopelessness. Hurt turns into cynicism, lack of trust, or worse. Anger turns into bitterness and hatred.*[126]

At the end of the day I don't want to remembered as depressed, hopeless, cynical, bitter and full of hate.

The losses are real. You may have lost literally everything. But to choose to sit in the middle of the rubble of the tower you so carefully constructed *and remain there* does no one any good. You will spend your days alone. You will deprive the world of what you have to offer for the years you have left.

Worst of all, bitterness just sucks. Who wants to spend the rest of their life in such a sucky, shitty place?

---

[126] Cloud, *9 Things You Simply Must Do to Succeed in Love and Life*, Kindle Location 355.

THINK ABOUT IT...

* On a scale of 0 to 10, (0 being not bitter at all to 10, absolutely completely bitter), how bitter are you?

   0—1—2—3—4—5—6—7—8—9—10

* From where you are today, how often and how far do you slide to the left (less bitter, more peace) or to the right (toward more bitterness)?
* What triggers your slides to the right?
* What thoughts, processes, situations or circumstances trigger a slide to the right? (I'm hoping that reading this book is included in this list!)

LIFE COMMITMENT:

Life sucks. But I will not make camp in the ruins. I'm moving on from here. I know it is a struggle to let anger and bitterness go. I commit to this battle for my heart. I have much to offer the world. Bitterness will not keep me from being who God wants me to be.

Wrestling with God

———⟡———

THE WORD

*I know, O Lord, that a man's life is not his
own; it is not for man to direct his steps.*

—JEREMIAH10.23

THOUGHT FOR THE DAY:

*One appreciates good weight equipment not
for any immediate pleasure it provides, but
for the ultimate benefit one receives.*

~ DALAI LAMA (WITH HOWARD CUTLER)

SO FAR IN OUR JOURNEY through manhood we've seen that boys
are born asking the same questions, *Am I good enough? What
does it take to be a man?* The boy answers those questions by
whatever standards the culture sets—a big truck, a snazzy
education, jumping over cows, enduring circumcision, etc.
The main idea drilled into all boys is to keep working hard,
keep rising, keep ascending.

At some point in life, however, usually between the
ages of 30 and 60, the tower a man so carefully constructed

according to society's standards, comes crashing down. An event, circumstance, or disaster tears into our tower, bringing it to the ground. That our tower is in ruins around us is a surprise to us and leaves us devastated.

At this point we have some choices to make. **Some men choose to <u>keep trying to ascend</u>.** Some men keep trying to *be the man*. They keep trying to achieve their idea of manhood by using the same standards as before—wealth, prestige, status, sexual prowess, physical fitness, knowledge, etc. They can't let go of the losses. They try to rebuild the same tower.

Most men, however, don't have the physical, financial or mental resources to start over. It was hard enough to think about building the tower when you were 20. But at least then you had energy, motivation, drive—and years—to get the job done. Given the present situation and limitations, **<u>bitterness</u> seems to be the only choice**. The work required to keep trying to ascend is too much. At this point, resigning oneself to 'reality' seems the natural and easy option.

We live with an internal struggle, a tug-of-war of sorts within our souls. Part of us wants an easy life. We long for a place to rest without a care in the world. We yearn for a break from the struggles of ordinary life. We work hard to have a few moments of peace and deep satisfaction.

On the other hand, deep down we long for a challenge. Do you really want to spend your days playing golf? *All your days?* Do you really find deep satisfaction in playing video games or watching endless football on TV? When we are in the struggle, we long for rest. When we are resting, we long for a challenge.

When a man's tower comes crashing down these two longings are accentuated. In the chaos we desperately seek a bubble of peace. Some try to find this bubble by escaping through alcohol or drugs.

At the same time, we know from our personal experience that there is deep satisfaction in overcoming looming obstacles. Though our lives are in ruins around us, something deep inside us senses the challenge and is invited into it.

It is at this point that a man can make the choice to keep trying to ascend (the first choice). If that doesn't work (which it won't for long), one realizes the futility of it all, and resigns himself to bitterness (the second choice).

There is a third way. That way is to *allow God to engage us in the struggle.*

In the first half of life the question we tried so hard to answer was *Who am I?* In the second half of life, when we are standing in the ruins of our failed attempt to answer that question, the next question becomes *Who is God and what does he want from me?*

We have been so busy building our tower in the first half of our lives that any real struggle with God was pushed aside. Now that our efforts are in ruins around us, God has room to engage us on the important questions.

Richard Rohr says, *Each of us is something greater than he or she dares to imagine, something beyond what meets the eye.*[127]

And John Eldredge states what that 'something' is: *Deep in his heart, every man longs for a battle to fight, an adventure to live, and a beauty to rescue. That is how he bears the image of God; that is what God made him to be.*[128]

---

[127] Rohr, Durepos, and McGrath, *On the Threshold of Transformation*, 41.

[128] John Eldredge, *Wild at Heart: Discovering the Secret of a Man's Soul* (HarperCollins: 2011), Kindle Location 88.

When we were boys growing into young men, something deep inside us called us to be exceptional. Something called us to give ourselves away in the battle. Something called us to heroically sacrifice ourselves for the world. We then tried it our way. Now, sitting in the rubble of our shattered boyhood dreams, *we are finally weak enough to be strong enough to come face-to-face with God.*

The male journey toward true manhood and maturity necessarily involves this face-off with God. It's the way we are wired. We simply don't get it until we have jumped into the ring and duked it out with Almighty God. Weird, huh? I can't explain it except that it seems our egos must be pummeled into the dust so that we finally have a heart that is open and receptive to God's love and work in our lives.

In the introduction to this daily guide I wrote,

> *If you ride this kayak all the way to the ocean, you will actually be thankful for the pain you are in right now because you will recognize that what you have gained in really knowing and being known by God is far better than anything bad the world can throw at you and anything good the world can entice you with.*

At the end of the day we want to be able to say with the Apostle Paul, *I have fought the good fight, I have finished the race.* Life *is* a fight! It *is* a race. Fights and races are never easy. But they pull us to something higher and better, and deep down. And we like that. We want that.

Think About It...

* The classic Bible story of a man wrestling with God is Jacob at the River Jabbok as he is about to face his brother Esau. Take a moment to read Genesis 32. What do you think is meant when the angel says to Jacob, *Your name will no longer be Jacob, but Israel, because you have struggled with God and with men and have overcome?* (Genesis 32.28)?
* What is at stake when we wrestle with God? What are we struggling about?

Life Commitment:

I tried it my way. Maybe God's way is better. To be convinced of this is a struggle for me. But I am willing to engage in this struggle.

Dirt

———— ❧ ————

The Word

When pride comes, then comes disgrace,
but with humility comes wisdom.

— Proverbs 11.2

Thought for the Day:

Egotism is a passionate and exaggerated love of self,
which leads a man to connect everything with his own
person, and to prefer himself to everything in the world.

~ Alexis de Tocqueville

If you are a farmer you know that everything depends on dirt.

But you don't have to be a farmer to know that dirt is not glamorous stuff. Dirt looks, well, dirty. It doesn't smell like Old Spice. It smells like Old Shit. Dirt is where dead things go. It's where we dump our waste. Dirt is beneath us. It's dark and dank. It's the place of rotting leaves and dead bugs and the repository into which we defecate.

The ground receives all that we don't want. We literally bury our trash in huge landfills and then cover them over with more dirt. No one hangs out at a landfill. Travel guides don't recommend a visit to the local trash pile. And the men who work there? We consider them invisible people, men less than ourselves.

But if you are a farmer *you know that life comes from dirt.* You know that the foundation of all the good stuff *above* the ground begins in the depth and the darkness and the dankness and the death of dirt that *is* the ground.

Our word *humility* comes from the Latin word *humus,* which means *dirt.*

Divorce pushes us face down into the dirt. Divorce is humiliating. Divorce is dark and dank. Divorce is death in a thousand ways. There is nothing glamorous or glittery about divorce. It is shit and it is the place of shit. Divorce is not new life, it's the place of rotting dreams and broken promises.

But... dirt is where old, dead, rotten things get transformed into nourishment for new life.

In wrestling with God you realize <u>dirt has value</u>. God reveals to you that, like the wise farmer, nothing good *above ground* happens without quality dirt *below ground.*

Could you rethink your position in life right now? Could you acknowledge that while you are in the dirt, good things happen in dirt and God is able to do good things in the dirty place you find yourself?

A mile-high glacier covered the northern half of the United States until about 10,000 years ago. The massive weight of the ice scoured the land down to bedrock. In my neighborhood in New Hampshire an open layer of rock bears the striated scars of where tons of ice dug out the granite thousands of years ago.

Because of this massive frozen bulldozer, all the soil in New England formed since that glacier receded 10,000 years ago. And there's not much of it. It's precious because it's scarce and it has been long in the making.

So too is the soil in your life that has been made from crushed dreams and broken relationships.

Chris Tiegreen writes, *High callings seem to require some low experiences. Revelations of light seem to come most often in places of mystifying darkness. And life seems to flourish most plentifully out of deathly wounds. Out of the depths, God speaks.*[129]

The reality is that life has pushed you face-down in the dirt. Why not let dirt do what dirt is meant to do? Why not let God take the dead, thrown-away things of your life and turn them into something new?

THINK ABOUT IT...

* Go outside and get a handful of dirt. Look at it closely. Smell it. Feel it. Now look around at the things growing out of that dirt. Can you believe such amazing things come out of something so lowly and distasteful as dirt?

* What can God do with the dirty place you are in right now?

---

[129] Tiegreen, *One Year Hearing His Voice Devotional*, 641.

PRAYER:

God, I have worked all my life to stay above ground. Now I am <u>in the ground</u>. But I know from your promises and from the dirt in my hand that there is tremendous value in dirt. I surrender to you. Do your magic in my life. Take my many deaths and transform them into amazing life.

Down = Up

---eee---

THE WORD

Do not conform any longer to the pattern of this world,
but be transformed by the renewing of your mind.

— ROMANS 12.2

THOUGHT FOR THE DAY:

We would rather be ruined than changed. We
would rather die in our dread than climb the
cross of the present and let our illusions die.

~ W. H. AUDEN

THE ABSOLUTE LAST PLACE ANY of us could imagine being
is where we are today. When we were 20-years-old, none
of us decided to intentionally end up in the dirt. Our
dreams, ambitions and goals did not include colossal failure. *But this is where we are, and, the reality is that this is where*
all men end up at some point along their journey. Somehow we
thought we would be the exception. We aren't and the fact
that we are now in the dirt proves it.

In this moment *we can choose to keep on trying the same old things that didn't work before.* We can try to rebuild our tower. But that's a lot of work and towers are always subject to come crashing back down.

In disgust we can choose option #2: *we can give up and become bitter.* We can curl our souls up into a hard little ball, keep our heads low, and be bitterly 'content' with dead dreams and a wasted life.

The *third way is to realize what every farmer knows: life comes from dirt.* But dirt is *down.* Dirt is low. Dirt is anything but glamorous. Dirt is not what dreams are made of. At least that's the way the world looks at it.

From God's perspective, however, he has you right where he needs you to do the amazing work of transformation, re-energizing and re-commissioning he has waiting for you.

In wrestling with God you realize the value of dirt and <u>you are willing to get dirty</u>.

That means taking the knee to God. It means bowing before him. It means surrendering to his ultimate authority in your life.

A few weeks ago I said that the longest distance is not from one end of the universe to the other (billions of light years). The longest distance in the universe is *the space from a man's knee to the ground, humbling ourselves before Almighty God.*

But this is exactly where God does his best and amazing work. God wants us to humbly jump in the dirt pile *not to humiliate us* but *to work in us.*

The good news is that none of this is a surprise to God, he has, after all, been here himself. He who humbled himself to become one of us—the greatest voluntary *demotion* of all—knows that *out of humiliation comes rebirth and renewal.*

For us to rise, he had to fall. For us to rise, we have to follow Jesus on the same journey—down, then up. Going down is exactly NOT what our culture defines as being a man. True men ALWAYS fight to stay on their feet, getting ever faster, smarter, richer. But we can't sustain it. WE ALL FALL. If we are smart, we recognize that Jesus, the manliest man who ever lived, voluntarily *fell* to show us the way *up*. If we are smart we will follow Jesus *down* in order for him to *lift us up.*

Unfortunately for us, we—especially men—don't work that way. Like a fullback breaking through the line, we fight with all we have to keep plowing forward, often blowing people away as we barrel through and over them. But just like that fullback, *we will be taken down.* And it hurts. It hurts a lot.

Divorce takes you down. It grinds your self-respect and dignity into the dirt. It leaves you 'shaken up' long after the play is over. It leaves your head spinning, wondering if you will ever be able to get back in the game.

So you are face down in the dirt, pounded there by your poor choices or because someone else pushed you there. *Don't despair and don't give up.* Jesus fell too, and he rose again. *So will you.*

Julian of Norwich wrote about:

By his permission, we fall; but we are kept in his blissful love with his might and wisdom; and by mercy and grace we are raised to many more joys. It is in rightfulness and mercy he wills to be known and loved, now and without end. And the soul that wisely beholds it in grace is well pleased with both and enjoys them endlessly.[130]

THINK ABOUT IT...

* We think we can avoid being face down in the dirt. Well, it happened. What do you think about dirt? Can this moment actually be good for you?
* If so, are you willing to bow to God's authority in your life to do the life transforming work that dirt does?

Life Commitment:
  Lord Jesus, you who were outrageously rich in all things became incomprehensibly poor for us, so that we, who were desperately poor in sin, might be made immeasurably rich in grace.[131]

---

[130] Julian of Norwich, *Revelations of Divine Love* (White Crow Books, 2011), , 80.
[131] Scotty Smith, *Everyday Prayers: 365 Days to a Gospel-Centered Faith* (Grand Rapids: Baker Books, 2011), 382.

Descent into Wisdom (1)

THE WORD

*A man's pride brings him low, but a
man of lowly spirit gains honor.*

— PROVERBS 29.23

THOUGHT FOR THE DAY:

If you ever find yourself in the wrong story, leave.

~ MO WILLEMS, GOLDILOCKS AND THE THREE DINOSAURS

W. H. AUDEN SAID, *WE would rather be ruined than changed. We
would rather die in our dread than climb the cross of the present and
let our illusions die.*[132]

Is Auden describing you? I don't think so, otherwise you
wouldn't be reading this book. Whatever the path ahead,
you have chosen *not* to keep trying to rebuild the same old
tower on which you worked so hard the first half of your life.
And though you may feel crushed, worried and ground into
the dirt, you are choosing *not* to end life a bitter old man.

---

[132] W.H. Auden, *The Age of Anxiety: A Baroque Eclogue*, ed. Alan Jacobs
(Princeton: Princeton University Press, 2011), 105.

The great news for us is that there is a third way. This third option is to humble ourselves before God and allow him to remake us into the men he always wanted us to be.

Our personal salvation project must always show itself to be almost totally wrong.... The pain of things falling apart is what we call suffering, and it is one of God's means to show us that life is always bigger than we imagine it to be.[133]

Life really *is* bigger than we imagined it could be. For us as men, it takes intense suffering to *humble* us enough so we will be *smart* enough to turn to the God who is *big* enough to *pull us up* enough to see the bigger picture. And when we get it—when we see the bigger picture and jump in with both feet—we realize that this whole thing is big enough to pull us forward out of the pit and into the future God has for us.

In the end, it is all about the source of our identity. Remember the question the boy asks himself, *Am I good enough to belong?* When our tower comes crashing down the resounding answer we hear back from the world is *Absolutely not. You failed.*

If we gain our identity from the world, we will be devastated. But if an unshakably positive identity comes from Almighty and Eternal God, what does it matter what the world thinks?[134]

The journey into wisdom begins with rejecting the quest to gain your identity from the world and, instead, truly embrace your identity graciously given by God. The first half of life was all about us. The second half of life is all about God.

---

[133] Rohr, Durepos, and McGrath, *On the Threshold of Transformation*, 61.

[134] *Fear of man will prove to be a snare, but whoever trusts in the Lord is kept safe.* (Proverbs 29:25.)

The first half of life is about building our own tower, hoping it will be good enough for the people in our little worlds to give us their approval. The second half of life is all about receiving the approval God already has of us.

In the first half of life we ask the question, *Who am I?* In the second half of life, we ask a bigger question: *Who is God?*

Am I good enough? is changed into *How can I embrace God's goodness in me?*

What do I do with my pain? changes to *How will God heal and use my pain?*

What do I do with my power? changes to *How will I join God in his use of power?*

Why not give up on your own tower and get to work on what God is building? He is a far better builder and what he is building will last forever.

To leave the ruins of your own tower and join God's project is to transition from the first half of life to the second half with grace and wisdom. Yes, it's humbling to leave your own project and join God's work crew, but in the end, it is the best and right choice.

THINK ABOUT IT...

* Think about your pain. Where do you hurt? What is the source of that hurt? How does the source of your hurt identify the source of your identity?

* What will you need to let go in order to leave the ruins of your own life and join God's great project?

LIFE COMMITMENT:

I've come a long way down from my heady days as a young man dreaming big dreams. But maybe my dreams then weren't big enough. And maybe I am not the real Dreamer anyway. I choose to leave the ruins of my life and join God's project. Partners with him, how can I go wrong? It really is his deal anyway.

Descent into Wisdom (2)

THE WORD

> *God chose the foolish things of the world to shame the*
> *wise; God chose the weak things of the world to shame the*
> *strong. He chose the lowly things of this world and the*
> *despised things—and the things that are not—to nullify*
> *the things that are, so that no one may boast before him.*

— 1 CORINTHIANS 1.27–29

THOUGHT FOR THE DAY:

> *In the divine economy of grace, sin and failure*
> *become the base metal and raw material*
> *for the redemption experience itself.*

~ RICHARD ROHR

TOWARD THE BEGINNING OF THIS journey we asked a simple question, *What does a win look like?* Let's ask that question again, except on a grander scale: *What does a win look like for all of life?* At the end of the day, what does a successful man look like? At the end of the day, how do you want to be remembered?

I have officiated many funerals for men and I have never extolled the selfishness, the raw power, the greed, or the anger of a man. At the end of the day, what we view as a wise man is the man who, from a platform of deep, inner strength, gives himself for others in solid, humble, and gentle ways.

Here, specifically, is what such a man looks like:

- He has found true life and he is settled in it.
- Because his source of power is God, not himself, he has no need to push, intimidate or manipulate.
- He is not a know-it-all. His knowledge runs broad and deep but he feels no need to be the smartest person in the room.
- His measures of success include faithfulness to God not accomplishments in the world. He doesn't need a dead animal's head on his library wall or a $100,000 car. The source of his identity is outside himself and the world, and is untouchable, unchangeable, and utterly and eternally secure.
- He is a Kingdom man, not a party man. He is a Kingdom man, not a company or union man. He does not give himself away to transient earthly entities such as corporations, armies, or nation-states.
- He has more life than when he was 25 and he knows it. Because his identity is secure and outside himself and the world, he has no need to protect it. He can give his life away because he knows there is more where that came from.
- Though he is no wimp, he is free from the need to compete. He can have peer-to-peer relationships with

other men because he doesn't to either beat them or subject himself to them.

* He is equally happy to either lead the team or to be a team player.
* His life is not his own. His life is not about him, it is about God. He lives to make God famous, not himself.[135]

Tony Dungy is such a man. Dungy did what only 31 other men have done: coach a football team to a win in the Super Bowl. But for him, this was not the apex of life:

Leading a team to a Super Bowl win is considered the pinnacle of an NFL coach's profession, and I'm fortunate enough to have done that. But that was never an all-encompassing quest for me. I knew it would not make my life complete if we won or leave me feeling unfulfilled if it never happened. I wanted to win, of course—I'm as competitive as the next guy. But significance isn't found in things like winning a Super Bowl—or whatever is considered to be the pinnacle of your career or ambitions. No, significance is found in focusing on the priorities you know are important: doing as good a job as you can do, spending quality time with people you love, and investing yourself in ministry opportunities and influencing others for good. In other words, real success is about doing what God has called you to do as well as you can.[136]

---

[135] Richard Rohr and Joseph Martos, *From Wild Man to Wise Man: Reflections on Male* Spirituality (Cincinnati: St. Anthony Messenger Press, 2005), Kindle Location 226-244.

[136] Dungy and Whitaker, *Uncommon: Finding Your Path to Significance*, Kindle Location 721 (emphasis mine).

THINK ABOUT IT...

- At the end of the day, what does a real winner look like? What is success?
- What must die in you for you to be reborn into this winner?

LIFE COMMITMENT:

At the end of the day, I want to be a winner in God's Kingdom. I submit to him and commit to his transforming work in my life.

God's Mission for You

—⊶∾⊷—

THE WORD

Then Jesus came to them and said, "All authority
in heaven and on earth has been given to me.
Therefore go and make disciples of all nations,
baptizing them in the name of the Father and of the
Son and of the Holy Spirit, and teaching them to
obey everything I have commanded you. And surely
I am with you always, to the very end of the age.

— MATTHEW 28.18-20

THOUGHT FOR THE DAY:

Humans don't mind hardship, in fact they thrive on it;
what they mind is not feeling necessary. Modern society
has perfected the art of making people not feel necessary.

~ SEBASTIAN JUNGER

I LIVE NEAR THE TEXAS Hill Country, famous for its spring-
time explosion of flowers, especially the bluebonnet. (By
the way, men who are well into the second half of their lives
can thoroughly enjoy beauty like wildflowers because we

don't consider such appreciation as unmanly). My work as a hospice chaplain takes me hundreds of miles through the hill country every week. The fields of bluebonnets are truly spectacular.

But this spring one bluebonnet caught my attention. I was hiking with my two sons at a state park along the Pedernales River. Over many millennia the river has carved a deep channel through the limestone. The river regularly floods and scours the riverbed down to bedrock. On this particular hike I was in the middle of the riverbed, a huge slab of limestone. But there in the middle of this solid rock riverbed was a lone bluebonnet.

By way of some undoubtedly torturous journey, a lone bluebonnet seed had found its way to a tiny patch of dirt, and there, in the midst of the chaos, this tiny seed had done its tiny seed thing—exploded forth into a bluebonnet of inestimable glory! A wayward bluebonnet seed and a patch of good dirt, however small, combined to do what it was it meant to do—sprout and grow into what God intended it to be.

Good dirt always makes something alive and amazing. Good dirt with a willing seed allow both to do what God intends it to do—grow.

This is true of you. You are in the dirt. Good! Now you are ready to live the life God intended. Now you are ready to be who God made you to be. Now you are ready to hear God's call on your life and find the intense, other-worldly satisfaction of fulfilling your eternal purpose.

In the first half of life the question we tried so hard to answer was *Who am I?* In the second half of life, when we are standing in the ruins of our failed attempts to answer that question, the next question becomes *Who is God and what does he want from me?*

God is good, that's who God is. And God is amazingly involved in every detail of your life. And God wants you to join him in his work on the world.

Remember my friend who gave the first half of his life to Verizon—and at the end of that run, felt empty? Most of us men do that—we give the first half of our lives away to something less than God, all in an attempt to 'make something of ourselves.' We've listened to what the world demanded, and if successful, discovered we climbed the wrong mountain. If unsuccessful, we are left alone and disillusioned.

But in God's goodness, the second half of your life can be spent giving yourself away to God's bigger, better and eternal mission! The second half of your life can be spent in the service of the God who has already accepted you and approves of you!

Rick Warren succinctly states:

God is at work in the world, and he wants you to join him. This assignment is called your mission. God wants you to have both a ministry in the Body of Christ and a mission in the world. Your ministry is your service to believers, and your mission is your service to unbelievers.[137]

---

[137] Warren, *The Purpose Driven Life*, Kindle Location 3999.

The deal is, however, that you come to God on his terms. God intervenes in our lives... but he is not coming on our terms; he is inviting us to join him on his terms. Do we invite God into our lives or do we accept God's invitation into his life?

The real question is *Can I trust God with the second half of my life?*

Those of us who have lived through the first half of life and then been devastated by the utter destruction of our towers, and then have then joined God on his mission for the second half of our lives can testify: **YES**! God is good and faithful and true and wild and amazing and awesome! We can affirm with Paul David Tripp:

> *The One who call[s us] created the world and holds it together by his will. He has power over all things spiritual and physical. He rules every situation, location, and relationship in which his call is to be followed. He is amazing in his wisdom, abundant in his grace, and boundless in his love. He is saving, forgiving, transforming, and delivering. What he says is always best and what he requires is always good. When he calls, he goes with you. What he calls you to do, he empowers by his grace. When he guides, he protects. He stands with power and faithfulness behind every one of his promises. He has never failed to deliver anything that he has promised. There is simply no risk in answering the call of the King of kings.*[138]

Yeah!

---

[138] Tripp, *New Morning Mercies*, Kindle Location 2680.

THINK ABOUT IT...

* What will you do now? What will you do with the rest of your life? Will you keep trying to be *the man* and end up an old fool? Will you sink into despair and bitterness? Or will you join God in the most amazing daring heart-thumping adventure?

* Merely to survive and preserve our life is a low-level instinct that we share with good little lizards, but it is not heroism in any classic sense. We were meant to thrive, not just survive. We are glad when someone survives, and that surely took some courage and effort. But what will do with your now resurrected life? That is the heroic question.[139]

LIFE COMMITMENT:

I am all in. I tried life on my own. It didn't turn out so well. But I know that for God to use me he had to break me. I'm broken but I am also ready for him to put me back together the way I was meant to be—and to give me a mission for the second half of my life. This won't be easy but it will be good. I'm ready.

---

[139] Rohr, Durepos, and McGrath, *On the Threshold of Transformation*, 21.

Peter's Journey

———— ✦ ————

THE WORD

As Jesus was walking beside the Sea of Galilee,
he saw two brothers, Simon called Peter and his
brother Andrew. They were casting a net into the
lake, for they were fishermen. "Come, follow me,"
Jesus said, "and I will make you fishers of men."
At once they left their nets and followed him.

— MATTHEW 4.18-20

THOUGHT FOR THE DAY:

Don't ask yourself what the world needs, ask
yourself what makes you come alive, because what
the world needs are men who have come alive.

~ JOHN ELDREDGE

THE APOSTLE PETER IS A case study in the spiritual journey of men.

As a young man he successfully fulfilled the role of a dutiful but not brilliant son in his Jewish culture. We assume he was a good fisherman, but we know he was not a scholar. He had already bumped into the limitation of having failed to reach the higher levels of education. But most boys didn't, so to continue the family tradition of fishing would have been acceptable. And it was good, manly work. Men fished. Being identified as such a man would have been good for a young man like Peter.

But then comes this young revolutionary named Jesus. Everything about Jesus appealed to the young, energetic, rambunctious Peter. Anything can be used by a young man to build his first-half-of-life identity, including religion, especially in a society steeped in religion.

But Jesus was more than religious—he was revolutionary. He was a rebel. And rebels draw young men like a magnet. The Jews were living under tyrannical Roman oppression. Jesus seemed to have what it would take to overthrow this evil Roman empire and bring back Israel's glory days.

The first half of life is all about us though the hero in every young man yearns to gain personal recognition through communal sacrifice. War neatly accomplishes this. The first half of life is about building our own tower to gain approval and recognition. In the first half of life we ask the question, *Who am I?* Jesus offered Peter the perfect opportunity to answer this question.

Peter, who are you?

I am a follower of the rebel Jesus who will lead us back to glory. And when all is said and done, I will be on top with Jesus!

It wasn't long into the journey before Peter was living the dream. When the disciples are stuck on a boat in a storm, Jesus comes walking to them on the water. (Matthew 14.22-33) Peter, ever adventurous and working hard to distinguish himself from the pack, says, *Lord, if it's you tell me to come to you on the water.* Jesus says, *Come on!*

You know the story—Peter takes those first steps on the water then realizes what he is doing, and—in fear—sinks in the waves. Jesus reaches down, pulling the soggy disciple from the water. Though gently rebuked by Jesus, Peter still has the intense satisfaction of having walked on water, if even for only a few steps. He was leader of the pack! He was the man!

A little while later Jesus pulls his disciples away to the mountains in the north. There Jesus asks them who they really think he is. Peter, always eager for approval, exclaims, *You are the Christ, the Son of the living God!* (Matthew 16.16) Then come words that must have been music to Peter's ears:

> *Blessed are you, Simon son of Jonah, for this was not revealed to you by man, but by my Father in heaven. And I tell you that you are Peter, and on this rock I will build my church, and the gates of Hades will not overcome it. I will give you the keys of the kingdom of heaven; whatever you bind on earth will be bound in heaven, and whatever you loose on earth will be loosed in heaven. (Matthew 16.-19)*

Wow! Peter had made it! Or so he thought. Peter was about to undergo the demolition of the tower he carefully and energetically constructed.

But for the moment, young Peter was at the top of his game. What could possibly go wrong?

THINK ABOUT IT...

* Think back again to your younger days. What expectations and dreams were given to you by your family? By your friends? By teachers and other influential people in your life?

* What dream or dreams did you buy into? What did you imagine your life would be as you entered adulthood?

* What dreams came true? What did you accomplish? How were you rewarded for what you accomplished?

* What dreams failed? What did you do with demolished dreams?

PRAYER:

God, renew and redirect the energy of my youth into energy given to you and your Kingdom.

Big Man Peter

~∞~

THE WORD

*Then Simon Peter, who had a sword, drew it and
struck the high priest's servant, cutting off his
right ear. (The servant's name was Malchus.) Jesus
commanded Peter, "Put your sword away! Shall I
not drink the cup the Father has given me?"*

—JOHN 18.10–11

THOUGHT FOR THE DAY:

*Fear not that your life will come to an end
but that it will never have a beginning.*

~ JOHN HENRY NEWMAN

THINGS WERE GOING WELL FOR Peter until he tried to stop Jesus.
Peter had a mission for Jesus. That's how we men think—*it's
all about me.* (Women don't start out that way. For them it
is all about the kids—that's the way God made them!) For
Peter the purpose of Jesus was to make Peter famous. Peter
would serve in Jesus' amazing kingdom after Jesus overthrew
the Roman empire

Peter reflected his way of thinking when he proclaimed at Caesarea Philippi that Jesus was the Christ. But then things began to go downhill for Peter. Right after Peter's amazing insight into Jesus' true identity, Peter gets Jesus completely wrong. It goes like this:

> *From that time on Jesus began to explain to his disciples that he must go to Jerusalem and suffer many things at the hands of the elders, chief priests and teachers of the law, and that he must be killed and on the third day be raised to life.*
>
> *Peter took him aside and began to rebuke him. "**Never, Lord!**" he said. "**This shall never happen to you!**"*
>
> *Jesus turned and said to Peter, "Get behind me, Satan! You are a stumbling block to me; **you do not have in mind the things of God, but the things of men.**"*
>
> *Then Jesus said to his disciples, "If anyone would come after me, he must deny himself and take up his cross and follow me. **For whoever wants to save his life will lose it, but whoever loses his life for me will find it.** (Matthew 16.21–25, emphasis mine)*

Jesus dying on a criminal's cross was definitely NOT how Peter envisioned his future. Peter had hitched his wagon to a winner, not a loser! Dying on a cross screamed LOSER!

But some things had to die in Peter before Jesus could use him to build his Kingdom.

The *first* thing that had to die in Peter was his young man dreams of personal glory.

The *second* thing that would have to die in him was the idea that being a true man meant always winning, always ascending, always being the leader of the pack. Peter just didn't get it.

Jesus and his disciples make their way to Jerusalem where Jesus is hailed as a hero (the Triumphal Procession, celebrated by the church as Palm Sunday). Peter liked that! But a few days later when Jesus tried to wash Peter's feet, he rebelled. The Master would *not* wash his feet! But Jesus insisted that the way up is down. Peter reluctantly relented.

Then came the arrest in the Garden. As Jesus is arrested, Peter steps up to defend his master by whacking off the ear of one of the servants of the High Priest with a sword. Instead of getting praised for his bravery, he gets rebuked.

But it only gets worse as the tide turns against Jesus. Everything Peter dreamed of—Jesus overthrowing the tyrannical Romans, Peter's place of honor and leadership in the new kingdom—was jeopardized as Jesus went to trial. As Jesus falls into the iron grip of the authorities and public opinion begins to turn, Peter becomes increasingly confused.

Peter's low point comes a few hours later. In a stunning turn of events, Peter actually turns against Christ. When pegged as a follower of Jesus, Peter disowns Jesus—not once but three times.

Where was Peter's mighty bravado? Where was his undying loyalty to his Master?

In that moment Peter's tower came crashing down. All his young man dreams and his young man energy failed him just at the point when he could have truly been a hero. The result? *[Peter] went outside and wept bitterly.* (Luke 22.62)

Peter was broken. Everything he had hoped for vanished in front of his eyes. His Master really would die on the cross, and just when Peter could have at last fulfilled his dream of being a hero, he blew it. Peter's carefully constructed identity was in tatters.

THINK ABOUT IT...

* If you had been Peter at the moment when the servant girl asked him about Jesus, what would you have said?

* Can you identify with Peter in his moment of anguish? When have you failed to be who you proclaimed yourself to be? When have you betrayed your core values?

* When have you experienced the destruction of your tower? When has your identity been threatened or destroyed? Did you 'weep bitterly'? If not, what did you do?

* Peter didn't know it then, but he would go on to be one of the top leaders of the church—far more useful and famous than he could have ever dreamed. How can knowing how God used Peter give you hope for your future?

LIFE COMMITMENT:
I commit to sticking with Jesus, though sometimes his way seems hard and even pointless.

Peter's Humbling

———∞∞∞———

THE WORD

Peter, however, got up and ran to the tomb.
Bending over, he saw the strips of linen
lying by themselves, and he went away,
wondering to himself what had happened.

— LUKE 24.12

THOUGHT FOR THE DAY:

The first thing God does is forcibly remove any insincerity,
pride, and vanity from my life. And the Holy Spirit
reveals to me that God loved me not because I was
lovable, but because it was His nature to do so.

~ OSWALD CHAMBERS

PETER'S LIFE WAS IN SHAMBLES. He had hopped on the Jesus train but now the train was off the rails and in the ditch.

Peter had stuck with Jesus. Peter had faithfully followed Jesus. Peter had defended Jesus. But Jesus didn't turn out the way Peter thought he would. Arrested, tried as a criminal, led off to die a criminal's death, Jesus had failed Peter and, in turn, Peter had miserably failed Jesus. Now Jesus was dead and the disciples were sure they were next.

Then came Sunday morning. Peter and the guys were hiding (yes, they were hiding) when women (yes, the women) came with the news: the tomb was empty. These women claimed angels had appeared to them declaring Jesus was back from the dead. They said the angels had told them, *Why do you look for the living among the dead?* (Luke 24:5)[140]

Peter was surrounded by death, most painfully, the death of the life he had invested in Jesus and the dreams he had given himself to. The question these women were asked by the angels must have resonated with Peter. *Peter, quit wasting your time lost in your shattered life and broken dreams. Peter, go to the cross with Jesus and let him put to death that tiny, insignificant little life you were living and let him resurrect you to the man you are called to be!*

When these women burst into the hideaway with the news of the empty tomb, Peter and John jumped up and ran to see. Peter took a look, and then *he went away, wondering to himself what had happened.* The question the angels asked of the women at the tomb is the same question

---

[140] It's worth noting that the cultural world of Peter had been turned upside down at the hands of women. It was a young servant girl who had first challenged Peter about knowing Jesus. She was able to quickly push him into denying Christ. And now it was women who were the first to see Jesus and tell the news to Peter. Peter must have been reeling in his male-dominated world at the impact women were having on his life!

Jesus asks of you: *Why do you look for the living among the dead?*

For us men, so much must die before we can be reborn into the life God intended for us. Our young man dreams of personal glory—the idea that being a true man meant always winning, always ascending, always being the leader of the pack—these must go to the cross and be crucified.

Peter had to be brought low before he could be lifted up. The same is true for us. The way up truly is down. You are down. Are you ready to find the way up?

Think About It...

* Imagine Peter hiding with the other disciples. What would he have been thinking? What would he have been feeling? How low would he have been?
* What emotions have you felt during your divorce? What thoughts have run through your head?
* Think about the words of the angels: *Why do you look for the living among the dead?* What is dead in your life? What would resurrection look like?

Life Commitment:
I believe in resurrection. I believe new things can come out of stuff that looks dead. I may feel dead inside but I believe Jesus can resurrect me.

Peter Restored

———— ∞ ————

THE WORD

I tell you the truth, a time is coming and has now come when the dead will hear the voice of the Son of God and those who hear will live.

—JOHN 5.25

THOUGHT FOR THE DAY:

The servant never sets the agenda—the master does.

~ HENRY BLACKABY

WHAT DOES GOD DO WITH us when we have failed miserably? What does God do with broken lives, shattered dreams, crushed spirits? What does God do with traitors and adulterers? What does God do with losers like Peter?

Peter found out in a literal 'come-to-Jesus' talk on the shore of the Sea of Galilee.

The disciples were fishing when they saw the resurrected Jesus on the shore. Jesus invites them to breakfast. Then Jesus pulls Peter aside.

Read what happens for yourself:

When they had finished eating, Jesus said to Simon Peter,
"Simon son of John, do you truly love me more than these?"
"Yes, Lord," he said, "you know that I love you."
Jesus said, "Feed my lambs."
Again Jesus said, "Simon son of John, do you truly love
me?"
He answered, "Yes, Lord, you know that I love you."
Jesus said, "Take care of my sheep."
The third time he said to him, "Simon son of John, do
you love me?"
Peter was hurt because Jesus asked him the third time,
"Do you love me?" He said, "Lord, you know all things; you
know that I love you."
Jesus said, "Feed my sheep. I tell you the truth, when you
were younger you dressed yourself and went where you want-
ed; but when you are old you will stretch out your hands,
and someone else will dress you and lead you where you do
not want to go." Jesus said this to indicate the kind of death
by which Peter would glorify God.
Then he said to him, "Follow me!" (John 21.15-19)

Peter must have worried about what Jesus would say to him. Finally the dreaded moment came. Remarkably, Jesus puts judgment aside and simply invites Peter into the second half of his life.

Peter's first half of life had been about Peter. But circum-stances demolished everything upon which Peter had built his life. Now Jesus asks Peter to give up his personal ambitions and join him on a journey where Jesus is truly in charge.

> *"Simon son of John, do you truly love me more than these?"* Peter, are you willing to give up your small dreams and join me in a grand adventure?
>
> *If yes, then you will have to die to yourself. Peter, when you were younger you dressed yourself and went where you wanted; but when you are old you will stretch out your hands, and someone else will dress you and lead you where you do not want to go.*
>
> *But, Peter, when you die you will have died an honorable death at the end of an honorable life in which you have given yourself to something far bigger than yourself.*

Jesus invites Peter into the second half of his life which is always a journey *downward* for men. We must let Jesus be the master. We allow him to shape, control and deploy our male energy. We commit to joining Jesus on his terms rather than demand he come to us on our terms.

Jesus gives you the same invitation he gave to Peter: *Follow me!*

When you say *yes* to following Jesus you deliberately give up your dreams, personal ambitions, and goals. You allow Jesus to become the Master of your life, your boss, your CEO.

If you haven't done that yet, do it now. Simply tell Jesus that you know he died for your sins on the cross, you believe he rose from the dead, and you are ready to follow him wherever he leads.

THINK ABOUT IT...

* Have you given your life to Jesus?
* If not, what is holding you back?

LIFE COMMITMENT:

I commit to following Jesus. I surrender my life to him. I want him to be the Lord, King, Boss, CEO, Leader of my life.

Your Soul is Like a Tire

———— ≋ ————

THE WORD

> *For this reason, since the day we heard about you, we*
> *have not stopped praying for you and asking God to fill*
> *you with the knowledge of his will through all spiritual*
> *wisdom and understanding. And we pray this in order*
> *that you may live a life worthy of the Lord and may please*
> *him in every way: bearing fruit in every good work,*
> *growing in the knowledge of God, being strengthened with*
> *all power according to his glorious might so that you may*
> *have great endurance and patience, and joyfully giving*
> *thanks to the Father, who has qualified you to share in*
> *the inheritance of the saints in the kingdom of light.*

— COLOSSIANS 1.9–12

THOUGHT FOR THE DAY:

> *Spiritual Disciplines are instruments of God's*
> *grace which, through the Spirit, transform us*
> *daily into people who reflect Jesus' love, obedience,*
> *humility, and connection to God.*[141]

---

[141] *Spiritual Disciplines*, (Peabody, MA: Rose Publishing, July 7, 2014).

YOUR SOUL IS LIKE A tire. No, I didn't say your soul is tired, though your soul may *feel* very tired. Let me suggest a different way to view your soul. Your soul is not *tired*, it is *flat*.

Ever since I can remember I have lived on my bike. Back in the day, we rode our bikes without helmets and common sense. There was nothing like flying my banana seat bike off a homemade plywood ramp and onto that ever so unforgiving asphalt! Now I ride 25 miles dodging cars, rocks and the heat.

If you are a cyclist *you know that your tires leak*. In fact, *every time I get ready for a ride I pump a little air in my tires.* Low tires translate into a slow and sluggish bike. Slow and sluggish is not me. I want to ride high and clean, fast and efficient.

Your soul is like a bike tire. It leaks. All kinds of things steal the air out of your soul—people poking at you, financial worries, expectations of others that go unmet. Most of our 'leakage' comes from within—*what we tell ourselves about ourselves.*

From the beginning we as boys are asking ourselves, *Am I good enough.* And if truth be told, our constant answer to ourselves is, *Not even close.* If you keep telling that to yourself long enough, you will have a flat soul. As in an all-the-way-to-the-ground flat soul.

Now you've been through a divorce. Divorce is a knife plunged into your soul—it takes you right to the ground.

When I arrived home on October 23, 2015 after 38 hours of travel from Tanzania only to be met in my garage by my wife telling me she had left me, that was a knife plunge straight to the soul. I went straight down to the ground. With my soul flat on the ground I knew I wasn't going anywhere for a while.

Every time I ride my bike I must put a little air in the tires. Every day you and I must put a little air back into our souls. If you don't, you will be flat. Tired, flat souls need air. Whether your soul is flat all the way to the ground or just a little low, what do you use to put the air back in?

In 'Christian speak,' the means by which we put air back into our souls are called *Spiritual Disciplines*. There are many spiritual disciplines but for you right here, right now, I want to recommend the following (we will explore each in more detail in the next few days):

- **Solitude**—Spending time alone to be with God.
- **Prayer**—Honest conversation with your True Father.
- **Fellowship**—Being with other Christians who nourish your soul through understanding, challenge and encouragement.[142]
- **Guidance**—Positioning yourself to follow God's best path for his glory, your good and the good of those around you.[143]
- **Study**—Reading and really thinking about what God is saying to you through his Word, the Bible.
- **Worship**—Giving back to God the worth he is due.
- **Confession**—Talking openly and honestly about your life with a trusted circle of friends.
- **Submission**—Humbling yourself before God, trusting that in God's economy, the way up is down.
- **Service**—Learning to live with an open hand.

---

[142] Bill Donahue, *Leading Life-Changing Small Groups: Groups that Grow*, (Zondervan, 2012), Kindle Locations 782-783.

[143] Richard J. Foster, *Celebration of Discipline* (Harper Collins, 2009), , 175.

I have ridden my bike hundreds of miles without a flat. But in one ride I had two! Life is like that. Whether cruising fast and efficient or stuck by the side of the road, you need air. Let God pump your soul back up.

THINK ABOUT IT...

* How much thinking do you do. Real thinking... about life, about decisions that must be made, about your place in the world, about your impact on the world, about your legacy?
* Of the spiritual disciplines listed, which do you think would be most helpful to engage in first?
* Which is the least appealing?

LIFE COMMITMENT:

My soul needs air. God can pump me back up, but only if I let his air in. I commit to these tools God has given me to get me back on the road again.

Getting to the Win

———⚬⚭⚬———

THE WORD

> *Blessed are those who hunger and thirst for*
> *righteousness, for they will be filled.*

> — MATTHEW 5.6

THOUGHT FOR THE DAY:

> *What kind of success are you hooking your*
> *heart to and how is it shaping the decisions*
> *you make and the actions you take?*

> ~ PAUL DAVID TRIPP

OVER 100 DAYS AGO AT the beginning of this journey we asked a simple question: ***What does a win look like?*** What does success look like to us right here, right now? From the reading from yesterday, we might ask the question this way: *What does a full and mature soul look like?*

We answered these questions in Days Five to Ten with five markers of success. They are listed below with some comments (quotes) from the readings from those days (5-10):

* ***Clarity*** — Clarity begins with how you view God. He is for you, remember? He didn't cause your pain but he can transform it. He will strengthen you so that in the end you will get through this. You need to be clear about these truths about God and about yourself. (Day 6)

* ***Passion*** — A win looks like being CLEAR about *where you are now* and clear about your PASSION *for your future.* (Day 7)

* **Solidarity with Others** — Everything in you will tell you to pull back from life. Don't do it. Instead, believe what King Solomon said: *Two are better than one, because they have a good return for their work: If one falls down, his friend can help him up.* (Day 8)

* ***Solid Decisions*** — Your goal is to *do the next right thing.* Your emotions may get in the way of making solid decisions. Ask God for direction and then get in touch with good people to stand with you and guide you. (Day 9)

* ***Integrity*** — Integrity means being solid through and through. It means that what you see on the inside is reflected on the outside. It means that if you cut a watermelon in half you find watermelon inside. It means being undivided and true. The only way to gain and maintain integrity is to *seek first [God's] kingdom and his righteousness.* (Day 10)

How do you get clarity, passion, life-building relationships, wisdom and integrity? The answer is that *you build habits of the heart* that will transform you into the man God intends you to be. These habits are called *Spiritual Disciplines.* Done consistently and frequently, these habits of the heart lead to transformation. These are habits that lead to success. These are the actions that shape your soul.

THINK ABOUT IT...

* What habits in your life have shaped your soul?
* What habits do you have now that have a direct impact on how you think, feel, and behave?

LIFE COMMITMENT:

My soul is in formation all the time. I choose to be deliberate in what I allow to shape my soul. I choose to pick up the tools in God's toolbox to make me into the man he designed me to be.

Training vs. Trying

———— ✺ ————

THE WORD

> *Therefore, my dear friends, as you have always*
> *obeyed—not only in my presence, but now much more*
> *in my absence—continue to work out your salvation*
> *with fear and trembling, for it is God who works in*
> *you to will and to act according to his good purpose.*

— PHILIPPIANS 2.12–13

THOUGHT FOR THE DAY:

> *A disciplined person is someone who can do the right thing*
> *at the right time in the right way with the right spirit.*

~JOHN ORTBERG

I WANT TO RUN A marathon. At least one. Maybe just one. Maybe more. But at the end of the day, I want to have run at least one marathon.

I know I can't run a marathon in hiking boots, so I bought some running shoes. I know I can't run in jeans, so I bought some running shorts (<u>not</u> the short-short kind!). Now that I have the right attire, am I ready to run a marathon?

If you answer *no* to that, then I have a good-old American answer for you: But I really really WANT to run this marathon! Surely if I just get out there and TRY hard enough, my intense desire to run the marathon will see me through to the end!

Desire is a wonderful thing. But desire alone will not see you through. *Trying* is a marvelous thing and nothing will happen if we don't give it a try. But no matter how much we want something or how hard we try to get it, *the best things in life demand more*. The good, lasting things demand that we put our *desires* and our willingness to *try* into the hard work of <u>*training*</u>.

You have been beaten down by life. Let me encourage you to recognize that reading this book is proof that you want something better. Working through this book is evidence that you can do the training necessary to take the next steps in your journey with God. But reading this book is only a beginning. The next steps demand more from you. Just like running a marathon, to reach the finish line requires serious training.

As you consider engaging in the serious training of the spiritual disciplines, commit to the hard work of these disciplines.

Is it worth it to get up an hour earlier so you can be alone with God to think, pray, read, and worship? When the alarm goes off you may not think so. That's when you have to remember that to reach maturity takes the little steps and sacrifices of training. You must believe that these moments of devotion will pay off in making you the man God intends you to be.

One thing is certain: Without training you will not become the man God intends you to be.

Bear Grylls is a man who knows the hard discipline of training! He writes this:

> *Time spent in preparation is never wasted. Before we tackle any mountain, real or metaphorical we have to arm ourselves as best we can—and that means preparing ourselves for what we face ahead.*
>
> *Having the right kit and knowing how to use it when it matters makes a big difference. Can you put up your tent in the dark, against the clock? If you're a soldier, can you reassemble your rifle blindfolded?*
>
> *A huge part of preparation is practice and, like they say, the harder you practise, the luckier you become.*
>
> *If you practise enough you will get proficient; if you practise a lot you will become an expert. It is how we are made.*
>
> *But then why aren't we all experts, you ask? Simple. Most people are too lazy to practise.*
>
> *Remember that the will to win means nothing without the will to train. You have to get out there and be prepared to suffer a little if you want to be properly prepped for a big mountain or task.*[144]

THINK ABOUT IT...

* Is it true that the American spirit of trying is enough?

---

[144] Bear Grylls, *A Survival Guide for Life*, 155-56. Reprinted by permission of Peters Fraser & Dunlop (www.petersfraserdunlop.com) on behalf of Bear Grylls.

* Have you tried something difficult without the necessary training to be successful? How did that work out?
* What have you invested your time in that took some serious training?
* Were you training for the right thing?

LIFE COMMITMENT:

To some extent, if it's going to be, it's up to me. In partnership with God, I commit to the hard work of training so that I can be the man God destined me to be.

Hearing God

———⊶∞⊷———

THE WORD

> *"Then you will call upon me and come and pray*
> *to me, and I will listen to you. You will seek me*
> *and find me when you seek me with all your*
> *heart. I will be found by you," declares the Lord,*
> *"and will bring you back from captivity."*

— JEREMIAH 29.12–14

THOUGHT FOR THE DAY:

> *People are meant to live in an ongoing conversation*
> *with God, speaking and being spoken to by him.*

~ DALLAS WILLARD

DO YOU BELIEVE GOD WANTS to speak to you? Many of us have been taught that we can and should talk to God (prayer) *but we should never expect him to talk back to us.* For years this is what I was taught, if not explicitly, then implicitly. If some-one ever said, "God told me..." they were to be regarded with suspicion.

But I was also taught that Christianity is a *relationship*, not a *religion*. As far as I could tell, relationships involved communication—two-way communication!

Jesus told his disciples, *My sheep listen to my voice; I know them, and they follow me. I give them eternal life, and they shall never perish; no one can snatch them out of my hand.* (John 10:27–28)

I didn't understand this shepherding thing until we lived in Africa for almost a year. I grew up in Texas where land is fenced. Sheep, cows and horses were kept in with a fence.

There are very few fences in Africa, however. One day while driving down the road in Tanzania I saw a little boy, about six years old, herding 50 cows, sheep, and donkeys down the side the road. The only tools this little boy had to manage all these animals were his voice and a small stick!

It was clear that the cows, sheep and donkeys knew the boy's voice and they listened to him. The boy was in constant communication with his animals, walking to and fro, chatting it up with them, gently pushing animals back in line with his stick. The shepherd wanted to speak to his sheep, and the sheep needed and expected to hear from him.

Here's the thing: *sheep don't come out of the womb knowing the shepherd's voice.* They must learn the voice of their shepherd, and since survival depends on knowing the shepherd's voice, they are motivated.

Jesus clearly said that our relationship to him is just like the sheep's relationship to their shepherd. Jesus wants to talk to us. He longs to have a relationship with us. He wants to guide us, protect us, comfort and heal us, just like the good shepherds back in his day. But we have to learn to hear his voice. To learn the voice of the shepherd takes several steps:

- **A desire to sit with the shepherd**. If you don't want to hear God speak to you, you won't. But if you don't have any desire to hear God, *ask him to give you a strong desire to want to know him and his voice.* God forms and shapes our desires. Expect to have an increasing desire to be with him!

- **Unhurried time sitting with the shepherd away from the thousands of voices and sounds that is the cacophony of modern life.** I love the New England forest. The woods behind our house in New Hampshire became sacred ground as I walked through and sat in the midst of the trees throughout the seasons. One thing I learned: *the longer you sit in the woods and just listen, the more sounds you will hear.* More than just hearing sounds, however, you will get to *know* that forest. Through the years my ears slowly tuned into the deep forest sounds around me—the black-capped chickadee to my left, the chipmunks behind me, the woodpecker 100 yards to the south. In the same way, to learn the voice of the shepherd takes time being still and listening.

- **Learning from his Word, the Bible.** The Bible is God's voice passed down through the centuries. It's his love letter and owner's manual wrapped up in one. The Bible is the primary way God communicates to us, but it is not the only way. To get a sense of God's voice, however, start with the Bible. Nothing you hear from God will contradict what the Bible says, but the Bible doesn't say everything he wants you to know, especially about the specifics of your own life. To hear

God's specific word to you immerse yourself in his words to all humanity.

* **Learning from others**. Others have journeyed this path before us. We can and must learn from those who have discerned the Shepherd's voice in the constant static of life.

* **Testing what you hear with others**. One of the jobs of the community of faith (the church) is to give us a place to test what we believe God is telling us. Imagine a flock of sheep. The shepherd calls out a command. At least that's what you *think* you heard. Unsure, you turn to the sheep next to you: *Was that our shepherd hollerin' at us?* The reply comes back: Y-e-e-e-e-e-e-p!

Bill Hybels writes:

> *If you were to study the major religions of the world, you would discover that most of them rely on an impersonal dynamic with their deity. Like the version of my Christianity of old, there are beliefs to be mastered and codes and rituals to be followed—and perhaps some rewards in this life or the next. But the stuff of genuine relationship between God and humankind? It is nowhere to be found.*
>
> *Biblical Christianity is a far cry from those systems....*
> *From Genesis to Revelation, the constant refrain of Scripture declares that our faith is relational—God listens when we speak through prayer, and we are to listen when he speaks through his whispers.*[145]

---

[145] Bill Hybels, *The Power of a Whisper* (Zondervan, 2010), 45.

THINK ABOUT IT...

- Do you believe God still speaks to people today?
- Do you believe God *can* speak to you today?
- Do you believe God *wants* to speak to you today?
- Do you want to hear what God has to say to you?

LIFE COMMITMENT:

This is an either-or kind of thing: I believe God still speaks today and that he actually wants to speak to me, or I don't. I choose to believe that God still speaks to his people, and that he wants to speak to me.

God Hears You

———∞———

THE WORD

*Trust in him at all times, O people; pour out
your hearts to him, for God is our refuge.*

— PSALM 62.8

THOUGHT FOR THE DAY:

*Gentlemen, I have lived a long time and am convinced
that God governs in the affairs of men. If a sparrow
cannot fall to the ground without His notice, is it
probable that an empire can rise without His aid? I
move that prayer imploring the assistance of Heaven
be held every morning before we proceed to business.*

~ BENJAMIN FRANKLIN, CONSTITUTIONAL
CONVENTION, JULY 28, 1787

WHEN AARON, MY SECOND SON, was about five years old, I was
to care for him for an entire Saturday. The day was spent doing stuff around the house and yard.

At that time Aaron asked a lot of questions and had lots of needs like any five-year-old. He would begin every single one of these questions or demands with a heart, "**DAD!**"

Dad, why do we have to mow the yard today?

Dad, when do we eat lunch?

Dad, look at that bird!

Toward the end of the day I was just finishing mowing. Aaron was in the backyard. Sure enough, I heard his little five-year-old voice holler, '**DAD!**'

After a day of what seemed like a thousand '**DAD!**'s, I'd had it! Hot, tired, covered in grass and dust, I had heard my name enough for one day!

But God is gracious. Before I could say something I would regret, it hit me: My Father in Heaven relishes it when I cry out to him! Unlike me, he <u>NEVER</u> tires of me hollering out to him! He actually <u>LIKES</u> it when I call out his name!

When I think about the countless times I had cried out to him, I was so grateful that he *always hears me when I pray*, and, what is more, *his greatest desire is for me to call out to him.*

Our sin is believing the lie that we can live as if God does not exist. Our greatest downfall is believing the lie that we are independent, the lie that we are not dependent on God for anything.

What an incredible lie! Every breath you and I take is a gracious gift from the Father! We have nothing that didn't come from God's gracious hand! Best of all, this same God who so generously provides us with all things wants—more than anything—to have a deep, abiding, personal love relationship with us.

The heart of any relationship is a foundation of trust expressed in frequent, passionate and honest communication.

All this to say, *God loves it when we cry out to him in our deepest need.*

Not only that, he relishes it when we praise him for an awesome sunset, a cup of hot coffee, a warm house on a cold day. Unlike me, he actually enjoys being 'bothered' by us when we holler out to him! God never tires of us calling his name.

This is the promise David gives to us in Psalm 62.8: *Trust in him at all times, O people; <u>pour</u> out your hearts to him, for God is our refuge.*

Yesterday we asked a simple question: Do you believe God still speaks today and that he wants to speak to you?

Today we ask the reverse question: Do you believe God hears us, and that he will hear you when you talk to him?

The answer to both questions is a resounding YES that rings throughout the universe and through all time: **<u>Our God hears us</u>**!

He hears us because he wants to hear us. He hears us because of all the things he created, he uniquely designed us to talk to him. *His ears are bent toward us, his heart leaning into ours to listen to us.*

THINK ABOUT IT...

* Do you believe the God of this universe hears you?

PRAYER:

God, I believe you hear me. Thank you that you never tire of me hollering out to you, even if what I holler sometimes isn't very civilized or even friendly toward you.

Alone or Lonely?

———— ∞∞∞ ————

THE WORD

*Very early in the morning, while it was still
dark, Jesus got up, left the house and went
off to a solitary place, where he prayed.*

— MARK 1.35

THOUGHT FOR THE DAY:

*Let us leave a little room for reflection in our lives,
room too for silence. Let us look within ourselves
and see whether there is some delightful hidden
place inside where we can be free of noise and
argument. Let us hear the Word of God in stillness
and perhaps we will then come to understand it.*

~ AUGUSTINE OF HIPPO

TODAY WE BEGIN LOOKING AT specific tools from God's toolbox that he will use to grow your relationship with him and
shape your soul for his Kingdom. Our foundation is laid:

* Like a bike tire, **our soul needs pumping up every day**. These disciplines are the pump that puts in the air.
* God uses the spiritual disciplines to get us to the *win*. He uses the disciplines to bring us to **clarity**, **passion**, **life-building relationships**, **wisdom** and **integrity**.
* We can have this amazing relationship with God all day long. To get there, however, takes more than *trying*. It takes ***training***. The spiritual disciplines are the training God puts us through.
* Like a good shepherd, **God wants to talk to us**.
* **God hears you** when you talk to him.

These truths are foundational to all that comes hereafter.

The first habit of the heart, the first lesson in our training is to practice the discipline of **SOLITUDE**.

Solitude is really simple: *Slow slow slow slow down.*

Actually, just stop. Stop your body. Quit moving your body. Quit fidgeting.

Stop your mind. Let the constant internal conversation in your head slow to a crawl. Stop the frantic thoughts. Quit thinking about what you have to do. Just stop it. You can do it. Push that stuff out of your brain.

Stop your eyes. Stop your eyes from roving to and fro. Relax your gaze upon God. Focus on him.

Stop your breathing. Well, don't *stop* breathing, but try to slow it down! Let all the air out of your chest. Now relax your chest. Now take a really deep breath. Let the air fill your lungs. Slowly let it go. In my personal walk with God, this moment of deeply relaxing my chest is the moment I know I have entered into real solitude and time with God.

The bottom-line is this: *You will NOT have a meaningful and fulfilling relationship with God unless you slow down and just sit still.* Don't complain that you can't hear God if, in reality, you are unwilling to stop moving enough to actually hear him. Just don't go there. Quit making excuses and slow down. Be still.

Psalm 46.10 says, *Be still, and know that I am God; I will be exalted among the nations, I will be exalted in the earth.*

The Hebrew word translated "be still" is *raphah*. This Hebrew word means *to sink down, to let drop, to relax, to withdraw, to abandon, to forsake, to let go, to be quiet.* Get the idea?

Being in solitude feels awkward at first just as walking through a forest for the first time feels strange and unfamiliar. But as you practice the discipline of solitude, you will become more comfortable with the silence. As you continue to sit in silence, the background static of your life will slowly recede and you will begin to 'hear' the deeper things of your own life.

As you keep practicing solitude, enough noise will drop out of your life to actually hear God's whisper. This is an amazing moment and you will know when it happens.

In that moment many things will change in your life. The most important change will be a deep inner awareness, untouchable by time and space and flesh, that you will be OK, that nothing can take God away from you, that all you really have is God and he is enough. More than enough. Nothing can touch that. It's worth the wait, believe me.

How to have time alone with God:

First, **choose a time**... morning, lunch, evening. I like morning. Really early morning. I promise that you won't die if you get up an hour earlier. No one died from getting up an hour early. You can do it. But if this doesn't work, try something different. Life is an experiment. If something doesn't work, ditch it. Try something else.

Next, **find a quiet place** free from distractions. Definitely do NOT sit close to your computer. Your computer or phone will beckon you. They will whisper to you, telling you how busy you are, how many things you have to get done today, how good you will feel if you just get started *right now* on getting things done. Don't give in. All that stuff can wait. Remember that when you die your inbox will be full. You cannot empty it today or ever.

Now, **settle your mind**. Ask God to quiet your thoughts. But don't worry if your brain is still cluttered. It's OK. Just showing up is a great start and God smiles despite all the crazy cluttered brain stuff going on between your ears.

Ask God to give you peace. Rest in his care. Breathe.

Listen to worship songs. Music has amazing power to settle your soul and put your mind back on track with God. If you are able to, **play** or **sing along** with the worship songs. Don't dismiss the power of worship music because you think it is unmanly to listen to Christian music. Again, lies from hell. We finally have some good Christian music! Enjoy!

Now take time to **pray** (more on that in the coming days).

Finally, **be open to variety**. God speaks in many ways. Don't be a slave to your routine. Just be WITH God... he loves to be with you!

Solitude means being alone but solitude is not lonely. God is there. But like a forest, you have to sit in it long enough to start to get a sense of the unseen but visible, the silent but raucous world the busy people miss.

THINK ABOUT IT...

* When was the last time you were really still (besides sleeping)?

LIFE COMMITMENT:

I want to know God. I mean, I want to KNOW God. I don't just want to know about him. I want to know him. I know this will take some time. I am willing to give solitude a whirl.

Slow Down Fast

—◦◦◦—

THE WORD

Give thanks to the Lord, call on his name; make known among the nations what he has done. Sing to him, sing praise to him; tell of all his wonderful acts. Glory in his holy name; let the hearts of those who seek the Lord rejoice. Look to the Lord and his strength; seek his face always.

— 1 CHRONICLES 16.8–11

THOUGHT FOR THE DAY:

Though we may be unfamiliar with the discipline of solitude, most of us recognize it as something we wanted when we were first in love. It didn't matter if the time spent together accomplished anything very useful or important to the world at large. It was simply the way we let our beloved know that he or she mattered. In order to show love, we sought time alone together.

~ ADELE CALHOUN

ARE YOU SICK AND TIRED of being sick and tired? Are you tired of being in the rat race, spinning the wheel ever faster but going nowhere? Are you tired of the frantic voices in your head pulling you in a million directions? If so, then solitude is for you.

Dallas Willard writes:

> *The body must be weaned away from its tendencies to always take control, to run the world, to achieve and produce, to attain gratification. These are its habitual tendencies learned in a fallen world. Progress in the opposite direction can only be made in solitude and silence, for they "take our hands off our world" as nothing else does.*[146]

Everything in your being will scream against spending quiet time alone with God. I know because I HATE being still. I like to get things done. And I like to get things done FAST. That *peaceful, easy feeling* is something I would like to have, but the people who know me would definitely *not* use these words to describe me.

So for me, solitude is a hard discipline. I have to force myself to sit down, shut up, and let God do his work in my soul.

But I can tell you this: I have NEVER taken slow time with God and regretted it. I have never gotten up from a time of silence, reading, worshiping and prayer and say, *That was a waste of time!*

But I still have to fight it. I still have to fight the urge to always be in motion. I have to fight the battle in my soul that says that I must accomplish something, I must do things to be a worthy person. In Willard's words, I enjoy having my 'hands in the world,' working, doing things, making a difference.

---

[146] Willard, *Renovation of The Heart*, Kindle Location 2462.

Why do we resist solitude?

We resist solitude because we have bought into the American lie that an unproductive life is not only a wasted life, it's not actually life. That's simply not true. This way of thinking implies that sitting still is unproductive. If we carried this lie to its logical conclusion we would have to kill people who can't produce. We don't put to death people in nursing homes because we know they have value outside of their ability to produce. If they have value, you do too apart from what you achieve and accomplish. And if you don't think people in nursing homes have value you need to go to your local nursing home and listen to these amazing people.

You are stamped with God's image. To be like God *is* the highest achievement. To be like God means pushing back against this lie that we must be productive to have worth. Being still with God is the most important thing you can do. Being still with God will lead to a transformed life with eternal consequences.

We resist solitude because we believe we are too busy. A pastor once told me that we do the things we want to do. He was exactly right. If you want to grow in your relationship with God you will make solitude happen. You will get up an hour earlier each day. You will get up knowing that God will give you the strength to make it through the day even though you now have less sleep. And if you keep it up, God will wake you up for his time with you—no alarm needed! If you can get up at 0400 to go fishing, you can get up at 0530 to spend time with God.

We resist solitude because we are afraid of what God may ask us to do. Many people gripe about God not talking to them. They whine that God doesn't speak to them the way he does to others. Sometimes we wish God would just get direct with us—that he would send us an email or text or something.

The truth is the Bible records plenty of times when God showed up to people in very direct and spectacular ways. The response of these people was furious back peddling! Moses and the burning bush come to mind (Exodus 3.1-4.17). Interestingly, Mary's response to Gabriel's visitation is a rare if not the single exception (Luke 1.26-38). We know that when God speaks to us we will be changed, and we hate change! Push against this. Trust God that the way he changes you will be for his glory and for your good.

We resist solitude because we are afraid of what others will think of us, especially those in our own household. We are afraid they will think we are mush balls or spiritual freaks. Spirituality is a touchy subject in our culture. If you start to get up early, someone will ask what you are doing. When you tell them, you may be afraid of their reaction.

If what they think is more important than knowing God, so be it. I can guarantee you, however, that you will *not* regret the impact you have on the lives of those you love when you are transformed by solitude. The people you live with may at first respond in strange and unpredicted ways. Don't worry about it. They will eventually be glad to see the changes God brings about in your life.

God will change you in amazing ways when you come to him with the intention of getting to know him and experiencing his awesome love for you.

Henri Nouwen writes, *Solitude is not a private therapeutic place. Rather it is a place of conversion, the place where the old self dies, the place where the new self is born, the place where the emergence of the new man and new woman occurs.*[147]

THINK ABOUT IT...

* If you are struggling with starting this first habit of the heart, what is holding you back?
* Getting started is tough. Commit to spending this time with God two days in the next week. See how it goes.

PRAYER:

I have tried the American way of doing life, which is to say, fast and furious. I want to slow down. God, give me the desire to be with you. Transform my mind to want to be still with you. Open up my schedule to make this happen. Give the people in my life understanding. Show me the way and I will walk in it.

---

[147] Quoted in Wicks, *Spiritual Resilience*, 118.

It's Not What You Think It Is

———— ✖✖✖ ————

THE WORD

*And when you pray, do not be like the hypocrites, for they
love to pray standing in the synagogues and on the street
corners to be seen by men. I tell you the truth, they have
received their reward in full. But when you pray, go into
your room, close the door and pray to your Father, who
is unseen. Then your Father, who sees what is done in
secret, will reward you. And when you pray, do not keep
on babbling like pagans, for they think they will be heard
because of their many words. Do not be like them, for
your Father knows what you need before you ask him.*

— JESUS, AS RECORDED IN MATTHEW 6.5–8

THOUGHT FOR THE DAY:

*On some given day when grace overtook
me and I returned to prayer, I half-
expected Jesus to ask, "Who dat?"*

~ BRENNAN MANNING

THREE OLD RANCHERS WERE SITTING in a Dairy Queen in a small West Texas town early on a Monday morning (as ranchers in small Texas towns are known to do). The topic of conversation was the preacher's sermon from the day before, which was prayer.

These old guys started to talk about the best posture for prayer.

The first rancher said, *I believe the best way to pray is with your head bowed and eyes closed.*

I think we should be kneeling beside our beds, like my mama taught me, said the second.

The third rancher chimed in: *The best way to pray is upside-down in a well!*

That third guy was on to something! The best prayers are when we *want* to pray, and for us humans, we most *want* to pray when we are upside-down in a well, that is, when life has kicked us in the teeth and we are down on the turf. Divorce is a face-down-in-the-turf moment. *Pray, man, pray.*

I've heard it said that too many people use God like a spare tire—pulling him out only when needed—instead of letting him be the driver. That may be true, but God wants us to cry out to him (see Day 117). When divorce slams into our life a good and right thing to do is pray. When you need a spare tire, a spare tire is a fantastic thing to have!

Our ultimate goal, of course, is to be in such a relationship with God that we carry on a conversation with him all through the day. Later we will talk about how to do that.

But for today, know that a lot of confusing things have been said about prayer. As with most things, however, prayer is much easier than we have been led to believe.

Prayer is simply talking to God and letting him talk to you.

There are **no special <u>words</u> or <u>phrases</u>** to use. Use whatever language God blessed you with to talk with him. He is as happy to hear your Bronx accent as he is to hear the finest Georgia drawl. Really. He doesn't care. He just wants you to show up.

There is **no special <u>place</u>** to pray. God is not more in a church than outside it. God is everywhere so you can pray to him anywhere. Place is simply not an issue.

You **don't have to go through any special <u>person</u>** to pray. You don't have to have a priest or a pastor to help you pray. In fact, those guys often get in the way. Just talk to God. That's it. You can tell him anything. It's that simple.

Anne Lamott writes, *I don't know much about God and prayer, but I have come to believe, over the past twenty-five years, that there's something to be said about keeping prayer simple.*[148]

Her three simple prayers are *Help, Thanks, Wow.*

Nice!

Jesus' disciples asked him to teach them to pray. Jesus gave them what Protestants call *The Lord's Prayer* and Catholics call *The Our Father.* The most stunning thing about this prayer is how short it is.

Back in that day the religious leaders addressed God like a subject would address their king—ridiculously long

---

[148] Anne Lamott, *Help, Thanks, Wow: The Three Essential Prayers* (London: Hodder & Stoughton, 2015), 1.

adjectives and titles, running on for what must have seemed like forever.

Jesus trashed that idea. He called God his *Abba*, his *Dad*. Dads want informal, intimate conversations with their kids. At least good dads do.

So that's how to pray. Just do it. Stop right now and just talk to God.

THINK ABOUT IT...

* What is prayer to you?
* Where and from whom did you learn to pray?
* What misconceptions about prayer were passed down to you?
* Did you pray a second ago when I said to stop and pray? If not, stop and pray. It's super simple.

LIFE COMMITMENT:

God, show me the truth about prayer. And... thanks for hearing the prayer I just prayed! Thanks for simple. I can do simple.

God Answers Our Prayers

—⚬⚬⚬—

THE WORD

The righteous cry out, and the Lord hears
them; The Lord is close to the brokenhearted
and saves those who are crushed in spirit.

— PSALM 34.17–18

THOUGHT FOR THE DAY:

I don't pretend to know how God makes it all
work, but somehow there are tangible benefits
when we pray in accordance with God's will.

~ TONY DUNGY

IT'S ONE THING TO KNOW that we can talk to God. It's another to know he hears us. *It is yet another to know if this conversation actually makes a difference.* Does God answer our prayers? Do our prayers matter?

One of the greatest mysteries of the universe is this: God hears our prayers and responds to each and every one with an answer.[149]

How can our Almighty Amazing Enormous God even care about us? We are unbelievably tiny and insignificant in an unfathomably vast universe! And yet, he does. If God knows the number of the hairs on our head (Matthew 10.30) he hears our prayers. The cry of your heart is more important than the number of hairs on your head. And if he hears your prayers, he promises to answer each one.

We claim by *faith* that Almighty God hears and answers our prayers. Anyone who walks with God for very long can also claim this by *experience*. God hates divorce, but he loves people who are going through divorce. He is close to the brokenhearted. He is close to you. He hears your prayers.

This morning I woke up worried and concerned about a situation. The problem is serious and if you knew it, you would know why I was distressed.

---

[149] Oswald Chambers writes: *God answers prayer in the best way—not just sometimes, but every time.* Oswald Chambers, *My utmost for His Highest: Selections for the Year* (Uhrichsville, OH: Barbour and Co, 1992), 353. Henry Blackaby writes: *It is overwhelming to consider that holy, Almighty God would speak directly to us! What a privilege that He would care enough to challenge our destructive thoughts or practices. No matter whether His words are praising us or chastising us, we ought to consider it joy to receive life-changing words from our Master! Every time we prepare to worship the Lord, we ought to do so with anticipation that Almighty God may have something to say to us. Whenever we open our Bibles, we should expect that God has something to tell us in our time with Him. We ought to be far more concerned with what God will say to us during our prayer times than with what we intend to tell Him. When you receive a word from your Lord, whether it be of praise or of correction, consider it joy that Almighty God would speak to you.* Henry T. Blackaby and Richard Blackaby, *Experiencing God Day by Day* (Nashville: B&H Publishing, 2006), Kindle Location 2605.

I sat down at 0500 for my time with God. I listened to a song (*Blessed Be Your Name* by Matt Redman), then I read this from Sarah Young's devotional, *Jesus Calling*:

> *When things don't go as you would like, accept the situation immediately. If you indulge in feelings of regret, they can easily spill over the line into resentment. Remember that I am sovereign over your circumstances, and humble yourself under My mighty hand. Rejoice in what I am doing in your life, even though it is beyond your understanding.*[150]

Bingo. God knew every aspect of my situation. He wasn't surprised by a single circumstance in my life. The negative things I am dealing with are not caused by God, but he knows about them and is already in my future working out solutions that will bring glory to him and good to me. When I sat down to spend time with him this morning, he knew exactly what I needed to take my heart off my worries and put my affections squarely on him. Knowing of his intimate knowledge and care of these details of my life brought peace to my soul.

If we could pull back the curtain on all that God is doing in your life, you would be as amazed as if you could somehow suddenly understand all the amazingly complex biological processes that keep your body alive. God is with you and in you. He is involved in every detail of your life.

Remember, this is NOT a WYSIWYG world (see Day 90). God is doing stunning things in your life and in your future. Because he is at work, we can trust his answers to our prayers.

So... how does God answers prayer?

---

[150] Young, *Jesus Calling*, Kindle Location 768.

Sometimes God answers with a **NO**.

Looking back on my life, I am so glad God gave me a NO to some of my requests! Like a parent who knows a steady diet of donuts is not good for a five-year-old, so God knows what is best for us. His 'no's' come to us for our good.

Sometimes God answers with a **SLOW**. We are on the right track but the timing is not right. He calls us to wait on him.

Wayne Stiles writes about waiting on God:

> *We want God to change situations. God wants us to change in them. We want relief. God wants repentance. We want happiness. God wants holiness. We want pleasure. God wants piety. It's like a game of Ping-Pong. Or tug-of-war.*
>
> *In the end, if we really knew the big picture, we too would want what God wants for us—and in the exact way and timing he wants it to occur. It's just that our pain often blinds us to that perspective. We see only the red light. God sees the purpose—his good and loving purpose—for the delay. And although we cannot understand why the light is there, we do know what the red light means. Wait. I'm convinced the primary way we apply God's providence to our lives is by waiting. We apply sovereignty by waiting on God.*[151]

Waiting is not an American virtue. But waiting on God to do the work he needs to do is crucial. When God gives you *wait* for an answer sit back and wait. Trust him with peace in your heart.

---

[151] Wayne Stiles, *Waiting on God: What to Do When God Does Nothing* (Grand Rapids: Baker Books, 2015), Kindle Location 93.

Sometimes God answers with a **GROW**. What we ask for is in his plan for us but we have to grow into it first. He has some soul-work that needs doing in our lives.

Oswald Chambers writes:

> *You did not do anything to achieve your salvation, but you must do something to exhibit it. You must "work out your own salvation" which God has worked in you already (Philippians 2:12). Are your speech, your thinking, and your emotions evidence that you are working it "out"? If you are still the same miserable, grouchy person, set on having your own way, then it is a lie to say that God has saved and sanctified you.*[152]

If you don't hear response to your prayer, submit to God's work of growth in your life.

Sometimes God answers with a **GO**. The purpose is right, the timing is right, and you're ready to go for it! This may be the answer we were hoping for. But ironically we may also feel a sense of hesitation because God's GO *always* means adjustments to our lives. If the answer is GO, trust God, make the adjustments in faith, and get moving!

Always remember this, however: God gave us the gift of free will. That means that God chooses not to coerce us or the people in our lives. If the answer to your prayer depends on someone else, that person must choose to follow God as well. If they don't obey God, however, be assured that God can take their NO and turn it into something good for his glory and your good.

---

[152] Chambers, *My Utmost for His Highest*, 135.

THINK ABOUT IT...

* What are you praying for right now?
* What have you sensed God's answer to be?
* What are your next steps?

LIFE COMMITMENT:

If God knows how many hairs I have on my head he knows every detail of my life. I can't explain it but I believe it. I am trusting him for however he chooses to answer my prayers. I know this: However he answers my prayers will be for his glory and for my good. This I believe.

God Conversations

———⬥⬥⬥———

THE WORD

*Be joyful always; pray continually; give
thanks in all circumstances, for this is
God's will for you in Christ Jesus.*

— 1 THESSALONIANS 5.16–18

THOUGHT FOR THE DAY:

*We can cultivate the habit of a Godward-directed
mind and heart. As we carry on the business of the
day, inwardly we keep pressing in toward the Divine
Center. At every opportunity we place our mind
before God with inward confessions and petitions.*

~ RICHARD FOSTER

IT WOULD BE A STRANGE thing indeed to talk with my child
in the morning before school and then ignore him the rest
of the day. We would consider it odd to sit down with an em-
ployee for a heart-to-heart talk and then proceed to pretend
as if she didn't exist the rest of the day. How odd it would be
to have coffee with my wife before the day begins and then
be silent toward her from that moment forward.

And yet, that is what we do with God! How wonderful it is to sit down with God in the early morning hours, coffee cup and Bible in hand, pouring out heart and soul to him. And then I turn the tables by acting as if the only time and place God could possibly show up is in that tiny time and place where I met him in the early morning!

God is bigger than that. But he's also small enough to be in every moment of your day. God relishes our attention to him as we go through every moment of the day. I know this sounds crazy but it is true.

Let me give you examples of how this might work:

When you see a beautiful sight such as a grassy hillside or a bank of flowers or a sunset or thunderstorm, praise God with something like, *Wow, that is cool! You are quite the artist!*

When you feel anger rising, bring it to him: *God, I am pissed. I can't believe _____. Help me settle down now.*

When you are at a crossroads... *Father, I'm not sure what to do here. I know you have a plan; show it to me.*

The point? God is everywhere and in everything. Like any good relationship, he wants you to acknowledge his presence and talk to and hear from him throughout the day. This is the *continuous prayer* Paul encourages in the verse above.

Brother Lawrence was a lay brother in the seventeenth century. He is famous for his book, *The Practice of the Presence of God.* In this book he writes,

> *By practicing God's presence and continuously looking at Him, the soul familiarizes itself with Him to the extent that it passes almost its whole life in continual acts of love, praise, confidence, thanksgiving, offering, and petition. Sometimes all this may merge into one single act that does not end,*

because the soul is always in the ceaseless exercise of God's divine presence.[153]

The main point about prayer is to PRAY! Just do it!

And, as you pray, don't worry about how it goes. Five hundred years ago John Calvin wrote these honest and encouraging words about prayer:

> *The prayers of believers do not always flow on with uninterrupted progress to the end... but, on the contrary, are involved and confused, and either oppose each other, or stop in the middle of the course, like a vessel tossed by tempests, which, though it advances towards the harbor, cannot always keep a straight and uniform course, as in a calm sea.*[154]

If John Calvin had trouble praying, you can too! Don't get discouraged, *just pray.*

Think About It...

* Stop right now and pray. Just talk to God. Then be still and give him space to speak to you or comfort you or whatever you need right now.

---

[153] Brother Lawrence, *The Practice of the Presence of God.* (Nabu Press, 2010), Kindle Location 386-388.

[154] John Calvin, *Calvin's Commentaries: The Gospels* (Grand Rapids: Associate Publishers and Authors, n.d.), 515. Quoted in Gary Thomas, *Authentic Faith: The Power of a Fire-Tested Life* (Grand Rapids: Zondervan, 2002), 205.

LIFE COMMITMENT:
God, thank you for hearing my prayers all the time! Remind me through this day to lean my heart toward you in prayer.

Guys, We are Lost

———∞∞∞———

THE WORD

*I will instruct you and teach you in the way you
should go; I will counsel you and watch over you.*

— PSALM 32.8

THOUGHT FOR THE DAY:

We're lost, but we're making good time!

~ YOGI BERRA

I HAVE EVERY MEANS OF geographical guidance known to humanity. I've always had a passion for maps, and now with GPS, I have a passion for maps *and* accompanying electronics!

I have several Garmin GPS units—one each for driving, hiking, biking and kayaking. And, yes, I still get lost! I just don't have that sense of direction that some folks are blessed with.

Once I was high above timberline in the Colorado mountains. The trail at the beginning of this six mile hike was wide and well-traveled. Not much need for GPS. But as I moved above timberline the trail petered out. If you have been above timberline you know that distances are distorted and the terrain can blend together. Narrow game trails crisscross, confusing the human trail.

To my astonishment, the map on my GPS unit showed the human trail! I walked with my head down looking at the GPS and trying to discern the trail in front of me. Several times I veered off the tiny path but by following the trail on the GPS, I could pick it up again. Sure enough, the GPS was true and I reached my destination.

The Global Positioning System consists of 24 transmitting satellites circling the earth twice a day at an altitude of about 12,000 miles. By locking onto three or more of these satellites, a GPS receiver can pinpoint your position to within a few feet or even closer.

If you had told someone 100 years ago that 24 manmade objects traveling in space at almost 9,000 miles per hour could tell me exactly where I was anywhere on earth, they would have laughed you off the planet!

Only a fool would walk off into the woods without reliable means of guidance. Unfortunately fools often do and have to be rescued. But who wants to be one of those guys? Ignorant or arrogance, or, most likely, both, will get you lost.

God doesn't want us to be fools. His wants to guide us in life. But to receive his guidance takes submission to his authority. To accept his guidance is to admit that he knows more than we do (implying we are not as smart as we think) and trust him to give us the right directions.

Here's a thought: *It is to God's benefit to guide us.* We are his special creation. The better we do this thing called life, the better he looks! And by following his guidance, we actually *do* better! Our lives are happier, healthier and longer both on earth and for eternity.

God's promise to you in Psalm 32.8 is clear: *I will instruct you and teach you in the way you should go; I will counsel you and watch over you.*

In this one brief sentence of 21 words, God tells us four times in four ways he will guide us:

> I will **instruct** you
> and **teach** you.
> I will **counsel** you
> and **watch over** you.

Clearly God wants to be the GPS of your life.

The next few days we will go over five specific ways God guides us. Today simply know this: Just like following my GPS was to everyone's advantage when I was trekking above timberline, so is it the best course of action for you and me to seek out God's good, true and benevolent guidance.

As I willfully and gladly submitted to my GPS unit in the Rockies, may you and I willfully and gladly submit to God's guidance wherever you are in your journey.

God *wants* to guide us for his glory, for our good and for the good of the world.

Think About It...

* Read over these words again: *Instruct, Teach, Counsel, Watch over.* What are the differences in these four ways of guidance?
* Have you experienced God's guidance in your life in one or more of these ways?
* What is holding you back from humbly and whole-heartedly giving the course of your life over to God?

Life Commitment:

I believe God wants to guide me for his glory, for my good and for the good of the world.

God's Owner's Manual

—∞∞∞—

THE WORD

*All Scripture is God-breathed and is useful for
teaching, rebuking, correcting and training in
righteousness, so that the man of God may be
thoroughly equipped for every good work.*

— 2 TIMOTHY 3.16–17

THOUGHT FOR THE DAY:

*God's regular channels of grace are his
word, his ear, and his people.*

~ DAVID MATHIS

FOR THE NEXT SEVERAL DAYS we will explore five ways God
guides us. We start with the Bible.

GOD GUIDES US THROUGH

- The **BIBLE**
- Prayer
- Circumstances

- People
- Common Sense

To be guided by God is to deliberately place yourself in a position to follow God's best path for his glory, your good and the good of those around you. The first and best position in which you and I must put ourselves is sitting with Bible in hand and the Holy Spirit in our heart.

The clearest presentation we have of God's path for us is the Bible. The Bible doesn't answer every question you will ever have but it answers more questions than any other worldview. The Bible is God's love letter to us. It's our owner's manual. It's always timely while remaining timeless. It's our map for life. It's our FAQ sheet.

While humans are mighty smart, we are not all mighty. Our power to reason has been damaged by sin. Henry Blackaby writes, *God's ways are not our ways (see Is. 55:8-9). You cannot discover these truths about God on your own. Divine truth must be revealed.*[155]

---

[155] Henry T. Blackaby, Richard Blackaby, and Claude V. King, *Experiencing God: Knowing and Doing the Will of God* (Nashville: B&H Publishing, 2008), 45. Wayne Grudem notes, *God communicates to people through different types of "general revelation"—that is, revelation that is given not just to certain people but to all people generally. General revelation includes both the revelation of God that comes through nature (see Ps. 19:1–6; Acts 14:17) and the revelation of God that comes through the inner sense of right and wrong in every person's heart (Rom. 2:15).* Wayne Grudem, *Systematic Theology: An Introduction to Biblical Doctrine* (Leicester: Inter-Varsity, 2007), 53. Blackaby notes that: *People who make decisions based merely on what seems most advisable to them will inevitably choose something inferior to God's best. History's overwhelming testimony is that the most brilliant human reasoning has proven inadequate to save humanity from its own frailty. To claim people can determine the best course of action apart from God's guidance is to ignore Scripture's clear teaching concerning humankind's degenerate condition (Jer. 17:9; Rom. 3:9–18). Numerous warnings throughout the Bible advise against making decisions apart from God's involvement: The writer of Proverbs warned: "There is a way which seems right to a man, but its end is the way of death" (Prov. 14:12). The apostle Paul speaks of*

God has not left us alone in the dark—he has given us the light of his Word. The gift of the Bible has come to us at great cost: countless men and women through the ages have sacrificed their lives to keep God's Word alive and accessible to us.

If you pray for God to reveal himself to you through the Bible, you will be amazed at what happens. Blackaby writes that, *When you understand the spiritual meaning and application of a Scripture passage, God's Holy Spirit has been at work. Remember: this understanding does not lead you to an encounter with God;* ***it is the encounter with God.*** *When God speaks to you through the Bible, He is relating to you in a personal and real way.*[156]

When that happens, the next step is do what God reveals to be your next step: Adjusting your beliefs to the truth God has revealed to you is the first step, but you also must respond to that truth in obedience. Then you will experience a closer relationship with God.[157]

Whatever we think God wants us to do, it will never contradict what God has revealed to us in the Bible. And whatever God reveals to you will lead you down the right path.

If you are new to the Bible, start reading the Gospel of John in the New Testament and the book of Palms in the Old Testament. Read in a newer translation such as the New International Version.

God as "able to do above and beyond all that we ask or think—according to the power that works in you" (Eph. 3:20). It is no secret that God's ways are vastly superior to our ways. It is inconceivable that God would ask his children to make independent choices that robbed them of the good he knew they could experience. While God does allow people the freedom to make their own decisions, Scripture clearly demonstrates that God also lets people know what his will is. Blackaby and Blackaby, *Hearing God's Voice* (Nashville: B&H Publishing, 2002), 5-6.

[156] Blackaby, Blackaby, and King, *Experiencing God*, 152, emphasis mine.
[157] Ibid., 153.

Think About It...

Today this section comes from the book already quoted, *Experiencing God* by Henry Blackaby:

*   What has God been saying to you through His Word?
*   How have you responded?
*   Are you spending time regularly reading your Bible so you can hear God speak?
*   If you haven't been hearing God speak to you through His Word, why do you think that is?
*   What might you need to do to change that?[158]

Life Commitment:

Of all the voices vying for my attention, I choose the Bible as my primary source of authority.

---

[158] Ibid.

It's OK to Ask for Directions

———∽∾∾———

THE WORD

My son, if you accept my words and store up my
commands within you, turning your ear to wisdom
and applying your heart to understanding, and if you
call out for insight and cry aloud for understanding,
and if you look for it as for silver and search for it
as for hidden treasure, then you will understand
the fear of the Lord and find the knowledge of
God. For the Lord gives wisdom, and from his
mouth come knowledge and understanding.

— PROVERBS 2.1–6

THOUGHT FOR THE DAY:

We have to get into the habit of carefully listening to
God about everything, forming the habit of finding
out what He says and heeding it. If, when a crisis
comes, we instinctively turn to God, we will know that
the habit has been formed in us. We have to take the
initiative where we are, not where we have not yet been.

~ OSWALD CHAMBERS

GOD GUIDES US THROUGH

- The Bible
- **PRAYER**
- Circumstances
- People
- Common Sense

IF GOD WANTS TO GUIDE us for his glory, for our good and for the good of the world, it would make sense that he delights in guiding us directly when we pray with him. Remember that prayer is two-way communication—prayer is a dialogue, not a monologue. God wants to tell you stuff as much as you want to talk to him.

Jesus said, *Which of you, if his son asks for bread, will give him a stone? Or if he asks for a fish, will give him a snake? If you, then, though you are evil, know how to give good gifts to your children, how much more will your Father in heaven give good gifts to those who ask him!* (Matthew 7.9–12)

He preceded this simple bit of logic with these imperatives and promises:

> *Ask and it will be given to you; seek and you will find; knock and the door will be opened to you. For everyone who asks receives; he who seeks finds; and to him who knocks, the door will be opened.* (Matthew 7.7–8)

In the midst of divorce your world has caved in around you. The foundations upon which your life was built are crumbling. You may feel you are in a free fall with no guidance or direction. It's right here and now that God wants to guide you. *From the words of Jesus we know that we can expect God to guide us through prayer. We can expect God to give us direction when we spend time alone with him.*[159]

How do you hear God's voice? My experience has been that I have 'heard' words in my head that are in my voice but are clearly not from me. I just know this distinction and really have other way to describe it.[160]

At other times, God's gentle voice has been accompanied by words from the Bible I have just read (or will read), a song I just listened to, and/or a passage in a book I am reading.

The main thing is this: Know that God can and wants to talk to you. Ask him to reveal himself to you through the Bible and through a personal experience with him.

These words ring true today: *God is speaking. The problem is people have become disoriented to his voice.*[161]

Go back and read again Day 115 about hearing God. Ask God to orient you to his voice. Then be still and listen.

THINK ABOUT IT...

* Ask God to guide you in a specific area of concern. Pray something like this: *God, I know you love me and*

---

[159] Need more encouragement to pray? *There are people who argue that God no longer speaks to people, but don't let anyone intimidate you about hearing from God. Deep within the heart of every believer is a desire and a need to commune with their God.* Blackaby, Blackaby, and King, *Experiencing God*, 119-120.

[160] Blackaby says: *How do you know what the Holy Spirit is saying? While I can't give you a formula, I can say that you will know His voice when He speaks (see John 10:4).* Blackaby and Blackaby, *Hearing God's Voice*, 159.

[161] Ibid., Kindle Location 53.

want to have a two-way conversation with me. Help me learn to discern your voice above all others. Align my desires with your desires. Let me see the world through your eyes. Help me want what you want. This morning I specifically ask you to tell me what to do about _____.

Help me hear your voice through the Bible. Help me hear your voice through prayer. And give me courage to go the way you show me. Above all, I desire your glory, and I completely trust that you desire my good.

LIFE COMMITMENT:

I believe God speaks today and that he wants to show me the way through prayer.

God Guides Us In Our Circumstances (1)

—⊗∞⊗—

THE WORD

Are not two sparrows sold for a penny? Yet not one of them will fall to the ground apart from the will of your Father. And even the very hairs of your head are all numbered. So don't be afraid; you are worth more than many sparrows.

— Matthew 10.29–31

THOUGHT FOR THE DAY:

It is true that we may desire much more. But let us use what we have, and God will give us more.

~ ADONIRAM JUDSON

GOD GUIDES US THROUGH:

* The Bible
* Prayer
* **CIRCUMSTANCES** (Part 1)

- People
- Common Sense

LISTED BELOW ARE SOME OF the events of my life from 2014 through 2017:

- June 2014: After twelve years as Senior Pastor of my church in New England, I was forced to resign by the leadership team, no biblical reason given. In over 35 years of ministry, I had never been terminated or forced to resign from any position I ever held. The church and I were stunned.
- December 2014: Unable to get a job as a pastor or staff member of a new church, we moved to Austin, Texas (our home town).
- June 2015: I became pastor of a small Baptist church south of Austin (a good thing!)
- October 2015: Upon returning home from a teaching trip to Africa, my wife of 32 years informed me that she had left me and had moved out while I was gone.
- December 2015: After only six months as pastor of my new church, I was forced to resign due to the pending divorce.
- May 2016: The divorce is final.

I think anyone would agree that this was a pretty sucky run of luck. *But God was not absent during this terrible time.* Instead, I keenly experienced his loving, comforting life-giving presence. Without him walking intimately with me, I would have taken my life. I'm serious about that.

Here are some other things that happened during that period:

- April 2015: I landed a part-time job as a hospice chaplain.
- November 2015: The part time position as hospice chaplain is becomes full-time.
- January 2015: I start as full time hospice chaplain. This was the perfect job for me at the time. I could be alone (driving 150 to 200 miles a day) and yet engage in meaningful conversations thus remaining in ministry, the vocational love of my life.
- May 2016: I sign up with the online dating service, eHarmony.
- June 2016: I meet Kelly, the love of my life. We start a relationship that becomes permanent.

If you weave the five positive events listed above into the timeline of the six traumatic events we started with, you would see God's gracious hand of providence and provision in my life. As life crumbled around me, God weaved new strands into the fabric of my existence in such a way that I knew he was watching over me.

God did not cause the bad things to happen in my life—people did. But God was able to intersperse his amazing provision and protection into my life through circumstances which he clearly orchestrated. I experienced God's amazing love, power, provision and protection through his intervention in my life.

In addition, God clearly called me to begin Men's Divorce Recovery. This book and the subsequent ministry are a direct result of God's call upon me in the middle of the hurricane that had become my life.

If you had told me in November of 2013 the events that were about to unfold in my life, I would have laughed you off the stage. Looking back now, however, I can see how God has been betwixt and between the threads of my life, weaving something far different than I could have imagined, but something amazing nonetheless.

THINK ABOUT IT...

* Draw a line down the middle of a piece of paper. On the left side write the bad things that have happened to you. On the right side, write down the positive events in your life.
* Now see how they intertwine and weave together.
* Can you see and believe God is speaking to you through these circumstances?

PRAYER:

God, help me see your hand in my life. Open my eyes to your working in every moment of my existence.

God Guides Us in Our Circumstances (2)

———∞∞∞———

THE WORD

*Consider it pure joy, my brothers, whenever you
face trials of many kinds, because you know that
the testing of your faith develops perseverance.
Perseverance must finish its work so that you may
be mature and complete, not lacking anything.*

— JAMES 1.2–4

THOUGHT FOR THE DAY:

*Whatsoever is good for God's children they shall
have it; for all is theirs to help them towards heaven;
therefore if poverty be good they shall have it; if
disgrace or crosses be good they shall have them; for
all is ours to promote our greatest prosperity.*

~ RICHARD SIBBES

GOD GUIDES US THROUGH:

* The Bible
* Prayer

* **CIRCUMSTANCES** (Part 2)
* People
* Common Sense

TODAY WE TAKE FLYING FOR granted but I never cease to be amazed when I ride on an airplane. Flying 600 mph five or more miles up in the air is astounding. Think of how few people in the history of the world have done this!

No matter how many times I have flown, looking down on the earth gives me new perspective. Highways become tiny ribbons across checkered farms. Houses and skyscrapers look like toys. I have often looked upon a city and considered the crises playing out below and thought of how insignificant and small these things seem from 35,000 feet.

In the same way, we should take a step back from our circumstances and try to consider our lives from God's perspective. The events in our lives may seem overwhelming to us but in the span of a lifetime and certainly in the space of eternity, a single event becomes a piece of a much larger puzzle.

Mentally stepping back from your circumstances gives fresh perspective and allows God to ease your mind and soul. Stepping back gives patience for his guidance through traumatic events.

Gary Thomas writes,

Regaining God's perspective—refocusing our spiritual eyesight—is one of the greatest blessings of the believer. It changes everything. If we don't consciously take a step back and adjust our vision, we'll live under a perpetual cloud of illusion. This is a conscious, meditative turning, a determined effort to set our sights on what really matters.

Will you pause for just a moment and consider where your eyesight may be growing dim? Are you blinded to God's daily blessings because you're too focused on financial concerns, health issues, or frustrated relationships? Have you stopped seeing people as important and instead stare persistently at possessions, power, and pleasure? Are your eyes so preoccupied by your comfort that they have grown too tired to look at your life and your circumstances from God's perspective?[162]

In this moment with God, take a step back. Consider these realities:

* **God is at work.** Look for his activity in your life. There are no accidents. God is never surprised. Whatever is happening in your life right now can and will be used by God in your life in ways you don't know yet.
* **God's work is for his glory, your good, and the good of the world.** You can't know how your present circumstances fit into his eternal plan. The promise, however, is that God will work every single event in your life for his glory and for your good.[163] God will

---

[162] Gary Thomas, *Holy Available*, 60.

[163] *And we know that in all things God works for the good of those who love him, who have been called according to his purpose. For those God foreknew he also predestined to be conformed to the likeness of his Son, that he might be the firstborn among many brothers. And those he predestined, he also called; those he called, he also justified; those he justified, he also glorified.* (Romans 8:28–30)

take the hard places of your life, and through you, help other people through their troubles.[164]

  ❋ **Look for God's invitation to join him in his work.** A bigger plan awaits and it is good. He will invite you into your new role and mission in his Kingdom.

After Katrina devastated the Mississippi coast our church traveled many times from New England to help. One day I was working in a school gym, the largest structure still standing in Lakeshore, Mississippi. Working beside me was an elderly man, thin, distinguished. His name was Bob, and I asked his story.

Bob, a retired attorney, was a longtime Christian hailing from Nebraska. His wife of many decades had died the year before. Despite this loss of half his heart, Bob knew God was not done with him. Bob stepped back and viewed his life from 35,000 feet. He saw his life from God's perspective and knew that God was not finished with him yet.

Instead of getting lost in his grief he asked God what he wanted him to do. The answer, at the moment, was to work in the gym in a community destroyed by a hurricane. So there was Bob, sorting through hundreds of donated items, as happy as happy could be because he knew his God was working in *all* his circumstances.

---

[164] *Praise be to the God and Father of our Lord Jesus Christ, the Father of compassion and the God of all comfort, who comforts us in all our troubles, so that we can comfort those in any trouble with the comfort we ourselves have received from God. For just as the sufferings of Christ flow over into our lives, so also through Christ our comfort overflows. If we are distressed, it is for your comfort and salvation; if we are comforted, it is for your comfort, which produces in you patient endurance of the same sufferings we suffer. And our hope for you is firm, because we know that just as you share in our sufferings, so also you share in our comfort.* (2 Corinthians 1:3–7)

THINK ABOUT IT...

* Use your imagination to lift yourself high above your life. Look to your left and see your birth. Moving your eye to the right, scan through your early childhood, teen years, young adulthood and then to today. Now look to your right, your future. This is how God sees your life—not this one tiny moment, but many moments strung together. He is in each one of these moments.

* Picture your future with God's plan overlaid upon it. What does God see for your future? Is it unclear? Ask him to show you. Ask him to give you strength to live the rest of your life in his perspective with more wisdom, grace and patience.

* Now ask him to let you see your present circumstances from his perspective. This is a big ask and God may or may not reveal anything. But one thing God will do—he will invite you to do the next right thing. He will invite you into a future with him as your guide.

LIFE COMMITMENT:

My life is smaller than I thought and yet bigger than I ever imagined. I believe God is in my circumstances and that he can use what has happened to me for his glory, for my good, and to make the world a better place. I submit to his plan for my life and I commit to keeping my spiritual eyes and ears open for his invitation to join him in his Kingdom work.

God Guides through People

———❧———

THE WORD

As iron sharpens iron, so one man sharpens another.

— PROVERBS 27.17

THOUGHT FOR THE DAY:

To give yourself the best shot of reaching your destination
and achieving all you are meant to in your life,
you need a great guide, someone who can lead you,
inspire you, comfort and strengthen you—especially
when the going gets tough, as it invariably will.

~ BEAR GRYLLS

GOD GUIDES US THROUGH:

- The Bible
- Prayer
- Circumstances
- **PEOPLE**
- Common Sense

THIS IS YOUR JOURNEY, AND yours alone. No one else can walk this path for you. But just because only you can make this journey doesn't mean you must make it alone. In fact, you *must* have companions or you won't make it.

I moved to New England in November. It wasn't long before the snow began to fall. Despite winter I was anxious to get out and explore. One frigid Saturday morning I took off to the Monadnock region of Southern New Hampshire to climb a mountain. The temperature was in the teens and the trail steep, rocky and icy.

As I hiked up the trail alone it began to dawn on me how cold it was, how much ice covered the trail and how hard the rocks were. Suddenly my feet felt unsure and my head vulnerable. I realized how a simple fall on the icy, rocky trail could turn into a disaster and even death for me. I like to hike alone, but doing this trail alone on a cold, icy day was stupid.

President Woodrow Wilson said, *We should not only use all the brains we have—but all that we can borrow.*

God designed the church to be the people whom he uses to support and guide us through tough times. Rick Warren writes, *When we place our faith in Christ, God becomes our Father, we become his children, other believers become our brothers and sisters, and the church becomes our spiritual family.*[165]

Having served in the church for over three decades, I know first-hand how far the church in America is from God's call and purpose in the world. But the church *is* the bride of Christ, and Jesus loves his bride, blemishes and all.

---

[165] Richard Warren, *The Purpose Driven Life*, 153.

Below are listed a few things the church can and should do for you:

The church supports me. Few churches know how to help the newly divorced but most churches have some people who are good at loving and supporting people through hard times of all kinds. Ask God to show you a church with people ready to help you.

The church keeps me on track. Left to myself, my thoughts, emotions and behavior can run away. I need others to hold me accountable and to nudge me when I am going the rails. Iron *does* sharpen iron. Trust that God will put people in your path to show you the right track to follow and a few folks who will block the trails that lead to destruction.

The church gives me a place to serve and a people to serve with. Winifred Newman said, *Vision is the world's most desperate need. There are no hopeless situations, only people who think hopelessly.* Because the church is led by God, the church has the right vision and mission. The church should be the most *hopeful* group of people in the world, *full of hope* for a dark world. By investing in a church, you join a people who are following God, however falteringly.

The church gives me opportunity to exercise grace. The church is far, far from perfect, especially the American church today. But where the church fails is my opportunity to show grace. Every time I show grace my soul is knit back together in small ways that, together, with other Christians, are making an amazing tapestry. It is good and right to be part of this tapestry, even if the underside is a mess of tangled threads.

THINK ABOUT IT...

* When I say the word *church*, what images, thoughts and emotions first come to mind?
* God wants you to be a part of his family, therefore you can expect God to guide you to one. Ask him to lead you to the local church he wants you to be a part of. Expect him to do it.

LIFE COMMITMENT:

Though the church is far from perfect, these are my brothers and sisters in Christ and I need them in my life. I commit to following God's leadership to the group of Christians to which he wants me to belong.

Use Your Head!

———⊶∞⊷———

THE WORD

*The Lord said to Joshua, "Stand up! What
are you doing down on your face?*

— JOSHUA 7.10–11

THOUGHT FOR THE DAY:

*Common sense in an uncommon degree
is what the world calls wisdom.*

~ SAMUEL TAYLOR COLERIDGE

GOD GUIDES US THROUGH:

* The Bible
* Prayer
* Circumstances
* People
* **COMMON SENSE**

ONCE I WAS FLUMMOXED OVER a situation at the church of
which I was pastor. When I have a problem, my typical answer
is to research it to death! So I began reading a book by F. B.

Meyer, a British pastor and scholar who bridged the 19th and 20th centuries. What attracted me to this book was its title: *The Secret of Guidance*. Expecting super-spiritual secrets on finding God's will, I was pleasantly surprised to read the following:

> *[God's] voice may come to us through the voice of sanctified commonsense, acting on the materials we have collected. Of course at times God may bid us act against our reason, but these are very exceptional; and then our duty will be so clear that there can be no mistake. But for the most part God will speak in the results of deliberate consideration, weighing and balancing the pros and cons.*[166]

Wow! This spiritual giant gave amazingly practical advice: *God gave me a brain—use it!*

Meyer goes on to write:

> *When Peter was shut up in prison, and could not possibly extricate himself, an angel was sent to do for him what he could not do for himself; **but when they had passed through a street or two of the city, the angel left him to consider the matter for himself.** Thus God treats us still. He will dictate a miraculous course by miraculous methods. But when the ordinary light of reason is adequate to the task, He will leave us to act as occasion may serve.*[167]

---

[166] F. B. Meyer, *The Secret of Guidance: Guideposts for Life's Choices* (Belfast, Northern Ireland: Ambassador, 2000), Kindle Location 95.

[167] Ibid. Emphasis mine.

God will guide you through amazing circumstances, splashes of insight and life-giving relationships. He will open his Word to you in ways that will astound you. But he also allows you to use the good and powerful 3.5 pounds of wonder between your ears. He gave you a brain. Use it!

THINK ABOUT IT...

* You have a lifetime of experience. What have you learned?
* If you are trying to decide on a course of action, use the SWOT method to help guide your decision. SWOT stands for Strengths, Weaknesses, Opportunities and Threats.[168]
* When factoring common sense into your decision making, keep in mind that our ability to think is damaged by sin and that we have an amazing capacity for self-deception. Use common sense *in conjunction with* the Bible, prayer, circumstances and other people to guide you.

PRAYER:

God, thank you for the power to think, a gift no other creature in the universe has! Help me use my head to guide my heart and my hands.

---

[168] See https://en.wikipedia.org/wiki/SWOT_analysis

Dig In! You Will Be Amazed!

———∞∞∞———

THE WORD

Do not conform any longer to the pattern of this
world, but be transformed by the renewing of your
mind. Then you will be able to test and approve what
God's will is—his good, pleasing and perfect will.

— ROMANS 12.2

THOUGHT FOR THE DAY:

When intellectuals' minds are awakened, when they
understand something new about God or his ways
with his children, then their adoration is unleashed.

~ GARY THOMAS

I HAVE THREE KIDS, THE youngest is 16 at the time of this writing. I've heard all three kids ask the same question as I have driven them to school or helped them with homework: *Why do I have to learn this? What good will this do me?*

While it is true that solving a quadratic equation is not something we use every day, our brains were meant to explore, consume, question and seek answers. How passionately we pursue answers will depend on how important we perceive the subject at hand to be. You may have never given a thought to prostate cancer until you are diagnosed with it. Suddenly pursuing knowledge of prostate cancer becomes all-consuming.

There is no more important subject than your soul and the relationship of your soul to God, to others and to the universe. The discipline of study is a commitment to pursue knowledge of these relationships.

Study starts with the Bible. Pray that God will give you an uncommon desire for the Bible and that he will create *time* and *space* for you to dig in. Ask him to show you *what* to study. I suggest the New Testament books of *John, James* or *Philippians* to start off with.[169]

Once you have a time and place, I suggest following Richard Foster's guidelines for studying the Bible:

* **Repetition**—Take a passage from the Bible and read it several times. Commit it to memory if possible. The power of memorizing is amazing! And you can do it! Don't underestimate the power of your brain.

---

[169] There are dozens of ways to study the Bible and just as many websites and other resources. Don't be intimidated by the plethora of offerings. The most important thing is to pick a portion of the Bible and dig in. To get an overview of the Bible I recommend *52 Greatest Stories of the Bible: A Devotional Study* (Kenneth Boa and John Alan Turner, *The 52 Greatest Stories of the Bible: A Devotional Study.* Baker Publishing Group, 2016). For a guide on different ways to study the Bible, check out *Rick Warrens Bible Study Methods: Twelve Ways You Can Unlock God's Word.* (Rick Warren. *Rick Warren's Bible Study Methods: Twelve Ways You Can Unlock Gods Word* (Grand Rapids: Zondervan, 2011). And don't think study is limited to just the Bible. I call nature the 67th book of the Bible.

- **Concentration**—Think about the passage. What kind of writing is this (narrative, history, poetry, exhortation, etc.). Who was it written to? What was the writer trying to convey?
- **Comprehension**—What does this passage mean on its own? What does the passage mean in the context of the rest of the book you are studying? In the rest of the Bible?
- **Reflection**—What does this passage mean for me? What is God saying to me?[170]

Jesus said, *You will know the truth, and the truth will make you free.* (John 8:32) Knowing the truth comes by studying.

Paul wrote to the young Timothy:

> *But as for you, continue in what you have learned and have become convinced of, because you know those from whom you learned it, and how from infancy you have known the holy Scriptures, which are able to make you wise for salvation through faith in Christ Jesus. All Scripture is God-breathed and is useful for teaching, rebuking, correcting and training in righteousness, so that the man of God may be thoroughly equipped for every good work. (2 Timothy 3.14–17).*

Even if you don't think of yourself as much of a reader, student or thinker, I promise that *you will be blessed if you take time to dig into God's Word!* He will honor your desire by opening your mind and your heart to his awesome truth.

---

[170] Foster, *Celebration of Discipline*, 64.

Don't underestimate the power of your brain to learn and grow through the discipline of study.

Think About It...

- Starting off with an hour a week, what time can you set aside to study the Bible?
- Where is a good place to study?
- What part of the Bible do you want to study?

Life Commitment:

There are many reasons I don't think I can study the Bible, but the reality is that God wants me to dig into his Word! Trusting in his desire for me to know truth and the brain he gave me, I commit to digging into the Bible for one hour this week to see what happens.

Give It Up! It's What You Were Made For

—— ✕✕✕ ——

The Word

God is great, and worth a thousand Hallelujahs.

— Psalm 96.4, *The Message*

Thought for the Day:

This world is full of fragile loves—love that abandons,
love that fades, love that divorces, love that is self-
seeking. But the unquenchable worshipper is different.
From a heart so amazed by God and his wonders
burns a love that will not be extinguished. It survives
any situation and lives through any circumstance.
It will not allow itself to be quenched, for that would
heap insult on the love it lives in response to.

~ Matt Redman

If there's one thing men don't like much, it's going to church. Every woman wants her man to go to church, and most men resist. In general, men don't like to sing. We also don't like to hear a talking head tell us what to do. We hate being asked for money. We don't want to waste time on a precious weekend when we have a million things to do before Monday morning rolls in on us again. I get that.

But worship is far more than a boring hour a week punching the 'God-clock.'

At its heart, worship is giving back to God the worth he is due. Worship is paying attention to God. Worship is turning your heart to God honestly, reverently, passionately, and unequivocally. Worship is engaging a wild and creative God with all we have, submitting to him not as his groveling subjects but as his free sons.

Given this definition, the habit of the heart we call *worship* is expanded. Corporate worship, what we call 'church,' is getting together with other people who love God to give him the worth he is due. And yes, we should go. Worshiping God together is the one thing we as the church do solely for God. If you don't want to go but you go anyway, what an offering to God!

But going to corporate worship (church) is more than that. It's pulling away from the busy-ness and business of earthly life to deliberately enter 'eternal' time. It's submitting to what God has chosen to say through the pastor that day. It's being with the people of God—all ages, shapes and colors.

Tripp writes:

> *God has designed us to regularly gather together and remember the things that are worth living for. Corporate worship reminds us of his power, glory, and grace. It reminds us of the depth of our spiritual needs. It reminds us of the eternity that is to come. It reminds us of salvation past, present, and future. And as it reminds us of these things, it clears up our values confusion once again, rescuing us*

from our wandering and often-fickle hearts, and pointing us to the One who rightly commands our allegiance and in grace gives us every important thing that we would ever need.[171]

Worship is a 24/7 way of life more than just a place to go once a week.

Other thoughts on worship...

* Worship is the heart of your time with God (See Day 121 on Covenant Prayer). A chunk of this time should be praise and thanksgiving. Listen to some Christian songs (we are fortunate to be living in a time when we have Christian music in every genre known to humanity). Pour out your heart to God. Read of his wonders.

* Get outside! Every part of nature points to the glory of God. It has been said that nature is the 67th book of the Bible. Amen!

* Make an offering of your time, talent and treasure. More on that in a couple of days.

* Cultivate a heart of gratitude toward every aspect of your life. Notice God at work throughout your days and nights.

Many times I have waked up on Sunday morning definitely NOT wanting to go to church, and I was the preacher! But not once did I go and regret it.

---

[171] Tripp, *New Morning Mercies*, Kindle Location 1891.

As a pastor I always told my people how proud I was that they had taken time from their busy schedules to sit with a bunch of other people and sing songs to God and then listen to me, a talking head, for 30 minutes.

Whether corporate or personal, worship is always a battle because the last thing the enemy wants is for you to pay attention to God. Resist the urge to turn away from God. Instead, turn your heart, soul and mind toward him and give him the worth he is due. When you do this either alone or with others at church, you push back the darkness.

THINK ABOUT IT...

* When you hear the word 'worship' what first comes to mind? What do you feel?
* Ask some other guys what they think about church.
* In what ways could you engage God today?

PRAYER:

God, I pay attention to a lot of things in my life. Give me a holy desire to pay more attention to you.

Sometimes You Just Have to Throw Up

———— ✿ ————

THE WORD

> *If we claim to be without sin, we deceive ourselves*
> *and the truth is not in us. If we confess our sins,*
> *he is faithful and just and will forgive us our*
> *sins and purify us from all unrighteousness. If we*
> *claim we have not sinned, we make him out to be*
> *a liar and his word has no place in our lives.*

— 1 JOHN 1.8–10

THOUGHT FOR THE DAY:

> *To confess your sins to God is not to tell him*
> *anything he doesn't already know. Until you confess*
> *them, however, they are the abyss between you.*
> *When you confess them, they become the bridge.*

~ FREDERICK BUECHNER

I WAS ON THE BEACH with my family. Then a beauty walked by. Then my choice: keep looking or find something else to look at/think about. My decision was to look away *because I knew if I didn't I would either have to confess to my accountability partner or lie to him.* Neither was a comfortable option.

At that time our church's men's group had a dynamic system of accountability partners. Groups of three men would meet every couple of weeks to share our victories and struggles and answer ten basic accountability questions.

These questions are as follows:

* Have you spent daily time in the Scriptures and in prayer?
* Have you had any flirtatious or lustful attitudes, tempting thoughts, or exposed yourself to any explicit materials which would not glorify God?
* Have you been completely above reproach in your financial dealings?
* Have you spent quality relationship time with family and friends?
* Have you done your 100% best in your job, school, etc.?
* Have you told any half-truths or outright lies, putting yourself in a better light to those around you?
* Have you shared the Gospel with an unbeliever this week?
* Have you taken care of your body through daily physical exercise and proper eating/sleeping habits?
* Have you allowed any person or circumstance to rob you of your joy?
* Have you lied to us on any of your answers today?[172]

---

[172] Rod Handley, *Character That Counts-Who's Counting Yours?* (Omaha: Cross Training Publishing, 2012), Kindle Location 1552.

Brothers, these are penetrating questions. These are hard questions. But there is a freedom in confessing to another brother, either that we have done well or that we have struggled.

Proverbs 28:13 says, *He who conceals his sins does not prosper, but whoever confesses and renounces them finds mercy.*

Remember the leaky bike tire? Sin puts holes in the tire. Confession plugs the holes and pumps you back up.

I admit that this doesn't make sense. To confess our sins and struggles to someone else seems more like taking an ice pick to our souls. But exactly the opposite is true. To come clean, to become vulnerable, to take off the mask is life-giving. Confession plugs the holes and pumps our souls back up.

We confess to others but our first confession is to God. John wrote If we confess our sins, he is faithful and just and will forgive us our sins and purify us from all unrighteousness. (1 John 1.9)

The Greek word we translate as *confession* is *homologeo*. It comes from two Greek words, *homo*, which means *the same*, and *logeo*, which means *to say*. Confession, then, means *to say the same thing about our sin as God does.* Confession is to come to a place in our minds where what we once thought was right, we now agree with God is actually wrong.

God already knows all this. When we confess our sins to him we aren't telling him anything new. But we *are* telling ourselves what God wants us to know about ourselves. He wants us to know when we sin because sin causes huge damage to ourselves, others, and our world. But he always wants us to know—to really *know*—that we are forgiven. He wants us to own up and move on. He wants us to feel and experience the amazing freedom of his forgiveness.

He wants this so much for you because he paid a terrible price for it: His Son died on the cross so that you can experience the freedom of his forgiveness. If you don't live in this freedom, Christ died for nothing.

The spiritual discipline of confession calls us to come clean with ourselves, with God and with others. When we come clean, *we are clean*. And clean is good.

THINK ABOUT IT...

* When you were caught doing something wrong, how did your parents react?
* Look over the ten questions listed above. Do a personal inventory. Ask God to reveal to you where you need to own up to falling short. Confess your sin to him. Ask him to give you a feeling of forgiveness and cleanness.
* Find out if your church has accountability groups for men. If your church doesn't have such groups, ask your pastor about it. Considering partnering with him and other men to start such groups.

LIFE COMMITMENT:

I am a son of God who sins. I confess my sins to God and others, and in so doing experience the freedom of forgiveness.

The Way Up Really Is Down. Really Down.

———— ∞∞∞ ————

THE WORD

Humble yourselves, therefore, under God's mighty
hand, that he may lift you up in due time.

— 1 PETER 5.6

THOUGHT FOR THE DAY:

How far you go in life depends on your being tender with
the young, compassionate with the aged, sympathetic
with the striving and tolerant of the weak and strong.
Because someday in life you will have been all of these.

~ GEORGE WASHINGTON CARVER

WE LOVE CONTESTS.

Every year in Egremont, Cumbria (England) people gather to see who can make the ugliest face. It's called the World Gurning Championship.

The Air Guitar World contest shows off the ability to play a guitar that isn't there. Same with the Air Sex Competition in New York City, except it is not a guitar that's missing. Then there is the Toe Wrestling Competition, the Worm Charming Championship (earthworms), Lawn Mower Races, Cherry Pit Spitting contest, Cockroach Racing and even the Bee Wearing Contest (held every year in China).

It seems everyone wants to be king of the hill so we keep making more hills. We all want to be the best at something, even if that 'something' is totally insignificant. Seriously? In a hundred years, does any of this really matter?

God calls us away from this silly need to be the king of the hill. He calls us to something much higher, much better, much more lasting and significant. But the call he gives to us is the downward call of humble submission rather than a frantic scramble to the top. He calls us on a journey of submission to him and his will for our lives.

Kristin Armstrong writes, *We need to allow God to lift us up instead of attempting to do it ourselves. Ours is a temporary high; His is a holy elevation.*[173] His is, indeed, a holy elevation.

The Discipline of Submission is a humbling yourself before God, trusting that in God's economy, the way up is down.

Submission goes against everything we are taught as men in our culture. We are told to climb the mountain even if that means leaving footprints on the backs (or necks) of those in our way.

God calls us to something higher, the path to which is something downward.

---

[173] Armstrong, *Happily Ever After,* Kindle Location 4161.

Submission is trusting that's God way is better than the world's way. Submission is giving up the constant need to assert ourselves, to make ourselves famous, to always get our way or put up a huge fuss if we don't.

The irony of submission is the amazing freedom we gain when we give up the impossible need to be the best, the richest, the brightest, the coolest, the smartest! In submitting to God we gain freedom from people. Again, ironically, in submitting to God's call to meet the needs of people, we gain freedom from them.

Martin Luther said, that *A Christian is a perfectly free lord of all, subject to none. A Christian is a perfectly dutiful servant of all, subject to all.*[174]

God doesn't waste pain, and God will not waste the pain of your divorce. One way God can redeem this pain in your life is to use it to pull you down so he can, in his time, lift you up.

THINK ABOUT IT...

* What do you do when you don't get your way?
* Would other people describe you as God-centered, people-centered or self-centered?
* How much of the mess you are currently in is because of your need to constantly assert yourself, to be on top, to get your own way?
* If submission is a new concept to you, try it out today! Ask God to place you in a situation today where you will have a choice between self-assertion or humble

---

[174] Martin Luther, The Freedom of the Christian, quoted in Foster, Celebration of Discipline, 110

submission. Choose submission and see what happens. I dare you!

Life Commitment:

Getting my own way has seemed like the only way. I will give up this tactic and try something new. I will give up the need to make myself famous, strong, smart, powerful and _____ (fill in the blank). Instead, I defer to God and his will for my life.

The Discipline of Gratitude

— ⬥⬥⬥ —

THE WORD

Give thanks to the Lord, for he is good.

His love endures forever.

— PSALM 136.1

THOUGHT FOR THE DAY:

No longer dependent on our good works and
performance, with the destination of our souls
secured for all eternity, you'd expect that the energy
of sheer gratitude, if nothing else, would propel us
to never-ending acts of worship and service.

~ NANCY LEIGH DEMOSS

NO SINGLE ATTITUDE ADJUSTMENT HAS more power to transform our lives than that of gratitude. And no single adjustment of attitude presents so stark a choice in real time.

Paul David Tripp writes, *Today you will spend solitary moments of conversation with yourself, either listing your complaints or counting your blessings.*[175]

---

[175] Tripp, *New Morning Mercies*, 478.

When it comes to our thought life, it really is *either/or.* *Either* I will choose to meditate on my complaints *or* I will choose to count my blessings.

The discipline of gratitude is a discipline and disciplines are hard. This discipline requires commitment, resolve, determination and strength to choose thankfulness over complaint.

At the heart of <u>in</u>gratitude is believing that the path your life has taken is out of God's control and/or that he cannot take the bad stuff and transform it into the good he promised in that famous verse, Romans 8.28. At the heart of ingratitude are faulty beliefs: God has lost control, he never had control, and/or he doesn't care.

To be grateful, then, is to replace this faulty belief system with the reality that nothing surprises God and that all that is happening in your life can be redeemed by God. The Apostle Paul reminds us that *we live by faith, not by sight.* (2 Corinthians 5:7)

To exercise this discipline is to believe that not *all* of life is terrible. Bad things have happened and the consequences of those bad things really are devastating. Though it may seem like we have lost everything through divorce, we haven't. We still have much in our lives for which you and I can be grateful.

Melodie Beattie summarizes the transformative power of gratitude: *Gratitude unlocks the fullness of life. It turns what we have into enough, and more. It turns denial into acceptance, chaos to order, confusion to clarity. It can turn a meal into a feast, a house into a home, a stranger into a friend.*[176]

---

[176] Melody Beattie, *"Melody Beattie Quotes."* BrainyQuote, accessed June 11, 2017. https://www.brainyquote.com/quotes/authors/m/melody_beattie.html.

To exercise this discipline is to choose to let go of some things.

* To be grateful requires letting go of *anger*, because you cannot be angry and grateful at the same time.
* To be grateful will mean letting go of *self-pity*, because gratitude is not on your pity party's guest list.
* To be grateful means letting go of *revenge*. The gladness in a grateful heart pushes out the bitterness that drives revenge.
* To be grateful is to *expand and project your perspective from this moment into eternity*, believing that in the long run, things will, indeed, work out for you.

This is a tough discipline for me. Anger, revenge, self-pity—I struggle with these. For my sake, I'm going to hammer this point home with this long but poignant quote from Richard Rohr:

> *Things go right more often than they go wrong. Our legs carry us where we are going, our eyes let us see the road ahead, and our ears let us hear the world around us. Our bodies, and our lives, work pretty much as they should, which is why we become so unsettled when we confront any failure or injustice. This is not so true for people born into intense poverty or social injustice, of course. And we had best never forget that.*
>
> *Nevertheless, we must stop a moment and look clearly and honestly at our life thus far. For most of us, life has been pretty good. We shouldn't be naive about evil, but perhaps the most appropriate attitude on a day-to-day basis should*

be simple and overwhelming gratitude for what has been given.[177]

THINK ABOUT IT...

+ Eugene Peterson writes, *All true prayer pursued far enough, becomes praise.*[178] What do you think he means by this?

+ You knew this was coming: Take a sheet of paper and make a list of things for which you can be grateful. Ask God to open your heart and show you the good things he has brought into your life. If you are struggling, check out this website: *http://www.lifehack.org/ articles/communication/60-things-thankful-for-life.html.* Caution: When you read a list like this you will come across items that you *don't* have! This may send you spiraling down into negative thinking. Skip over those items quickly, and move on to the things you *do* have. If a list like this does more damage than good, skip the list!

+ Note: If you are stuck in a pattern of negative, cynical thinking, you may be depressed. If you know you should be grateful but your mind can't go there despite your best efforts, see a counselor/therapist and your medical doctor. Living with depression sucks, and counseling, along with medication (if needed)

---

[177] Rohr, Durepos and McGrath, *On the Threshold of Transformation*, 285.

[178] Eugene Peterson, *God's Message for Each Day: Wisdom from the Word of God* (Nashville: Thomas Nelson, 2006), 239.

can literally save your life. There is no shame in getting the help you need.

PRAYER:

God, open my heart and mind to your goodness in my life. Push away anger, thoughts of revenge and indulgences in self-pity to make way for glad thoughts of the good in my life.

Living with an Open Hand

———❦———

The Word

> *Command those who are rich in this present world*
> *not to be arrogant nor to put their hope in wealth,*
> *which is so uncertain, but to put their hope in*
> *God, who richly provides us with everything for our*
> *enjoyment. Command them to do good, to be rich in*
> *good deeds, and to be generous and willing to share.*
> *In this way they will lay up treasure for themselves*
> *as a firm foundation for the coming age, so that*
> *they may take hold of the life that is truly life.*

— 1 Timothy 6.17–19

Thought for the Day:

> *Our real success is measured by how we touch and enrich*
> *people's lives—the difference we can make to those who*
> *would least expect it, to those the world looks over.*

~ Bear Grylls

It really is a matter of where the heart is: *either* my heart
is leaning toward God *or* away from him.

Nothing has more power to pull our hearts away from God than money and things. We live in a material world that operates on currency. We can't get away from money and stuff. But money and stuff have amazing power to drag our affections away from the vertical (God) to settle for shallow, horizontal lives of meaninglessness and temporary satisfaction.

Klaus Bockmuehl wrote, *Living for yourself is too notoriously small an aim for any human soul.*[179] And yet the power of money pushes us to be satisfied with our small selves.

How does God reorder our affections? The answer is through the discipline of living with an open, generous hand. This is a discipline, and, as noted yesterday, disciplines, are by nature, hard.

- **Begin by looking up.** Look *up* to God (the vertical), asking him to do the work of reordering your affections and desires. Ask him to bring balance (see the verse above) to how you think about money and stuff. This is a work of God in your heart. As such, you must submit to his will in this area.[180]
- Continuing your gaze upward, **ask God to help you distinguish between true needs and mere wants**. This is a crucial distinction because the gap between our perceived needs and our wants creates the space

[179] Quoted in Gary Thomas, *Authentic Faith*, 126.

[180] Paul David Tripp writes, *Grace works to rescue you from you by progressively breaking your bondage to the created world and turning the deepest affection of your heart toward God.* Tripp, *New Morning Mercies*, Kindle Location 2394.

of discontent that pulls our hearts toward material-ism.[181] Richard Carlson notes that

> *An excellent measure of happiness is the differential between what you have and what you want. You can spend your lifetime wanting more, always chasing happiness—or you can simply decide to consciously want less. This latter strategy is infinitely easier and more fulfilling.*[182]

* Now look around you. Going back to yesterday, **practice the discipline of gratitude**. Remember its power to transform your attitude. What has God given you? Tim Keller wisely notes that *If you have money, power, and status today, it is due to the century and place in which you were born, to your talents and capacities and health, none of which you earned. In short, all your resources are in the end the gift of God.*[183] All comes from God. A huge mistake is to think otherwise.

* Next, **ask God to rightly order your view of money**. Francis Bacon was on target when he said that

---

[181] Tripp notes that, *When you tell yourself that something is a need, three things follow. First, you feel entitled to the thing, because, after all, it is a need. Second, because it is a need, you feel it's your right to demand it. And third, you then judge the love of another person by his or her willingness to deliver the thing. This not only happens in our relationships with one another, but more important, it happens in our relationship with God. When you name something as a need and God doesn't deliver it, you begin to doubt his goodness. What is deadly about this is that you simply don't run for help to someone whose character you've come to doubt.* Tripp, *New Morning Mercies*, Kindle Location 1967.

[182] Richard Carlson, *Don't Sweat the Small Stuff...and It's All Small Stuff Simple Ways to Keep the Little Things from Taking Over Your Life* (New York: Hyperion, 1997), 232.

[183] Tim Keller, *Generous Justice: How God's Grace Makes Us Just* (New York: 2010: Penguin Publishing Group), 89.

money is a terrible master but an excellent servant.[184]
Money is a commodity, a tool, but it has the power to become your master. Ask God to change your view of money to see it as *only* a tool.

* By looking up (the vertical) you have now gained God's perspective on money and stuff. Through his eyes you can now see the horizontal through his eyes. Continuing your gaze around you (the horizontal), *use your money and stuff to meet the needs of those around you.* Loosen the grip of money on your life by giving. Giving becomes the true test of whether you are practicing the discipline of generosity. Your checking account will clearly express where your heart is.

* Now enjoy the freedom of having loosened the grip of money on your life!

* **But beware... the pull of money is constant and unrelenting**. By practicing the discipline of living with an open hand on a regular basis (read: weekly) you consciously direct your heart back to God and away from lesser things.

Think About It...

* Take a look at your checking account. Where is your heart? What things do you value the most, really?
* If you won the lottery, what would you do with it?

---

[184] Francis Bacon, accessed October 3, 2017, https://www.goodreads.com/quotes/446478-money-is-a-great-servant-but-a-bad-master.

* Don't just think about it... DO IT! Give to your church right now. Stop right here, right now, and send money to your church.

PRAYER:

God, I live in a material world but I was made for more than this. Set my heart upon you. Pull my gaze upward and show me the right way to view money and things. Give me an open heart that reflects your open and generous heart toward me.

How Alpha Males Can Help One Another Instead of Tearing Apart One Another

—⊶⊷—

THE WORD

A friend loves at all times, and a
brother is born for adversity.

— PROVERBS 17.17

THOUGHT FOR THE DAY:

A true friend never gets in your way unless
you happen to be going down.

~ ARNOLD GLASOW

THE MAN SITTING ACROSS FROM me in the diner was exceptional. He was educated, smart, sharp-looking. He worked as an engineer his entire career. He had run for and been elected to serve on the local school board several times. He lived for adventure—scuba diving wrecks in the cold and dangerous waters off New England was nothing to him. he had a woodworking shop that turned me green with envy. He was successful and well-liked.

But then his life fell apart. He was laid off from his job. His marriage disintegrated. His tower came crashing down.

He came to our church broken and busted up. There he found a group of guys walking the same journey—broken and busted up—*but lending each other a hand up the mountain.*

As we talked that early morning in the diner, he told me about some men he had known for decades. He thought they were his friends. Even though they knew his life was crumbling around him, *not a single one even acknowledged the pain he was going through.*

In his loneliness he was hungry for someone to give a damn, someone who would see past the tough exterior and shine a light on his crushed heart without shaming or embarrassing him.

Males are hard-wired to compete against one another. Because of our competitive spirit, we find it difficult, if not impossible, to connect with one another. To show vulnerability is to expose a weakness, a weakness that has the potential to be exploited by another man. In our dog-eat-dog world, any advantage we give another man may lead to our demise. Hence the image of the successful American male whose outer shell is impenetrable, able to take whatever is thrown at him and shrug it off.

What a load of crap! There is no lonelier experience than divorce. It crushes your heart. Men, we hurt and it is OK to acknowledge that. What takes more courage—to *pretend* everything is OK or to actually speak the truth about what is happening inside?

I get that no one wants to be around a constant whiner. No one seeks out the company of an incessant complainer.

All of us have our physical aches and pains, but I doubt if you want to hear about my sore knee, achy back, mild headache or itchy toe. But if I am face-down on the ground with chest pains and barely able to breathe, I better let someone know I'm in distress and dammit, you better pay attention to me!

God will bring into your life another man or a small group of men to help get you off the pavement and to the ER. Don't resist what God provides. Willingly and gladly participate in the spiritual discipline of fellowship.

Henry Blackaby writes,

> *The Christian life is a pilgrimage. At times the road is difficult, and we get lonely. Sometimes we may become discouraged and consider abandoning the journey. It is at such times that God will place a friend alongside us. One of God's most precious gifts to us is friends who encourage us and lovingly challenge us to keep going. According to Scripture, a friend is one who challenges you to become all that God intends.*[185]

And, God will use you to pick another guy up off the pavement. Tony Dungy notes that *Dale Carnegie said you can make more friends in two weeks by genuinely showing interest in them than you can make in two years by trying to get them interested in you.*[186]

---

[185] Blackaby and Blackaby, *Experiencing God Day-By-Day,* Kindle Location 2347.

[186] Tony Dungy and Nathan Whitaker, *The One Year Uncommon Life Daily Challenge,* Kindle Location 297.

The discipline of fellowship is being with other Christians who nourish your soul through understanding, challenge and encouragement.[187]

Think About It... for today's *Think About It* we return to Day 8. If you didn't do this exercise *then*, I encourage you to do it *now...*

* On a scale of 0 to 10, (0 being not lonely at all to 10, absolutely completely lonely), how lonely are you?

    0 —1—2—3—4—5—6—7—8—9—10

* List two guys you know you can call anytime day or night for help.

    _____ Phone# _____
    _____ Phone# _____

* If the two lines above are BLANK, list two guys who you **THINK** might be willing to be your friend:

    _____ Phone# _____
    _____ Phone# _____

* Call the first one on your list. Take him to lunch or something. Be creative. It really can't be that hard to get together. Dogs do it. We can too.

* If none of the above work (or you just want to talk) give me a call or send me an email!

---

[187] Bill Donahue, *Leading Life-Changing Small Groups*, Kindle Locations 782-783.

LIFE COMMITMENT:
I don't want to be a whiner but I do want to get better and stronger. I believe God places other men in my life to help me accomplish those two goals.

Habits of the Heart

─────── ✺ ───────

THE WORD

For this very reason, make every effort to add to your
faith goodness; and to goodness, knowledge; and to
knowledge, self-control; and to self-control, perseverance;
and to perseverance, godliness; and to godliness,
brotherly kindness; and to brotherly kindness, love. For
if you possess these qualities in increasing measure, they
will keep you from being ineffective and unproductive
in your knowledge of our Lord Jesus Christ.

— 2 PETER 1.5–8

THOUGHT FOR THE DAY:

Everyone is in a process of spiritual formation. We
are being shaped into either the wholeness of the
image of Christ or a horribly destructive caricature
of that image—destructive not only to ourselves but
also to others, for we inflict our brokenness upon
them.... The direction of our spiritual growth infuses
all we do with intimations of either Life or Death.

~ M. ROBERT MULHOLLAND JR.

OVER 20 DAYS AGO (beginning with Day 114) we began our spiritual training with this commitment: *In partnership with God, I commit to the hard work of training so that I can be the man God destined me to be.* To get there, we committed to exercising the habits of the heart we call spiritual disciplines which are instruments of God's grace which, through the Spirit, transform us daily into people who reflect Jesus' love, obedience, humility, and connection to God.[188] (See Days 112-138)

We said that **our souls are like a bike tire**—they naturally leak a little, so every day I must pump them back up. The spiritual disciplines are the daily shots of 'air' that keep my soul solid and ready for the rides.

We recognized that to meet the challenges before us as divorced men—namely to survive with grace and then thrive beyond our fall—trying is not enough. **Success comes when we couple training with trying**.

Practicing the spiritual disciplines is God's way of training our souls for being successful in the things that matter. Listed below are the disciplines we discussed. As you look through this list, ask God to show you which disciplines he wants to you focus on now.

☐ Solitude (Days 117-118)
☐ Covenant Prayer (Days 119-121)
☐ Conversational Prayer (Day 122)
☐ Guidance (Days 123-129)

---

[188] *Spiritual Disciplines*, Rose Publishing July 7, 2014.

- ☐ Study (Day 130)
- ☐ Worship (Day 131)
- ☐ Confession (Day 132)
- ☐ Submission (Day 133)
- ☐ Gratitude (Day 134)
- ☐ Generosity (Day 135)
- ☐ Fellowship (Day 136)

THINK ABOUT IT...

- ✦ Which way is your heart leaning: toward God, or away from him?
- ✦ If away from him, ask God to give you a desire for him.
- ✦ Ask God to show you the pathway to know him better. Ask him where to start on these spiritual disciplines.
- ✦ This much we know: Training begins with time alone with God. Commit to spending a few minutes several days a week alone with him.

PRAYER...

God, though so much seems like it has been stripped away in my life through divorce and other tragedies, you have never left me. I want to know you more. Shape my soul to be like Jesus. Plant a deep desire to know you more and more.

God Wants Love, Not Fear

———❦———

THE WORD

There is no fear in love. But perfect love drives
out fear, because fear has to do with punishment.
The one who fears is not made perfect in
love. We love because he first loved us.

— 1 JOHN 4.18–19

THOUGHT FOR THE DAY:

Define yourself radically as one beloved by God. This
is the true self. Every other identity is illusion.

~ BRENNAN MANNING

SO IN THE END, WHAT God desires more from us than anything is a vital, dynamic living relationship based on his acceptance and love of us, not based on fear or dread. This is a hard thing to grasp. We've been taught by the church (whatever church you may have been a part of) and our culture that God is distant, angry, and, above all, demanding that our behavior conform to his standards.

After decades of listening, reading, preaching, hard experience, counseling others and being counseled, I am convinced that **God's desire is to woo us to heaven rather than scare us out of hell.** God wants to guide us for his glory, for our good and for the good of the world based on a foundation of love, not fear. God is for us, not against us. He wants us to be madly in love with him because he is madly in love with us.

Do you understand this? Do you understand that this is all about a relationship? Do you understand that when you are in a vital relationship with God based on love, the behavior issues fall into place?

The church keeps telling us to make apples so we go looking for some apples. When we manage to grab a few and hold them up, we are given a pat on the back and told that we are good apple trees.

God's way is to change old sin-filled spiritual DNA to 'apple tree' DNA. Then, when we *are* apple trees, making apples is not hard—it's what apple trees do. God rewrites our spiritual DNA through a love relationship. When our spiritual DNA is rewritten, we produce spiritual fruit because that is what we do, and it's not hard.

Unfortunately, most of us have been taught that to be good Christians, we must produce fruit that we are simply not wired to produce. Then when we fail, we are punished. This is like cutting down a peach tree because it doesn't make apples.

Richard Rohr makes this point well:

> *Living merely for reward or in avoidance of punishment has allowed us to become absentee landlords of our own lives.*

We just muddle through, safe in the promise of a heavenly reward if we do our best. So we go to church on Sunday—we get the reward later and avoid punishment—fire-insurance religion instead of any real freedom or love.

God friendship is its own reward now. If you have it now, you will have it then, and that is called heaven. If you don't have it now, apparently you don't want it very much, and that is hell. But both heaven and hell are first of all now, and not delayed rewards or punishments.

Is my faith rooted primarily in punishment and reward, or have I experienced faith for the sake of an ongoing communion with my creator?.... God has to be greater than the greatest love you have ever experienced.... God's constant posture toward us is love.[189]

The Spiritual Disciplines are not designed to make us miserable. These habits are not duties to fulfill or to be punished if we fall short. They are not a long checklist of even more things to do as part of an already over-crowded day. The disciplines are places in our soul that we plow up in order for God to plant the seeds that grow into what he wants us to be—*and what he wants us to be is always best for ourselves and others.* This is a good, joyful, fun and right place to be!

Richard Foster writes,

God has given us the Disciplines of the spiritual life as a means of receiving his grace. The Disciplines allow us to place ourselves before God so that he can transform us.... The Disciplines

---

[189] Rohr, Durepos and McGrath, *On the Threshold of Transformation*, 55, 57, 75.

are *God's way of getting us into the ground; they put us where he can work within us and transform us. By themselves the Spiritual Disciplines can do nothing; they can only get us to the place where something can be done. They are God's means of grace.... God has ordained the Disciplines of the spiritual life as the means by which we place ourselves where he can bless us.*[190]

Be blessed!

THINK ABOUT IT...

* Do you think of God as another impossible-to-please authority in your life or as your joy-filled dad who likes you and wants to be with you?

LIFE COMMITMENT...

I commit to this radically freeing reality that God loves me, and his love is the basis of all reality and the thing for which I am most grateful and the position in which I most want to live.

---

[190] Foster, *Celebration of Discipline*, 7.

Thinking About Forgiveness (Again)

———— ∽◈∾ ————

THE WORD

Get rid of all bitterness, rage and anger, brawling
and slander, along with every form of malice. Be
kind and compassionate to one another, forgiving
each other, just as in Christ God forgave you.

— EPHESIANS 4.31–32

THOUGHT FOR THE DAY:

Failing is painful. It fuels the "shouldas and couldas,"
which means judgment and shame are often lying in wait.

~ BRENÉ BROWN

FORGIVENESS IS HARD. IT IS, frankly, impossible without God. God works in us through a process that moves at its own pace. Grief is like that. You can't make anyone get through the grieving process faster, though some well-meaning folks will surely try. *It was her time to go... She is better off now... You can always have another child.* You can't grieve faster than our built-in processes allow any more than you can make a child grow taller faster than that kid's potential.

But you can slow down the grieving process, you can stunt a kid's growth, you can put roadblocks in the path to forgiveness.

Here are some more thoughts on forgiveness:

* Don't rush this process.
* Be careful who you listen to. Some well-meaning folks in the Christian community will tell you that you MUST forgive. They will then cite scriptures that warn of eternal damnation if you don't forgive those who hurt you. At the same time, the world will tell you to get revenge. A common trope in all forms of American entertainment is the revenge trope. It feels good when the villain gets it. When people tell you what you must do, consider their words but hold them loosely. Always remember that *Ignorance isn't bliss, it's just loud.*
* The deeper the hurt, the longer the path to and through forgiveness.

Carefully consider again the questions we asked many months ago:

* How have I experienced forgiveness from others in my life?
* What barriers to forgiving others are in my life right now?

- What will I gain by forgiving the people in my life who have hurt me?
- What would I gain by not forgiving them?

THINK ABOUT IT...

One of the best books on forgiveness is *The Book of Forgiving: The Fourfold Path for Healing Ourselves and Our World* by Desmond Tutu and his daughter, Mpho Tutu.[191] This book is about the fourfold process they used in dealing with the atrocities committed during Apartheid in South Africa and the healing that saved the nation from a bloodbath when Nelson Mandela came to power.

The Tutus do not gloss over the intense difficulty of forgiveness. Evidence of that is found in this prayer by Mpho Tutu. It is the *Prayer before the Prayer*. If you can't see your way to forgiveness right now, that's OK. This *Prayer before the Prayer* will resonate with you.

PRAYER BEFORE THE PRAYER

I want to be willing to forgive
But I dare not ask for the will to forgive
In case you give it to me
And I am not yet ready
I am not yet ready for my heart to soften
I am not yet ready to be vulnerable again
Not yet ready to see that there is humanity
in my tormentor's eyes

---

[191] Desmond Tutu and Mpho A. Tutu, *The Book of Forgiving: The Fourfold Path for Healing Ourselves and Our World* (London: William Collins), 2015.

Or that the one who hurt me may also have cried
I am not yet ready for the journey
I am not yet interested in the path
I am at the prayer before the prayer of forgiveness
Grant me the will to want to forgive
Grant it to me not yet but soon

Can I even form the words Forgive me?
Dare I even look?
Do I dare to see the hurt I have caused?
I can glimpse all the shattered pieces of that fragile thing
That soul trying to rise on the broken wings of hope
But only out of the corner of my eye
I am afraid of it
And if I am afraid to see
How can I not be afraid to say Forgive me?

Is there a place where we can meet?
You and me
The place in the middle
The no man's land
Where we straddle the lines
Where you are right
And I am right too
And both of us are wrong and wronged
Can we meet there?
And look for the place where the path begins
The path that ends when we forgive[192]

---

[192] Ibid., 9-10.

LIFE COMMITMENT...

I commit to praying this Prayer before the Prayer. I commit to taking first steps on the journey to forgiveness.

Losses—Concrete and Abstract

THE WORD

Though the fig tree does not bud and there are no
grapes on the vines, though the olive crop fails and
the fields produce no food, though there are no sheep
in the pen and no cattle in the stalls, yet I will rejoice
in the Lord, I will be joyful in God my Savior. The
Sovereign Lord is my strength; he makes my feet like
the feet of a deer, he enables me to go on the heights.

— HABAKKUK 3.17–19

THOUGHT FOR THE DAY:

Heartbreak knocks the wind out of you, and the
feelings of loss and longing can make getting out
of bed a monumental task. Learning to trust and
lean in to love again can feel impossible.... In those
moments when disappointment is washing over us
and we're desperately trying to get our heads and
hearts around what is or is not going to be, the death
of our expectations can be painful beyond measure.

~ BRENÉ BROWN

As YOUNG MEN WE WORK hard to acquire, to gain, to gather. We get an education, we get a reputation. We get a job, we get money. We get a wife, we get kids. We get a house. We get friends. We get status and standing. The first half of life is about getting, gathering, collecting. Midlife is the pinnacle of our gathering. We have a house that is almost paid for. We have a career that is at its zenith. We are well respected and well paid. We have kids who are getting married and having grandkids for us. We have growing 401k's and a hopeful future filled with happy grandkids, financial security, rest and fun.

At least that's the dream. The reality is that while the first half of life is about getting, the second half of life is about losing. All that is gained in the first half of life is lost as we grow older, until, finally, we lose our bodies and leave the world and everything we accumulated behind.

Divorce accelerates the losses of the second half of life and, because divorce often happens at midlife—at the supposed pinnacle of all we have worked so hard to acquire— the losses seem doubly painful.

I have felt deeply—*really deeply*—the losses caused by divorce. I ache in the places where words cannot go. I lost my family, my career, my reputation, my income. These losses hurt so much because they are real. I have felt angry, lonely, exhausted, shamed, embarrassed and sad. I count my losses and alternate between intense anger and sadness.

The journey to healing encompasses and embraces the realities of these losses. You cannot gloss over them, cover them up, numb them away with drugs or forget about them with a new hobby, girlfriend, job or career.

The reality is that we are all on a pathway of loss. As a hospice chaplain I see people at the end of their lives. Most of these folks are old, some are very old. Some are wealthy, very wealthy. Some live in shacks (literally). Some are white, many are Hispanic, a few are black. Some have had amazing careers. Others have spent most their adult lives in prison. In the end, death takes away all they have ever been. Death leaves behind all they worked for. Every person on the planet is on a pathway to the loss of all they have acquired on earth.

While divorce accelerates this journey, it is a journey we must all face. How can you and I navigate this journey with grace? How can we finish well?

Trust in God. You will lose every material thing that you own right now, including your body. Without God, what do you have? The journey through the pain and loss of divorce can lead you away from reliance upon your own power to the wisdom of relying completely on God's amazing power. This is a journey we all must eventually take *so why not start this journey now?*

Give it to God. Let God take your pain, heartache and worries. When you let go and relax into him, you are relinquishing dependence on your own power and letting him handle things in his power. Your mind clears, your tight chest loosens up, and you are off the ledge once again. Time after time I have heard God say to me, *Hold on, I've got you, I am sustaining you, I will see you through this, you will get through* *this!* And he has. That's the cool thing—he has done it! So I can trust him to keep doing it.

Know everything that is lost will be restored, now or later. Read Hebrews 11. The writer tells tales of mighty men and women of faith who, through their amazing commitment to God, made huge differences on earth. But keep reading. The last part of Hebrews 11 tells of anonymous men and women who suffered terribly for their faith. Lost, alone, forgotten to the world, they were not forgotten by God. Hebrews 11:40 says, *God had planned something better for us so that only together with us would they be made perfect.* God has something better planned for you.

You will regain what you have lost. For some of us, our restoration will be like Job's, who received on earth double what he had lost (Job 42.10). Others of us will see our reward on the other side. Either way, it is good.

Choose happiness today. The losses are real, deep and they hurt. You may have lost nearly everything. But to choose to sit in the midst of the ruins of the tower you so carefully constructed *and remain there* does no one any good. If you choose to sit in the rubble, you will spend your days alone. You will deprive the world of what you have to offer for the years you have left. Instead, reframe the inner dialogue in your head and heart using the tools of gratitude and hope.

The Apostle Paul had it right when he wrote, *I consider my life worth nothing to me; my only aim is to finish the race and complete the task the Lord Jesus has given me—the task of testifying to the good news of God's grace.* (Acts 20.24)

THINK ABOUT IT...

* In this time of loss, what loss (your role as husband, role as father, your reputation, standard of living, money to settle your divorce and pay your lawyer, living arrangement, etc.) has hurt (or is hurting) the most? Why does that particular loss hurt so much?
* Is it possible for anyone to really know God without experiencing deep, soul-wrenching loss?
* What does trusting God and giving it to him look like to you?

PRAYER...

Dear Heavenly Father, You created me for a specific purpose. I am Your masterpiece. You have plans to prosper me and to give me hope and a future. It is my heart's desire to accomplish what you created me to do. You know what would satisfy the deepest longings of my heart. And if I take delight in You, You will give me the desires of my heart. Even when adversity comes against me and keeps me from fulfilling my dreams and desires, You promise that my gifts and calling will never be withdrawn. Help me to trust in You with all my heart and not lean on my own understanding. As I seek Your will for my life, You promise to teach, guide and instruct me in which path and direction to take. Thank you, God. You restore my dreams and satisfy the desires of my heart.[193]

---

[193] Violet James, *God Restores: Prayers & Promises for Restoration* (Maximum Potential: 2017), 7.

When You Hurt Your World Shrinks

———❦———

THE WORD

Then Job took a piece of broken pottery and scraped
himself with it as he sat among the ashes.

—JOB 2.8

THOUGHT FOR THE DAY:

When we're in the middle of adversity, it feels all
consuming. Faith flickers, hope falters, courage burns
low. It sometimes seems as if the dark times will never
end. And these are the hours when the enemy of our
soul whispers his lies of discouragement and despair.

~ JONI ERICKSON TADA

THE DAY BEFORE I PREACHED a sermon about marriage and divorce I glued two pieces of wood together lengthwise. During
the sermon I illustrated divorce by ripping the boards apart.
I said something like this: *The biblical word describing marriage*
is the word for 'glue.' When we divorce, we believe we can cleanly
and neatly separate. But divorce is not neat or clean. It is like these

two boards, glued together. When I rip them apart, they tear at each other, leaving a mess.

The people left church that day with one image in their minds: the boards being ripped apart and the mess they left behind. When we suffer, all we initially see and deeply experience are the rips and tears in our lives.

Suffering shrinks our world...

Time slows down to *this moment*. If we think about the *past* it hurts—either we deeply regret the mistakes that led to our divorce or we grieve the hard work we put in to avoid such a catastrophe.

The *future* is so uncertain and painful, we can't think about it. Whatever we had planned for our future is now off the table. The pain of the past and the uncertainty of a frightening future compress time to the terrible *now*.

When we hurt, **space** also compresses. Forget the vacation trip to Colorado, forget the plans to remodel the kitchen, forget organizing my desk. Pain is the heat that shrinks our space around us.

This was driven home to me when I was asked by a family to visit their 32-year-old son who was dying of a rare form of cancer. I went to the hospital, introduced myself, and began to chat it up. He seemed disengaged from what I was saying. Then, without a word, he stood up, pulled up his hospital gown, and urinated into a plastic urinal as if I wasn't there.

For this 32-year-old man, time and space had shrunk to this moment and to his hospital bed. He didn't care about anything I said. He just needed to pee, so he did. Two days later he died.

When the Old Testament figure of Job had lost everything, his world shrank to an ash heap (see the scripture for today).

If this is the way you feel, then...

* Know that this is where you are at the moment—it is normal to feel like time and space have shrunk to this moment and this little space.
* When the terrible pain of divorce is upon you, you may feel like time needs to shrink to nothing and that you need to leave the space. We call this option *suicide*, and it is a bad and terrible idea. It is OK to experience compressed time and space, just don't let the pain squeeze the life out of you. If you feel like this at this moment, read the next point...
* You will not always feel like this. The process of healing will re-expand time and enlarge your space. *I promise you that you will not always feel like this.* But if you are considering suicide as a viable option to your suffering, call the National Suicide Prevention Hotline now: 800-273-8255. You can call me as well.[194]

Think About It...

* If you are new to divorce, have you experienced how pain can shrink your time and space?

---

[194] 978.204.0480. Visit www.mensdivorcerecovery.org for more information and resources for help.

* If you are further down the road of recovery, are you experiencing an expansion of time and enlarging of your space?

LIFE COMMITMENT...

It is normal for pain to compress time and shrink my space. I commit to living through this moment, but I pray to God that he will deliver me from this pain, and I trust he will do it. I will hold on.

When You Hurt You Become Super Sensitive

———— ∞ ————

THE WORD

Why is life given to a man whose way is hidden,
whom God has hedged in? For sighing comes
to me instead of food; my groans pour out like
water. What I feared has come upon me; what I
dreaded has happened to me. I have no peace, no
quietness; I have no rest, but only turmoil.

— JOB 3.23–26

THOUGHT FOR THE DAY:

We rarely start with God. We start with the
immediate data of our lives—a messy house, a
balky car, a cranky spouse, a recalcitrant child.

~ EUGENE PETERSON

I HAVE WALKED WITH MANY men and women through the
heartbreak of divorce. One couple in particular comes to

mind. Both were super-achievers. Each had tried to overcome tremendous adversity the world's way, and had ended up in more pain than when they started. They finally found Christ and things between them improved.

But staying together was not to be. For whatever reasons, anger rose up and lashed out and both found themselves filing restraining orders against the other as tensions exploded.

It was a long and painful season for them both. The church staff and I reached out in every way possible. We met with them, recommended counselors, nursed each through their pain. Church folks watched after their kids when things were imploding at home. All this to say, we gave them our best time and energy.

So it came as a shock when a fellow staff member and I received a scathing seven page single-spaced email from the wife. My staff member walked into my office and stated that this was the longest email she had ever received! After all the time and energy we had put into this woman, my first response was anger. But then we realized the pain this woman was in had made her hurt so deeply that the smallest thing would seem super painful to her. Intense pain had made her super sensitive.

When your world comes crashing down time and space shrink and you may become hyper-sensitive to your environment and those around you. I know I did. I couldn't believe that most of my friends made no effort to reach out. And most of those who did venture forth simply didn't get the intense pain I was in. It pissed me off.

Looking back now I understand a little better. I now realize how my pain drove me to seek someone, *anyone*, who would understand. Few did. But the few who did saved my life.

If the people in your life seem insensitive or not to care, don't be surprised. Some really don't care. Some may care but are uncomfortable sitting with someone who is in such intense pain. Others shy away because they don't want to be reminded of what could happen to them.

But a few will get it. A few will understand. Thank God for these few. Seek them out. Ask them questions. Let them into your heart.

And release everyone else from the burden of sharing your burden. God knows who you need to help you through. Find those folks and be grateful to them and to God for what they give you.

THINK ABOUT IT...

- Who among your friends and/or family has failed to reach out to you? Release them from your anger. They don't understand and you can't make them understand. Instead...

- ... Ask God to send you a few, maybe even just one, to get you through. And...

- ... Determine that you will not be insensitive to the hurting. Further down the path, when God puts hurting people in front of you, love them as you have been loved.

PRAYER...

Not everyone will understand. Not everyone will get it. God, thank you for the few who do. As I heal, help me to be one of those 'few' to the hurting and suffering in this world.

When You Hurt You May Lash Out

⎯⎯∞∞⎯⎯

THE WORD

Teach me knowledge and good judgment
for I believe in your commands.

— Psalm 119.66

THOUGHT FOR THE DAY:

There are too many people today who instead of
feeling hurt are acting out their hurt; instead of
acknowledging pain, they're inflicting pain on
others. Rather than risking feeling disappointed,
they're choosing to live disappointed.

~ BRENÉ BROWN

NO ONE LIKES TO TAKE their dog to the vet, least of all, the dog! We have all been shocked when our normally loving and tail-wagging dog suddenly bares his teeth and emits a low, menacing growl. What causes a friendly animal to transform into a frightening beast? The short and simple answer is, *pain*. When normally benign animals are cornered or hurt, they turn ugly. So do we. Hurt people hurt people.

When my life crashed around me my first reactions were benevolent. I tried to understand why others were coming against me. I tried to be gracious to those who had betrayed me. But then the reality of what I had lost began to sink in and I became angry.

I can illustrate this through a Facebook Messenger conversation with a longtime friend. It started with me explaining what had happened in my life the past two years. My friend acknowledged the difficulty of the situation, then wrote,

I will remind you that our God is big. Really big. He came to reconcile and leaves us with a ministry of reconciliation. He is most glorified when we are most like him.

My response?

If I did not know God was big I would have a .40 caliber bullet through my head a few months ago. Having to go through this with you just brings it all back so maybe I should just give the lite answer when someone I know hasn't heard.

It should come as no surprise that I didn't get a response from him.

What happened in this conversation? My friend tried to understand, then he off-loaded the 'Sunday School answer' to my pain in a way that I heard as condescending and trite. This infuriated me more, and when he let the conversation drop, my anger only increased. I did *not* feel like a minister of reconciliation. I felt like I wanted to hurt him and all those who had wounded me so deeply.

When we are in severe pain we need to express it in ways that don't further alienate us from those around us trying to help. Ask God to give you the one or two people who can absorb your pain without further hurting you.[195]

And then release anger through other means. For me, my bike is my outlet. I let the anger flow from my head down through my legs and into the pavement. My record rides have come when I have been most angry. I can't over-emphasize the value of sweating. Men were made to fight. Channel that urge away from others and into the pavement or weights or yoga. *When you are angry and frustrated, get moving.*

And if you are on the receiving end of someone who has been severely wounded, *leave the trite answers at home.* Instead, absorb their pain, even if it is directed at you. Hurt people lash out. Let them. Then, when the time is right, God will use you to mitigate some of their pain.

THINK ABOUT IT...

* What do you do when you are really hurt?
* What are some physical ways you can let pain out that are legal and only moderately dangerous?
* Who is the friend or counselor who is mature enough to sit with you in your pain?
* Who in your life needs you to sit with them in their pain?

---

[195] Brene Brown writes, *Most of us were never taught how to hold discomfort, sit with it, or communicate it, only how to discharge or dump it, or to pretend that it's not happening.* Brene Brown, *Rising Strong* (Random House, 2017), Kindle Location 859.

Life Commitment...

I commit to releasing my hurt in as constructive a way as possible.[196]

---

[196] To read more, go to this website: http://www.charismanews.com/opinion/the-pulse/53573-15-ways-hurting-people-hurt-people.

When You Hurt You May Be Willing to do Anything to Get Out of the Pain

—∞∞∞—

THE WORD

> *Blessed is the man who does not walk in the counsel*
> *of the wicked or stand in the way of sinners or sit*
> *in the seat of mockers. But his delight is in the*
> *law of the Lord, and on his law he meditates day*
> *and night. He is like a tree planted by streams of*
> *water, which yields its fruit in season and whose*
> *leaf does not wither. Whatever he does prospers.*

— PSALM 1.1–3

THOUGHT FOR THE DAY:

> *Our search for significance shows up*
> *in a lot of misdirected ways.*

~ TONY DUNGY

AS WE ALL KNOW, THE Chinese characters for the word *crisis* mean *danger* and *critical point.*[197]

---

[197] See this article for a brief discussion about the common misinterpretation of this phrase: https://en.wikipedia.org/wiki/Chinese_word_for_%22crisis%22

Crises push us to critical points where we can choose well or not.

Perhaps it was a crisis in your marriage that led you to choose to cheat on your spouse, and your divorce is the result. Perhaps you are the victim of a wayward or misguided spouse, and the divorce was a complete surprise to you. Either way, you and I have choices to make from this point forward. The problem is that our intense pain can push us to make poor decisions with long-term consequences. The intensity of the pain can falsely make you believe you must make decisions *now*.

If there ever is a time when you need to slow down and seek God's wisdom and the wise direction of others, this is it. Don't make any huge decisions now. Stop, pray, talk with wise friends, seek out a counselor. Don't make any major decisions when you are hurting the most.

Paul Tripp says, *We all tend to surrender to and serve what we think will give us life.*[198] In your pain you may be led to believe that what gave you life before has radically failed, and it's time to try something new. If what you believed would give you life is anything less than God, then, yes, it is time to try something new, or rather, *Someone* new. God is ready for you to surrender to him and find your life and significance in him.

One thing is guaranteed: If we seek we will find life in things lesser than God, we will be disappointed, betrayed, damaged, and eventually, destroyed. Alcohol, drugs, sex, shopping, work, hobbies... these *horizontal* things will not deliver what only our vertical God can deliver.

---

[198] Paul David Tripp, *New Morning Mercies*, Kindle Location 4163.

And remember this: *Thinking and doing are two different things.* You have probably *thought* of doing one or more (or all) of the things listed above. But *thinking* and *doing* are two different things. You may *think* of doing a lot of things. Just *don't do* them.

Consider these things in your moment of crisis:

* How do you want to be remembered?
* How do you want your kids to think of you now?
* What is the cost of choosing poorly now?

Divorce strips away the things that gave us significance. Take the advice of Wayne Stiles who writes, *We need a different goal: faithfulness rather than significance.*[199]

In your time of crisis, choose to be faithful to God. In the end, faithfulness to him will pay off *now* and for *eternity.*

The most common ways men use to escape pain are pornography and alcohol. Below are resources to help you succeed against these quagmires of disaster:

* Alcohol and Drug Addiction: Alcoholics Anonymous: *www.aa.org*; Celebrate Recovery (Christian-based recovery program for all addictions meeting in local churches): www.celebraterecovery.com
* Pornography: *www.2.bebroken.com* (Be Broken Ministries) and *www.faithfulandtrue.com* (Faithful & True Ministries)

---

[199] Stiles, *Waiting on God*, 24.

Think About It...

* Consider these good words from Paul David Tripp:

> *No person can be the source of your identity.*
> *No one can be the basis of your happiness.*
> *No individual can give you a reason to get up in the morning and continue.*
> *No loved one can be the carrier of your hope.*
> *No one is able to change you from the inside out.*
> *No human being can alter your past.*
> *No person is able to atone for your wrongs.*
> *No one can give your heart peace and rest.*[200]
> *Asking another human being to do those things is like requiring him to be the fourth member of the Trinity and then judging him when he falls short. It simply cannot and will not work.*[201]

Life Commitment...

I commit to finding my significance in God and not in another person, place or thing. From this point on my choices will be driven by being faithful to God, not easing my pain.

---

[200] Tripp, *New Morning Mercies*, Kindle Location 3962.
[201] Ibid., Kindle Location 3960.

When You Hurt You May Question Everything

———— ✺ ————

THE WORD

> *Trust in the Lord with all your heart and lean not on*
> *your own understanding; in all your ways acknowledge*
> *him, and he will make your paths straight. Do not be wise*
> *in your own eyes; fear the Lord and shun evil. This will*
> *bring health to your body and nourishment to your bones.*

— PROVERBS 3.5–8

THOUGHT FOR THE DAY:

> *We say that there ought to be no sorrow,*
> *but there is sorrow, and we have to accept*
> *and receive ourselves in its fires.*

~ OSWALD CHAMBERS

THEY SAY THAT THE LITTLE toe was given to us by God to show us where the furniture is in the middle of the night. If I slam my toe into furniture in the dark, the pain transmitted to my brain will cause me to question several things. *Have I lost my sense of direction in the dark? Has someone moved the furniture without me knowing? Am I getting old and losing my mind?*

The point is, every pain we experience causes us to question something. The deeper the pain, the more penetrating the questions.

When I was a chaplain at Children's Medical Center in Dallas I talked with a very confused father. His daughter was dealing with juvenile diabetes, and she was struggling. Her struggle was serious but not life threatening. Just a few hundred feet away was the liver transplant unit. *There* the kids were fighting for every moment of life.

But this dad was angry and upset, disproportionally so. As he looked out the window he shook his head and said to me, *I don't get it. I started going to church. I started giving money, lots of money. And my daughter is still sick.*

Without knowing it, this father had tried to bargain with God: *God, I will give my life to you, I will give my money to you. And if I do my part, you must do your part, and your part is to take this sickness away from my daughter.*

When his daughter remained sick, he questioned God. Instead of questioning God, he should have questioned his bargain with God. God cannot be manipulated into doing our bidding.

But this dad was hurting for his daughter, and his pain caused him to ask some tough questions.

Don't be surprised if you find yourself doubting beliefs you have deeply held. I know I did. I had given my life to the church. When I was booted out of the church I had faithfully served, I had serious doubts about the church at large. I had followed the right path regarding marriage. I had followed the rules. But my marriage didn't turn out the way I had been promised it would. All I had believed in about marriage was up for review in my mind's eye.

When your ground is shaken, allow yourself to ask the hard questions, *but always come back to God*. Even if you doubt him, come back to him and ask him to give you just what you need to settle your heart and quiet your mind.

Take a look at Psalm 73. Here is a man who, in his pain, was questioning everything. Finally, he says, *When I tried to understand all this, it was oppressive to me till I entered the sanctuary of God; then I understood...* (Psalm 73:16–17)

God doesn't mind our questions. In the midst of our hard questions he always invites us into his sanctuary to experience his love and grace.

Think About It...

* What foundational beliefs have you questioned through this painful process?
* How can you know what beliefs should be ditched and which should be kept?

Life Commitment...

I commit to the truth. I commit to shedding old, false beliefs and finding the truth in God.

When You Hurt You Don't Care

———ᘓᘓᘓ———

THE WORD

My people are fools; they do not know me. They are
senseless children; they have no understanding. They
are skilled in doing evil; they know not how to do good.

—JEREMIAH 4.22

THOUGHT FOR THE DAY:

Discouragement focuses more on the broken glories
of creation than it does on the restoring glories
of God's character, presence, and promises.

~ PAUL DAVID TRIPP

AS LONG AS YOU ARE feeling your pain, you care. As long as you are questioning what you believe in, you care. As long as you are fighting to do the next right thing, you care. As long as you are struggling with decisions, you care.

But if you stop feeling, if you stop questioning, if you stop thinking, if you stop struggling, you don't care anymore. Even a man stuck in self-pity cares—if only for himself.

A man who doesn't care is a dangerous man indeed.

But it's easy not to care. It is easy to throw up your hands and walk away—*the world (and God) be damned.* It's easy to fall into the pity pit and curl up in a ball and die. The easy way is not to care. The easy way is to give in to despair. The easy thing is to give up.

When you feel like that, *or if you stop feeling anything,* stop, pray, and find someone to talk with. And if you haven't gotten to this place, know that you very well might. Several times.

Don't give in to this strong pull to give in to the despair. Know that our enemy (Satan) wants to destroy you. His primary targets are families, churches, fathers, mothers, children. If you are human you are a target, and Satan's goal is destruction.

Push back. You are in a fight bigger than yourself. More is at stake than your immediate pain. What you do, how you respond, the choices you make will reverberate far wider *now* than you know and far *longer* than you can imagine.

Don't let your pain shrink your time and space to this tiny moment and this pinpoint of space. Allow God to expand your perspective of time—there is more to your life than this painful, present *now.*

Allow God to enlarge your space. If you give in to despair your space shrinks to nothing. If you push back and allow God to lead you through this, your place of positive, life-giving influence will expand far beyond what you can imagine.

Think About It...

* When have you despaired? What triggered that emotion? An email from your ex? A text from your bank

warning of an overdraft? A bill from your lawyer? An ignored call to your child?

* What did you do? Dwell on it? Or give it to God?
* If you feel your time shrinking, pray. Breathe deeply. Relax into God and allow him to love you back into a larger time frame. If you feel your space shrinking, take a walk. Get outside and let God use the beauty of his creation to expand your space.

PRAYER...

God, I am tempted to give in to the despair. The pain is too much, or so it feels that way right now. Give me strength to push back. Give me hope. Give me encouragement—put courage into my heart again. Help me see the bigger picture. Help me see beyond this moment. Help me see the future you have for me. Help me see the influence you can have through me to my children and to the world. Deliver me from the enemy.

The Four P's of Identity

——— ∞∞∞ ———

THE WORD

*Those who are led by the Spirit of God are sons of
God. For you did not receive a spirit that makes you
a slave again to fear, but you received the Spirit of
sonship. And by him we cry, "Abba, Father."*

— ROMANS 8.14–15

THOUGHT FOR THE DAY:

*We are never-ending. We are warriors and
creators. We are divine and sacred and worthy.
You are worthy without caveat or exception.*

~ TERESA PASQUALE

FROM THE MOMENT OF OUR birth we are seeking our identity.
The first task is to separate ourselves from our parents. But to
define ourselves by what we are *not* leaves a huge hole. We fill
that hole with things from the horizontal. Richard Rohr writes:

> *Without a transcendent connection, each of us is stuck in his
> own little psyche, struggling to create meaning and produce*

an identity all by himself. When we inevitably fail at this—because we can't do it alone—we suffer shame and self-defeat. Or we try to pretend that our small universe of country, ethnicity, team, or denomination is actually the center of the world. This can bear dire results. We need a wider universe in which to realize our own significance and a bigger story in which to find meaning. Not only does a man need to hear that he is beloved, that he is a son, he needs to believe that he is a beloved son "of God." [202]

Rohr identifies a man's horizontal pursuit of identity by the 'Four P's': *Possessions, Perks, Prestige, and Power.*[203]

Perhaps you are divorced because you sought your identity through one or more of these Four P's to the detriment of your marriage and family. Maybe you worked too many hours to attain these Four P's and the price was your family. Or maybe you have attained these Four P's, only to have divorce strip them away.

In the end, for every person on the planet, the great awakening is that *finding happiness, satisfaction and contentment in the horizontal is empty and fruitless.* The horizontal is composed of the *gifts.* True happiness, satisfaction and contentment are found (vertically) in the *Giver.*

And what does the Giver think about us? He radically, wildly, passionately loves us and pursues us!

The Bible says that Jesus began his ministry with his Baptism. Matthew says that *As soon as Jesus was baptized, he went up out of the water. At that moment heaven was opened, and he saw the Spirit of God descending like a dove and lighting on him.*

---

[202] Rohr, Durepos and McGrath, *On the Threshold of Transformation,* 254.
[203] Ibid., 95.

And a voice from heaven said, "This is my Son, whom I love; with him I am well pleased." (Matthew 3.16–17)

The amazing thing about this is that God named Jesus his Son and stated his love, pleasure and acceptance of him *before Jesus did anything.*

The same is true of us. *Because* you are a child of God, you are of immeasurable worth and happiness to God. And you are a child of God because he has named you his son and paid the price through Jesus to make you his child.

Brennan Manning writes, *It takes a profound conversion to accept that God is relentlessly tender and compassionate toward us just as we are—not in spite of our sins and faults (that would not be total acceptance), but with them. Though God does not condone or sanction evil, He does not withhold His love because there is evil in us.*[204]

Your identity is in God, the Giver, not in acquisition of the gifts. Your identity is as a child of God, not a product of this world. Your identity is rooted in the eternal, not the temporal. No one can take your identity in God away from you. He holds you safe and secure.

Think About It...

* Go back and read the section of this devotional on being accepted by God (Days 34-39).
* Think about what you have lost because of your divorce. What role did those things play in defining

---

[204] Brennan Manning, John Blase, and Jonathan Foreman, *Abbas Child: The Cry of the Heart for Intimate Belonging* (Colorado Springs: NavPress, 2015), 19.

you? How can firmly rooting your identity vertically in God replace the pain of losing these horizontal things.

* In 100 years, what will the Four P's have given you?
* In 100 years, what will having rooted your identity in God have given you?

LIFE COMMITMENT...

Though building my identity around Possessions, Perks, Prestige, and Power is tempting, I choose to find my identity in God and in him alone.

God is Your Anchor

———∞∞∞———

THE WORD

We have this hope as an anchor for the soul, firm and
secure. It enters the inner sanctuary behind the curtain,
where Jesus, who went before us, has entered on our behalf.

— HEBREWS 6.19–20

THOUGHT FOR THE DAY:

Ultimately, spiritual maturity is not about memorizing
the Bible and mastering the spiritual disciplines. These
are healthy things to do, but they are still only means
to a greater end, which in itself is learning to love with
God's love and learning to serve with God's power.

~ GARY THOMAS

FOR A FEW YEARS I had the privilege and joy of restoring a
28-foot sailboat and learning to sail it. There is nothing like
the feeling of a massive boat moving silently through the water under the power of the wind alone.

After the boat was habitable, my two older children and I would spend nights on Lake Travis. Lake Travis was formed upon the completion of Mansfield Dam in 1941. The dam backed up water between limestone hills. Most of the shoreline of Lake Travis is rocky cliffs. Spending the night on the lake made me suddenly aware of the extreme importance of correctly setting the anchor of my boat so we didn't end up smashed into those rocky cliffs!

I had never given much thought to how to anchor a boat. I just thought you tossed the anchor overboard and it would hold. But when you are on a sailboat surrounded by rocks, correctly setting the anchor takes on new meaning. The last thing you want is to wake up with the boat smashing against the rocks with your two kids inside.

On one trip a cold front was predicted to come in that Friday afternoon. Sure enough, the winds went from a southerly breeze of 10 mph to a northerly howler of at least 25 mph. We were determined to spend the night on the boat anyway, so we motored to our favorite spot. But I knew that with a strong northerly wind predicted through the night, setting the anchor was critical. I took my time choosing the spot and then worked to make sure the anchor would hold.

Through the night the wind buffeted our boat but the anchor held. The next morning we were where we planned to be—safe in the cove, ready for a breakfast of pancakes and sausage. All through the night the winds had buffeted our sailboat. And through the night our boat swung back and forth, *but not too far back and forth because the anchor held.*

If you have set your anchor on one of the Four P's, Possessions, Perks, Prestige, and Power, you have wrongly set your anchor. The only anchor for your soul that will hold is God himself.

We have this hope as an anchor for the soul, firm and secure.

The Greek word translated *firm* is formed from the negative of *fail*. In other words, the writer says that Jesus is our anchor that will not fail. The Greek word we translate as *secure* means *stable* and relates to walking on stepping stones that are sure and secure. In other words, both from the negative and the positive side, the writer of Hebrews is confirming for us as clearly as possible that God is our only hope, an anchor that will hold us secure in the storm.

Like my sailboat, you and I may swing about when the winds blow, but if we remain anchored in God we will not be set adrift to crash into the rocks.

THINK ABOUT IT...

- Into what is your anchor set? Is your anchor holding?
- What steps can you take to set your anchor in God? (Reading this book is a good start!)
- Go back and re-read Day 83. How can anchoring yourself in God help you live between fear and hope?

LIFE COMMITMENT:

God is my anchor, my rock, my sure foundation. He will not be moved. Though I may waver between hope and fear, God will not waver. He holds me secure.

Stay

———⟨❀⟩———

THE WORD

The thief comes only to steal and kill and destroy; I have
come that they may have life, and have it to the full.

—JOHN 10.10

THOUGHT FOR THE DAY:

It is crucial to see that deciding against the principle
of suicide creates its own practical strengths: it
commits one to the human project and to one's
own life in a way that gives rise to solidarity
and resilience. And when one speaks of such
commitment to living, others may be encouraged to
live and to find the resources to survive pain.

~ JENNIFER MICHAEL HECHT

NATIONAL SUICIDE PREVENTION LIFELINE: **800-273-8255**

Divorced or separated men have a 39% higher suicide rate
than their married counterparts. They are also more likely

to take part in risky activities which increases their chance of early death.[205]

If you have thoughts of taking your life you are not alone nor are you abnormal. I believe that the vast majority of people think of taking their own life at some point in their lives.

I know I did. For about four days a few months after my divorce was final, suicide became one of several options. What was strange about this was how casually I thought of this option. As I considered what to do, suicide seemed a viable choice. Death by my hand was laid out there with the other options on how to move forward out of the pain.

A newly divorced man named Philip writes:

As a divorced man, I can honestly say I contemplated suicide for the first time in my life during the first year or two of my separation. It's incredibly difficult to have your entire family life—children, home and even wife—pulled away from you. Prior to the divorce, I was very happy, making a good salary and living in a nice neighborhood. Soon after the divorce, I was saddled with very high child support payments, debt from legal fees and barely enough left over to pay the rent of my small one bedroom apartment.[206]

[205] *"Why Divorce is bad for a man's health: Separation increases the risk of early death, substance abuse, suicide and depression,"* Emma Innes, last updated October 2, 2013, accessed October 20, 2017, http://www.dailymail.co.uk/health/article-2440005/Divorce-mans-health-Separation-increases-risk-death-substance-abuse-suicide-depression.html

[206] *"Why does divorce make men more suicidal than women?"* Jack Cafferty, last updated March 11, 2010, accessed July 13, 2017, http://caffertyfile.blogs.cnn.com/2010/03/11/why-does-divorce-make-men-more-suicidal-than-women/.

Tremendous pain is caused through divorce because divorce creates so much loss. Add to this that our society has minimal ability to deal with this loss, largely ignoring the immense pain caused by divorce. We are, by nature, wired to get out of pain, and suicide is one way to escape.

H. Norman Wright says that there are four main reasons for suicide:

- **Depression [Rage]**—The person is sitting on a high level of unacceptable rage that has developed because of a series of events in life over which he or she has no control. Eventually this repressed rage is turned against himself or herself in suicide.
- **Relief of Pain**—Those with high levels of pain usually have three choices: a psychotic distortion that reduces the pain, drugs or alcohol, or suicide. They often say, *"I don't want to die, but I don't know any other way out—I just can't stand it."*
- **Revenge**—Some [people] feel overwhelmed by hurt or rejection from another person. Their desire to hurt back is stronger than the desire to live.
- **Hopelessness**—Twenty-five percent of those who commit suicide do so after giving it quiet consideration and weighing the pros and cons of living and dying.[207]

Teacher, author, and historian Jennifer Michael Hecht lost two friends to suicide. In her own grief she decided to

---

[207] H. Norman Wright, *The New Guide to Crisis and Trauma Counseling* (Ventura, CA: Regal Books, 2003), Kindle Locations 3120-3126.

research and write about it. She wrote her thoughts in a blog called "The Best American Poetry." In the blog she made an appeal to those contemplating suicide:

> *I want to say this, ... Don't kill yourself. Life has always been almost too hard to bear, for a lot of the people, a lot of the time. It's awful. But it isn't too hard to bear, **it's only almost too hard to bear**...*
>
> *I'm issuing a rule. You are not allowed to kill yourself. When a person kills himself, he does wrenching damage to the community. One of the best predictors of suicide is knowing a suicide. That means that suicide is also delayed homicide. You have to stay.*
>
> *I'm throwing you a rope, you don't have to explain it to the monster in you, just tell the monster it can do whatever it wants, but not that. Later we'll get rid of the monster, for now just hang on to the rope. I know that this means a struggle from one second to the next, let alone one day at a time.*
>
> *Don't kill yourself. Suffer here with us instead. **We need you with us, we have not forgotten you**, you are our hero. Stay.*[208]

When I was struggling those four days, here is what I kept in my head in order to choose to stay:

* ***I will get through this.*** Life has always been almost too hard to bear for a lot of the people, a lot of the time.

---

[208] Jennifer Michael Hecht, *Stay: A History of Suicide and the Philosophies Against It* (New Haven: Yale University Press, 2015), 7-8 (emphasis mine).

It's awful. But it isn't too hard to bear, it's only *almost* too hard to bear. What I feel today will not be what I feel tomorrow.

* ***If I take my life, this is what I will be remembered for.*** No matter all my accomplishments, the first thing people will think of when my name is mentioned will be that I took my life. I did not want that.

* ***By taking my own life, I may contribute to someone else's suicide.*** Survivors of those who take their lives are more likely to take their own life. I didn't want to potentially contribute to the death by suicide of anyone among my family or friends.

* ***I will deprive the world of what God has planned to do through me.*** I have much to offer this world. God showed me that I had many years to serve him and that many people would be helped if I chose to stay.

When I thought of these realities, suicide remained an option, but one among many options. If I had not considered these realities, suicide as an option could have become my *only* option, at least in my mind.

If you are thinking of suicide as one of several options, pay attention to your thinking. If you have come to the conclusion that suicide is your *only* option, your thinking has become distorted and you need immediate help. ***Call the suicide prevention hotline at the top of this page immediately.*** Don't hesitate. Put this book down and call ***now.***

Don't turn temporary moments of personal anguish into a permanent state of calamity for those around you.

THINK ABOUT IT...

- Go back and read Day 93. (Don't put a period where a comma belongs.)
- Is suicide one of several options you are considering? God has bigger plans for you than you can imagine. Don't cheat the world of what you have to offer.
- In your mind, is suicide becoming the *only* option? You need help. Call the suicide hotline above.

LIFE COMMITMENT...

"Life has always been almost too hard to bear, for a lot of the people, a lot of the time. It's awful. But it isn't too hard to bear, it's only almost too hard to bear." *I commit to bearing through this terrible time of life, knowing that what is now will not always be. God is my hope. He will see me through to new life and new hope. I choose to stay.*

Suicide—Assessing Your Risk

―∞∞―

THE WORD

The Lord is close to the brokenhearted and saves those
who are crushed in spirit. A righteous man may have
many troubles, but the Lord delivers him from them all.

— PSALM 34.18–19

THOUGHT FOR THE DAY:

It can be a tremendous comfort to learn
that great minds have concluded that no
individual need wonder whether his or her
life is worth living. It is worth living.

~ JENNIFER MICHAEL HECHT

NATIONAL SUICIDE PREVENTION LIFELINE: **800-273-8255**

On September 25, 2000, Kevin Hines jumped off the Golden
Gate Bridge. He hit the water 220 feet below and lived to
tell about it. He is only one of 33 among an estimated 2,000
people to have survived the fall. As I read his story his words
leapt out at me:

In the midst of my free fall, I said to myself these words, words I thought no one would ever hear me repeat: "What have I done? I don't want to die. God, please save me!" As I fell, I somehow possessed the mind-set that all I wanted to do was live—by any means necessary.[209]

I wonder how many of the more than 30,000 people who take their lives every year in the United States have had the same thought the second after they jumped or pulled the trigger or hit the tree or swallowed the pills or cut their wrists.

Are you thinking of taking our life? Take your thoughts seriously.

If you are thinking any of the following thoughts or taking any of the following actions, you are at a higher risk for attempting to take your life by your own hand. Ask yourself these questions:

* How much of your 'brain space' is taken up by thinking of suicide? Are you thinking of *how* to do it? Are you considering what people would say?

* Are your thoughts turning into *plans*? Have you thought of a *time* and a *place*? Have you thought of how you would do it? Have you thought of how you would get the means to do it?

* *Are you preparing others for your leaving?* Have you told anyone you will miss them? Have you written out your will? Have you given away personal belongings? Have you

---

[209] *"He jumped off the Golden Gate Bridge . . . and lived!"* New York Post, last updated June 20, 2013, accessed July 13, 2017, http://nypost.com/2013/06/30/he-jumped-off-the-golden-gate-bridge-and-lived/. See also his book, Kevin Hines, *Cracked, Not Broken: Surviving and Thriving After a Suicide Attempt*, (Lanham, MD: Rowman & Littlefield Publishers, 2013).

obtained the means to do it such as purchasing a gun or obtaining pills? Have you rehearsed how you will do it?

* ***Have you decided if you want your attempted suicide to be your final act on earth***, or do you plan for it to be only self-injurious, not lethal?

If you answered yes to any of these questions, I urge you, I plead with you, get help immediately. Call this number: **800-273-8255**.

I want you to stay. I got up at 4:45 every morning for months so that I could write this book *so that you would choose to stay*. One reason I chose to stay is to help others in the same situation choose to stay. You are wanted and needed. Please stay.

What the Psalmist wrote 3,000 years ago is as true today as it was then: *The Lord is close to the brokenhearted and saves those who are crushed in spirit. A righteous man may have many troubles, but the Lord delivers him from them all.* (Psalm 34.18–19)

In 1997 my 50-year-old sister, Jackie, took her life. Don't do what my sister did. Please stay. I did, and I am glad I did.

Think About It...

* Go back over the questions listed above. If you are considering suicide as an option I urge you get help. Call the hotline. Call a pastor, a trusted and wise friend, a counselor.

Life Commitment...

I commit to staying. The world needs me.

Suicide—Get help

———⟨∞⟩———

THE WORD

> *So do not fear, for I am with you; do not be dismayed,*
> *for I am your God. I will strengthen you and help you;*
> *I will uphold you with my righteous right hand.*

— ISAIAH 41.10

THOUGHT FOR THE DAY:

God's agenda is never elimination but transformation.

~ RICHARD ROHR

NATIONAL SUICIDE PREVENTION LIFELINE: **800-273-8255**

Jesus said as recorded by the apostle John: *The thief comes only to steal and kill and destroy; I have come that they may have life, and have it to the full.* (John 10.10)

Brother, you are in a war and Satan is your enemy. Satan hates God, but since Satan can't destroy God, his driving passion is to deface God by defacing and/or destroying you. Suicide is the ultimate destruction of God's amazing creation.

King David wrote: *When I consider your heavens, the work of your fingers, the moon and the stars, which you have set in place, what is man that you are mindful of him, the son of man that you care for him? You made him a little lower and crowned him with glory and honor.* (Psalm 8:3–5)

Wow! You and I are God's amazing creation! No wonder Satan wants to take you out! **Don't let him!**

In my office I have a plastic anatomical human skull that can be taken apart. Inside is a model of the brain. Sometimes when people come into my office who are troubled and depressed, I take out my plastic skull and pull out the brain.

I say to them:

> *I know you are suffering and that you are in pain because of your loss. But did you know that you still have this amazing thing between your ears—your brain! Your brain is the second most incredible thing in all the universe. Did you get that? That three-pound mass of cells in your head is the second most astounding thing in the entire universe! The first is, of course, God himself. Whatever you have lost, you still have this amazing thing! And, you have God! What can be better than that?* [210]

To take your life by suicide is to destroy this second most amazing thing in all the universe! Don't do it. Don't give Satan the victory. Don't let the thief come in and destroy. Instead, cry out to God. He WILL rescue you!

Yesterday I listed some questions to help you assess how much of a risk for suicide you are.

Have you thought about those questions since then?

---

[210] See Day 18.

Whatever your answers, I urge you to get help. The journey you are on is a journey only you can make. Only you make the journey but you don't have to make the journey alone.

God knows the battle for your soul. God knows the war against your life. He wants you to win. He is on your side. Because he is for you, God will put resources in your path that will help you survive this journey and thrive on the other side. This book is one of those resources. It's no accident that you are reading this. God knew you would need this book to make it through this ordeal. He called me to write it and he called you to read it. This IS evidence of God's loving care for you!

In addition to written resources, God has placed many other resources for you to tap into during this hard time. I urge you, please reach out and get the help you need. The following are some suggestions. Perhaps these suggestions will be prompts God is putting in your path to help you right now.

- **Pray** to God. He is listening and much closer to you than you can imagine. He is eager to help you and see you through this. See Day 116.
- **Friends**. We all need a few trusted, loyal, wise friends. Who can you call in the middle of the night who will listen to you, accept you for who you are, and help get you through? Not everyone will help you but God will give you a few who will.
- **A Pastor**. Pastors are today's unsung heroes. Most pastors are amazing people who have given themselves to helping people win victories over the enemy. If you don't have a church, ask around to find a

church known for their love for God and their love for people. It takes courage to jump in, but do it. God works through his church. His church is there for you. If available, find a church with a strong and lively men's ministry.

* **A Counselor** or **Therapist**. God has put smart people on this planet who have committed themselves to helping people get through hard times. Ask around for a counselor or therapist who is known for his/her skills in helping people through hard times. You want someone who is tender and compassionate. You also want this person to be honest and be able to gently confront you when necessary.

* This **website** has hotlines for all kinds of problems: https://brokenbelievers.com/2011/01/23/247-crisis-lines/

For years I have told depressed people the same thing: *Don't believe everything you are telling yourself right now. Your thinking is distorted. Instead, listen to what others are saying to you.*

How you are *thinking* now will change. You will have more positive thoughts as time goes by. Hold on!

How you are *feeling* now will change. You will feel better! Hold on!

Jennifer Hecht succinctly states: *Though we may refuse a version of life, we must also refuse voluntary death.*[211]

You are right to be upset about how your life is right now. Don't choose to change the state of your life, however, by ending it. That is a worse choice with far worse

---

[211] Hecht, *Stay*, 183.

consequences. Instead, hang on, get the help you need, and watch God do his amazing work in your life.

THINK ABOUT IT...

* Go back and read Day 18. You're amazing! Focus on what you have, not what you have lost.
* Get help. Really. Help will help more than you imagine right now.

LIFE COMMITMENT...

I commit to getting the help I need to get through this.

Homicide

—◦◦◦—

THE WORD

*Now Cain said to his brother Abel, "Let's go out to
the field." And while they were in the field, Cain
attacked his brother Able and killed him. Then the
Lord said to Cain, "Where is your brother Abel?" "I
don't know," he replied. "Am I my brother's keeper?"
The Lord said, "What have you done? Listen! Your
brother's blood cries out to me from the ground."*

— GENESIS 4.8–10

THOUGHT FOR THE DAY:

*The great malady of the twentieth century, implicated
in all of our troubles and affecting us individually
and socially, is "loss of soul." When soul is neglected,
it doesn't just go away; it appears symptomatically in
obsessions, addictions, violence, and loss of meaning.*

~ THOMAS MOORE

ON SEPTEMBER 9, 1996, A beautiful young 23-year-old girl
was shot and killed. The killer was her ex-boyfriend. He then
turned the gun on himself.

Ami had just graduated with a degree in social work and had worked as a volunteer with the Austin Police Department. She had helped AIDS victims and disabled children and adults.[212] Ami's huge and generous heart was stopped by the irrational rage of an angry young man.

As pastor to this family I saw firsthand the unbelievable damage caused by homicide. One thing I learned was that *painful circumstances can lead to murder.* No one would have guessed that Ami's murderer would have committed such a radical act.

Murders happen when people are enraged and take their rage to the next level. People don't just kill people. The pathway to murder starts with rage.

Are you angry at what has happened to you? In your anger do you have thoughts of taking someone's life?

Perhaps your wife cheated on you. Are you thinking of killing her lover? Do you have thoughts of killing her? If so, you would not be the first, and if you carried it out you would not be the first to commit murder in these circumstances. The reason I point this out is simply that murder happens, and murder usually begins with an angry male. Consider these statistics:

* Males were convicted of the majority of homicides in the United States, representing 90.5% of the total number of offenders. (2014 stats)
* Females were most likely to be victims of domestic homicides (63.7%) and sex-related homicides (81.7%).

---

[212] *"Ami Lunsford Memorial Scholarship in Victim Services,"* accessed July 14, 2017. http://www.bing.com/cr?IG=8BF3D1A1E87C4D6BAF9D269-446BF9619&CID=356862F851646250018F68475062631A&rd=1&h=PH 5-feb3x01j4K1YVOvuEZ9hJYaZj2j1OBAeL9eCpNo&v=1&r=http%3a%2f%2fendowments.giving.utexas.edu%2f5384%2f&p=DevEx,5064.1.

* Male perpetrators constituted 96% of federal prosecution on domestic violence.[213]

All this to say, it is possible that someone reading this could be thinking of homicide. If you are one of those people, don't do it. I bring this up because murders happen when ordinary men are extraordinarily wounded. Hurts lead to rage which can lead to the actual act of murder. When murders are traced back through their line of formation, it's clear that most men who commit murder did not start out thinking they would. Their rage carried them along until the deed was done.

Believe it or not, there is actually help for those considering homicide. The following website is a great resource even if you are not thinking of murder as an option to handling your problems: http://www.savingcain.org/preventing-murder.html

The author if this website, Yale lecturer James Kimmel, Jr, writes:

> *Research scientists have discovered that when we have been hurt or wronged, the desire to harm others activates the same pleasure centers of the brain activated by narcotics. This suggests that the desire to kill is a biological craving created inside the brain. If you are thinking about killing, you are*

---

[213] *"Sex differences in crime,"* Wikipedia, June 29, 2017, accessed July 14, 2017, https://en.wikipedia.org/wiki/Sex_differences_in_crime, from https://www.bjs.gov/content/pub/pdf/htus8008.pdf, Rep. No. NCJ 236018 (2011). *Homicide Trends in the United States, 1980-2008: Annual Rates for 2009 and 2010,* U.S. Department of Justice Office of Justice Programs, Bureau of Justice Statistics by Alexia Cooper and Erica L. Smith, BJS Statisticians.

not "evil." You are experiencing a brain-created desire to harm others and yourself. If your brain created it, then your brain can also make it go away. Help is available right now. The desire to kill can be overcome. [214]

THINK ABOUT IT...

* Have you thought of killing someone because of the pain you are in?
* If you are thinking of homicide, go to the website *http://www.savingcain.org/preventing-murder.html* and follow the steps to getting the help you need.
* Remember that Satan's greatest desire is to destroy God's amazing creation. Don't let him win the victory. Self-destruction (suicide) and murder (homicide) are never part of God's plan. God is *for life*, yours and others.

LIFE COMMITMENT...

God, help me see your incredible hand on my life. Preserve my life so I can give your life to others.

---

[214] http://www.savingcain.org/preventing-murder.html

The Place of Wisdom

THE WORD

*At this, Job got up and tore his robe and shaved his
head. Then he fell to the ground in worship and
said: "Naked I came from my mother's womb, and
naked I will depart. The Lord gave and the Lord has
taken away; may the name of the Lord be praised."*

—JOB 1.20–21

THOUGHT FOR THE DAY:

*In the mouth of society are many diseased teeth,
decayed to the bones of the jaws. But society makes
no effort to have them extracted and be rid of the
affliction; it contents itself with gold fillings.*

~ KAHLIL GIBRAN

IN HIS JUNE 3, 2017 commencement speech at his son's graduation from Cardigan Mountain School, an elite school for
boys in New Hampshire, Chief Justice John Roberts gave
some unusual advice:

From time to time in the years to come, I hope you will be treated unfairly, so that you will come to know the value of justice. I hope that you will suffer betrayal because that will teach you the importance of loyalty. Sorry to say, but I hope you will be lonely from time to time so that you don't take friends for granted. I wish you bad luck, again, from time to time so that you will be conscious of the role of chance in life and understand that your success is not completely deserved and that the failure of others is not completely deserved either.

And when you lose, as you will from time to time, I hope every now and then, your opponent will gloat over your failure. It is a way for you to understand the importance of sportsmanship. I hope you'll be ignored so you know the importance of listening to others, and I hope you will have just enough pain to learn compassion. Whether I wish these things or not, they're going to happen. And whether you benefit from them or not will depend upon your ability to see the message in your misfortunes.[215]

This was not the usual commencement address which celebrates everyone's 'specialness' and that anyone can achieve the impossible if they only dream big enough.

Roberts spoke to these young men through the lens of an elder. His is the voice of a man well into the second half of his life. The heart of his advice is that the tough places are where wisdom is born and matured.

Oswald Chambers says it like this:

---

[215] Katie Reilly, "'*I Wish You Bad Luck.' Read Supreme Court Justice John Roberts' Unconventional Speech to His Son's Graduating Class*," last updated July 5, 2017, accessed July 17, 2017, http://time.com/4845150/chief-justice-john-roberts-commencement-speech-transcript/.

We say that there ought to be no sorrow, but there is sorrow, and we have to accept and receive ourselves in its fires.... You cannot find or receive yourself through success, because you lose your head over pride. And you cannot receive yourself through the monotony of your daily life, because you give in to complaining. The only way to find yourself is in the fires of sorrow. Why it should be this way is immaterial. The fact is that it is true in the Scriptures and in human experience.[216]

He goes on to say, *Sorrow removes a great deal of a person's shallowness, but it does not always make that person better. Suffering either gives me to myself or it destroys me.*[217]

These are hard things to hear because our culture tells us that we deserve not to suffer, that suffering can be avoided with hard work and the right insurance, and that pain can be eliminated with the right medication.

These are all myths. Suffering and sorrow are part of our journey. Embrace your sorrows as the place where wisdom is truly born and matured. Chambers is brutal: *Why it should be this way is immaterial.* It IS this way, so embrace it and learn from it. Don't waste your pain.

THINK ABOUT IT...

* Whether or not you waste your pain is up to you. If you have chosen to allow God to use your pain and suffering to grow you, what lessons have you learned so far?

---

[216] Chambers, My Utmost for His Highest, 177.
[217] Ibid.

LIFE COMMITMENT:

I realize that suffering and sorrows are part of the human deal. I choose to embrace this reality and allow God to use my suffering to make me a source of wisdom and strength to others.

Shadow Mission

⸺∞⸺

The noble man makes noble plans,
and by noble deeds he stands.

— ISAIAH 32:8

THOUGHT FOR THE DAY:

You and I were created to have a mission in life. We were made to make a difference. But if we do not pursue the mission for which God designed and gifted us, we will find a substitute. We cannot live in the absence of purpose. Without an authentic mission, we will be tempted to drift on autopilot, to let our lives center around something that is unworthy, something selfish, something dark—a shadow mission.

~JOHN ORTBERG

SO FEW MEN, IT SEEMS, end well. My observation is that financial success, in particular, does something to a man that takes him off course. I have seen noble men make noble plans and then, instead of standing, they fall by the wayside, destroyed by going off track.

To end well we must know and follow our purpose, the mission to which God calls us. Then we must relentlessly pursue that purpose to the end.

The last letter the Apostle Paul wrote was to the young Timothy. As Paul approached death he said,

> *For I am already being poured out like a drink offering, and the time has come for my departure. I have fought the good fight, I have finished the race, I have kept the faith. Now there is in store for me the crown of righteousness, which the Lord, the righteous Judge, will award to me on that day— and not only to me, but also to all who have longed for his appearing.* (2 Timothy 4:6–8)

At the end of the day, I want this said about me.

Do you know your purpose? God made you for a mission bigger than your personal pursuits. If you don't know your purpose, you will expend your time and energy on things less than that for which you were made. (See Days 14, 94, 107, 112)

Once we know our purpose, however, we must stick to it. It is easy to get off track.

Tony Dungy writes,

> *Joe Marciano, an assistant coach for me in Tampa, had a saying that always resonated with our team: "Death by inches." When a team is winning, coaches have a tendency to let little details slide by because things are going well. Then suddenly we're in a losing streak and can't figure out why. It's because those small, infrequent mistakes that didn't get*

corrected have become the norm, and the team can't get that sharpness back. Death by inches.[218]

Our Enemy gets us off track by selling us a 'shadow mission,' a mission that might sound godly but which takes us just a few degrees off course.

On July 28, 1976, Air Force Captain Eldon W. Joersz and Major George T. Morgan flew the Lockheed SR-71 (known as the "Blackbird") at a speed of 2,193.2 mph, setting the world record for air-breathing manned aircraft. The Blackbird is a reconnaissance aircraft designed to out race any missiles fired at it. At such high speeds, however, the slightest change in direction can quickly lead to a trajectory wildly off-course. It only takes a few degrees.

The same with us. How do we know if we are getting off-course? If our choices are directed toward our own selfish desires or designed to boost our egos we are buying into our shadow mission. If our choices are primarily about us, we are buying into our shadow mission rather than the bigger mission God has for us.

I knew a wonderful Christian man who made a lot of money and was extraordinarily generous with his money. He supported missionaries around the world as well as dozens of local projects. But late in life he was tempted sexually. He ended up in a strip club. When confronted, he claimed that his mission was to go into the strip club to be a witness for Jesus. He even bought one of the waitress's 10-year-old son a Bible! He was off-course and didn't even know it.

---

[218] Dungy and Whitaker, *The One Year Uncommon Life Daily Challenge,* Kindle Location 1677.

God uses troubles in our lives to give us course corrections. Let God do his work in your life. Don't let your problems throw you further off course. The consequences are disastrous.

THINK ABOUT IT...

* What is your God-given purpose for your life?
* Are you on-course? How do you know?
* How would you know if you are off-course?

LIFE COMMITMENT:

From Tony Dungy: *You know where God wants you to go. You know the life He wants you to live. Be aware and wary of the small things that can lead you off track.*[219]

---

[219] Ibid.

God Restores

———⟨∞⟩———

THE WORD

> *And the God of all grace, who called you to his eternal*
> *glory in Christ, after you have suffered a little while,*
> *will himself restore you and make you strong, firm and*
> *steadfast. To him be the power for ever and ever. Amen.*

— 1 PETER 5.10–11

THOUGHT FOR THE DAY:

> *Fell sorrow's tooth doth never rankle more*
> *Than when he bites, but lanceth not the sore.*

~ SHAKESPEARE
THE LIFE AND DEATH OF RICHARD THE SECOND
ACT I, SCENE III.

DIVORCE IS ABOUT LOSS. WHETHER you are the primary cause or not, divorce results in devastating losses (see Day 140). Is it possible to regain what has been lost?

Our English word *restore* comes from the French, from *re* which means *back again* and *stauro* which means *to stand, to be firm.*[220]

Divorce knocks us off our feet. In the old days, to be knocked to the ground in battle was the quickest way to death. For a warrior to live, he had to get back up on his feet. God will do this for you—he will pick you up and restore you to a position of strength stronger than you had before.

Don't take my word from it. Consider these promises from God's Word:

And the God of all grace, who called you to his eternal glory in Christ, after you have suffered a little while, will himself restore [mend] you and make you strong [stable], firm [to make strong of soul and body so you can stand up] and steadfast [to establish]. (1 Peter 5.10–11, AMP)

Though you have made me see troubles, many and bitter, you will restore my life again; from the depths of the earth you will again bring me up. You will increase my honor and comfort me once again. (Psalm 71:20–21)

I will repay you for the years the locusts have eaten—the great locust and the young locust, the other locusts and the locust swarm— my great army that I sent among you. You will have plenty to eat, until you are full, and you will praise the name of the Lord your God, who has worked wonders for you; never again will my people be shamed. Then you will know that I am in Israel, that I am the Lord your God, never again will my people be shamed. (Joel 2.25–27)

---

[220] *"Restore,"* Online Etymology Dictionary, accessed July 19, 2017, http://www.etymonline.com/index.php?allowed_in_frame=0&search=restore. Our English word *restaurant* comes from the same root as our word, *restore,* and means *food that restores.*

"But I will restore you to health and heal your wounds," declares the Lord, "because you are called an outcast, Zion for whom no one cares." (Jeremiah 30.17)

Instead of their shame my people will receive a double portion, and instead of disgrace they will rejoice in their inheritance; and everlasting joy will be theirs. (Isaiah 61.7)

Return to your fortress, O prisoners of hope; even now I announce that I will restore twice as much to you. (Zechariah 9.12)

The Lord is my shepherd, I shall not be in want. He makes me lie down in green pastures, he leads me beside quiet waters, he restores my soul. (Psalm 23.1–3)

Does God automatically restore what we have lost? The answer is no. What are the conditions, then, for restoration? The following verses show us:

* ***Repent**, then, and turn to God, so that your sins may be wiped out, that times of refreshing may come from the Lord, and that he may send the Christ, who has been appointed for you—even Jesus. He must remain in heaven until the time comes for God to restore everything, as he promised long ago through his holy prophets.* (Acts 3.19–21)

  God wants us to come to him in humility and submit to his Lordship. Just as a train must submit to the rails to run free and do what trains do best, so we willingly 'place' ourselves on God's 'rails' in order to move forward.

* ***After Job had prayed for his friends**, the Lord made him prosperous again and gave him twice as much as he had before.* (Job 42.10)

Part of our restoration will be moving forward in the process of forgiveness. Job had some friends who were unhelpful to him in his time of need. When Job forgave them, God was free to move forward toward Job's restoration.

* But **seek first his kingdom and his righteousness**, *and all these things will be given to you as well.* (Matthew 6:33)

As you give yourself to God your priorities will change. The things of God will become primary in your life. God's Kingdom will become your first focus. As that happens, the things of earth will grow less important, and you will know and experience God's gracious provision for your every earthly need.

The next few days we will talk about how you can regain what you lost through your divorce. It all begins with your willingness to allow God to lead you: *Our response to God determines His response to us.*[221]

Kristin Armstrong has these hopeful words for us: *God will restore your life. In all the ways you think you need it, and in intimate areas where you aren't even aware of your need.*[222]

THINK ABOUT IT...

* What have you lost?

---

[221] Blackaby and Blackaby, *Experiencing God Day-By-Day*, Kindle Location 3450.

[222] Armstrong, *Happily Ever After*, Kindle Location 3377.

* What do you expect God to restore to you?
* What steps do you need to take to make room in your life for God to work? How do you place yourself on God's 'rails' so your train can move freely and fast fulfilling your purpose?

PRAYER...

Restore to me the joy of your salvation and grant me a willing spirit, to sustain me. (Psalm 51.12)

Regaining Your Footing

---∞∞∞---

THE WORD

Therefore, my dear brothers, stand firm. Let
nothing move you. Always give yourselves fully
to the work of the Lord, because you know that
your labor in the Lord is not in vain.

— 1 CORINTHIANS 15.58

THOUGHT FOR THE DAY:

If you have an unsatisfied heart now, outward
accomplishments won't change a thing. Know who
you are on the inside and what God has done to make
you who you are. That's where your identity comes
from. Who you are is not a vocational question.
Your identity is defined by the God who made you,
and it doesn't change with circumstances.

~ TONY DUNGY

IT WAS 1992, THE BARCELONA Olympics. British runner
Derek Redmond started off strong in the 400 meter semi-fi-
nals, but at the 150-meter mark his hamstring ripped. Pain
drove him to the ground. As the medical crew approached

to carry him from the track, Redmond waved them off, deciding that even if he limped across the finish line dead last, he *would* finish. In that moment he says that he thought to himself, *I remembered where I was—the Olympics—and I knew I had to finish.*

Redmond stood up and started hobbling down the track. It was then that his dad, Jim Redmond, ran onto the track, pushing past a security guard to get to his son. Father and son finished the race, Derek leaning on his father's shoulder for support. The crowd, 65,000 strong, jumped to their feet, cheering on father and son.

You may feel you are down on the track with your dreams shattered, your soul ripped to shreds, and no hope of finishing. In this moment *remember **where** you are and **who** you are and **who God your Father is**.*

You are God's son, a trophy of his grace, a man of God who has a mission to accomplish, a purpose to fulfill.

He is there, next to you, hand outstretched, to lift you back to your feet and get you to the finish line.

Derek Redmond says that as his dad helped him toward the finish line, his father said to him, *Don't worry, you've got nothing to prove, you are a champion to us, we'll be back to do this together.*

I can't think of any words I would want to hear more from my dad if I were limping along the track in front of 65,000 people.

God says the same to you: *Don't worry, you've got nothing to prove, you are a champion to us, we'll be back to do this together.*[223]

---

[223] Watch this video to hear Redmond explain that day: https://www.youtube.com/watch?v=kjkBPthoYVg

Ask God to give you strength to get back on your feet. Ask God to give you a steady hand to right yourself as you stand. Ask God to point you in the right direction. And ask God to give you a shoulder to lean on as you head toward the finish line.

There was no prouder man in Barcelona than Jim Redmond on the day he helped his son across the finish line. God feels the same about you.

Think About It...

* In your mind picture the entire race Derek Redmond ran that day. Where are you on that race? At the starting line? Hurtling down the first 150 meters? Or down on the track in agony trying to decide what to do? Limping along alone toward the finish line? Leaning on dad's shoulder as you move down the track?
* Where does God fit into your race?
* What do you believe God is saying to you right now?

Life Commitment...

I commit to crossing the finish line. I may be slow and a bit gimpy, but I will cross the finish line with God at my side.

Regaining Your Hope

———∞∞∞———

The Word

May the God of hope fill you with all joy and peace
as you trust in him, so that you may overflow
with hope by the power of the Holy Spirit.

— Romans 15.13

Thought for the Day:

Hope in the Christian's life is not wishful
thinking. It is confident expectation.

~ Henry Blackaby

Hope is a hard and strange and marvelous thing. On one hand, we must live in what we call the 'real' world, that is, the world where pain really hurts, decisions have consequences, and the future seems up for grabs.

On the other hand, the Christian lives in the *real* real world. He/she knows that this is not a WYSIWYG world (see Day 90)—what seems permanently devastating can be used by God in amazing ways to turn our lives and circumstance around.

Our only hope is that God is not surprised by our circumstances, he loves us, is for us, and died and rose again to be with us is. But this radical hope in a materially invisible God is sometimes challenging to maintain through hard times.

The writer of Psalm 43 demonstrates the emotional roller-coaster of living through tough times while still grounding his hope in God:

> *Vindicate me, O God, and plead my cause against an ungodly nation; rescue me from deceitful and wicked men.*
>
> *You are God my stronghold.*
>
> *Why have you rejected me? Why must I go about mourning, oppressed by the enemy?*
>
> *Send forth your light and your truth, let them guide me; let them bring me to your holy mountain, to the place where you dwell.*
>
> *Then will I go to the altar of God, to God, my joy and my delight. I will praise you with the harp, O God, my God.*
>
> *Why are you downcast, O my soul? Why so disturbed within me?*
>
> *Put your hope in God, for I will yet praise him, my Savior and my God.* (Psalm 43:1–5)

J. A. Motyer writes of this Psalm: *Realism continues, balancing the problems of the present with the prospect of the future.*[224]

---

[224] J. A. Motyer, "The Psalms," in *New Bible Commentary: 21st Century Edition*, ed. D. A. Carson et al., 4th ed. (Downers Grove: Inter-Varsity Press, 1994), 513.

Let's walk through this Psalm: The Psalmist is hurting. He has been falsely accused and the cost has been high. Real life is incredibly painful for him in the moment. For you and me, divorce has caused real pain and huge losses. But then, is not God still God? The writer thinks so: *You are God my stronghold.*

But the question remains: *Why all this pain?*

The writer does what we do—he swings between anger and hope, frustration with God and radical reliance upon him:

> *Why have you rejected me? Why must I go about mourning, oppressed by the enemy? Send forth your light and your truth, let them guide me; let them bring me to your holy mountain, to the place where you dwell.*

The writer then imagines himself further down the road. The pain is less and God is victorious:

> *Then will I go to the altar of God, to God, my joy and my delight. I will praise you with the harp, O God, my God.*

The writer then reflects back on his previous thoughts and admonishes himself with these words:

> *Why are you downcast, O my soul? Why so disturbed within me? Put your hope in God, for I will yet praise him, my Savior and my God.*

If your emotions are swinging wildly between amazing hope and black despair, you are not alone. Everyone swings between hope and fear (See Day 83). The difference between those with God and those without is that ***those whose hope is in God come back from the brink of despair to rest in God***. We settle our souls upon God and find him a place of amazing refuge, comfort, strength and enduring hope.

Eugene Peterson writes,

> *Without hope a person has basically two ways to respond to the future, with __wishing__ or with __anxiety__. **Wishing** looks to the future as a fulfillment, usually miraculous, of desire. **It expends its energy in daydreaming and fantasy.** **Anxiety** looks to the future as a demonstration of inadequacy—present weakness is projected to the point of disaster.*
>
> *Hope is a response to the future that has its foundation in the promises of God. **It looks at the future as time for the completion of God's promise.** It refuses to extrapolate either desire or anxiety into the future, but instead **believes that God's promise gives the proper content to it.**[225]*

Your future belongs to God. **Wishful thinking** will not deliver you out of your troubles and, instead, set you up for unrealistic expectations. **Anxiety** will take energy away from what you need to do now. Instead of dreaming about a blissful future or losing yourself in anxiety, ***lean back into God. Settle your hope upon him*** and expect him to do amazing things.

---

[225] Peterson, *God's Message for Each Day*, 233. Emphasis mine.

Why are you downcast, O my soul? Why so disturbed within me? **Put your hope in God**, *for I will yet praise him, my Savior and my God.*

THINK ABOUT IT...

- Are you living in a fantasy world or, at the other extreme, overcome by anxiety?
- What does resting in God look like to you? How has God helped you so far?

PRAYER...

Lord God, only you can deliver me out of my troubles. My hope is in you, and my promise is that you get all the praise when I get out of this mess.

Regaining Your Strength

———∞∞∞———

THE WORD

*Do you not know? Have you not heard? The Lord
is the everlasting God, the Creator of the ends of
the earth. He will not grow tired or weary, and his
understanding no one can fathom. He gives strength
to the weary and increases the power of the weak.
Even youths grow tired and weary, and young
men stumble and fall; but those who hope in the
Lord will renew their strength. They will soar
on wings like eagles; they will run and not grow
weary, they will walk and not be faint.*

— ISAIAH 40:28–31

THOUGHT FOR THE DAY:

*It is not the critic who counts; not the man who points
out how the strong man stumbles, or where the doer of
deeds could have done them better. The credit belongs
to the man who is actually in the arena, whose face
is marred by dust and sweat and blood; who strives
valiantly... who at the best knows in the end the*

> *triumph of high achievement, and who at the worst,*
> *if he fails, at least fails while daring greatly.*

~ Teddy Roosevelt

Life is hard enough as it is. Just the day-to-day regimen of work, family life and attention to personal needs takes an enormous investment of energy. At the time of my divorce I was using 110% of my energy. Then came the news that fateful Friday afternoon. The next weeks and months would see my available energy drop to half or less of what it had been. Divorce sucks the life right out of your life.

Logistically, energy must be diverted to figuring out the legal and financial aspects of this new reality.

Emotionally, whether you wanted it or not, anxiety, worry and despair take the wind out of your sails. Just when you need *more* energy to meet enormous challenges, your energy level drops dramatically. Charles Spurgeon said, *Anxiety does not empty tomorrow of its sorrows, but only empties today of its strength.*[226] No truer words could be said.

When divorce comes into your life, here are some tips on wisely investing the energy you have and working to get your strength back:

- **Invest in time with God.** Spending time with God will give you energy, not take it away. Getting up an hour earlier to be with God will *not* make you more tired. Your true strength comes from God. Time with him will put energy *into* you, not take it away.

---

[226] Quoted in Wayne Cordeiro, *Leading on Empty: Refilling Your Tank and Renewing Your Passion* (Minneapolis, MN: Bethany House, 2009), Kindle Location 835.

- **Lower your expectations of what you can accomplish.** No one expects a patient who just had open-heart surgery to run a marathon the next day. Or week. Or year. Dial back what you expect to get accomplished. This will most likely *not* be the most productive time in your life. That's OK. As you heal, strength will return. There will be times of amazing productivity in the future. It is winter, now, however, not spring.
- **Invest in your children.** Divorce takes energy away from kids and puts it squarely on adults. Your kids are hurting and now, more than ever, need your attention. Don't rail about your spouse to them. Love them, listen to them, hug them.
- **You must keep working**, so think about what you must do at work toget you by. When you are working, *work*. Concentrate, focus, get the job done. Don't waste time at work worrying about your personal life.
- As painful and distasteful as it is, **invest concentrated energy on the legal and financial aspects** of divorce. Bear down and focus. Push through.
- **Exercise.** I can't emphasize enough how sweating will give you energy. Don't go for the marathon, just move some every day. A little goes a long way.
- **Sleep.** A common experience for the newly divorced is to want to curl up in bed and escape through sleep. This is normal since your mind is working hard to process all that is happening. Sleep, but don't sleep too much. If you *just* want to sleep that could be a

sign of depression. You will need more sleep but not too much.

* **Don't waste your energy** or money on anxiety, drugs, alcohol, pornography, buying stuff or escaping to the Caribbean. That's stupid and only makes things worse. *Don't make things worse.*

Pastor Wayne Cordeiro writes:

Each of us has a finite amount of energy to invest each day, and how we invest that will make all the difference.... I measure my energy in bursts or pockets of energy. I have found that I have about seven bursts of energy each day that I can invest. I must choose wisely where and when to invest these pockets of life vitality, because (as the used-car dealer says on the TV ads) when they're gone, they're gone.[227]

You *will* get your strength back. It will take some time but you will be strong again. Invest the energy you have now wisely.

THINK ABOUT IT...

* How is your energy level?
* What things deserve your pockets of energy right now?
* What can you quit doing or leave off your schedule?

---

[227] Ibid., Kindle Location 1653.

Dale J. Brown, Ph.D.

PRAYER...

God, I am beat. Restore to me my strength. Let me draw upon you and invest what you give me in what matters most.

Regaining Your Financial Health

———⊗⊗⊗———

THE WORD

*I know what it is to be in need, and I know what
it is to have plenty. I have learned the secret of
being content in any and every situation, whether
well fed or hungry, whether living in plenty or in
want. I can do everything through him who gives
me strength.... And my God will meet all your needs
according to his glorious riches in Christ Jesus.*

— PHILIPPIANS 4.12–13, 19

THOUGHT FOR THE DAY:

*Wherever God sends us, He will guard our lives.
Our personal property and possessions are to be a
matter of indifference to us, and our hold on these
things should be very loose. If this is not the case, we
will have panic, heartache, and distress. Having the
proper outlook is evidence of the deeply rooted belief in
the overshadowing of God's personal deliverance.*

~ OSWALD CHAMBERS

DIVORCE TAKES MONEY AWAY IN amazing ways. Standards of living drop for both parties when divorce hits. This is a hard reality.

I have a good friend who was making well into the six figures when his wife divorced him. The financial impact on him was extreme as it is for all of us. Anxiety over finances can be overwhelming and depressing. Push back on financial anxiety with these realities:

- **Know that God will provide**. The overarching theme of the Bible is that God loves us. The two most poignant and tangible ways God shows his love for us are his presence with us and his provision for us. All through the Bible we see God providing for his people, often when it looked like all the resources were dried up. Pray to God for his provision. And start giving. Choose an amount to give away, and despite the seeming lack of logic in doing it, give it away. God blesses an open hand (see Day 135).
- **Know that loss is part of everyone's life**. You may have believed that your financial trajectory would always be up and to the right on the chart. You worked hard, you saved, you invested. Divorce takes much of that away and can really hurt. Know this: financial reversals for many reasons are part of nearly everyone's life. They survived and so will you.
- **This is an opportunity to re-evaluate what is important**. Money is king in our culture. I'm convinced

that our culture esteems a rich scoundrel over a poor saint. That's the world's view. God's view is that he owns every single resource and he can give and take away at will. He will not leave us without, but he also wants us to think about our money and other resources.

Patrick Morley reminds us that

All the benefits of prosperity are temporal. All the risks of prosperity are eternal. No matter how affluent and influential we become in the prosperous, material world, we will not find eternal profit from temporal kingdoms. Despite all our prosperity, we must still come daily to the foot of the Cross of the Lord Jesus Christ to inherit an eternal kingdom.... Tread lightly in temporal kingdoms, for all our plans will come to an end, and then we die. The only profit that matters is an eternal one.[228]

* **Follow God's path for you.** If you submit to the Lordship of Christ in your life, your financial picture may look very different in the future, but if Christ is Lord of your life, *whatever your finances are, you will be happy and satisfied.* Trust in God to provide.

Carefully and prayerfully consider what Jesus said,

Therefore I tell you, do not worry about your life, what you will eat or drink; or about your body, what you will wear. Is not life more important than food, and the body more important than clothes? Look at the birds of the air; they do not sow

---

[228] Patrick Morley, *Devotions for The Man in The Mirror* (Grand Rapids: Zondervan, 2015), Kindle Location 174.

or reap or store away in barns, and yet your heavenly Father feeds them. Are you not much more valuable than they? Who of you by worrying can add a single hour to his life?

And why do you worry about clothes? See how the lilies of the field grow. They do not labor or spin. Yet I tell you that not even Solomon in all his splendor was dressed like one of these. If that is how God clothes the grass of the field, which is here today and tomorrow is thrown into the fire, will he not much more clothe you, O you of little faith?

So do not worry, saying, 'What shall we eat?' or 'What shall we drink?' or 'What shall we wear?' For the pagans run after all these things, and your heavenly Father knows that you need them. But seek first his kingdom and his righteousness, and all these things will be given to you as well. Therefore do not worry about tomorrow, for tomorrow will worry about itself. Each day has enough trouble of its own. (Matthew 6.25–34)

The key is to lay it all before God, seeking his will first.

THINK ABOUT IT...

* How has God provided for you in the past?
* What are your chief financial concerns right now?
* Pray to God, giving your financial worries to him. Ask him to re-order your priorities. Ask him to give you strength to follow his plan for your money.

LIFE COMMITMENT...

I commit my financial concerns to God, expecting him to meet all my needs but not all my wants. I ask him to help me know the difference.

Regaining Your Standing with Your Kids

———— ⬥⬥⬥ ————

THE WORD

He will turn the hearts of the fathers to their children,
and the hearts of the children to their fathers; or
else I will come and strike the land with a curse.

— MALACHI 4:6

THOUGHT FOR THE DAY:

In my career, there's many things I've won and
many things I've achieved, but for me, my greatest
achievement is my children and my family. It's
about being a good father, a good husband, just
being connected to family as much as possible.

~ DAVID BECKHAM

I GAVE MYSELF AS MUCH as possible to my children. Divorce
suddenly ripped one of them away from me just at the time
in life I believed he needed me most. Divorce left my two
older children wondering what happened to their family
and who I was as a dad and husband. Being a good husband
and father were high values to me. Divorce seemed to tell

my children and the world that I had failed on both counts. That was a huge blow.

As the pain of divorce ripped through me I was angry. It was difficult not to express that anger to my children. Because I was ambushed by my ex-wife I wasn't given the opportunity for any discussion with her or with my children. I was suddenly left without wife and the one child remaining at home was now gone with her. I had to do something, say something. Your situation is different, but the confusion is the same. Now, imagine being one of your kids. They are struggling with the same turbulence and confusion as you are.

I don't know your situation with your children. What I *do* know your kids need you to do these things for them:

* **Love your kids.** One of the most painful results of divorce is the separation of children from their parents. Our kids are hurting *but they probably won't show it*. Most kids can't express their emotions with words (most of us adults can't either!). Children go silent. Adults misinterpret this silence. When asked how their kids are doing, most couples will say that their chilcren are 'handling it really well.' Their evidence for this assessment is that their children aren't saying much. The kids aren't saying much because they are hurting inside! They are as lost, confused, disoriented and wounded as anyone else. Your children NEED YOUR LOVE, understanding, attention, and lots of hugs. Put yourself in their shoes and love accordingly.
* **Assure your kids that this is not their fault.** It is common for kids to blame themselves. Go overboard in

assuring them the divorce is not their fault. And it is NOT their fault. Adults caused this disaster. The adults need to own it.

- **Be willing to answer any questions your kids have.** The right knowledge can help children disentangle themselves from the mess. Be willing to own up to your piece, give a fair assessment of your spouse's role, and then promise to move forward together.

- **Develop a new and independent relationship with each child.** As I struggled with trying to figure out how to be with my kids, especially my then 15-year-old son, a wise woman gave the following advice: *You can and need to develop an independent relationship with each of your children.* Up to this moment in my life my kids had been *our* kids. My relationship with them had always been in the deeply embedded context of their mother. Divorce changed all that. I needed to develop a separate relationship with my children completely independent of their mother.

- **Tell them the truth.** Have enough respect for your children to tell them the truth. Our children are far more capable of receiving the truth and correctly processing it than we give them credit for. Be honest with your kids as far as is appropriate (telling your five-year-old that you had an affair and that's why mommy kicked you out is not appropriate).

As I write this I am about to embark on a four-day trip to the Texas coast with my two sons, age 16 and 26. As I prayed about this trip I asked that God would give me the best words to say throughout the trip—words of encouragement, affirmation, and blessing. I prayed God would put moments in our trip when I would be able to speak honestly about the divorce, assuring them that this was not their fault. I prayed that God would empower our time together and enable me to lead them as their father in spite of what has happened.[229]

Think About It...

* Think back to your childhood. What scared you? What made you anxious?

* How did the adults in your world help or hurt you when various crises came into the family?

* Take some time to really put yourself in your children's place. If you were them, what would you be thinking and feeling? What would you want your dad to *say* to you? What would you want your dad to *do* for you?

* Make a plan. Plan when you will see them, what goals you have for their relationship with you, what you will say to them, what you will do as you listen to them.

---

[229] The following are good resources for helping your kids through divorce: John W. James, Russell Friedman and Leslie Matthews, *When Children Grieve: For Adults to Help Children Deal with Death, Divorce, Pet Loss, Moving, and Other Losses* (San Francisco: HarperCollins, 2001); Jean McBride, *Talking to Children About Divorce: A Parent's Guide to Healthy Communication at Each Stage of Divorce: Expert Advice for Kids' Emotional Recovery* (San Antonio: Althea Press, 2016).

LIFE COMMITMENT...

I commit to my children. I commit to praying for them by name every day. I commit to being fully invested in their lives by giving them undivided attention, listening to them and expressing my love for them. I realize that how they see me as their earthly father will influence their view of their Heavenly Father. I commit to representing God to them as best as I can.

Regaining Your Manhood

———— ✦✦✦ ————

THE WORD

*Be on your guard; stand firm in the faith; be men
of courage; be strong. Do everything in love.*

— 1 CORINTHIANS 16.13–14

THOUGHT FOR THE DAY:

*The masculine identity in America and other Western
nations is confusing, nebulous, and arbitrary, and
often seems politically incorrect in modern society.*

~ BRET STEPHENSON

DIVORCE IS AN EPIC FAIL on many levels but certainly in the area
of what it means to be a man. Nothing pulls at our manhood so
much as divorce. The reality for us is that our divorce happened
for whatever reason. What has happened has happened. But
what *will* happen is up to us.

I was once friends with a golfer on the Senior Pro Tour.
I picked his brain about a lot of things, because, as we all
know, golf can teach us valuable stuff about life. I asked him
what he did when he hit a really bad shot. He said, *Well, Dale,*

I've seen men wrap golf clubs around trees in anger. But I never did that. I just figured that it was best to not worry about how the ball got there. Instead, I needed to play the ball from where it lay.

When divorce pushes us face-down, we have choices to make. Like Derek Redmond in the 1992 Olympics, we can choose to be taken out of the race on a stretcher or we can choose to get up and move forward with God's help. Your goal from this point forward should be to be a better man, that is, to get up and move forward. Your goal should be to finish well (See Day 94).

To illustrate what this might look like for you, I pulled this quote by Brett Stephenson about the nature of manhood in our culture. As you read it, consider what makes a good man, and think about what kind of man you want to be from here on out. If you ask God for help, he will give it. He will show you the next steps to take to either become the man he intended you to be or to regain the manhood you lost when divorce took you down.

> *The concept of masculinity in our culture has shifted dramatically over time. As we become less and less clear with each generation on what healthy masculinity is, it becomes hard to agree on what is expected of boys as they mature. Differences in just a couple of generations serve as testament to this.*
>
> *For example, in the world of movies there have always been heroes for us to identify with. Typical movie heroes of the 1940s were Bogart, John Wayne, Cary Grant, and Clark Gable. They were strong and tough, but not necessarily the biggest and baddest guys around. They often portrayed fairly ordinary men; their personification of ideal masculinity arose from their*

*confidence, their **values**, and their **resolve**. Contrast that with the profile of modern heroes like Arnold Schwarzenegger in the eighties and nineties and Vin Diesel and The Rock today. The current model of a hero is truly larger than life, often assisted by technological invention such as bionics, genetic manipulation, and/or some serious weaponry. This new breed of hero, unlike those of yesteryear, is an image unattainable by the common boy who doesn't have personal trainers and mega-million-dollar computer effects to enhance him.[230]*

A random Google search for 'values of a man' yielded this result. These are worthy goals for each of us. Where we fall short, may God give us wisdom and strength to move forward.

* Loyalty
* Respect
* Action
* Ambition
* Compassion
* Resilience
* Risk
* Centeredness
* Self-esteem
* Wisdom[231]

---

[230] Bret Stephenson, *From Boys to Men*, 25. Emphasis mine. Used with permission.

[231] Patrício, Vasco, *"10 Values Every 20-Something Man Should Strive To Embody,"* last updated August 6, 2015, accessed July 21, 2017, http://elite-daily.com/life/10-values-gen-y-men/635340/.

THINK ABOUT IT...

* What kind of man would your friends say you are? Your kids? Your ex-wife?
* What kind of man do you want to be a year from now? Five years?
* How do you want to be remembered?

PRAYER...

God, give me wisdom, insight, revelation, motivation, and strength to become a better man. I answer to you first. I want to be a godly man.

Regaining Pride—The Right Kind!

———— ⚬⚬⚬ ————

THE WORD

When pride comes, then comes disgrace,
but with humility comes wisdom.

— PROVERBS 11.2

THOUGHT FOR THE DAY:

Failing in love is better than succeeding in pride.

~ EUGENE PETERSON

MY FIRST REAL HEAD-ON CONFRONTATION with my pride happened at 22,000 feet in a twin-engine Beechcraft King Air somewhere over Zimbabwe. Our 7-year-daughter lay on a stretcher in front of me, delirious, stomach distended with an unknown diagnosis and terrifyingly uncertain prognosis.

After graduation from seminary we had followed God's call to teach for a year in Tanzania. On Valentine's Day, 1996, Lindsey became sick to her stomach. The next 48 hours would see her condition rapidly deteriorate. We decided to drive to Nairobi for help. In Nairobi the doctors encouraged us to evacuate her to South Africa.

The story has a happy ending. We landed in Johannesburg where Lindsey received amazing medical care. She recovered and is now a beautiful, brilliant biologist working at a biotech startup in Boston. That's a story for another book.

Up to that moment on the plane from Nairobi to Johannesburg I was certain of my identity and proud of it. I was a newly graduated Ph.D. who was on the cusp of what was sure to be a brilliant career as a pastor after a teaching stint in the wilds of Africa. I was full of energy, confidence, intelligence and pride. Things had gone my way and I was sure the positive trend would continue

But as I looked with despair at my daughter on the stretcher, God hammered into me the stark reality that none of the things I was proud of in my life—none of my accomplishments, none of my schooling or experience—could help her as she lay on the brink of death. As I watched Lindsey writhe in pain on the stretcher, I was brought to my knees in humility.

Oswald Chambers writes,

> *The underlying foundation of Jesus Christ's kingdom is poverty, not possessions; not making decisions for Jesus, but having such a sense of absolute futility that we finally admit, "Lord, I cannot even begin to do it." Then Jesus says, "Blessed are you . . ." (5:11). This is the doorway to the kingdom.*[232]

---

[232] Chambers, *My Utmost for His Highest*, 203.

Men hate this. We were born to win. We live for competition. We dream of being strong and victorious. But Jesus shows us another way. The way up is down. The way to wisdom is across the river of pain. We learn when we fall. We find God and our true strength when we fail.

Pride is the opposite of all that. But can we have any kind of pride at all?

Nehemiah was commissioned by God to lead in rebuilding the destroyed city of Jerusalem. When he first saw the city he was dismayed. Instead of being discouraged, however, he was energized.[233] He gathered the leaders and said to them, *You see the trouble we are in: Jerusalem lies in ruins, and its gates have been burned with fire. Come, let us rebuild the wall of Jerusalem, and we will no longer be in disgrace.... The God of heaven will give us success.* (Nehemiah 2:17, 20).

With God's command, strength and protection, the people rebuilt the walls. It was an extraordinary feat that took enormous energy and courage. Its success was due to God's help and the hard work of the people. Together, something amazing was accomplished that still inspires almost 2,500 years later.

Nehemiah had much to be proud of, but his was the right kind of pride. Thanks went to God *first* because it was God's strength supplied to his people that made the task possible. But it was also the effort of the people that built the wall.

---

[233] The story of Nehemiah is found in the Old Testament of the Bible titled *Nehemiah*. It's a quick, worthy and exciting read.

Like Jerusalem, your life may be in shambles. But with God's help and your cooperation and energy, something new can rise from the ashes. You have been brought low, but God will not leave you there. In due season he will lift you up and together, you and God will look back on something amazing you built together. This is the right kind of pride, pride in our amazing God and what he can do through willing, available *and humble* servants.

> *Humble yourselves, therefore, under God's mighty hand, that he may lift you up in due time. Cast all your anxiety on him because he cares for you. Be self-controlled and alert. Your enemy the devil prowls around like a roaring lion looking for someone to devour. Resist him, standing firm in the faith, because you know that your brothers throughout the world are undergoing the same kind of sufferings.*
>
> *And the God of all grace, who called you to his eternal glory in Christ, after you have suffered a little while, will himself restore you and make you strong, firm and steadfast. To him be the power forever and ever. Amen.* (1 Peter 5.6–11)

THINK ABOUT IT...

* How has human pride caused you to be where you are today?
* Have you embraced the 'humbling'?
* What could God be calling you to join him to do today?

PRAYER...

Lord God, I have been brought low. It hurts. But what would hurt more is if I waste this pain by wallowing in it. Instead, I submit to this humbling and ask you to take the pieces of my life and accomplish what you will to build your Kingdom. Whatever good comes of the rest of my life, I give you the credit and glory.

Regaining Your Courage

———⊸≋⊶———

THE WORD

Have I not commanded you? Be strong and courageous.
Do not be terrified; do not be discouraged, for the
Lord your God will be with you wherever you go."

—JOSHUA 1.9

THOUGHT FOR THE DAY:

Courage is not the absence of fear, but rather the judgment
that something else is more important than fear.

~ AMBROSE REDMOON

THE AMERICAN HERITAGE DICTIONARY SAYS that *courage is the state or quality of mind or spirit that enables one to face danger, fear, or vicissitudes with self-possession, confidence, and resolution; bravery.*[234]

The root of our word courage comes from the Latin *cor* which means *heart.* Your heart is your inner being, your thoughts, your desires and your will. We can have a strong

---

[234] *The American Heritage Dictionary*, s.v. "courage," accessed July 25, 2017, https://ahdictionary.com/word/search.html?q=courage&submit. x=0&submit.y=0.

heart, which means a heart that is sure, confident and leaning in the right direction. Or your heart can be weak—fearful, timid, flighty, and leaning in the wrong direction.

Painful and frightening life experiences weaken our heart. Just like a blow to the leg weakens it and makes walking difficult, so hard experiences take courage out of our hearts and make living difficult.

Discouragement takes courage out of our heart. Encouragement puts courage back in the heart. God wants your weakened heart to have courage. Courage comes into your heart when you believe the right things about God and about yourself.

Are you strong enough to get through this? Your answer will reveal what you believe about your strength.

Does God have your best interests in mind, making all things work for his glory, your good and the good of the world? A resounding *Yes!* to that question will put courage into your heart. A wavering or faltering *Maybe* will take courage away.

Let God put courage back into your heart.

To have courage, believe in a mission bigger than yourself.

Courage is not the absence of fear, but rather the judgment that something else is more important than fear. What is more important than your fear? I suggest first thinking of your kids. They are far more important than anything you can fear. I suggest thinking of the amazing good God can do in your life if you give yourself to him and the task he has for you in his Kingdom. If one life is significantly changed because of your story, isn't that one life worth pushing past this fear?

Audrey Lorde writes, *When I dare to be powerful, to use my strength in the service of my vision, then it becomes less and less important whether I am afraid.*[235]

What are you really living for? The suffering of divorce can clarify the answer to this question for you. When you have a mission and purpose bigger than yourself, courage comes flowing in!

Believe in a God big enough to accomplish his mission through you.

God is far beyond anything you and I can imagine. I believe one of our first responses to arriving in heaven and seeing God's glory will be, *Why did I worry so much? Why was I so discouraged?*

Consider these passages from the Bible:

But God made the earth by his power; he founded the world by his wisdom and stretched out the heavens by his understanding. (Jeremiah 10.12)

Finally, be strong in the Lord and in his mighty power. (Ephesians 6.10)

For God did not give us a spirit of timidity, but a spirit of power, of love and of self-discipline. (2 Timothy 1.7)

Believe in a God who will, in the end, make things right.

If you have been treated unfairly you may be tempted to put your energy into revenge. The goal of revenge is making someone pay. It's working hard to make things just. In the end this is a wasted expenditure of energy. We will

---

[235] "Audre Lorde Quotes." BrainyQuote, accessed July 25, 2017. https://www.brainyquote.com/quotes/quotes/a/audrelorde357287.html.

explore this more the next few days as we look at the issue of forgiveness.

Bear Grylls writes, *Real courage is about how we react in the face of overwhelming odds. And it is impossible to be courageous if you aren't also afraid. Courage involves facing our fears, and walking through them. It is not about having no fear, but it is about doing what is necessary despite the fear.*[236]

Let God put courage into your heart today.

THINK ABOUT IT...

* What is most frightening to you?
* How can one or more of the truths above address your fear?
* What action(s) do you need to take to demonstrate power over your fear?

LIFE COMMITMENT...

I am not a coward and I will not be ruled by fear. My God will move me boldly into the future he has for me, and I want to be there with him, side-by-side.

---

[236] bear grylls, *a survival guide for life*, 183. reprinted by permission of peters fraser & dunlop (www.petersfraserdunlop.com) on behalf of bear grylls.

Forgiveness—*It's a Journey*

———❧———

THE WORD

Bear with each other and forgive whatever grievances
you may have against one another. Forgive as the Lord
forgave you. And over all these virtues put on love,
which binds them all together in perfect unity. Let the
peace of Christ rule in your hearts, since as members of
one body you were called to peace. And be thankful.

— COLOSSIANS 3.13–15

THOUGHT FOR THE DAY:

I've been engaged in a full professional rumble
with the concept of forgiveness for ten years.

~ BRENÉ BROWN

I HAVE READ MULTIPLE BOOKS on forgiveness. I have
preached many sermons on forgiveness. I have counseled
myriads of people on forgiveness. I can preach it and teach
it. But when it comes to the hard work of actually forgiving,

one thing is blatantly obvious: *Forgiveness is a journey and it's an uphill slog.*

There's a reason I only *mentioned* forgiveness back on Day 60. I only mentioned it because forgiveness is a seed that needs to first be planted in the hostile soil of anger, resentment and bitterness. Like any seed, forgiveness takes a long time to germinate and push toward the sunlight.

At Day 139 I re-introduced the idea of forgiveness to keep the seed alive in you. I tried to water the soil around the seed you planted back at Day 60.

Now it's time to wrap our minds and hearts around what forgiving those who have hurt us can look like if you continue to let the seed grow.

The best authority on this subject I have found is Everett Worthington, Jr., professor of psychology at Virginia Commonwealth University. He has studied forgiveness for several decades. In the midst of his research and teaching on forgiveness, he had the severest of occasions to practice it. In 1996 his mother was brutally murdered in a botched home invasion. If anyone can teach us about forgiveness, it is Dr. Worthington.

Worthington notes that *Forgiveness is a complex, primarily emotional event. It's not just a change in the beliefs that we should forgive.... It is not merely a change in attitude or an act primarily of the will apart from our feelings.*[237]

Everett affirms that forgiving someone who has hurt you takes time and looks different in each situation. He insists

---

[237] Everett L. Worthington, *Forgiving and Reconciling: Bridges to Wholeness and Hope* (Downers Grove: InterVarsity Press, 2003), 141.

that forgiveness is worth pursuing but he is realistic in stating that forgiving those who wound us is difficult and increases in difficulty the deeper the wound. This is important information for those who are victims, that is, those who need to forgive someone, and those who are perpetrators, that is, those who are seeking forgiveness from their victim.

I have been a Christian for almost 40 years. I have been a pastor/teacher for 35 years. Despite what should be a strong foundation from which to forgive, I have struggled. I want to forgive and I know I should, but when I think about what others have done to me and the enormous price of their actions against me, I seethe with anger and burn with resentment. *Wanting* to forgive and know that I *should* forgive have not been enough for me to reach forgiveness. I need more info, and Dr. Worthington provides it.

A key insight is that there are two kinds of forgiveness we can move toward.

The first, called **Decisional Forgiveness**, involves our head and our will. Worthington writes that *When we grant decisional forgiveness, we agree to control our negative behavior (avoidance or revenge) toward the other person and restore our relationship to where it was before the transgression occurred.*[238]

In my situation, decisional forgiveness is expressed in what I have tried *not to do*. I have tried not to lash out through emails or other means at those who have hurt me. So far I have mostly succeeded in this. When I have failed (four or

---

[238] Ibid., 41. He is clear that the *ideal* would be a restored relationship with those who wronged us, but in reality, the ideal of full restoration and reconciliation is seldom reached.

five times), I regretted it. The negative feeling of regret has checked my subsequent urges to lash out (more on that in a few days when we talk about revenge).

Regarding my divorce, decisional forgiveness has expressed itself in not complaining about my ex to my children. I had one good talk with each of my children, expressing my own deep woundedness at what happened. After that talk, I have restrained from saying the many things I want to say. I know there will be a time in the future for more discussion, but the immediate aftermath of the divorce is not the time to download on your kids (see Day 160).

The **second kind of forgiveness has to do with our emotions, our heart, our gut**. Worthington calls this <u>Emotional Forgiveness</u>. With the head we decide not to lash out and we decide to pursue, at the right pace, emotional forgiveness. We agree to let God work in our hearts to move us toward emotional forgiveness.

Worthington explains:

> *[Emotional] forgiveness is defined as the emotional juxtaposition of positive emotions (such as empathy, sympathy, compassion, agape love or even romantic love) against (1) the hot emotions of anger or fear that follow a perceived hurt or offense or (2) the unforgiveness that follows ruminating about the transgression, which also changes our motives from negative to neutral or even positive.*[239]

---

[239] Ibid.

He goes on to say:

> *[In Emotional Forgiveness], positive emotions are juxta-posed against—or experienced at the same time as—the negative emotions. At first, the positive emotions reduce the intensity of the negative emotions. If the emotional juxtaposition is strong enough and lasts long enough, the unforgiveness is changed so that it can never be experienced in the same way again. Emotional "replacement" has occurred. In the most complete forgiveness, the positive emotions of empathy, sympathy, compassion, agape love or romantic love remain without any negative feelings. Instead of wishing to avoid or seek revenge against the transgressor, the forgiver is left with feelings of good will toward the person who hurt him or her. Complete (emotional) forgiveness is experienced.*[240]

Can you imagine having positive feelings toward your ex? Can you imagine feeling warmly toward those who have hurt you? With God's help, we can get there. But this is a slow process. Worthington writes, *You won't suddenly become a more forgiving person... forgiveness will grow like fruit in your life if the plant from which it is to grow is nurtured.*[241]

THINK ABOUT IT...

* What is Decisional Forgiveness? Have you decided to practice this kind of forgiveness? If so, what does

---

[240] Ibid.
[241] Ibid., 149.

that look like to you? If not, what is holding you back?

* What is Emotional Forgiveness? Where are you on this journey? Filled with anger, hate, resentment, bitterness? Or is your heart softening?

LIFE COMMITMENT...

I commit to this journey of forgiveness. I don't want to spend the rest of my days filled with pain, anger, resentment and bitterness.

Unforgiveness—*Drinking Your Own Poison, Building Your Own Prison*

———

THE WORD

For I see that you are in the gall of bitterness
and in the bond of iniquity.

— Acts 8.23 (ESV)

THOUGHT FOR THE DAY:

Every major difficulty you face in life is a fork in
the road. You choose which track you will head
down, toward breakdown or breakthrough.

~ John Maxwell

IF ANYONE HAD CAUSE FOR resentment and bitterness, it was Nelson Mandela. He watched his people driven into the ground by Apartheid, and then he did something about it. He was imprisoned 27 years for his troubles. Imagine losing 27 years of your life *for standing up for the right thing.* And yet Mandela wrote, *Resentment is like drinking poison and then hoping it will kill your enemies.*[242] It was a lesson learned through breaking one hard rock at a time on Robben Island.

Desmond Tutu, in his book on forgiveness, wrote of Mandela:

> *When Nelson Mandela went to jail, he was a very angry man. This global role model of forgiveness [Mandela] was not very forgiving on the day he stepped onto Robben Island to begin his prison sentence. It took the many years in jail, years he spent cultivating a daily practice of forgiveness, for him to become the luminous example of tolerance who was able to put our wounded country on the road to reconciliation and healing. The man who walked into prison was not the man who invited his prison guard to be a VIP guest at his inauguration. That took time and effort.*[243]

Unforgiveness is like building a prison for the person who hurt you, only to find, when you are done, that you're trapped in this prison cell of your own making. It's like concocting a poison to kill your enemy, only to discover that it is killing you.

Unforgiveness is bad for you. Worry, anxiety, bitterness and rage do things to your body such as activate the endocrine system leading to increased heart rate, blood pressure, etc. When activated repeatedly, this "fight or flight"

---

[242] *"A quote by Nelson Mandela."* Goodreads, accessed August 22, 2017, https://www.goodreads.com/quotes/144557-resentment-is-like-drinking-poison-and-then-hoping-it-will.

[243] Tutu and Tutu, *The Book of Forgiving*, 217.

response wears on the body and slowly leads to damage.[244] Unforgiveness can actually kill you.

Unforgiveness is like giving an unruly and obnoxious tenant space in your head rent free.

Unforgiveness binds you to the past, sucking up time and energy you could and should be investing in your future.

And so the arguments go for forgiving those who have wounded us.

What motivates us to the path of forgiveness? It's difficult but not impossible to talk yourself into forgiveness using all the rational arguments for it. But as I heard a preacher say, *Soul wounds are emotional, not rational.*[245] The psychological and physical health benefits of forgiving may not be enough to convince us. Smart people know smoking and overeating will kill them, but they do these things anyway.

People won't stop smoking or overeating, however, unless they are armed with knowledge to build a foundation for the final leap to give it up.

Given that the mind *does* have some power to persuade our will to act despite—or sometimes contrary to—our emotions, think about the damage done by living in unforgiveness and the rational reasons to forgive listed above. Maybe they will convince you. I hope so because this is the easiest and quickest way to forgiveness.

But most offenses cause wounds that are not easily or quickly dealt with. Unforgiveness is a result of ruminating on

---

[244] Mike Fillon, *"Holding a Grudge Can Be Bad for Your Health,"* last updated February 25, 2000, accessed August 22, 2017, http://www.webmd.com/depression/news/20000225/holding-a-grudge-can-be-bad-for-your-health#1.

[245] Trey Steele, in a sermon at Real Life Church, heard August 21, 2017, Austin, Texas.

what happened to you and the feelings associated with the hurt. The deeper the hurt, the greater the losses from that hurt, and the more difficult it is to stop ruminating.

If I cut my finger, it will hurt and I will notice it, but it will heal in a few days. If my leg is cut off, it will hurt a lot for many days, and its healing will be slow and painful. Even when the pain goes away I will know I am missing a leg every time I try to stand up. I will struggle to stop ruminating about my missing leg and the reasons for its loss.

As we continue giving consideration to forgiveness, take a moment to think about where you are on this journey. Can you choose forgiveness for your own sake? Or is the pain too deep to stop deliberating about what has happened to you?

For your own mental and physical health, the best thing would be to let the pain go, but that may not be possible for you at this time. If you can't talk yourself into forgiveness from the standpoint of logic because the pain is too much, don't beat yourself up about it. Just keep asking God to soften your heart and give you a desire for forgiveness. And keep learning about what forgiveness is all about.

This is a journey, and journeys take a while. Be patient with yourself.

THINK ABOUT IT...

* Forgiveness is good for you. It is freeing, liberating, exhilarating. Unforgiveness is bad for you. It wastes time, takes up brain power you could devote to your future, and it wears your body out. Do you believe

these things with your head? Can you embrace them with your heart?

* If not, be patient with yourself. Allow God to continue his work in you. As someone said, *Soul business is slow, slow business.*

LIFE COMMITMENT...

I acknowledge that forgiving those who have hurt me is in my best interest. If I cannot embrace this reality now, I will be patient with myself and allow God to continue working on my heard and my heart.

Unforgiveness—*Making Them Pay*

—∞∞∞—

THE WORD

> *Do not repay anyone evil for evil. Be careful to do what*
> *is right in the eyes of everybody. If it is possible, as far as*
> *it depends on you, live at peace with everyone. Do not*
> *take revenge, my friends, but leave room for God's wrath,*
> *for it is written: "It is mine to avenge; I will repay," says*
> *the Lord. On the contrary: "If your enemy is hungry,*
> *feed him; if he is thirsty, give him something to drink. In*
> *doing this, you will heap burning coals on his head." Do*
> *not be overcome by evil, but overcome evil with good.*

— ROMANS 12.17–21

THOUGHT FOR THE DAY:

> *We realize that it is not up to us to take revenge on*
> *others who have wronged us, or even to want to do*
> *so, because God has reserved that right for himself.*

~ WAYNE GRUDEM

LIFE IS NOT FAIR. HOW many times have we said this to our children when they don't get their own way or a teacher gives them a bad but undeserved grade, or a friend is mean to them? And yet when we are treated badly, we rage. The reason we rage is because we know, deep down, that life should be fair. If we normalize unfairness, things will only get much worse in our world.

Unfairness creates what Worthington calls an 'injustice gap.' He describes it this way: *When a transgression occurs, things are put out of balance... a transgression creates an injustice gap— the difference between the way I want events to settle out ideally and the way I perceive them to be at present.*[246]

The deeper the offense, the wider the gap. The wider the gap, the stronger the natural and instinctive urge to close the gap by seeking justice. One way to close the injustice gap is to make the perpetrator(s) pay.

The negative feeling of unforgiveness seeks to express itself through actions.[247] The purpose of these actions is to balance the scales of justice, that is, to close the injustice gap. We say, *Don't get mad, get even.* That is, *bring the universe back into even balance.*

The problem with trying to balance the scales ourselves is that it doesn't work. Consider the following:

* **Revenge is not satisfying.** Revenge is like the emotion of anger. I am *always right when I am in the heat of anger,* but inevitably I have realized afterwards that anger is self-justifying and never leads to positive outcomes.[248] Revenge may feel good for a moment, but

---

[246] Worthington, *Forgiving and Reconciling*, 37.

[247] Remember that the emotion of unforgiveness is developed over time by ruminating on the offense which created anger, resentment and bitterness.

[248] *For man's anger does not bring about the righteous life that God desires.* (James 1.20)

in the end, it leaves a sour taste in our mouth and can do serious harm to ourselves and others.

* **Revenge doesn't pull people together.** If you are seeking to rebuild a relationship with someone, revenge will not build a bridge. Revenge builds a wall over which we keep tossing grenades hoping to blow up the other person. On the other hand, you may not care about the other person's well-being. You may want them dead. But in the end, doesn't the world have enough violence? Wouldn't it be better to be a part of stitching the world back together rather than ripping it apart?[249]

* **Revenge can't make up for the intangible losses.** Will getting even get your reputation back, or further damage it? Will exacting revenge erase the hurt done to you by the offending party or just add to everyone's pain? Sometimes we think revenge will inflict so much hurt on the offender that he/she will see the light and repent, crawling back to us in submissive confession. Rarely does this occur! While you have been plotting your revenge they have been busy justifying their every move, or just moving on.

* **Revenge usually can't make up for material losses.** Will "making them pay" put dollars in your checking account lost to divorce? In fact, seeking revenge will take away needed energy and brain space to invest your life in making up for these material losses. As American writer Patricia Cornwell says, *Survival*

---

[249] *Justice rarely leads to reconciliation, even when justice can be achieved (such as with a fair trial). At best it brings an uneasy truce. In most relationships, justice never really is experienced. When one side believes justice has been done, the other side doesn't.* Worthington, *Forgiving and Reconciling*, 183.

was my only hope, success my only revenge.[250] The best revenge is to be the best person you can be.

• **Thoughts of revenge give power to the person who has wounded you.** Marc and Angel Chernoff write: *The person you liked or loved in the past, who treated you like dirt repeatedly, has nothing intellectually or spiritually to offer you in the present moment, but more headaches and heartache.*[251] Plotting revenge is wasted time and energy. It's allowing the past to dominate your present and thus rob you of your future.

• **To balance the scale through revenge is to take the low road, not the high road.** As Marcus Aurelius said, *The best revenge is to be unlike him who performed the injury.*[252] Like anger, revenge seems to be the "manly" thing to do because it feels powerful. But as is so often the case, bad things happen when power is misused. Don't abuse your power. Channel your energy into making a better you and a better future *for* you.

---

[250] *"Patricia Cornwell Quotes,"* BrainyQuote, accessed August 24, 2017, https://www.brainyquote.com/quotes/quotes/p/patriciaco701486.html?src=t_revenge.

[251] Marc and Angel Chernoff, *"18 Things to Remember When Your Heart is Breaking,"* last updated February 16, 2015, accessed October 27, 2017, http://www.marcandangel.com/2015/12/16/18-things-to-remember-when-your-heart-is-breaking/.

[252] *"Marcus Aurelius Quotes,"* BrainyQuote, accessed August 24, 2017, https://www.brainyquote.com/quotes/quotes/m/marcusaure383110.html?src=t_revenge.

Think About It...

   ✦   On a scale of 0 to 10, (0 = *I have no desire for revenge* to 10 = *I am close to murder*), how strong is your desire for revenge?

0—1—2—3—4—5—6—7—8—9—10

   ✦   If you are in the 5 to 10 range, list two things you believe revenge will give to you:

1. _____
2. _____

Now go back and read (above) what we said about revenge. Imagine that you have carried out your plan for revenge. What does the outcome look like? How do you feel? How do the people in your life feel about you, such as your kids, your co-workers, your friends, your church?

   ✦   Is revenge worth it?

Prayer...

I want them to pay. I need someone to pay. God show me another way.

Forgiveness—*Releasing to God's Judgment*

---⚬⚬⚬---

THE WORD

*When they hurled their insults at him, he did not
retaliate; when he suffered, he made no threats. Instead,
he entrusted himself to him who judges justly.*

— 1 PETER 2.23

THOUGHT FOR THE DAY:

*We have reached acceptance when we finally
recognize that paying back someone in kind will never
make us feel better or undo what has been done.
To quote the comedian Lily Tomlin, "Forgiveness
means giving up all hope for a better past."*

~ DESMOND TUTU

REVENGE IS A DEAD-END STREET. As we try to balance the
scales of justice in our own power, we realize that making the
offender pay may give a temporary high, but in the end, it is
a lose-lose for everyone.

But the incredibly strong pull to close the injustice gap, born out of our good and right sense of fairness, remains. How can the gap be closed?

Looked at from a different angle, we need to put the thoughts of what happened to us out of minds. Franklin Jones notes, however, that *You never realize what a good memory you have until you try to forget something.*[253] As hard as you try, you can't put what happened out of your mind. In fact, the harder you try to not think about something, the more you think about it.

The only way to not think about our thoughts is to do something with them.[254] This is a conundrum. We want to close the injustice gap. We also know we are incapable of closing this gap on our own. Because of these mental dynamics, it appears we are stuck with thoughts that we know are bad for our mental and physical health, buy we also can't get rid of them. The answer is an infusion of help from outside ourselves.

Ironically, this infusion of help comes from the fact that God is Judge and that there is a judgment.

Theologian Wayne Grudem explains this dynamic much better than I can:

> *We realize that it is not up to us to take revenge on others who have wronged us, or even to want to do so, because God has reserved that right for himself. "Beloved, never avenge yourselves, but leave it to the wrath of God, for it*

---

[253] *"Good Memory Quotes,"* BrainyQuote, accessed August 25, 2017, https://www.brainyquote.com/quotes/keywords/good_memory.html.

[254] See Day 19.

is written, 'Vengeance is mine, I will repay, says the Lord'" (Rom. 12:19).

In this way whenever we have been wronged, we can give into God's hands any desire to harm or pay back the person who has wronged us, knowing that every wrong in the universe will ultimately be paid for—<u>either it will turn out to have been paid for by Christ when he died on the cross (if the wrongdoer becomes a Christian), or it will be paid for at the final judgment</u> (for those who do not trust in Christ for salvation). But in either case we can give the situation into God's hands, and then pray that the wrongdoer will trust Christ for salvation and thereby receive forgiveness of his or her sins.

This thought should keep us from harboring bitterness or resentment in our hearts for injustices we have suffered that have not been made right: God is just, and we can leave these situations in his hands, knowing that he will some-day right all wrongs and give absolutely fair rewards and punishments. In this way we are following in the example of Christ, who "when he was reviled, he did not revile in return; when he suffered, he did not threaten; but he trusted to him who judges justly" (1 Peter 2:22–23). He also prayed, "Father, forgive them, for they know not what they do" (Luke 23:34; compare Acts 7:60, where Stephen followed Jesus' ex-ample in praying for those who put him to death).[255]

God is the ultimate judge and only he can judge. Only he has all the *information* about the situation and only he has the *power* to execute perfect judgment. Only he has the knowl-edge and power to close the injustice gap. On our own, we

---

[255] Grudem, *Systematic Theology*, 1146-1147. Emphasis mine.

simply don't have enough knowledge and power to close the gap. But he does, and because *only* he does, we should give it over to him.

The reality is that *he will close the gap.* God *is* the Judge of the universe and *he will judge.* Whether this happens or not is not up to if we believe it will happen. It *will* happen. Our choice is to believe in God's ability and power to close the gap or to keep holding onto the belief that we can close the gap in our own power.

If we release the urge we feel to close the gap to God, we will make major strides toward both decisional and emotional forgiveness. If we don't, we will continue suffering needlessly.

And, in a more striking way, we will be profaning the cross of Christ. That is, if we continue in our desire to make them pay for what Christ has already paid for on the cross, we are emptying the cross of Christ of meaning.

Sociologist Brené Brown heard a sermon on forgiveness. Her pastor said, *In order for forgiveness to happen, something has to die. If you make a choice to forgive, you have to face into the pain. You simply have to hurt.*[256]

She goes on to write:

> *Forgiveness is so difficult because it involves death and grief.... The death or ending that forgiveness necessitates comes in many shapes and forms. We may need to bury our expectations or dreams. We may need to relinquish the power that comes with "being right" or put to rest the idea that we can do what's in our hearts and still retain the support or approval of others. Joe [her pastor] explained, "Whatever it*

---

[256] Joe, Brené Brown's pastor, quoted in Brown, *Rising Strong*, Kindle Location 859.

is, it all has to go. It isn't good enough to box it up and set it aside. It has to die. It has to be grieved. That is a high price indeed.[257]

In their book, *The Book of Forgiving,* the Tutus list some of things we may have to give up: the right to revenge, the expectation of an apology, an expectation that the person who hurt you will understand the pain they have caused.[258]

The beautiful thing is that because God is the Perfect Judge, we can release these things into his amazing care.

This, my friend, is where true freedom is found.

THINK ABOUT IT...

* Do you believe you can close the injustice gap in your own knowledge and power? If so, how will that happen?
* Do you believe God knows everything about your situation? Do you believe he has the power and desire to ultimately set things right?
* Grudem writes: ... *ultimately God's universe is fair, for God is in control, and he keeps accurate records and renders just judgment. When Paul tells slaves to be submissive to their masters, he reassures them, "For the wrongdoer will be paid back for the wrong he has done, and there is no partiality" (Col 3:25). When the picture of a final judgment mentions the fact that "books were opened" (Rev. 20:12; compare Mal. 3:16), it reminds us (whether the books are literal or*

---

[257] Ibid., Kindle Locations 2173-2179.
[258] Tutu and Tutu, *The Book of Forgiving,* 44.

symbolic) that a permanent and accurate record of all our deeds has been kept by God, and ultimately all accounts will be settled and all will be made right.[259]

Do you believe that, in the end, God will act such a way that everyone will say, at the end of the day, that God is fair?

PRAYER...

God, you alone are the Perfect Judge. You alone have the knowledge and the power to set things right. You alone have the knowledge and power to close the injustice gap. I surrender to you my own delusional thinking that I can do what only you can do. I put to death my desire to be you. I put to death my desire to close the gap in my own power.

---

[259] Grudem, *Systematic Theology*, 1146.

Forgiveness—*Christ's Sacrifice*

———⊷⊶⊷———

THE WORD

> *Then he took the cup, gave thanks and offered it to*
> *them, saying, "Drink from it, all of you. This is my*
> *blood of the covenant, which is poured out for many*
> *for the forgiveness of sins. I tell you, I will not drink of*
> *this fruit of the vine from now on until that day when*
> *I drink it anew with you in my Father's kingdom."*

— MATTHEW 26.27–29

THOUGHT FOR THE DAY:

> *He fills us with His Spirit, covers us with His*
> *protection, drenches us with His love and favor,*
> *and walks with us through our adversities. To lose*
> *everything and gain Jesus is no loss at all.*

~JONI ERIKSON TADA

ONE OF MY JOBS WHILE attending seminary was hanging wallpaper. I called Daryl and Sally in response to an ad they had posted on the seminary job board, and they gave me the job. I worked for three summers hanging wallpaper in new construction. It was hot, dusty work but I enjoyed doing something with my hands.

For the most part, Daryl and Sally were good people and we got along famously. But that changed the third summer when they went on vacation. They left me in charge of all the wallpaper in a new subdivision. When they returned from vacation I suspected they had not paid me what was agreed upon. My suspicions were confirmed when I talked with the construction supervisor.

I was livid. I angrily confronted them on the phone. After that confrontation they ignored my calls. My wallpapering days with them were over. The monetary loss was not huge, $300, but for a seminary student back in 1987, it hurt. In addition, they took two of my ladders and other equipment.

My anger knew no bounds. I was undone. But then one day I read the following parable found in Matthew 18:

Peter came to Jesus and asked, "Lord, how many times shall I forgive my brother when he sins against me? Up to seven times?"

Jesus answered, "I tell you, not seven times, but seventy-seven times.

Therefore, the kingdom of heaven is like a king who wanted to settle accounts with his servants. As he began the settlement, a man who owed him ten thousand talents was brought to him. Since he was not able to pay, the master ordered that he and his wife and his children and all that he had be sold to repay the debt.

The servant fell on his knees before him. 'Be patient with me,' he begged, 'and I will pay back everything.' The servant's master took pity on him, canceled the debt and let him go.

> *But when that servant went out, he found one of his fellow servants who owed him a hundred denarii. He grabbed him and began to choke him. 'Pay back what you owe me!' he demanded. His fellow servant fell to his knees and begged him, 'Be patient with me, and I will pay you back.' But he refused. Instead, he went off and had the man thrown into prison until he could pay the debt. When the other servants saw what had happened, they were greatly distressed and went and told their master everything that had happened.*
>
> *Then the master called the servant in. 'You wicked servant,' he said, 'I canceled all that debt of yours because you begged me to. Shouldn't you have had mercy on your fellow servant just as I had on you?' In anger his master turned him over to the jailers to be tortured, until he should pay back all he owed.*
>
> *This is how my heavenly Father will treat each of you unless you forgive your brother from your heart."* (Matthew 18.21–35)

God's Spirit hit me between the eyes with the words of Jesus. How could I *not* forgive Sally and Daryl for their small offense when I had been forgiven of so much more? I immediately wrote them a note. I shared with them my experience of reading this parable and I told them that I released them from any debt they owed me. I also told them that if I saw them again, I would treat them as if the incident had never occurred.

I never heard from Daryl and Sally but I felt good in my heart. I felt clean and free. And I never got angry about this again. In addition, God more than restored my lost income and equipment.

In the end, you and I forgive because we have been forgiven of much more than has been done to us. The price Christ paid for our forgiveness was far beyond anything you and I could ever pay. Jesus died the most agonizing death anyone has ever died so that we can be forgiven: *God made him who had no sin to be sin for us, so that in him we might become the righteousness of God.* (2 Corinthians 5.21)

Though undeserved, all my sins have been forgiven by God through the indescribable sacrifice of his own Son. Since I have been forgiven of much, I am obligated to forgive others of much lesser sins.

The problem, of course, is the size of the thing that needs to be forgiven. Back in 1988 it was $300. Now my losses are counted in the hundreds of thousands of dollars. Thirty years ago it was a side job. Today it is my career. I could forgive *then* when the cost was low. Can I forgive *now* when the cost is exponentially higher?

I am on the journey of forgiveness as are you. I am committed to the journey and know that one day God's Spirit in me will do his work in my soul so that I feel about the people in my life who betrayed me the same way I feel about Sally and Daryl. I know I will get there because Jesus has forgiven me of much more than has been done to me. I know I will get there because I don't want to be the unforgiving servant in the parable. God is taking the seeds of my desires and growing them into full-blown forgiveness.

THINK ABOUT IT...

On Day 60 I introduced the concept of forgiveness, a seed planted in your soul. In the 'Think About It' section for that day, I asked the following questions, questions worth considering again today:

- How have you experienced forgiveness from others in your life?
- What barriers to forgiving others are in your life right now?
- What will you gain by forgiving the people in your life who have hurt you?
- What would you gain by not forgiving them?

To review again what Jesus has done for you, read Days 61-69.

LIFE COMMITMENT...

At the end of the day, I don't want to be the unforgiving servant in the parable told by Jesus. Today I ask God to close the gap between how I feel now and what will eventually be complete emotional forgiveness. I submit to his work in my soul and anticipate the day I can be free in completely forgiving those who have wounded me.

Forgiveness—*Knit Back Together*

———⟨∞∞⟩———

THE WORD

*I urge Euodia and Syntyche to iron out their differences
and make up. God doesn't want his children holding
grudges. And, oh, yes, [fellow worker], since you're
right there to help them work things out, do your best
with them. These women worked for the Message
hand in hand with Clement and me, and with
the other veterans—worked as hard as any of us.
Remember, their names are also in the Book of Life.*

— PHILIPPIANS 4.2-3 (MSG)

THOUGHT FOR THE DAY:

*We must develop and maintain the capacity to
forgive. He who is devoid of the power to forgive is
devoid of the power to love. There is some good in the
worst of us and some evil in the best of us. When we
discover this, we are less prone to hate our enemies.*

~ MARTIN LUTHER KING, JR.

IN MY YOUNG DAYS AS a seminary student I helped start a church. One Sunday we were called away to our home church for a special business meeting. In Church World, special business meetings are usually not pleasant. When we arrived a police officer was standing at the back of the church. We were told he was there 'just in case.' When a police officer is at a church business meeting 'just in case,' something is terribly wrong and out of place.

And so it is with any break between people. The Gospel of Jesus Christ is about people moving toward God and one another. When people are moving away from one another, something is fundamentally and foundationally wrong. Jesus died on the cross so we *could* and *would* move toward each other. *Any breach between humans is a travesty and a tragedy and a violation of all God made us for and all he gave his Son for.* As Gandhi is purported to have said: *An eye for an eye will make the whole world blind.*

In the end, I want to be remembered as a healer. I want to be part of stitching the world back together, not continuing to pull the fabric of life apart.

The Tutus write:

> *None of us wants to have our life story be the sum of all the ways we have been hurt. We are not created to live in suffering and isolation. We are created to live in love and connection with one another. When there is a break in that connection, we must have a method of repair.*[260]

---

[260] Tutu and Tutu. *The Book of Forgiving*, 46.

Forgiveness is that 'method of repair.'

Worthington notes that *When transgressions rip apart relationships, forgiveness is the seamstress who reweaves the jagged tear in trust, thread by thread. Forgiveness restores the unraveled seam of love and irons out the wrinkles of residual anger.*[261]

At the same time, forgiveness is perhaps the biggest challenge any of us will face. It's a journey fraught with steep grades, switchbacks, dangerous ridges and slippery footholds. Forgiveness is more complex than people imagine.

Some people will tell you that you should just forgive and move on. My response to this command is as follows: Thank you for your concern, but let me ask you two things: (1) What have you lost and (2) have you forgiven those who have caused you these losses.

If the person ordering me to forgive and forget has experienced extreme loss and has moved successfully through the journey, I will be happy to listen to them. But just the fact that they glibly have ordered me to *forgive and forget* is a pretty good indication they have not suffered severe loss and, therefore, have not climbed up the Everest called Forgiveness. Forgiveness is a tall, steep and treacherous mountain. It *can* be climbed but it is not nearly as easy as most people think.

Recall that the mountain of forgiveness is climbed in two phases: **Decisional Forgiveness** and **Emotional Forgiveness** (see Day 164).

---

[261] Worthington, *Forgiving and Reconciling*, 238.

Decisional Forgiveness is deciding not to harm the other person. It is deciding not to take revenge upon them and undermine them.[262]

Emotional forgiveness is accomplished when the negative emotions you have toward the offender are replaced by positive feelings of empathy and compassion.[263] This, indeed, is hard to do.

In the end, the journey of forgiveness is long. It's hard. Use the resources I have cited in this section on forgiveness. And, as always, I recommend finding a competent therapist or counselor to help you journey up this huge mountain.

THINK ABOUT IT...

* Have you decided to practice Decisional Forgiveness? In what ways have you not sought revenge? How does it feel to release the need to get revenge?
* Have you decided to practice Emotional Forgiveness? What feelings do you have regarding your ex and those involved in your divorce? Would you commit

---

[262] Worthington: *When we grant decisional forgiveness, we agree to control our negative behavior (avoidance or revenge) toward the other person and restore our relationship to where it was before the transgression occurred. We hope later to reduce or eliminate our negative emotions and motivations—that is, our desires to act— if possible. However, we usually realize that it will take a lot longer to change emotions and motivations than to say we intend to control our behavior. There is a great distance between head and heart.* Worthington, *Forgiving and Reconciling*, 41.

[263] Worthington: *In the most complete forgiveness, the positive emotions of empathy, sympathy, compassion, agape love or romantic love remain without any negative feelings. Instead of wishing to avoid or seek revenge against the transgressor, the forgiver is left with feelings of good will toward the person who hurt him or her.* Worthington, *Forgiving and Reconciling*, 42.

to asking God to replace your negative emotions with positive feelings toward your ex and others who have wounded you?

* If you are the offender, how can you seek forgiveness from your ex in a way that is healing?

LIFE COMMITMENT...

I don't want my 'life story to be the sum of all the ways [I] have been hurt' (Tutu). As far as I am able and as much as God can empower me, I want to be a mender of the fabric of life, not one who continues to rip it apart.

Fathered by God

———◦◦◦◦◦———

THE WORD

I myself said, 'How gladly would I treat you like sons.'

—JEREMIAH 3.19

THOUGHT FOR THE DAY:

A boy learns who he is and what he's made of from a man.

~ JOHN ELDREDGE

MY DAD WAS A TOUGH guy to figure out. On one hand, he was amazingly driven, smart, gregarious and generous. At the same time he was hyper-critical, verbally abusive, and emotionally immature. I spent many an hour trying to figure him out, sometimes just for the sake of survival.

Most of us have long histories with our dads and our histories have defining moments.

One of those defining moments for me was when it was discovered that my 84-year-old father had been frequenting strip clubs. When I was told this, I was stunned. I couldn't imagine being 84-years-old and *wanting* to be in a strip club.

But then came the profound disappointment: *How could this guy do this to me and the rest of his family?*

At one time my dad had led the deacons at my home church, and this was a huge church. He had made and given away tons of money from his huge Christian heart. He had strict views about sexuality and divorce. And yet here he was, going to strip clubs. As happens with these stories, there is much more than meets the eye. I won't go into the sordid details, but suffice it to say that my dad had been lured down his shadow mission and his life was not ending well.

What did all this do to me?

First, *I realized that finishing well was not guaranteed.* As a man, I renewed my commitment to finish this thing called life soaring rather than crashing.

Second, *it renewed my commitment to help other men finish well.* As pastor of a church with a men's ministry with 100 guys in it, I wanted each of them to finish the race with head held high and integrity intact.

Third, *it profoundly impacted the way I viewed my dad.* His poor choices created a vacuum in me. While my father was deeply flawed as a dad, at least he had been there and provided for us. The discovery of his wayward behavior sucked the positive stuff I felt about him right out of me.

One morning I was sitting in my office praying. I lifted this huge disappointment up to God. I opened my empty heart to him. And then God said to me, *"I am your father. Your dad was your dad on earth, deeply flawed, mixed up, confused. Don't measure me by him. Measure him by me. I am your father and no one can take me away from you."*

Wow. God had really spoken to me and filled my empty, disappointed heart with himself! The promise of 2 Corinthians 6.18 became a stunning reality in my life: *I will be a Father to you, and you will be my sons and daughters, says the Lord Almighty.*

I immediately took whatever needs I was hoping to have filled from my earthly father and dumped them into the lap of my heavenly Father. God took them with joy and has been my true Father ever since.

John Eldredge describes what he calls 'unfinished men,' men who were not fathered well by their dads.

He writes: *We no longer live, either as a society or even as the church, with a father-view of the world, the view centered in the presence of a loving and strong father deeply engaged in our lives, to whom we can turn at any time for the guidance, comfort, and provision we need.*[264]

He goes on to make the point that our earthly fathers can't give us what we need, but our heavenly Father can and *wants to.* The process God puts us through to teach us about himself, ourselves, and life is our trials.

Eldredge says,

> *So much of what we misinterpret as hassles or trials or screw-ups on our part are in fact God fathering us, taking us through something in order to strengthen us, or heal us, or dismantle some unholy thing in us. In other words, initiate us—a distinctly masculine venture.*
>
> *You are the son of a kind, strong, and engaged Father, a Father wise enough to guide you in the Way, generous*

---

[264] John Eldredge, *Fathered by God: Learning What Your Dad Could Never Teach You* (Detroit: Gale Cengage Learning, 2009), Kindle Location 49.

enough to provide for your journey, offering to walk with you every step.[265]

God our Father invites us into his story, a story much grander, more enduring, and far more challenging than our own little lives. He invites us to a life of significance, all the while promising to equip us for the journey ahead and promising *never* to abandon us or be cruel to us in any way.

Because you are sons, God sent the Spirit of his Son into our hearts, the Spirit who calls out, "Abba, Father." So you are no longer a slave, but a son; and since you are a son, God has made you also an heir. (Galatians 4.6–7)

Think About It...

+ If your dad was in your life, what did he give to you? What did he fail to give to you?
+ In what ways do you think you have been acting out trying to get from your dad what he never gave to you or could give to you?
+ If your dad is still alive, what is your relationship with him now? How would you want it to change? What steps could you take to initiate this change?
+ What does it mean to be fathered by God?

Prayer...

God, you are my Father. Reveal yourself to me as my Father. Show me what being your son and having you

---

[265] Ibid, 12-13, 27.

All In for Jesus

—⊸≪≫⊸—

THE WORD

> But whatever was to my profit I now consider loss for
> the sake of Christ. What is more, I consider everything
> a loss compared to the surpassing greatness of knowing
> Christ Jesus my Lord, for whose sake I have lost all
> things. I consider them rubbish, that I may gain Christ
> and be found in him, not having a righteousness of my
> own that comes from the law, but that which is through
> faith in Christ—the righteousness that comes from God
> and is by faith. I want to know Christ and the power
> of his resurrection and the fellowship of sharing in his
> sufferings, becoming like him in his death, and so,
> somehow, to attain to the resurrection from the dead.

— PHILIPPIANS 3.7–11

THOUGHT FOR THE DAY:

> Obedience is not a stodgy plodding in the ruts of
> religion, it is a hopeful race toward God's promises.

~ EUGENE PETERSON

AT SOME POINT IN LIFE we must make a major decision. After we make this huge decision, the rest of life is filled with many decisions either supporting or undermining this decision. The decision of which I speak is what to do with Jesus.

Are you all-in for Jesus? Have you given control of your life over to him? Is he your leader now? Have you bent your knee before him in submission, then experienced him raising you up to a new, challenging, fulfilling life?

Or, is one foot in the 'religious' world and your other foot still in the secular world? Are you still trying to play both sides? Are you sitting on the fence? Guys, we know what sitting on the fence can do to us, and it's painful just to think about!

Another way to ask this question is: Imagine you are on your deathbed. In that moment, who or what will you be trusting in to get you to the other side? Luck? Your 'good' life or good deeds? A philosophy that claims that when you die you just go away? Or Jesus?

God calls you to himself through his Son Jesus who gave himself on the cross so that you could, in humble, exhilarating gratitude, give yourself back to him.

Chris Tiegreen asks this penetrating question:

Imagine God giving you these two options: (1) to live a mediocre existence without too many highs or lows; or (2) to lay it all on the line and experience ultimate joy and rewards along with genuine sacrifices. Which would you choose? Most of us would say we want the second option—to live life to its fullest, in spite of the costs. But that's exactly the choice

God gives us, and most of us tend to opt for average on a daily basis.[266]

Jesus doesn't call you to average. He calls you to himself to allow him to propel you into his Kingdom in whatever way he chooses. One thing I have learned: following Jesus completely is not easy by any means, but it is *best*.

When Jesus walked the earth he was constantly calling people to decision:

> *Then Jesus said to his disciples, "If anyone would come after me, he must deny himself and take up his cross and follow me. For whoever wants to save his life will lose it, but whoever loses his life for me will find it. What good will it be for a man if he gains the whole world, yet forfeits his soul? Or what can a man give in exchange for his soul?"* (Matthew 16.24–26)

What is so precious on earth that you want to hold onto it at the price of your soul? What has the world given you that is so worth keeping? Why not surrender to Jesus and follow him wherever he leads?

Oswald Chambers said that…

> *It is only through abandonment of yourself and your circumstances that you will recognize Him. You will only recognize His voice more clearly through recklessness—being willing to risk your all.*

---

[266] Tiegreen, *One Year Hearing His Voice Devotional*, 685.

> *As soon as we abandon ourselves to God and do the task*
> *He has placed closest to us, He begins to fill our lives with*
> *surprises.*
>
> *God ventured His all in Jesus Christ to save us, and*
> *now He wants us to venture our all with total abandoned*
> *confidence in Him.*[267]

God risked all for us. He calls us to surrender our lives completely to him. This is risk. This is adventure. This is the thing for which you were made.

THINK ABOUT IT...

- When did you surrender to Jesus? If you can't remember the experience, you may not have done this yet.
- What is holding you back? What are you afraid you will lose?
- If you are struggling with this decision, seek out a pastor or a good friend whom you know has taken the plunge.

LIFE COMMITMENT...

I surrender. I give up my little life to become part of God's bigger, eternal reality. I realize I am giving up on my own petty desires and dreams, but in the end, I want to be able to say with the Apostle Paul, "I consider [it all] rubbish, that I may gain Christ and be found in him...."

---

[267] Chambers, *My Utmost for His Highest*, 169, 120, 129.

DAY 172

Occupation or Vocation?

———◈◈◈———

THE WORD

> **Fight** the good fight of the faith. **Take hold** of the eternal
> life to which you were called when you made your good
> confession in the presence of many witnesses. In the
> sight of God, who gives life to everything, and of Christ
> Jesus, who while testifying before Pontius Pilate made
> the good confession, **I charge you to keep** this command
> without spot or blame until the appearing of our Lord
> Jesus Christ, which God will bring about in his own
> time—God, the blessed and only Ruler, the King of
> kings and Lord of lords, who alone is immortal and who
> lives in unapproachable light, whom no one has seen
> or can see. To him be honor and might forever. Amen.

— 1 TIMOTHY 6.12-16, EMPHASIS MINE

THOUGHT FOR THE DAY:

> Grace not only forgives you, but enables you to
> live for something hugely bigger than yourself.
> Why go back to your little kingdom of one?

~ PAUL DAVID TRIPP

LET'S GO BACK TO OUR mission statement:

> *Men's Divorce Recovery exists to empower divorced men through support, encouragement and knowledge to __survive and thrive beyond their divorce__ to become resilient, strong and wise assets to their world.*

God has something much bigger for you than just punching a clock until you can hit a little white ball around a nicely manicured lawn. He calls us to a life of risk and adventure, not for our own sakes, but for the sake of the world.

Divorce may be tearing you down so God can rebuild you into the man he called you to be—a strong, confident man, given over to God and to the world he created, using your male energy for others instead of yourself.

Do you merely have an *occupation?* Or has God called you into his *vocation?* The root meaning of the word *vocation* means *voice.* You hear it in other words like *vocal.* To fulfill God's mission in your life means *hearing his voice in your life and following the thing into which he calls you* (see Day 116).

How do you live in the power and energy of your *vocation* rather than merely live in the drudgery of an *occupation?*

First, Till the Soil.

If the farmer wants a crop in the fall he tears up the soil in the spring. God can't plant a vision, a dream, a mission into a hard, bitter, crusty heart. Take the plow to your heart. We do that by practicing the Spiritual Disciplines, the *habits of the heart* that make room for God to speak to us (see Days 113-138). If you plow the soil of your heart God will honor your movement toward him by speaking to you.

Be patient. The farmer doesn't plow and plant on Monday and get the harvest on Friday!

Second, Listen for God's Call.

The call of God upon our lives is *God's call.* He initiates and invites. We don't come up with a good idea and then ask God to bless it. That would be us inviting God to join us in *our* mission. No, this is about God, not us. Let God speak. Expect him to speak! He has a huge mission in this world! Why would he not call you to your place in that mission?

Henry Blackaby writes:

The most dramatic changes in your life will come from God's initiative, not yours. The people God used mightily in Scripture were all ordinary people to whom He gave divine assignments that they never could have initiated. The Lord often took them by surprise, for they were not seeking significant mandates from God. Even so, He saw their hearts, and He knew they were trustworthy.

The Lord may be initiating some new things in your life. When He tells you what His plans are, trust Him and walk closely with Him. Don't let the busyness of your present activity keep you from experiencing all that God has in store for you. You will see Him accomplish things through your life that you never dreamed were possible (Eph. 3:20).[268]

Third, Trust.

Trust that the call is from God. God wants you to do his will. He is for you! He wants you to succeed for his Glory, for your good, and for the good of the world!

---

[268] Blackaby and Blackaby, *Experiencing God Day-By-Day*, Kindle Location 3510.

Trust that he will accomplish his will through you. I heard the testimony of a man named Jimmy Heald. By all accounts, Jimmy should be dead. Growing up with drug abusing parents, his dad was murdered when Jimmy was a boy, his mom hooking. But God reached Jimmy, rescued him, and set him on a path to becoming a staff member of a large, growing new church, all in the course of a few years! Jimmy could testify from his own amazing experience: *If God is calling me to it he will see me through it.*[269]

Fourth, Obey.

C.S. Lewis throws down the challenge before us: *[God] is calling us. It remains with us to follow or not, to die in this winter, or to go on into that spring and that summer.*[270]

Divorce brings winter, but if we wait patiently, winter turns to spring. This is *always* true in the earth, but *only* true in our lives if we plow the soil, let God plant the seed, and then obey him through the summer to the harvest. If God calls, obey. Don't hesitate.

THINK ABOUT IT...

* Have you heard God speak to you?
* Have you heard God call you to a ministry inside the church or beyond its walls?
* Consider this statement by Rick Warren: *God never wastes anything. He would not give you abilities, interests,*

---

[269] Sermon by Jimmy Heald, Real Life Church, Austin, Texas, 2017

[270] C. S. Lewis and Walter Hooper, *The Business of Heaven: Daily Readings from the Writings of C.S. Lewis* (London: Fount, 1999), Kindle Location 1828.

talents, gifts, personality, and life experiences unless he intended to use them for his glory.[271] What abilities, interests, talents, gifts, and life experiences do you have that God is calling you to use for others?

LIFE COMMITMENT...

Life is too short to spend it on myself. I give myself to God, asking him to plant the seed of his vision for my life in my heart. I will hear and respond to him in obedience.

---

[271] Rick Warren in Erik Rees, *S.H.A.P.E.: Finding and Fulfilling Your Unique Purpose for Life* (Grand Rapids: Zondervan, 2006), 6.

Risk

———∾∾∾———

THE WORD

Now the men of Judah approached Joshua at Gilgal,
and Caleb son of Jephunneh the Kenizzite said to him,
"You know what the Lord said to Moses the man of
God at Kadesh Barnea about you and me. I was forty
years old when Moses the servant of the Lord sent me
from Kadesh Barnea to explore the land. And I brought
him back a report according to my convictions, but my
brothers who went up with me made the hearts of the
people melt with fear. I, however, followed the Lord my
God wholeheartedly. So on that day Moses swore to me,
'The land on which your feet have walked will be your
inheritance and that of your children forever, because
you have followed the Lord my God wholeheartedly.'
"Now then, just as the Lord promised, he has kept me
alive for forty-five years since the time he said this to
Moses, while Israel moved about in the desert. So here
I am today, eighty-five years old! I am still as strong
today as the day Moses sent me out; I'm just as vigorous
to go out to battle now as I was then. Now give me
this hill country that the Lord promised me that day.
You yourself heard then that the Anakites were there

and their cities were large and fortified, but, the Lord
helping me, I will drive them out just as he said."

— JOSHUA 14.6–12

THOUGHT FOR THE DAY:

You cannot reach the big summits if
you do not accept the big risks.

~ BEAR GRYLLS

AT THE AGE OF 85 most of us see ourselves sitting around taking it easy. Not Caleb. He was 85-years-old when he chose the risky, death-defying, God-honoring route of taking a mountain that had been promised to him 45 years before.

The setting was this: 45 years before this moment when old Caleb demanded he be allowed to storm a mountain occupied by the enemy, Moses had sent the 12 spies into the Promised Land. When these spies returned, they agreed that the land really *was* awesome, but it was also populated by giants. The land was bountiful, but occupied by the enemy.

Ten spies said it was impossible to take the land. Two spies, Joshua and Caleb, proclaimed God bigger than the giants (See Numbers 13-14). Ten spies recommended retreat. Joshua and Caleb recommended faith! The people chose retreat. They rebelled and God punished them: The entire generation that rejected him would die in the desert.

Only two, Joshua and Caleb, would be allowed to enter the Promised Land 45 years later.

And so it happened. Four decades later, Joshua led a new generation across the Jordan River, and so began the conquest. But Caleb remembered the promise made to him that he would have Hebron as his inheritance. One problem: Hebron sat atop a mountain and was still occupied by the enemy.

Dauntless, Caleb claimed his promise and, in total faith to God, sallied forth to take the land.

The Bible describes it like this:

> *Then Joshua blessed Caleb son of Jephunneh and gave him (Caleb) Hebron as his inheritance. So Hebron has belonged to Caleb son of Jephunneh the Kenizzite ever since, because he followed the Lord, the God of Israel, wholeheartedly. (Hebron used to be called Kiriath Arba after Arba, who was the greatest man among the Anakites.)*
>
> *Then the land had rest from war.* (Joshua 14.13–15)

Notice:

Hebron <u>has belonged to Caleb</u>... Nothing belongs to us if we don't take the risk to take it. What is God calling you to? Dare to risk it! Helen Keller said, *Life is a daring adventure or nothing at all.*

... <u>because he followed the Lord</u>, the God of Israel, <u>wholeheartedly</u>. It's all in for God, no straddling the fence, no one foot here, another there, no divided loyalties, no wavering commitment. Give it all and he will give it back.

Hebron <u>used to be called</u> Kiriath Arba... Did you notice that little phrase *"used to be called"*? God's desire is to take your yesterdays *and leave them there*. If you give your life to him, he will put the words *"used to"* in front of all the pain of your divorce.

Hebron used to be called Kiriath Arba <u>after Arba, who was the greatest man among the Anakites</u>... Wow! Not only was Hebron occupied, it was occupied by the greatest warrior of the Anakites! An old 85-year-old is going to take the city from the greatest warrior the Anakites have? Yes, because God was on Caleb's side. The Lord PLUS an old 85-year-old man took the city from Arba, *the greatest man among the Anakites.* God is in the business of slaying giants.

Bear Grylls writes:

> *The great climbers know that great summits don't come easy—they require huge, concerted, continuous effort. But mountains reward real effort. So does life and business. If you risk nothing, you gain nothing. Having a big goal is the easy bit. The part that separates the many from the few is how willing you are to go through the pain.*[272]

---

[272] Bear Grylls, *A Survival Guide for Life,* 191. Reprinted by permission of Peters Fraser & Dunlop (www.petersfraserdunlop.com) on behalf of Bear Grylls.

Think About It...

* What do you risk by following God?
* What do you risk by not following him?

Life Commitment:

I commit to the adventure before me. Adventures require faith, hope, initiative, energy, sweat, pain. But I would rather die trying than miss out on what God has for my future with him.

Expectations of Yourself

———— ∽∞∾ ————

THE WORD

And we, who with unveiled faces all reflect
the Lord's glory, are being transformed into
his likeness with ever-increasing glory, which
comes from the Lord, who is the Spirit.

— 2 CORINTHIANS 3.18

THOUGHT FOR THE DAY:

Do I really dare to let God be to me
all that he says he will be?

~ OSWALD CHAMBERS

AS YOU MOVE INTO THE future, what can you expect of yourself? Of others? Of God? We will answer these questions the next several days.

What does your future look like to you right now? If you're in the middle of a divorce or just divorced, the future can look distressingly bleak. The losses are piling up and those losses have a way of snuffing out what tiny rays of hope that may remain.

Don't despair. Whatever is *now* will change. Whatever you feel will *not last forever*, or even for very long. Whatever losses you have incurred can be restored with God's help and blessing.

What can or should you expect from yourself in this time? Expectations can be disappointing if we set them as standards by which we choose to measure ourselves. On the other hand, expectations can and should be aspirational— expectations can lift us up to think and do things that are good for us. Expectations can be targets to aim for. We know that without a target we lose focus and direction. Without goals we are always successful... at nothing. Expectations help us set targets that pull us forward.

With these things in mind...

Expect yourself not to give up. Paul J. Meyer, founder of the Success Motivation Institute, says, *"Ninety percent of those who fail are not actually defeated. They simply quit."*[273] Most people don't quit. Most people keep going. Be one of those people. Though it feels like it is almost too much to bear, at some point you will realize that it was *only* almost too much to bear. You will get through this.

Expect yourself to grow. Tell yourself that you will be a different person at the end of all this, and that you *want to* and *will be* a *better* person. You owe that to yourself, to your kids, and to the world at large.

Expect yourself to know God better. Like Jacob by the Jabbok River (Genesis 32.22-32), expect to wrestle with God. Like Jacob, expect God to both wound you and bless you. Expect God to take you down a bit and lift you up a lot. See Day 103.

---

[273] Quoted in John C. Maxwell, *The Maxwell Daily Reader*, 220.

Expect to feel better. The sting of grief and loss will lessen in frequency, intensity and duration.

But expect to hurt. There is no way to simply forget all this and not hurt anymore. As time goes by, the pain will be less intense and less frequent.

Expect yourself to be a contributor to the world. Expect God to invite you into a partnership with him that will bring him glory, bring you good and bring good through you to the world. Expect God to make this a win-win for everyone. Expect to feel good about living the second half of your life for someone other than yourself.

I like the encouragement John Maxwell brings to us:

You certainly can't control the length of your life—but you can control its width and depth.

You can't control the contour of your face—but you can control its expression.

You can't control the weather—but you can control the atmosphere of your mind.

Why worry about things you can't control when you can keep yourself busy controlling the things that depend on you?[274]

THINK ABOUT IT...

* On a scale of 0 to 10, how hopeful are you about your future, zero being completely unhopeful and 10 being completely confident of God's plan for you and your future healing?

---

[274] Ibid., 193.

0—1—2—3—4—5—6—7—8—9—10

* Read through the expectations listed above. Which of these expectations do you see happening in your life right now? Which are on the radar? Which seem beyond reach?
* Ask God to move you toward each one of these expectations.

Life Commitment:

I hurt but I know it won't be forever. I am down but I know I will get back up. I have been wounded but I know someday I can forgive. I have sinned greatly, but I know I am forgiven and I can make amends. I am hopeful about what God will do in my future, and I expect both him and I to make it together. The best is yet to be.

Expectations of Others

⊸≋≋⊸

THE WORD

Now while [Jesus] was in Jerusalem at the Passover Feast,
many people saw the miraculous signs he was doing and
believed in his name. But Jesus would not entrust himself
to them, for he knew all men. He did not need man's
testimony about man, for he knew what was in a man.

—JOHN 2.23–25

THOUGHT FOR THE DAY:

Maybe ever'body in the whole damn
world is scared of each other.

~ JOHN STEINBECK, *OF MICE AND MEN*

WE ARE ALL EMPTY CUPS desperately wanting to be filled.
Our problem is that we go to the wrong source for filling.

We mistakenly expect other people to be faucets of
clean, clear, soul-quenching water. What we fail to realize
is that *they* are empty cups as well and *they are seeking to be*
filled from us! When our expectations of other people are

not met, we are hurt, angry and disappointed. We blame the other for not meeting our expectations.

It is at this point that we might try to get our cups filled with *things*, rather than relationships. We call this *addiction*. The heart of addiction is that we build a relationship with an object (drugs, alcohol, stuff, work, etc.) and make people objects.[275]

Paul David Tripp is right when he says, *Many people say they believe in God, but they shop horizontally for what can be found only vertically.*[276] Satisfaction, security, strength and fulfillment can only be found in a solid relationship with God. God certainly uses people in our lives to fulfill some needs in our lives, but the people are the gift.

In the hands of God, people can become amazing sources of help to us and we to them. But they are the gift, God is the Giver. We trust God to place people in our lives to meet certain needs, and we trust God to place us where we can be of most help to others. But we understand that God is the

---

[275] Craig Nakken, *The Addictive Personality: Roots, Rituals, and Recovery.* (Center City, MN: Hazelden, 1988). Nakken writes, *Addiction is an emotional relationship with an object or event, through which addicts try to meet their needs for intimacy. When looked at in this way, the logic of addiction starts to become clear. When compulsive eaters feel sad, they eat to feel better. When alcoholics start to feel out of control with anger, they have a couple of drinks to get back in control. (22) My definition of addiction... is as follows: addiction is a pathological love and trust relationship with an object or event. (24) Because addiction is an illness in which the addict's primary relationship is with objects or events and not with people, the addict's relationships with people change to reflect this. Normally, we manipulate objects for our own pleasure, to make life easier. Addicts slowly transfer this style of relating to objects to their interactions with people, treating them as one-dimensional objects to manipulate as well.* Nakken, *The Addictive Personality*, 26.

[276] Tripp, *New Morning Mercies*, Kindle Location 3701.

source and that because of our sin, his tools are flawed and temporary.

With this in mind, what can you expect of people? **We can expect them to meet some needs in our lives but not *every* need.** God uses people to meet some of our needs, but God is always the source.

Because all people are sinners (Romans 3.23) **we can expect people to fail us.** We remember the wisdom of John Gardner: *Most people are neither for you nor against you; they are thinking of themselves.*[277] We really want to believe people will be strong, loyal, honest and true to us. This will not be this side of heaven.

A Buddhist saying has helped me: *The glass is already broken.* In other words, at some point, the glass that holds my water will break. When it does, I am not surprised because I knew this moment would come. People will disappoint. If you expect this, you won't be as overwhelmed when it happens.

We can learn to walk the line between trust and cynicism. God calls us to love and trust one another. But he also knows that trust is earned and can be broken. Trust *first* in God, and when people disappoint, expect it and forgive. In doing this, we can walk the fine line between blind trust of people and we can stay away from the depressing pit of cynicism.

There is hope, but it begins with God and then moves to people as he places in our lives. When people disappoint, God is there to catch us, renew us, and get us ready for our next encounters where we have the opportunity to be to

---

[277] *"John Gardner's Writings,"* accessed August 06, 2017, http://www.pbs.org/johngardner/sections/writings_speech_1.html.

people what they need, which is to say, we have the opportunity to represent our kind, benevolent awesome God to others.

THINK ABOUT IT...

* What are you expecting from others?
* How and when have people let you down?
* How can you learn to walk with realistic hope and expectations of others and stay out of the pit of cynicism?

LIFE COMMITMENT:

My commitment is first to God then to others. I will get my soul filled from God and then let him use me to fill others and let him use others to fill me. I will remember that he is the Giver and people, including myself, are the gifts.

Expectations of Your Children

―⟨∞⟩―

THE WORD

> *Fathers, do not exasperate your children; instead, bring
> them up in the training and instruction of the Lord.*

> — EPHESIANS 6.4

THOUGHT FOR THE DAY:

> *Children ought not to be victims of the
> choices adults make for them.*

> ~ WADE HORN

A YOUNG WOMAN NAMED LESLIE writes:

> *One of the most painful and significant events in my life
> was my parents' divorce. It felt as if my family had died and
> my whole life as I knew it would change forever. For me,
> the divorce was sudden and unexpected. My father left the
> house one night and would never return as the Dad I grew
> up with. He had fallen in love with someone else, which
> shattered all my thoughts and feelings about what a happy
> marriage my parents had. They were supposed to be together*

forever... "until death do us part." My body literally went into shock, and I cannot recollect what I did for days or weeks after hearing the news about my parent's separation. I was about to graduate from high school, and the last few weeks of school were a daze.

All I could think about was when would my dad return to my mother and this whole nightmare be over. *I had my high school prom to go to, which I hated and did not want to attend. I don't even remember if any family member said good-bye to me as I embarked on what was supposed to be a night to remember.*

I remember my father driving to the house for visits with my mother. My siblings and I would wait to see him, and sometimes he would leave the house without ever saying hello or good-bye. ***None of us could really be there for each other because we were all hurting over a relationship that was unique and special to each one.***[278]

So many times I have sat with couples wrestling with divorce. The common theme in these counseling sessions was *selfishness.* As I listened to the husband and wife take turns stabbing each other, all I could hear was a radical self-centeredness that left little room for concern for their children.

At some point I would ask, *So, how are the kids doing through all this?*

The typical response was, *They are doing OK.*

To which I would reply, *How do you know?*

To which they would say, *They seem to be handling it fine.*

---

[278] John W. James and Russell Friedman, *When Children Grieve: For Adults to Help Children Deal with Death, Divorce, Pet Loss, Moving, and Other Losses* (New York, NY: HarperCollins, 2001), 199-200. Emphasis mine.

To which I would reply, *How do you know?*

To which they say, *Well, they aren't saying much.*

Really? Mom and dad are the bedrock of every child's life. They are born completely dependent on you! You are the first people they know and trust. And yet you believe they are OK because they aren't saying anything as the foundation of their lives crumbles before them?

Leslie's heartfelt re-telling of how she experienced her parent's divorce is revealing:

> *It felt as if my family had died and my whole life as I knew it would change forever....*
>
> *My body literally went into shock, and I cannot recollect what I did for days or weeks after hearing the news about my parent's separation....*
>
> *All I could think about was when would my dad return to my mother and this whole nightmare be over....*
>
> *None of us could really be there for each other because we were all hurting over a relationship that was unique and special to each one....*

If you think your child is not suffering through this time, you are badly mistaken. Your child is probably experiencing the very feelings Leslie experienced, but he/she doesn't know how to put his/her feelings into words. As adults we find putting appropriate words to our emotions challenging. How can we expect children to express themselves at all? Instead of trying, they clam up. We assume their silence means they are fine. Big mistake.

When I have counseled self-centered couples fighting with one another, more than once I have said, *You are expecting your children to act like adults while you act like children. It is time you act like adults and let your children be children!*

Whatever you are experiencing emotionally, no matter your level of pain, guilt, shame, embarrassment, anger, etc., **you must be a dad to your children.** They are hurting more than you know. They deserve your love.

So the real question is not, What can you expect from your children? but **What can your children expect from you?** Your children should be able to expect...

* **Your time and attention.** You *must* make time for each child. This will be difficult but it must be a priority. When you are with your children they should expect your full attention. They are hungry for your attention but they may not know how to express it. Assume they desperately need you because they really do.

* **Your tenderness.** This is not a time to be hard, tough or thick-skinned. This is a time for tenderness, compassion and an open heart. This is a time to acknowledge that things are hard. Say something like this: <u>Name of your child</u>, *this is a hard and terrible time for all of us. I am so sorry for what you are going through. I know it must be painful beyond words. I am happy to hear whatever words you have to say. I will always be here for you. This is not your fault. We will get through this together.*

* **Access to counseling.** Read Leslie's story again. She needs and deserves a safe place to pour out her heart. She wrote, *None of us could really be there for each other because we were all hurting over a relationship that was unique and special to each one.* You can be there

for your kids, and you should, but patients in the ER don't and can't help one another. Doctors and nurses do. Offer counseling for your kids and do whatever it takes to make it happen. Spend the money. Take the time to get them to the appointments.

* Reassurances that they will be taken care of.

This is <u>not</u> a time to...

* **Rag on your ex.** There will be a time for you to share your side of what happened, including personal confession where you have failed. Now is not the time. If you can't say anything nice about your ex, don't say anything at all.
* **Make false promises.** We all want to reassure our children, but we can't make promises we can't keep. Don't say, *I think mom and I are going to get back together* if it is not true.
* **Compensate by spending lavishly on your kid.** Kids see right through that. They want love, not things.

Think About It...

* One of the most important things you can do during this time is to put yourself in your child's place. If you were your child, what would you be thinking? If you were your child, what would you be feeling? What would you be afraid of?
* Now, with a heart of compassion, go love on your kids. They deserve the best you have to give to them.

LIFE COMMITMENT:

My kids deserve my best and I will give it to them no matter what it takes.

Expectations of God

---∽∼∞∼∽---

THE WORD

In the day when I cried out, you answered me,
and made me bold with strength in my soul.

— PSALM 138.3

THOUGHT FOR THE DAY:

The Lord will make a way for you where no foot
has been before. That which, like a sea, threatens to
drown you, shall be a highway for your escape.

~ CHARLES SPURGEON

ON OCTOBER 3, 2003 PERFORMER Roy Horn was attacked by a tiger while performing the famous Siegfried & Roy show in Las Vegas. Fortunately Roy survived. Many people blamed the tiger. But comedian Chris Rock nailed it when he said, *That tiger ain't go crazy; that tiger went tiger!*[279]

Tigers do tiger things. Guess what? *God does God things.*

---

[279] Chris Rock, *"Chris Rock Tiger Gone Crazy,"* https://www.youtube.com/watch?v=kGEv5dC0lo4, accessed October 22, 2017.

And what God does is show up in the middle of our crises, traumas and disasters. The reality is that we don't usually come to God in good times. We come to God when our lives fall apart. It's just the way it is.

When it all hits the fan, we get humble and needy. At that point the smart people cry out to God and God rescues us. These are the places where we can expect God, our Rescuer, to do his rescuer thing.

So what can you expect of God as you continue down this pathway?

Expect God to show up.

Every Christmas we celebrate that God showed up. Christmas is all about God's Son, *wrapped in flesh*, leaving heaven and inserting himself into the mess of humanity, not just to visit but to stay with us: *The Word became flesh and made his dwelling among us. We have seen his glory, the glory of the One and Only, who came from the Father, full of grace and truth.* (John 1.14)

Jesus didn't do a lot of explaining about why the darkness is dark. But he knew that light pushes out darkness. You may not know why your life is the way it is right now, but Jesus is light and he will show up with you to push back the darkness.

Expect God to comfort you.

Divorce hurts. Even the 'manliest' of men get hurt. And when we are hurt we want comfort. Take King David, for example. There was no more manly man than King David. He kicked the butt of a giant warrior over nine feet tall. He led men into battle many times. When it comes to manly men, David rates! Yet he wrote about God: *He heals the brokenhearted and binds up their wounds.* (Psalm 147:3) Yep, manly men hurt, and manly men need God to heal our manly, broken hearts.

If you let God comfort you, you will have an experience like no other.

Eugene Peterson observes that *We don't have to wait until we get to the end of the road before we enjoy what is at the end of the road.*[280] Heaven is a pain-free place of comfort. You can enjoy heaven on earth *now*. God loves to comfort his people.

Expect God to make a way.

The Israelites were up against the Red Sea on one side and a charging Egyptian army on the other. When all seemed lost, God made a way. He is doing this for you and will continue to do it for you, for his Glory, for your good and for the good of the world. (See Exodus 14-15)

Expect God to call you.

God doesn't waste pain. Only you can waste your pain by not following God's mission for your life. Our world is a damaged and hurting place. God calls his people to be *wounded healers* to our dark world. God will take what has happened to you and call you to help others who only you can help:

> *Praise be to the God and Father of our Lord Jesus Christ, the Father of compassion and the God of all comfort, who comforts us in all our troubles, so that we can comfort those in any trouble with the comfort we ourselves have received*

---

[280] Eugene H. Peterson, Dale Larsen, and Sandy Larsen, *A Long Obedience in The Same Direction: 6 Studies for Individuals or Groups, With Guidelines for Leaders & Study Notes* (Downers Grove, IL: InterVarsity Press, 1996), Kindle Location 1711.

from God. For just as the sufferings of Christ flow over into our lives, so also through Christ our comfort overflows. (2 Corinthians 1.3–5)

Expect God to empower you.

If God calls you he will equip and empower you. He certainly did this for me. After my divorce I was physically, emotionally and spiritually exhausted. And yet I heard his clear call to write this book. Then he not only gave me the energy to get up at 4:45 every morning to write it, he woke me up to get on with it!

Tony Dungy writes:

When we focus on the obstacles in front of us, they seem to grow larger and larger until we give up. But if we focus on what God can do through us—and on His promise that if we delight in Him, He will give us the desires of our hearts—we become confident and able to achieve whatever we were designed to achieve. Start each day by focusing on what needs to occur that day. Set your mind on what you are attempting to achieve and where you want to go. If it's a God-honoring goal and you are following His leading, believe that He wants you to achieve it. And you will begin to see your heart's desires fulfilled.[281]

---

[281] Dungy and Whitaker, *The One Year Uncommon Life Daily Challenge*, Kindle Location 2468.

THINK ABOUT IT...

* How is God showing up in your life right now?
* If you don't see him at work in your life, find a trusted friend or pastor to help you see God's hand in your life. We live in a muddy, foggy world. God is at work but sometimes we need help seeing him do his God thing.
* Have you heard God's call on your life? If not, give him time. In his timing he will call you.

PRAYER:

God, my life is in tatters. So much has been lost. So much damage has been done. But despite the hurt and pain, I believe you not only will show up in my life, I believe that you <u>want</u> to show up. I open my life and heart to you. I desire your comfort. I know you will call me. And I look forward to you rebuilding, renewing and restoring my life, for your Glory, for my good, and for the good of the world.

Steady Strum

———

THE WORD

*By the grace God has given me, I laid a foundation
as an expert builder, and someone else is building
on it. But each one should be careful how he builds.
For no one can lay any foundation other than
the one already laid, which is Jesus Christ.*

— 1 CORINTHIANS 3.10–11

THOUGHT FOR THE DAY:

*The Mission of Men's Divorce Recovery is to Empower
Divorced Men through Support, Encouragement and
Knowledge to Survive and Thrive beyond their divorce to
become Resilient, Strong and Wise Assets to their World.*

I'VE BEEN PLAYING THE GUITAR for only a few years and it's
been good for my soul.

As a new student to the guitar, I have realized that it
takes both the left and right hands doing the right things at
the right time to make good sound. But both hands do different things.

The foundation of good sound are the notes that the left hand establishes as the fingers push down on the strings on the fretboard. To make good sound, the fingers must be on the fretboard pushing down hard in the right place at the right time. No matter how great my strumming, if my fingers on the left hand are weak and/or misplaced, the sound will be muddled and out of tune.

At the same time, the right-hand strums or picks. Unlike the fingers of the left hand—which must be firm, secure, stable and tight—the right hand is free to strum or pick as the song dictates.

What is true of my guitar is true of my life. On the one hand, my life must be secured to the right foundation. Like the fingers of my left hand on the fretboard, I must have a firm grasp of my values, my convictions—the things in my life I am willing to die for and I will not give up at any cost. I must be clear and firm about the principles, values and core truths that define the 'sound' of my life. Some men have found it helpful to ask God to give them a Mission Statement for their life. God clearly gave me mine: *My Life Mission is to Fervently love God and People, expressing this love Frequently and persevering in it Forever.*

I have not always strummed well to this mission statement, but at least I have something to ground me.[282]

With my foundation firmly in place, I am free to strum or pick as life demands. Sometimes I can strum my life with a slow, steady peaceful rhythm. At other times I have

---

[282] For help with developing your own Mission Statement, see Rick Warren, *The Purpose-Driven Life* (Cleveland: Findaway World, 2005), 312-319.

to strum hard and fast to make the music that fits the moment. At other times, finessed picking sounds best. As a guitarist, I am still working on strumming. Finessed picking is sometime in my future!

As we come to the close of this devotional, think about what core truths. What are your values? Are you pushing down hard on these values? Are these truths deeply ingrained in our soul and second nature to you?

How about your strumming? Do you know when to strum slow and when to strum fast?

Think About It...

♦ Do you have a Mission Statement? If not, check out *The Purpose-Driven Life* by Rick Warren to figure yours out.

Life Commitment:
I may not be Jimi Hendrix, on a real guitar, but with God's help and the right values, I can strum well to life.

Moving into the New Normal

———— ∞∞∞ ————

THE WORD

*When you were dead in your sins and in the
uncircumcision of your flesh, God made you alive
with Christ. He forgave us all our sins, having
canceled the charge of our legal indebtedness, which
stood against us and condemned us; he has taken it
away, nailing it to the cross. And having disarmed
the powers and authorities, he made a public spectacle
of them, triumphing over them by the cross.*

— COLOSSIANS 2.13-15

THOUGHT FOR THE DAY:

*Attitude is everything—or at least a great, big
piece of everything! Check your attitude as you do
small tasks and then take on greater things.*

~ TONY DUNGY

TWICE IN TWO YEARS I experienced moments that I knew
everything changed for me, and not for the better.

The first was December 16, 2013. By the time I left what should have been a routine meeting of my church's elders, I understood that I could not trust them or my staff anymore. At that point everything I had believed in and worked so hard for was radically changed. The foundation of my vocational life was shattered. The future of what I had worked so hard for was completely up for grabs.

The second came nearly two years later. On October 23, 2015, I arrived home after a two-week teaching trip to Africa only to have my wife meet me in the carport of the church parsonage and tell me she had left me. As I walked into the house I knew that my life was further radically changed. I knew that I was losing things I had worked hard to achieve. I knew the losses would pile up and would be felt for years to come. I knew that the things by which I identified myself were being stripped away before my eyes.

The journey since those moments has been like something I have never experienced. I cannot find words to wrap around the heartache and pain.

But this I know: *God has walked with me every step of this treacherous path.* Whatever was normal before is gone and can't be recovered. But with God at my side, he is moving me into a new 'normal,' whatever 'normal' is.

You can't let what has happened to you or what you have done to others stop you in your tracks now. Too much is at stake and God has so much planned for you.

Life is more like pedaling a bike uphill than it is a cruise downhill. If you are going uphill and you stop pedaling, you tump over! So... keep pedaling!

In the end, I want to be able to say with the Apostle Paul: *I have fought the good fight, I have finished the race, I have kept the faith.* (2 Timothy 4:7)

THINK ABOUT IT...

- What is 'normal' to you?
- How has your life been turned upside-down?
- What could a new 'normal' look like to you?
- What steps do you need to take today to move into the future God has for you?

LIFE COMMITMENT:

God is for me. He has a future for me that includes a deeper, richer, more profound life. I want to live for him and eternity rather than for myself and this brief life on earth. I want to fight the good fight, finish the race, keep the faith.

The Next Right Thing

———∞∞———

THE WORD

*In all my prayers for all of you, I always pray with
joy because of your partnership in the gospel from
the first day until now, being confident of this,
that he who began a good work in you will carry it
on to completion until the day of Christ Jesus.*

— PHILIPPIANS 1:4-6

THOUGHTS FOR THE DAY:

*Perhaps it's not such a bad thing to come to
the end of your rope if at the end of your rope
you find a strong and willing Savior.*

~ PAUL DAVID TRIPP

*You will find yourself at your wits' end but at the
beginning of God's wisdom. When you come to your
wits' end and feel inclined to panic—don't! Stand
true to God and He will bring out His truth in a way
that will make your life an expression of worship.*

~ OSWALD CHAMBERS

With time, great good can come from great sorrow.

~ Desmond Tutu

*Every spiritual problem has an individual genesis
and therefore requires an individual exodus.*

~ Gary Thomas

AHHH, WHAT A TIME IN which to live! Everything seems to be getting stronger and lighter with so many choices it leaves the head spinning! One such product caught my attention recently: Duct Tape.

Amazingly enough, modern duct tape was the brainchild of Vesta Stoudt, mother of two Navy sailors in World War II. Working in a factory making ordnance, she had the idea for duct tape as a way to seal ammo boxes so that the boxes would stay closed but could also be easily opened during battle.

She wrote the President who forwarded her idea to the War Production Board. They sent it to Johnson & Johnson who developed duct tape.[283] Today duct tape comes in so many colors and patterns it boggles the mind. Not only is it strong, it is pretty. Go figure.

Competition to produce ever-better duct tape is fierce. I recently saw one such product: T-Rex Duct Tape. I haven't bought any yet but I probably will before the zombie apocalypse. It pays to be prepared.

---

[283] *"Duct tape."* Wikipedia. July 28, 2017, accessed August 11, 2017. https://en.wikipedia.org/wiki/Duct_tape.

What caught my eye about the T-Rex Duct Tape ad was its tag line: *T-Rex Ferociously Strong Tape... All Weather, Works Longer, Holds Stronger.*

Guys, I want to be like T-Rex Duct Tape: *Ferociously Strong, All Weather, Works Longer, Holds Stronger.*

In the end, this is who God calls us to be: *Ferociously Strong, All Weather, Working Longer, Holding Stronger.*

The circumstances of my life caused me to change residences five times in 38 months, and this for a guy who really likes to hang out in the same place forever! In my last move I ran across a box that had been sealed long ago with duct tape. The gray plastic top layer was faded to white or completely. The fabric showed underneath. But it was still holding.

The grind of life can weather us. Traumatic events like divorce can rip us apart. But in the end, we want to be *Ferociously Strong, All Weather, Working Longer, Holding Stronger.*

By now this truth has sunk into you: Whatever happens *circumstantially* in your life is secondary to what is going on *spiritually.* And above all, by now you understand that what God wants—more than anything—is for **you to come to him so he can invade your soul and grow you into the man he calls you to be.**

Circumstances are what they are. I certainly didn't want to lose two churches and a wife in 18 months. In fact, I worked like heck to keep that from happening, but it happened anyway. I didn't choose to have my life turned upside-down and to lose hundreds of thousands of dollars in the process. But it happened.

What I did choose to do was to go to God. In him I found something, or rather Someone, who could never be taken away from me: I found my Heavenly Father, my *true* Father, glad to receive me, eager to comfort me, and firmly calling me into a future with him.

I know God did not cause my life to fall apart—people did. But I also know God is the pro at taking the horrible things in our lives and, with our cooperation, turning them into amazing displays of his grace, love and strength.

Tony Dungy captures this reality:

Have you thought about all the events that led up to this moment in your life—why you're here, how you've been shaped, what caused you to read this book or seek God's plans for your life? Have you wondered how much of it is accidental or random and how much is designed? I believe God knew exactly where you would be right now and exactly what you would be like. He knew about your passions and gifts and the platform you have. In fact, I believe He was very purposeful in designing your life. He made you to be uniquely significant and to have an eternal impact on the world around you.[284]

When life comes crashing in we can either choose hope or despair, action or depression, life or suicide.

In the introduction of this book I wrote:

Right now you are in pain and you are looking for relief. Know this: Our God who created a world of immense variety has many tools to get back on your feet and back in the game.

---

[284] Dungy and Whitaker, *The One Year Uncommon Life Daily*, Kindle Location 202.

*And he will do it! **You will get through this!** But right now you are face down on the turf wondering if your playing days are over. They're not. You are God's son, and he doesn't leave his kids on the field alone and bleeding. His specialty, in fact, is taking wounded warriors and rehabilitating them into magnificent men who give back to the very world that beat them to the ground.*

My hope and prayer is that you know this reality more *now* than when you began reading this book.

Life will continue to be a challenge. As long as we have breath on this planet we will struggle. But how much better to know this world is not all there is? How much better is God's invitation into a future with him? How much better to know that God can turn your pain into promises for others? How much better to know that your life counts and can be spent doing things of eternal significance?

It all begins when we say *Yes* to God. As Henry Blackaby points out, *Our response to God determines His response to us.*[285] Have you said *yes* to God? He has already said *yes* to you! With God at your side your future is far brighter and more significant and meaningful than you can imagine!

In the old days they said... *Nulla tenaci invia est via...* (*For the tenacious, no road is impassable*).

In today's language we might say: *Ferociously Strong, All Weather, Working Longer, Holding Stronger.*

---

[285] Blackaby and Blackaby, *Experiencing God Day-By-Day*, Kindle Location 3450.

THINK ABOUT IT...

* Where are you with God?
* What are your next steps? See the resources and suggestions at the end of this book and on Men's Divorce Recovery website (www.mensdivorcerecovery.org).

LIFE COMMITMENT:

I am a wounded warrior and being rehabilitated into a magnificent man who will give back to the very world that beat me to the ground. In God's strength and love, I am ferociously strong, working longer, holding stronger.

NEXT STEPS

Men's Divorce Recovery exists to Empower
Divorced Men through Support, Knowledge &
Encouragement to Survive & Thrive Beyond their
Divorce to Become Resilient, Strong & Wise Men

IT'S ONE THING TO GET this info in your head. How do you let it soak down into your heart and out through your hands in your daily life? Try these next steps to continue your journey of hope and healing.

STAY **CONNECTED** to a community of men committed to finishing well despite the traumas we have been through:

* MDR **WEBSITE**: MensDivorceRecovery.org
* MDR **Facebook page**: https://www.facebook.com/mensdivorcerecovery/

ATTEND AN MDR EVENT:

* An MDR weekend conference.
* A 6-Week Recovery Group. (Recovery groups include S-GROUPS (Survive Groups) for men in the immediate crisis of divorce and T-GROUPS (Thrive Groups) for men ready to take the next step with God)

* An MDR Retreat.
* An MRD week-long extended Expedition. See the website for conference, retreat, expedition and group dates and locations.

Keep putting the good stuff in your head! **<u>READ</u>**:

* *The Quick Start Guide for Divorced Men: Help and Hope Now* if you haven't already.
* The second volume of *Daily Survival Guide for Divorced Men: Surviving & Thriving Beyond Your Divorce.*
* The <u>newsletter</u> and <u>blog</u> found here.
* <u>Watch our Videos</u> and listen to the <u>podcasts</u> on specific topics related to divorce and recovery, accessible through the website, Facebook and LinkedIn.
* Go to counseling! I know this is hard but you will be rewarded for the time and money you invest in yourself, and you have potential to avoid the same mistakes of your past and give a much better life to your children now and a partner in the future. Contact me for references in your area.

Men's Divorce Recovery website (mensdivorcerecovery. org).

WORKS CITED

Anderson, Neil T. and Joanne Anderson. *Daily in Christ: A Devotional*. Eugene: Harvest House Publishers, 1993.

Armstrong, Kristin. *Happily Ever After: Walking with Peace and Courage Through a Year of Divorce*. New York: Faith Words, 2008

Auden, W.H. *The Age of Anxiety: A Baroque Eclogue*. Edited by Alan Jacobs. Princeton: Princeton University Press, 2011.

Berry, Wendell. *The Selected Poems of Wendell Berry*. Berkeley: Counterpoint, 1998.

Blackaby, Henry T. and Richard Blackaby. *Experiencing God Day by Day*. Nashville: B&H Publishing, 2006.

———. *Hearing God's Voice*. Nashville: B&H Publishing, 2002.

Blackaby, Henry T., Richard Blackaby, and Claude V. King. *Experiencing God: Knowing and Doing the Will of God*. Nashville: B&H Publishing, 2008.

Bly, Robert. *Iron John: A Book About Men*. Boston, MA: Da Capo Press, 2015.

Boa, Kenneth and John Alan Turner. *The 52 Greatest Stories of the Bible a Devotional Study.* Baker Publishing Group, 2016.

Briggs, J. R. *Fail: Finding Hope and Grace in The Midst of Ministry Failure.* Downers Grove, 2015.

Brother Lawrence, *The Practice of the Presence of God.* Nabu Press, 2010.

Brown, Brené. *Rising Strong: How the Ability to Reset Transforms the Way We Live, Love, Parent, and Lead.* New York: Random House, 2017.

Carlson, Richard. *Don't Sweat the Small Stuff...and It's All Small Stuff Simple Ways to Keep the Little Things from Taking Over Your Life.* New York: Hyperion, 1997.

Chambers, Oswald. *My utmost for His Highest: Selections for The Year.* Uhrichsville, OH: Barbour and Co, 1992.

Chesterton, G. K. *Orthodoxy.* Centrehouse Press, 2017.

Henry, Cloud. *9 Things You Simply Must Do to Succeed in Love and Life: A Psychologist Probes the Mystery of Why Some Lives Really Work A=and Others Don't.* Detroit: Gale, Cengage Learning, 2008.

Cordeiro, Wayne. *Leading on Empty: Refilling Your Tank and Renewing Your Passion.* Minneapolis, MN: Bethany House, 2009.

Darwin, Charles, *Life and Letters of Charles Darwin.* Rare Books Club, 2016.

Descartes, René. *The Passions of The Soul: And Other Late Philosophical Writings*. Oxford: Oxford University Press, 2015.

Donahue, Bill. *Leading Life-Changing Small Groups: Groups that Grow*. Zondervan, 2012.

Driscoll, Mark. *Who Do You Think You Are? Finding Your True Identity in Christ*. Nashville: Thomas Nelson, 2013.

Dungy, Tony and Nathan Whitaker. *The One Year Uncommon Life Daily Challenge*. Carol Stream, IL: Tyndale House Publishers, 2011.

Eisenhower, William. "Fearing God," *Christianity Today*, March 1986.

Eldredge, John, Fathered by God: Learning What Your Dad Could Never Teach You. Detroit: Gale Cengage Learning, 2009.

———. *Wild at Heart: Discovering the Secret of a Man's Soul*. HarperCollins: 2011.

Foster, Richard J. *Celebration of Discipline*. Harper Collins, 2009.

Grylls, Bear. *A Survival Guide for Life: How to Achieve Your Goals, Thrive in Adversity, and Grow in Character*. New York: William Morrow, 2014.

Grudem, Wayne. *Systematic Theology: An Introduction to Biblical Doctrine*. Leicester: Inter-Varsity, 2007.

Handley, Rod. *Character That Counts-Who's Counting Yours?* Omaha: Cross Training Publishing, 2012.

Hecht, Jennifer Michael, *Stay: A History of Suicide and the Philosophies Against It.* New Haven: Yale University Press, 2015.

Hybels, Bill. *The Power of a Whisper.* Grand Rapids: Zondervan, 2010.

James, John W. and Russell Friedman. *When Children Grieve: For Adults to Help Children Deal with Death, Divorce, Pet Loss, Moving, and Other Losses.* New York, NY: HarperCollins, 2001.

James, Violet. *God Restores: Prayers & Promises for Restoration.* Maximum Potential: 2017.

Kahneman, Daniel. *Thinking, Fast and Slow.* New York: Farrar, Straus and Giroux, 2015.

Keating, Thomas. *The Human Condition: Contemplation and Transformation.* New York: Paulist Press, 1999.

Keller, Tim. *Generous Justice: How God's Grace Makes Us Just.* New York: 2010: Penguin Publishing Group.

Lamott, Anne. *Help, Thanks, Wow: The Three Essential Prayers.* London: Hodder & Stoughton, 2015.

Lewis, C. S. and Walter Hooper. *The Business of Heaven: Daily Readings from the Writings of C.S. Lewis.* London: Fount, 1999.

————. *Of Other Worlds: Essays and Stories*. San Francisco: HarperOne, 2017.

————. *Poems*. San Diego: Harcourt Brace & Co., 1992.

————. *Selected Literary Essays*. New York: Cambridge University Press, 2013.

Manning, Brennan, John Blase, and Jonathan Foreman. *Abbas Child: The Cry of the Heart for Intimate Belonging*. Colorado Springs: NavPress, 2015.

Martin. Keturah C. *Jesus Never Wastes Pain but Can Bring Eternal Gain*. Bloomington, IN: Xlibris Corp, 2014.

Maxwell, John C. *The Maxwell Daily Reader: 365 Days of Insight to Develop the Leader Within You and Influence Those Around You*. Nashville: Thomas Nelson, 2007.

————. *Failing Forward: Turning Mistakes into Stepping-Stones for Success*. Nashville: Thomas Nelson Publishers, 2000.

McBride, Jean. *Talking to Children About Divorce: A Parent's Guide to Healthy Communication at Each Stage of Divorce: Expert Advice for Kids' Emotional Recovery*. San Antonio: Althea Press, 2016.

Merton, Thomas, *The Seven Storey Mountain*. London: SPCK, 2009.

Meyer, F. B. *The Secret of Guidance: Guideposts for Life's Choices.* Belfast: Ambassador, 2000.

Morley, Patrick. *Devotions for The Man in The Mirror.* Grand Rapids: Zondervan, 2015.

Motyer, J. A. *New Bible Commentary: 21st Century Edition.* Edited by D. A. Carson et al., 4th Edition. Downers Grove: InterVarsity Press, 1994.

Nakken, Craig. *The Addictive Personality: Roots, Rituals, and Recovery.* Center City, MN: Hazelden, 1988.

O'Donohue, John, *Anam Ċara: A Book of Celtic Wisdom.* New York: Harper Perennial, 2004.

Ortberg, John, *When the Game is Over, It All Goes Back in the Box.* Grand Rapids: Zondervan, 2007.

———. *You Have a Soul: It Weighs Nothing but Means Everything.* Grand Rapids: Zondervan, 2014.

Pascal, Blaise, *Pensées.* Harmondsworth: Penguin Books, 1966.

Peterson, Eugene H., Dale Larsen, and Sandy Larsen. *A Long Obedience in The Same Direction: 6 Studies for Individuals or Groups, With Guidelines for Leaders & Study Notes.* Downers Grove: InterVarsity Press, 1996.

Eugene Peterson, *God's Message for Each Day: Wisdom from the Word of God.* Nashville: Thomas Nelson, 2006

Pritchard, Ray. *An Anchor for the Soul: Help for the Present, Hope for the Future*. Chicago: Moody Publishers, 2011.

Rohr, Richard, Falling Upward: *A Spirituality for the Two Halves of Life: A Companion Journal*. London: Society for Promoting Christian Knowledge, 2013.

———. *Things Hidden: Scripture as Spirituality*. Cincinnati: St. Anthony Messenger Press, 2007.

Rohr, Richard and Joseph Martos. *From Wild Man to Wise Man: Reflections on Male Spirituality*. Cincinnati: St. Anthony Messenger Press, 2005.

Rohr, Richard, Joseph Durepos, and Tom McGrath, *On the Threshold of Transformation: Daily Meditations for Men*. Chicago: Loyola Press, 2010.

Seven Areas of Life Training. Victorious Christian Living International. Accessed February 03, 2017. http://www.vcli. org/salt/.

Smith, Colin S. and Tim Augustyn. *The One Year Unlocking the Bible Devotional*. Carol Stream, IL: Tyndale House, 2012.

Smith, Scotty. *Everyday Prayers: 365 Days to a Gospel-Centered Faith*. Grand Rapids: Baker Books, 2011.

Stecker, Chuck. *Men of Honor Women of Virtue: The Power of Rites of Passage into Godly Adulthood*. Denver: Seismic Publishing Group: 2010.

Stephenson, Bret. *From Boys to Men: Spiritual Rites of Passage in an Indulgent Age*. Rochester, VT: Park Street Press, 2006.

Stiles, Wayne. *Waiting on God: What to Do When God Does Nothing*. Grand Rapids: Baker Books, 2015.

Stoltz, Paul Gordon. *Grit: The New Science of What It Takes to Persevere, Flourish, Succeed*. Climb Strong Press, 2014.

Thomas, Gary. *Authentic Faith: The Power of a Fire-Tested Life*. Grand Rapids: Zondervan, 2002.

———. *Holy Available: What If Holiness Is About More Than What We Don't Do?* Grand Rapids: Zondervan, 2009.

———. *Sacred Marriage: What If God Designed Marriage to Make Us Holy More Than to Make Us Happy?* Grand Rapids: Zondervan, 2015.

———. *Simply Sacred: Daily Readings*. Grand Rapids: Zondervan, 2011.

Tiegreen, Chris. *One Year Hearing His Voice Devotional: 365 Days of Intimate Communication with God*. Carol Stream, IL: Tyndale Momentum, 2015.

Thoreau, Henry David. *Works of Henry David Thoreau*. Hustonville, KY: Golgotha Press, 2010.

Thurber, James. *Secret Life of Walter Mitty*. Penguin Books, 2016.

Chris Thurman, *The Lies We Believe*. Nashville: T. Nelson, 2003.

Tozer A. W. *The Knowledge of The Holy: The Attributes of God, Their Meaning in The Christian Life*. New York: Harper & Row, 1961.

Tripp, Paul David. *New Morning Mercies: A Daily Gospel Devotional*. Wheaton, IL: Crossway, 2014.

Tutu, Desmond and Mpho A. Tutu. *The Book of Forgiving: The Fourfold Path for Healing Ourselves and Our World*. London: William Collins, 2014.

Warren, Rick. *Rick Warren's Bible Study Methods: Twelve Ways You Can Unlock Gods Word*. Grand Rapids: Zondervan, 2011.

———. *The Purpose Driven Life*. Cleveland: Findaway World, 2005.

Walton, John H. *The Lost World of Genesis One: Ancient Cosmology and the Origins Debate*. Downers Grove: IVP Academic, 2009.

———. *The Lost World of Adam And Eve: Genesis 2-3 and the Human Origins Debate*. Downers Grove: IVP Academic, 2015.
Wicks, Robert J. *Spiritual Resilience: 30 Days to Refresh Your Soul*. Cincinnati: Franciscan Media, 2015.

Willard, Dallas. *The Divine Conspiracy: Rediscovering Our Hidden Life in God*. San Francisco: HarperSanFrancisco, 1998.

———. *Hearing God: Developing A Conversational Relationship with God*. Downers Grove: InterVarsity Press, 1999.

———. *Renovation of The Heart: Putting on The Character of Christ.* Colorado Springs: NavPress, 2002.

Worthington, Everett L. *Forgiving and Reconciling: Bridges to Wholeness and Hope.* Downers Grove: InterVarsity Press, 2003.

Wright, H. Norman. *The New Guide to Crisis and Trauma Counseling.* Ventura: Regal Books, 2003.

Young, Sarah. *Jesus Calling: Enjoying Peace in His Presence: Devotions for Every Day of the Year.* Nashville: Integrity Publishers, 2016.

ABOUT THE AUTHOR

DALE J. BROWN, PHD, EARNED his bachelor's degree from the University of Texas and the master of divinity and doctorate of philosophy degrees from Southwestern Baptist Theological Seminary. Brown has pastored six churches in Texas and New England; lived and taught abroad; served as a chaplain for hospices, hospitals, and volunteer fire departments; and led men's retreats and conferences. He has ministered in multiple prisons and worked with sex offenders and victims. His passion is to help men make a lasting impact on the world and to finish well.

Brown has three children: Lindsey, Davis, and Aaron. In his free time, Brown enjoys hiking, hunting, backpacking, guitar, swing, and two-step.

91768485R00417

Made in the USA
Columbia, SC
22 March 2018